# THE FUTURE OF TRADE UNIONISM

# The Future of Trade Unionism

## International Perspectives on Emerging Union Structures

*Edited by*
MAGNUS SVERKE

LONDON AND NEW YORK

First published 1997 by Ashgate Publishing

Reissued 2018 by Routledge
2 Park Square, Milton Park, Abingdon, Oxon, OX14 4RN
52 Vanderbilt Avenue, New York, NY 10017

*Routledge is an imprint of the Taylor & Francis Group, an informa business*



Publisher's Note
The publisher has gone to great lengths to ensure the quality of this reprint but points out that some imperfections in the original copies may be apparent.



A Library of Congress record exists under LC control number: 97073409

ISBN 13: 978-1-138-35083-0 (hbk)
ISBN 13: 978-1-138-35084-7 (pbk)
ISBN 13: 978-0-429-43565-2 (ebk)

# Contents

## Part IV
## Member-union relations

# List of contributors

*Torben Andersen*, Institute of Organization and Management, Aarhus School of Business, Aarhus, Denmark.

*Julian Barling*, School of Business, Queens University, Kingston, Ontario, Canada.

*Reynald Bourque*, School of Industrial Relations, University of Montreal, Montreal, Quebec, Canada.

*Donna M. Buttigieg*, Department of Management and Industrial Relations, University of Melbourne, Parkville, Victoria, Australia.

*Victor M. Catano*, Department of Psychology, Saint Mary's University, Halifax, Nova Scotia, Canada.

*Gary N. Chaison*, Graduate School of Management, Clark University, Worcester, Massachusetts, USA.

*Jennifer Curtin*, Public Policy Program, Australian National University, Canberra, Australia.

*Annelies Daalder*, Motivaction Amsterdam B.V., Amsterdam, the Netherlands.

*Kay Devine*, Faculty of Business, University of Alberta, Edmonton, Alberta, Canada.

*Patrizio Di Nicola*, Work & Technology Research Association, Rome, Italy.

*Peter Ewer*, Union Research Centre on Organisation and Technology, Melbourne, Australia.

*Clive Fullagar*, Department of Psychology, Kansas State University, Manhattan, Kansas, USA.

*Daniel G. Gallagher*, Department of Management, James Madison University, Harrisonburg, Virginia, USA.

*Raymond Harbridge*, Industrial Relations Centre, Victoria University of Wellington, Wellington, New Zealand.

*C. Gail Hepburn*, Department of Psychology, Queens University, Kingston, Ontario, Canada.

*Winton Higgins*, School of History, Philosophy and Politics, Macquarie University, Sidney, Australia.

*Anthony Honeybone*, Industrial Relations Centre, Victoria University of Wellington, Wellington, New Zealand.

*Roderick D. Iverson*, Department of Management and Industrial Relations, University of Melbourne, Parkville, Victoria, Australia.

*Boris Kagarlitsky*, Institute of Political and Labour Studies, Russian Academy of Sciences, Moscow, Russia.

*E. Kevin Kelloway*, Department of Psychology, University of Guelph, Guelph, Ontario, Canada.

*Catherine A. Loughlin*, Department of Psychology, Queens University, Kingston, Ontario, Canada.

*Ian Macun*, Sociology of Work Unit, University of Witwatersrand, Johannesburg, South Africa.

*Paul Marquardt*, Department of Psychology, Kansas State University, Manhattan, Kansas, USA.

*James E. Martin*, School of Business Administration, Wayne State University, Detroit, Michigan, USA.

*Michael McMillan*, United Food and Commercial Workers Local 951, Grand Rapids, Michigan, USA.

*Rudolf Meidner*, National Institute for Working Life, Solna, Sweden.

*Renaud Paquet*, Department of Industrial Relations, University of Quebec-Hull, Hull, Quebec, Canada.

*Wolfgang Pollan*, Austrian Institute of Economic Research, Vienna, Austria.

*Yonatan Reshef*, Faculty of Business, University of Alberta, Edmonton, Alberta, Canada.

*Claude Rioux*, Federation of Paper and Forest Workers, Quebec, Quebec, Canada.

*Robert R. Sinclair*, Department of Psychology, University of Tulsa, Tulsa, Michigan, USA.

*Anders Sjöberg*, National Institute for Working Life, Solna, Sweden.

*Renee Slick*, Department of Psychology, Kansas State University, Manhattan, Kansas, USA.

*Canan Sumer*, Department of Psychology, Kansas State University, Manhattan, Kansas, USA.

*Magnus Sverke*, Department of Psychology, Stockholm University, Stockholm, Sweden.

*Judith W. Tansky*, Department of Management, James Madison University, Harrisonburg, Virginia, USA.

*Lois E. Tetrick*, Department of Psychology, University of Houston, Houston, Texas, USA.

*Coen van Rij*, Centre for European Studies and Employment Relations, University of Amsterdam, Amsterdam, the Netherlands.

*Diane Veilleux*, School of Industrial Relations, University of Montreal, Montreal, Quebec, Canada.

*Kurt W. Wetzel*, College of Commerce, University of Saskatchewan, Saskatoon, Saskatchewan, Canada.

*Charlotte Yates*, Labor Studies/Political Science, McMaster University, Hamilton, Ontario, Canada.

# Preface

This book has emanated from the research project Emerging Union Structures which started in 1991 at the Swedish National Institute for Working Life (formerly called the Swedish Center for Working Life and the Swedish Institute for Work Life Research). In 1992, Gary Chaison at Clark University in Worcester, Massachusetts, hosted an international workshop — the Symposium on Emerging Union Structures: An International Comparison — at which we were given the opportunity to discuss our research on union structural change and member attitudes and behaviour with colleagues from Canada and the U.S. In connection with the completion of the research project in 1995, Anders Sjöberg and myself organized the Second International Conference on Emerging Structures in Stockholm, Sweden.

The chapters in this volume were selected from around 70 papers presented at this conference and have been revised to fit into the themes of the book. The contributors, who represent eleven different countries, are renowned experts in the field of trade union research. As an editor, one of my major pleasures (and major challenges as well) has been to integrate theoretical and empirical evidence from a wide variety of cultural settings, research traditions and scientific disciplines into one single volume. This international and interdisciplinary perspective represents a fundamental prerogative of the book. The contributions have resulted in a rich description of the varied environmental challenges trade unions are facing, strategical and structural attempts of unions to meet these challenges, and member-union relations in a rapidly changing industrial relations climate. The chapters have been written so as to be of relevance for researchers, students and practitioners (both management and union) interested in industrial relations and organizational behaviour.

A number of actors have facilitated my work on this book. The National Institute for Working Life sponsored the conference upon which the book is based and also provided financial support to make the book possible. Ann-Britt Hellmark and Cecilia Runström have assisted me in the editorial work. Ann-Britt has also been responsible for proof-reading the chapters and for linguistic revisions of contributions by non-native English writers, and her work has been important for the realization of the book project. Hans Anderson, Eva-Carin Barbara and Carina Ericson prepared the camera-ready copy. Niklas Bruun, Lars Grönkvist, Lena Karlsson, Lars Magnusson, Gunilla Ohlsson and Birger Viklund at the Institute provided administrative support. I am indebted to them all.

My thanks also go to my former colleagues in the Emerging Union Structures project, Bengt Abrahamsson, Kristina Ahlén, Arne H. Eriksson and Anders Sjöberg, for providing a stimulating research environment; Anders has been my co-author and a valuable discussion partner, and Bengt continues to be a source of inspiration, even after he left the project to become rector at Växjö University. I am also grateful to Johnny Hellgren, Stockholm University, for his preparedness to always listen to my ideas about the book, to Gary Chaison, Clark University, for inspiring suggestions, and to Rudolf Meidner at the Institute for sharing with me his knowledge about the tradition and vision of the Swedish labour movement.

Lastly, I would like to acknowledge the never-ceasing support of my wife, Ingrid, and my daughters, Emeli, Elina and Ebba.

*Magnus Sverke*

# Part I
# INTRODUCTION

# 1 Emerging union structures: An introduction

*Magnus Sverke*

Throughout the world, the features that for a long time have characterized industrial relations appear to be undergoing a radical change. Internationalization of capital, intensified global competition, technological change, industrial restructuring, decentralized employment relations and the introduction of flexible production systems are all examples of external challenges that trade unions have been facing for the past several years (Hyman, 1994; Kochan, Katz, and McKersie, 1986; Visser, 1994). These environmental changes have been accompanied by declines in several sectors within the manufacturing industry while a major expansion has occurred in the service sector. Simultaneously, the traditional distinctions between different industry sectors and between blue- and white-collar work have been loosened. Sectorial decline, unemployment, and blurred jurisdictional boundaries have led to eroded recruitment potentials and decreasing membership rates for many unions.

How far, then, have trade unions succeeded in adjusting to the rapidly changing industrial relations climate? There is no single comprehensive answer to this question. As noted in several recent volumes (e.g. Hyman and Ferner, 1994; Kester and Pinaud, 1996; Niland, Lansbury and Verevis, 1994; Strauss, Gallagher and Fiorito, 1991; Tetrick and Barling, 1995), it is apparent that the nature and severity of the environmental threats and challenges differ between countries as well as between unions. Depending on factors such as the severity of change, the degree to which unionism has a historical role in

Magnus Sverke, Department of Psychology, Stockholm University, 106 91 Stockholm, Sweden.

the country, employer and legislative resistance to unionism, and the strength of the particular union, the new situation can either be a grave threat or represent a challenge which can be turned into an opportunity.

Unions have effected various structural reforms, such as mergers, in order to come to grips with rapidly changing environmental conditions and declining membership numbers. Such structural reforms are, in turn, likely to affect the membership. On the other hand, members' support for union goals and willingness to participate in industrial action are of fundamental importance for unions. As noted by Davis (1994, p. 115), the 'future condition and character of unions will necessarily depend upon their ability to attract and retain members'. An understanding of the changing environmental conditions and the effects they have on unions and their members, therefore, would require theoretical and empirical evidence from both the macro and the micro level.

This book discusses the conditions for contemporary and future unionism in the light of recent economic, political and managerial changes. It presents theoretical and empirical research from Australia, Austria, Canada, Denmark, Italy, the Netherlands, New Zealand, Russia, South Africa, Sweden and the United States. Part II provides a rich international description of threats and challenges to contemporary and future unionism. It also gives a background to remaining parts in which the consequences of the challenges, and union attempts to overcome them, are further investigated. Part III focuses on union strategical and structural change. It contains chapters addressing issues such as union amalgamations, political unionism, strategic planning, decentralized wage bargaining, and strategies for implementing gender equality within unions. Part IV is concerned with the consequences of the changing union environment for member-union relations. It focuses on members' attachment to, active involvement in, and willingness to belong to unions. Some chapters also address the effects of union membership for employee role fulfilment, of employment characteristics for union attachment, and of structural and strategical union interventions for members' perceptions of their unions.

## The central role of union structure

In Chapter 2, Gary Chaison inquires into the role of union structure in unions' attempts to meet the threats and challenges of the environment. As a consequence of declining membership numbers, many unions have been forced to consider structural reforms in order better to adjust to the changing environmental conditions. Chaison also observes that decentralized employment relations and collective bargaining practices have faced unions with the dual challenge to both decentralize the authority required for local level bargaining and to centralize the resources needed to develop long-term strategies and support local unions.

There has been a tendency, Chaison notes, to use structural reforms as a means to reduce the number of small unions, increase the share of total membership in the largest unions, and rationalize overlapping union jurisdictions. Obviously, large unions benefit from economies of scale and have the opportunity to increase staff expertise and experience, but smaller unions may have a structure that fosters union identity, encourages participation and better allows for representing members' interests. The homogeneity of member interests in industrial unions may result in greater bargaining strength, while the heterogeneous membership bases of general unions might provide opportunities for union officers to centralize decision making and, thereby, possibly reduce membership participation. On the other hand, unions with narrow jurisdictions are dependent on one particular industry or craft, and thereby more susceptible to technological change. Chaison's chapter provides a research agenda and raises a number of important questions about how the emerging structures of unions may affect factors such as the implementation of union goals and strategies, the ability to represent increasingly heterogeneous member interests, the strength and bargaining power of unions, and the attitudes and behaviours of the members. These questions permeate the research presented in the remainder of chapters in this book.

## Threats and challenges to contemporary trade unionism

In connection with the gobalization of the economy and the intensified international competition, trade unions all over the world have been faced with a number of threats and challenges to traditional ways of organization and interest representation. In some countries, the existence of unions has long been recognized and accepted by both employers and governmental laws. In other countries, the notion of unionism is a new one and unions are fighting hard for the right to organize the workforce. In still other countries, the conditions of previously strong union movements have changed dramatically, resulting in severe membership losses and even in discontinuations of whole organizations. The chapters in Part II provide an overview of how the changing environmental conditions affect trade unionism in a variety of countries.

In Chapter 3, Rudolf Meidner discusses threats and challenges to contemporary Swedish trade unionism. Sweden is known to be a corporatist society with a high degree of unionization. As Meidner notes, the Swedish Model of interest representation — characterized by an active manpower policy, centralized wage bargaining and the wage policy of solidarity, and with full employment and general welfare as its goals — has served as a source of inspiration for both industrial relations scholars and trade union leaders in many countries. Although, in comparison with other countries, Sweden's traditionally high degree of unionization remained almost unaffected by the last international crisis in the late 1980s (Visser, 1994), Meidner argues that a number of environmental changes (e.g. the intensified internationalization, a decline in the manufacturing industry, an increasing unemployment level and a trend towards decentralized bargaining) have undermined the solidaristic wage policy and, therefore, threatened the Swedish model. Only by adopting strategies encompassing a return to full employment, a reconsideration of the principle of solidarity and coordinated wage claims, a strive for new forms of financial participation and a closer cooperation between blue- and white-collar unions, can the Swedish union movement, he suggests, be revitalized.

Wolfgang Pollan (Chapter 4) describes the development within another corporatist society, Austria. His focus is on the nationalized industries, which used to employ almost one third of the workforce, and their role in Austria's system of Social Partnership. As Pollan shows, even if the Social Partnership, with its strong emphasis on wage restraint, has endured for almost four decades, a number of recent changes have challenged the Austrian industrial relations system. One such change is that since the mid-1980s the traditional informal consensus regarding wage restraint has given way for large wage differentials. The recent privatization of the nationalized industries is another important factor which has affected the Social Partnership system. These changes do not necessarily imply the end of the partnership, Pollan argues, but labour market flexibility, decentralized bargaining and increasing wage differentials put unions under strong pressure and definitively indicate that Austria is on its way to a new industrial relations system.

In Chapter 5, Patrizio Di Nicola discusses recent changes in the Italian union movement. He argues that the proletarian model, characterized by egalitarianism and with a strong social appeal, was an important factor behind the rising union density in the 1970s, but that it also may have been responsible for the membership decline in the 1980s when wage differentials were called for. Despite an increasing proportion of instrumental and passive members in Italian unions, company level bargaining appears to be vital and workers — unionized as well as non-unionized — are willing to support strikes. Di Nicola furthers the idea that Italian workers have moved from membership in unions to selective support for union action, from formal to informal representation. He envisions a future characterized by decentralization, local level bargaining and more informal relationships with the unions.

Chapter 6 provides an analysis of the dramatic decline in New Zealand unionism during the past decade. Raymond Harbridge and Anthony Honeybone demonstrate that in comparison to changes in the labour market and in the public opinion, the removal of the external legitimacy of unions through impaired labour laws has been the major determinant of this decline. Whereas formerly there was a legislative basis of compulsory unionism and inclusive bargaining, the Employment Contracts Act of 1991 has led to decollectivization and a weakening of New Zealand unions. The 1990s has witnessed a dramatic decline in union density, and collective bargaining has gradually been replaced by individual employment contracts. Harbridge and Honeybone argue that in order to meet the demands of the changed industrial relations system, New Zealand unions must find new and better forms of organizing and recruitment if they are to prosper in the new environment.

In Chapter 7, Reynald Bourque and Claude Rioux illustrate how technological change confronts trade unions with challenges to traditional forms of structure and organization, and exemplify with the development in the pulp and paper industry in Quebec, Canada. Decentralization and new, flexible approaches to work organization has led to an increasing number of local agreements and a higher degree of autonomy for union locals. Bourque and Rioux observe that in many cases unions have adjusted their structures to the changed environmental conditions by broadening their agenda to encompass market imperatives and the objective of increased control over the work organization. The trend towards decentralization, they conclude, suggests the emergence of a new representational model in which a strategic alliance between the local union and the employer is maintained, and also calls for a new structural balance between local and central levels within unions.

Chapter 8 focuses on the emergence of a new industrial relations system in Russia. Boris Kagarlitsky provides a vivid description of how the breakdown of the former political system, the passage to a market economy an d the profound privatization have affected the labour market climate and the preconditions for union representation. Russia's official unions declared their independence of the communist party in 1990, which restricted their agenda to distributive and welfare issues. At the side of the official unions, a new independent union movement, with broader political ambitions and with roots in the support of the *perestroika*, gradually began to grow in the late 1980s. However, Russia's tripartite system, which 'was meaningless when the three parties were not distinct ... [because the] ... overwhelming majority of enterprises remained in state ownership, while the trade unions remained representatives of management, not of workers' (Clarke and Fairbrother, 1994, p. 377), has definitively restricted the roles of traditional as well as alternative unions. Kagarlitsky observes that unions were even more weakened in 1993, partly as a function of a conflict with the government but primarily because the Russian economy was so bad that workers' demands for reforms became more or less impossible to realize. Thus, a major challenge for Russia, as for eastern Europe in general (Héthy, 1994), appears to be to achieve both economic and political stability, and unions still have to find their role in this process.

In Chapter 9, Ian Macun sketches the development in the South African trade union movement from 1979, the year when unionism for black workers was legally recognized. He shows that, in contrast to many other countries, South African unionism has flourished and union density has increased steadily since then, despite high levels of unemployment and a poor economic performance in the 1980s and 1990s. Also in contrast to most industrialized countries, South Africa has a very large number of trade unions, most of which are small and unaffiliated to the major confederations. Obviously, the 'voice' mechanism of unions (Freeman and Medoff, 1984), but also other factors such as the legislative reforms, have been important for achieving growth. Within the federations, the affiliated unions are characterized by a high degree of autonomy. Although the affiliate-driven confederations have rationalized their structures and there has been a tendency from small craft unions to large multi-unions, primarily through merger, Macun argues that extended cooperation between federations as well as more centralized policy-making are required in order to increase the unity and power of the South African trade union movement.

## Union strategical and structural change

As is apparent from the chapters in Part II, major economic, political and social transformations are having profound implications for industrial relations and the conditions for union organization. Unions throughout the world are faced with new threatening and challenging environmental circumstances, some of which have a more or less universal applicability, while others are unique to specific countries. As was highlighted by Chaison in Chapter 2, unions have considered, and applied, a variety of strategical and structural reforms in their attempts to adjust to the rapidly changing environment. The chapters in Part III analyze how several important forms of union strategical and structural change have been implemented in different countries.

One crucial form of union structural change concerns rationalized jurisdictions and membership growth through merger (Chaison, 1986). Charlotte Yates and Peter Ewer (Chapter 10) investigate how Australian and

Canadian unions have applied amalgamations in response to environmental transformation and membership decline. They identify more than a hundred mergers in Australia from the mid-1980s to the mid-1990s and more than seventy mergers in Canada during this period. A major difference between the two countries, Yates and Ewer argue, is that in Australia mergers have been pursued through a maintenance of centralized structures and in combination with recruitment based on services to the memberships, whereas in Canada there has been a lack of federational structure policies which has led to a variety of organizational strategies. Even if unions in both countries have striven for a European type of industrial unionism, the merger waves have rather resulted in general unions with blurred jurisdictions and heterogeneous membership bases. This raises the question, Yates and Ewer note, of how union identities can be reformulated to encompass the diverging interests of a heterogeneous membership body in order to secure members' commitment to, and support of, the union organization.

In Chapter 11, Dianne Veilleux and Renaud Paquet focus on the degree of autonomy of local unions of national and international unions in Canada. Their analysis of the constitutions of thirteen of the largest and most representative unions in Canada shows that these unions overall exercize a more or less exclusive control over their locals, that the degree of autonomy does not differ between national and international unions, that local union autonomy varies considerably among industrial unions, and that nationally certified unions in the federal public service grant very little autonomy to their locals. As emphasized in this chapter, the balance between local and central level authority is vital to union organization because the local union is the organizational unit which recruits new members, negotiates the terms of employment and represents members' professional interests, while centralization is inevitable for the furthering of union solidarity and for increasing bargaining power. Veilleux and Paquet note that the trend towards decentralization may provide local unions with an opportunity to redefine their roles in the union structure, but whether local unions aspire increased decentralization, and how this can be achieved while preserving union solidarity, remains to be seen.

Chapter 12 provides an in-depth analysis of one particular aspect of decentralization in another country — the local pay bargaining system in the Danish public sector — and its potential implications for union organization and representation. Torben Andersen identifies three characteristics of this decentralized pay bargaining system: the decentralized bargaining structure has resulted in decentralization of bargaining competence from federations to unions; the extended coverage of pay bargaining has provided local levels with more flexibility, and; the new pay system, payment by qualifications and results, has paved the way for a more individualized wage determination. Although still only a marginal proportion of wages are distributed from local wage pools, these have, Andersen argues, had a profound effect on the strategies and behaviour of local management and unions. While the analysis indicates that local wage pools to some extent may reinforce existing relationships between management and employees, Andersen maintains that they have the additional potential to increase member participation and to improve bargaining qualifications. In the long run this could provide an opportunity to develop competencies also in other areas, such as work organization and production issues.

The next two chapters focus on strategies to improve the representation of women's interests in trade unions. As emphasized in both these chapters, the representation of women is both a question of justice — all workers should have the right and opportunity to participate in union activity — and a necessity if the interests of women are not to be overlooked. Winton Higgins (Chapter 13) analyzes a large female dominated Swedish public sector union which has union feminism, the achievement of gender equality, as a highly prioritized issue on its agenda. In order to overcome problems of under-representation of women on union posts, the union has implemented a variety of strategies (e.g. women's networks, mentor schemes, training programmes and more informal meeting formats) which have facilitated women's participation in union activity. The union has also been involved in issues of work organization; it has initiated bottom-up projects aiming at improving both the cost-efficiency and the service quality in the public sector. Higgins shows that the union has been feminized in recent years — the number of women in representative positions has increased and the union was the first within the blue-collar federation to have a woman on the top post. His analysis also stresses the importance of building a commitment to reform into the very structure of the union if strategical change is to be successfully implemented.

Departing from the observation that a lack of responsiveness by trade unions to women's interests undermines their legitimacy as democratic institutions, Jennifer Curtin (Chapter 14) investigates whether unions in Sweden and Australia encourage women to participate and if the structures of unions allow for the representation of women and their interests. She notes that Swedish trade unionism, as a function of its underlying universal class politics, is more gender neutral and focuses on general issues of equality rather than on women's issues, while in Australian unionism there has been a tradition of representing the identities of women in gender specific terms. However, in both countries women are under-represented at most levels of the union hierarchy, but there has been a tendency to come to grips with this problem through changed meeting times and styles, education and networks for moral support. Curtin concludes that better representation of women and their interests not only is crucial for the effectiveness and legitimacy of trade unions, but also may attract more potential women members.

Since the strategies for achieving goals, the bargaining structure and the organizational structure of unions are all interrelated (Kochan and Katz, 1988), and represent 'choice variables' over which unions can exercise discretion in adjusting to changing environmental conditions (Fiorito, Gramm and Hendricks, 1991), planning for the implementation of desired strategies and structures is an issue of fundamental concern for trade unions. In Chapter 15, Kay Devine and Yonatan Reshef provide a framework for the understanding and analysis of union planning. They identify three major types of planning: reactive (i.e. quick and *ad hoc* reactions to unexpected events), operational (i.e. plans that guide daily operations such as budgeting, bargaining and staffing) and strategic planning (i.e. a formulation of strategies that is based on a vision, derived from various alternatives and encompasses member interests from all levels of the organization). Their empirical analysis shows that strategic planning is more frequent at higher levels in the union hierarchy while union locals, partly as a function of limited resources, mainly engage in reactive and operational planning. However, rather than primarily reacting to external changes, union leaders at all levels must, Devine and Reshef argue, rethink and reformulate basic assumptions about union practices and more frequently apply strategic planning in order proactively to meet the challenges of a rapidly changing environment.

## Member-union relations

While the chapters in Part II describe the threats and challenges posed by a rapidly changing industrial relations climate, the chapters in Part III illustrate some of the strategic and structural changes unions have implemented in handling these threats and challenges. Naturally, both sets of factors discussed in the previous parts — changing employment relations and structural reforms — will have consequences for members' attitudes towards, and involvement in, their unions (Barling, Fullagar and Kelloway, 1992; Hartley, 1995). As Chaison observes in Chapter 2, the critical question is how macro-level changes are related to micro-level outcomes. The chapters in Part IV investigate member-union relations in terms of factors such as attachment to unions, joining and leaving unions and participation in union activity. They also examine how members are affected by employment conditions, union structural change and strategy implementations.

In Chapter 16, Kevin Kelloway, Julian Barling and Victor Catano provide an introduction to the concept of union attitudes. They note that union attitudes have a central role in the unionization process in that individual attitudes towards labour unions are related to key aspects of unionization (e.g. joining, commitment, participation and decertification). Although specific attitudes, such as job dissatisfaction and the perception that the union is instrumental in redressing specific dissatisfactions, have been found to be better predictors of these key criteria as compared to general attitudes, Kelloway et al. argue that general union attitudes may serve a gate-keeping role through which union and job experiences are translated into attachment to, or disengagement from, the union. The critical role of favourable general attitudes towards unions thus suggests, Kelloway et al. conclude, that strategies aimed at improving both workers' knowledge about unions and the public image of the labour movement are important, not least today when unions are being attacked by media, legislation and employers.

Coen van Rij and Annelies Daalder (Chapter 17) examine the applicability of business-cycle models, in which economic developments are assumed to affect aggregate unionism, for micro-level unionization decisions of individuals. Given that these models of union growth and decline are based on assumptions of individual worker decisions (Visser, 1988), van Rij and Daalder evaluate the relative importance of macro-economic factors and micro-level characteristics in the prediction of unionization decisions using data from the Netherlands, where union membership is optional. The results show that individuals' opinions (e.g. attitudes towards unions), experiences of unions (e.g. meeting attendance), social environment (e.g. level of unionization at the workplace) and personal characteristics (e.g. gender and employment history) are more important than macro-economic factors (e.g. aggregated levels of unemployment, prices) in explaining micro-level decisions of individuals to join and leave trade unions. Still, the macro-economic factors included in business-cycle models are important, van Rij and Daalder argue, because they shape the environment in which individuals' experiences and attitudes are formed.

In Chapter 18, Gail Hepburn, Catherine Loughlin and Julian Barling take another perspective on union joining and inquire into the factors which may lead individuals to abstain from voting in union certification elections. A better understanding of this issue is, as emphasized by the authors, of fundamental concern for trade unions because certification elections are typically determined by such small margins that the number of abstainers may influence the election outcome if they decide to vote. Using a Canadian sample, Hepburn et al. find that workers' levels of job satisfaction, general attitudes towards unions and perceptions of peer pressures regarding unionization, differentiate between those who vote for the union, those who vote against and those who abstain from voting, in that abstainers have more neutral views while voters tend to hold more extreme positions. Even more important, abstainers are found to differ from voters irrespective of the direction of the vote — those who abstain express much less interest in the election and perceive their vote less likely to make a difference to the election outcome. Thus, a crucial issue for unions (and management), Hepburn et al. conclude, is to identify potential abstainers and convince them of the instrumentality of their vote.

The next two chapters focus on the nature of union attitudes and make a distinction between ideological and instrumental attitudes. Clive Fullagar, Renee Slick, Canan Sumer and Paul Marquardt (Chapter 19) investigate to what extent these two dimensions of union attitudes can be explained from cultural beliefs. Their empirical analyses, which are based on a U.S. sample, imply that in cultures which are of a collectivist nature and where there are large power distances, union attitudes will tend to be ideological, whereas in cultures characterized by an individualistic orientation, union attitudes are more likely to be of an instrumental kind. Magnus Sverke and Anders Sjöberg (Chapter 20) examine how ideological and instrumental commitment to the union are related to members' involvement in union activity. Using three samples of Swedish blue-collar workers, they find that ideological commitment, an identification with the values of the union, appears to be crucial for the decision to engage in union activity, while instrumental commitment, a calculative attachment based on the benefits associated with membership, predicts only those forms of union involvement which are associated with relatively low degrees of personal effort, such as the propensity to retain union membership and to participate in union meetings. Both these chapters stress the importance of assessing the relevance of the distinction between ideological and instrumental attitudes to countries characterized by varying degrees of business unionism and social movement unionism.

In Chapter 21, Robert Sinclair, James Martin, Lois Tetrick and Michael McMillan examine the role of union stewards in union functioning and test a model of stewards' satisfaction with the union, participation in union activity and perceptions of union performance. As the authors note, stewards are generally recognized to have an important role in shaping members' attitudes and behaviour, but only a limited amount of research has been directed at unravelling the antecedents and consequences of stewards' behaviour. Sinclair et al.'s longitudinal data from a sample of stewards in the U.S. demonstrate the influence of stewards' satisfaction and participation on perceptions of union performance. The results imply, the authors argue, that positive exchange relationships of stewards with the union, as manifested in their satisfaction with the union, are likely to lead to increased participation for both stewards and rank and file members which, in turn, could be expected to result in improved union performance.

The next two chapters address the fundamental issue of the relationship between employee and member roles by examining the effects of union membership on employee behaviour (Chapter 22) and of employment status on members' attachment to the union (Chapter 23). Donna Buttigieg and Roderick Iverson (Chapter 22) provide a test of the exit-voice hypothesis in an Australian work setting. Departing from the work of Freeman and Medoff (1984) and the observation that unionized workers tend to express higher levels of job dissatisfaction but to have lower turnover rates than non-unionized workers, they examine the impact of union membership on job satisfaction and two forms of exit, voluntary absenteeism and intention to quit. After controlling for a variety of job attributes, contextual variables and individual characteristics, their empirical results show that union membership does not predict job satisfaction, but that both job satisfaction and union membership predict exit behaviour, as measured by voluntary absenteeism and intention to quit. Buttigieg and Iverson's findings, that members and non-members do not differ in terms of job satisfaction, and that union members are more inclined to make use of the exit option, raise some interesting challenges to traditional assumptions of exit-voice theory.

In Chapter 23, Daniel Gallagher, Judith Tansky and Kurt Wetzel focus on the recent managerial trend towards the restructuring of employment contracts in order to increase flexibility through key-time employment (cf. Hartley, 1995). Given that many unions have historically opposed part-time employment as a threat to full-time jobs or as a means to undermine worker power, Gallagher et al. inquire into the relationship between employment status and union attachment. They find that full-time workers tend to express higher levels of union commitment than their part-time counterparts. The results also show that, after controlling for the effects of demographic, tenure, socialization and union performance variables, employment status is not related to attitudinal commitment (loyalty to the union), but, in two of the three Canadian samples used, to more active forms of commitment (responsibility to the union and willingness to work for the union). Gallagher et al. conclude that differences in union commitment between full-timers and part-timers may vary depending on the dimension of commitment under examination, and that, most importantly, even when significant, employment status *per se* has only a limited effect on members' commitment to their union.

The two final chapters employ quasi-experimental designs and investigate how members are affected by structural (Chapter 24) and strategical (Chapter 25) reforms of their union. In Chapter 24, Magnus Sverke and Anders Sjöberg examine the short-term effects of a merger between two Swedish blue-collar unions on members' attitudes towards, and active involvement in, the union. As noted both in this chapter and elsewhere (e.g. Chaison, 1986), mergers represent a frequently occurring form of union structural change, and they are generally seen as tools for improving cost effectiveness, bargaining power and membership growth, but very little is known about how they influence the membership. In contrasting members of the merging unions with members of a comparison union both before and shortly after the merger, Sverke and Sjöberg find that the merger had negative, albeit small, effects on members' union meeting attendance, but that it did not affect their attitudes towards the union or the frequency of union office holding. This suggests, they argue, that membership growth, economies of scale, and more powerful and centralized governing structures through mergers can be achieved while preserving pre-merger levels of union attitudes and participation if the structural change is well implemented and anchored among the memberships.

Victor Catano and Kevin Kelloway (Chapter 25) observe that in times of rapidly changing economic, political and social climates, unions can choose between passively reacting to impaired employment conditions or actively undertaking systematic strategical efforts to counteract the impairments. They study a political action campaign, designed in opposition to the privatization of public companies and the down-sizing of services in a Canadian province, of a union representing the government employees, and evaluate whether the campaign had an effect on the members. Catano and Kelloway find that the campaign was successful in that members' attitudes about privatization and towards the government became more negative in comparison to their beliefs prior to the campaign. The results also indicate that members became more definite in their perceptions of the union's power, and that they supported the idea of using union dues for funding political action. The study implies, Catano and Kelloway argue, that unions can take action to change the beliefs and attitudes of their members.

## Concluding remarks

The chapters in this volume identify specific factors that have affected unionism in single countries, but they also suggest a number of general threats and challenges to contemporary and future trade unionism. For many unions in many countries, economic, political, legislative, social, and managerial changes have resulted in membership decline. This is especially unfortunate given that unionization and collective bargaining coverage is fundamental for democratic worker representation in the workplace (Kochan and Wever, 1991).

The chapters also provide important insights into the character and consequences of the strategical and structural reforms that unions have implemented to adjust to the rapidly changing environment and to reverse the declining trends. In this respect, union mergers have frequently been used as a means of maintaining, or obtaining, sufficient size. Although a large number of members may result in economies of scale and allow for providing services to the membership, an increased size through mergers typically also implies a broadening of jurisdictions and an associated diversity of member interests. A large number of members is, undoubtedly, necessary for union strength, but it is not a sufficient condition. Since the power of an organization may be viewed as a multiplicative function of resources and mobilization (Blalock, 1967), a large number of members constitutes an important resource. But the mobilization of this resource into action also suggests that a strong union requires members' support for union goals as manifested in their active participation in the fulfilment of these goals. The strength of a union is, as noted by among others Gallagher and Strauss (1991, p. 139), to a large extent dependent upon the union's 'ability to mobilize its members not only in strikes but also in policing the collective agreement, filing grievances, and serving in the capacity of union stewards or committee members'. Thus, a challenge for trade unions is to find ways of representing increasingly heterogeneous interests and translate them into all-encompassing identities in order to create the fundamental basis of members' involvement in the union.

As emphasized in several chapters, the trend towards more individualized employment relations call into question the traditional ways of union organization and interest representation. The gradual replacement of central bargaining with more decentralized forms requires a corresponding decentralization of the structures and decision-making authorities of unions, but, at the same time, it also calls for the centralization of expertise, coordinating capacities and long-term strategy making. As Kochan and Wever (1991, p. 374) noted, 'to address changes in employer strategies and human resource policies, unions must significantly broaden their own involvement at levels "above" and "below" collective bargaining'.

Such broadening at the strategic level not only involves providing bargaining support, coordinating members' interests and maintaining worker unity, but also suggests that unions must rethink and reformulate their goals and strategies, and build a commitment to implementing these into the very structure of the organization. In doing this, they can choose between a number of identities (cf. Hyman, 1994). Is the main objective of the union to provide its members with services and benefits? Is work organization issues and productivity coalitions with management its primary goals? Does the union have alternative social, economic or political visions? The research presented in the present volume indicates that unions consider various strategies, or combinations of strategies, aimed at establishing the desired union identity, and that such strategies can be successfully implemented.

A broadening at the workplace level points to the necessity of winning members' support. Decentralized collective bargaining practices require the voluntary efforts of an increasing number of members serving as union representatives. The chapters included here provide important insights into the psychological mechanisms that may lead members to involve actively in their unions. Not least importantly, they also suggest that members' relations with their unions can be influenced by structural and strategical efforts of unions.

To conclude, this volume provides a rich description of threats and challenges to contemporary and future unionism, and presents research addressing how the changing environmental conditions affect unions and their members. It also demonstrates the importance of applying an international and multi-disciplinary perspective on the analysis of these issues. The inclusion of both macro- and micro-level research deepens the understanding of the mutual relationships between the conditions of the industrial relations environment, the structural and strategical changes of unions, and the attitudes and behaviours of members.

## References

Barling, J., Fullagar, C. and Kelloway, E. K. (1992), *The union and its members: A psychological approach*, Oxford University Press, New York.

Blalock, H. (1967), *Toward a theory of minority group relations*, Wiley, New York.

Chaison, G. N. (1986), *When unions merge*, Lexington Books, Lexington, MA.

Clarke, S. and Fairbrother, P. (1994), 'Post-communism and the emergence of industrial relations in the workplace', in Hyman, R. and Ferner, A. (eds.), *New frontiers in European industrial relations*, pp. 368–397, Blackwell, Oxford, UK.

Davis, E. (1994), 'Trade unionism in the future', in Niland, J. R., Lansbury, R. D. and Verevis, C. (eds.), *The future of industrial relations: Global change and challenges*, pp. 115–134, Sage, Thousand Oaks, CA.

Fiorito, J., Gramm, C. L. and Hendricks, W. E. (1991), 'Union structural choices', in Strauss, G., Gallagher, D. G. and Fiorito, J. (eds.), *The state of the unions*, pp. 103-137, Industrial Relations Research Association, Madison, WI.

Freeman, R. B. and Medoff, J. L. (1984), *What do unions do?*, Basic Books, New York.

Gallagher, D. G. and Strauss, G. (1991), 'Union membership attitudes and participation', In Strauss, G. Gallagher, D. G. and Fiorito, J. (eds.), *The state of the unions*, pp. 139–174, Industrial Relations Research Association, Madison, WI.

Hartley, J. (1995), 'Challenge and change in employment relations: Issues for psychology, trade unions, and managers', in Tetrick, L. E. and Barling, J. (eds.), *Changing employment relations: Behavioral and social perspectives*, pp. 3-30, American Psychological Association, Washington, DC.

Héthy, L. (1994), 'Tripartism in eastern Europe', in Hyman, R. and Ferner, A. (eds.), *New frontiers in European industrial relations*, pp. 313–336, Blackwell, Oxford, UK.

Hyman, A. (1994), 'Changing trade union identities and strategies', in Hyman, R. and Ferner, A. (eds.), *New frontiers in European industrial relations*, pp. 108–139, Blackwell, Oxford, UK.

Hyman, R. and Ferner, A. (eds.) (1994), *New frontiers in European industrial relations*, Blackwell, Oxford, UK.

Kester, G. and Pinaud, H. (eds.), (1996), *Trade unions and democratic participation in Europe: A scenario for the 21st century*, Avebury, Aldershot, UK.

Kochan, T. A. and Katz, H. C. (1988), *Collective bargaining and industrial relations*, Irwin, Homewood, IL.

Kochan, T. A., Katz, H. C. and McKersie, R. B. (1986), *The transformation of American industrial relations*, Basic Books, New York.

Kochan, T. A. and Wever, K. R. (1991), 'American unions and the future of worker representation', in Strauss, G., Gallagher, D. G. and Fiorito, J. (eds.), *The state of the unions*, pp. 363-386, Industrial Relations Research Association, Madison, WI.

Niland, J. R., Lansbury, R. D. and Verevis, C. (eds.) (1994), *The future of industrial relations: Global change and challenges*, Sage, Thousand Oaks, CA.

Strauss, G., Gallagher, D. G. and Fiorito, J. (eds.) (1991), *The state of the unions*, Industrial Relations Research Association, Madison, VI.

Tetrick, L. E. and Barling, J. (eds.) (1995), *Changing employment relations: Behavioral and social perspectives*, American Psychological Association, Washington, DC.

Visser, J. (1988), 'Trade unionism in Europe: Present situation and prospects', *Labor and Society*, Vol. 14, pp. 125-182.

Visser, J. (1994), 'European trade unions: The transition years', in Hyman, R. and Ferner, A. (eds.), *New frontiers in European industrial relations*, pp. 80–107, Blackwell, Oxford, UK.

# 2 Reforming and rationalizing union structure: New directions and unanswered questions

*Gary N. Chaison*

There is a resurgence of interest in union structure among legislators, union officers, employers and the academic community. In many countries, research is planned or underway on such issues as the effects of union size and type, the composition of labour movements, union processes for governance and administration, inter-union relations, and union members' commitment, satisfaction and participation.

This concern with aspects of union structure is the result of the confluence of two historical trends. First, as most unions either failed to grow or lost members since the early 1980s, they were forced to consider structural changes that would enable them to survive in hard times. Should they merge with other unions, combine their smaller locals, centralize administration for greater financial control, or diversify their membership base to protect against sudden membership losses, among other options? Little can be done about recessions and rising foreign competition, but structure remains a 'choice variable', something over which unions can exercise discretion as they adjust to a threatening environment (Fiorito, Gramm and Hendricks, 1991).

Second, in many industrialized countries collective bargaining has become decentralized as negotiations shifted from national and industry levels to company and workplace levels (Katz, 1993; Niland, 1994). This was usually caused by employers who sought greater flexibility in compensation and settlements more closely related to the conditions of the firm or workplace. Unions now have to negotiate at local levels where they have had little experience and where they customarily see their role as enforcing rather than

---

Gary N. Chaison, Graduate School of Management, Clark University, Worcester, MA 01610, USA.

determining settlements. At the same time, they have had to strengthen their national organizations. Niland (1994, p. 461) observed the dual pressures on union structure:

> The leadership and structural challenge is to both decentralize the power and authority needed to bargain at enterprise level, and centralize the provisions of staff expertise and other resources needed to develop long-run strategies and advise local union entities on the increasingly complex array of technical, economic and organizational issues that confront labor today. How this is eventually settled in each case will say much about the likely future relevance of trade unions in modern industrial society.

The concern for union structure has inspired several proposals for reform and rationalization. These include not only reports of commissions on the state of industrial relations and labour markets, but also the strategic studies of labour federations, government white papers that precede new labour laws, studies commissioned by employer associations, and the commentaries of union officers.[1] Macro-level changes, such as the reduction in the number of unions, are usually linked to micro-level outcomes, for instance, better representation at the workplace or fewer inter-union disputes. The proposals raise difficult, controversial questions and reveal gaps in our understanding of union structure.

## The elements of union reform

Regardless of their author or country of origin, a common thread — three fundamental premises — runs through the vast majority of reform proposals. First, *union fragmentation,* the presence of many small unions, *should be reduced.* Second, *union concentration,* the share of total membership in the largest unions, *should be increased.* Third, *union jurisdictions should be rationalized* by reducing overlap in union memberships and having one or a few unions in each industry or group of related industries.

### *Union fragmentation*

Small unions are characterized as ineffectual, unable to meet the rising costs of union administration, lacking economies of scale in operation, and providing a limited array of membership services. Fragmented labour movements are said to be in disarray, torn by continuous inter-union disputes and too weak to repel employers' and governments' attacks on unionism (Chaison, 1980, 1986; Stewart, 1989).

The alleged threshold of union effectiveness apparently varies from country to country. In Canada, small unions were created from the numerous regional public employees' unions and breakaway sections of U.S.-based international unions. Unions with fewer than 25,000 members were said to be unable to function effectively on a national basis (Chaison, 1980).[2]

In the United States, smallness seems to be a problem for unions with less than 50,000 members. For example, a federation officer observed:

> The largest drop in union membership has been in the smallest unions, who don't have the resources to organize and to fight employers determined to get rid of them. In this tough climate, it's hard to imagine that a national organization with less than 50,000 members can really do much more than hold its own (Noble 1986, p. 5).

An article in the *New York Times* reported:

> Small unions — those with 50,000 or fewer members — have fallen on troubled times. Their numbers are shrinking and the resources for serving their members and organizing workers are often insufficient to meet the demands of today's labor movement (Shabecoff 1980, p. 19).

In Australia, employers, union officers and legislators shared the belief that under a centralized system of wage determination, effective worker representation was beyond the reach of the smallest unions. It was unclear how small was too small. The minimum size for unions to register with the federal government and be full participants in the labour relations system was increased from 100 members to 1,000 members in 1988 and 10,000 members in 1991. But as the emphasis shifted toward representation at the enterprise level, the minimum size returned to 100 members in 1993 (Stewart, 1989; Niland and Spooner, 1992).[3]

### *Union concentration*

Advocates of structural reform envision compact, streamlined labour movements — constellations of mega- or super-unions surrounded by either nothing or by a few small, highly specialized unions. For example, in the United States, the president of the Laborers International Union said Americans should consider the European approach of having about 15 unions in each country ('Labor letter', 1993).[4] The head of the British GMB, a proponent of the 'super-bloc' model, envisioned a British labour movement centred around four general unions, each having more than 2 million members ('British unions divided on mergers', 1989).

In the later 1980s, the leaders of the Australian Council of Trade Unions (ACTU) revealed a blueprint for a labour movement of twenty or fewer large unions to be formed through complex sequences of mergers. Restructuring was nearly completed by the end of 1993; there were 18 industry-wide, multi-industry or multi-craft unions, of which 17 were formed from mergers of 110 unions since 1989 (Australian Council of Trade Unions, 1994).

### *Union jurisdiction*

It is often proposed that jurisdictions be rationalized by reducing overlap in union memberships and having one or a few unions in each industry or group of related industries. This is accomplished by transferring members from one union to another or, more practically, encouraging mergers among unions in similar jurisdictions.

The realignment of jurisdictional boundaries is intended to reduce both multi-unionism, i.e. the presence of many unions at an individual workplace or enterprise, and union rivalry in the recruitment of new members or the assignment of work (jurisdictional or demarcation disputes). Rationalization of jurisdiction is nearly synonymous with industrial unionism and enjoys popular support. Gill and Griffin (1981, p. 365) commented on the trend in Australia:

> This consistent commitment to industry-based unions is momentous, as it is seen in the interests not only of workers and employers but also of the system and the process of adjusting to change. More generally, the analysis is set in a consensual framework and reforms are posited as part of the system's need for order.

The British also see a compelling logic in industrial unionism, a way to modernize their antiquated union structure of numerous small regional and craft unions. In the late 1970s, an employer association complained of too many unions with overlapping boundaries, an Employment Secretary spoke of the need to 'frame and create a rational structure', and a retired union leader saw 'an obvious need and desire to combine to produce one union for all workers in a particular industry' (Lover, 1980, p. 98).

At the heart of proposals for the reform, we find the related goals of fewer small unions, more large unions, and less jurisdictional overlap. But beyond these are three fundamental questions that are rarely addressed: Should the reform of union structure be legislated in the public interest? What is the future of the small union in the restructured labour movement? Is it too late to rationalize union jurisdiction?

## Should the reform of union structure be legislated in the public interest?

Gill and Griffin (1981, p. 363) observed that 'public policy toward union structure can only be indirect: as an analogy a liberal state can facilitate marriage but it cannot compel it'. I believe this underestimates both the intentions and the powers of the state. Governments can and have compelled changes in union structure by equating structural change with the furtherance of the public interest and by controlling access to representational status. The public policy of union mergers is a good illustration of this point.

In the United States, legislation does not compel mergers in general or between specific types of unions. Mergers are treated as internal union affairs. The National Labor Relations Board is concerned with whether a merger is carried out in accordance with the provisions of the unions' constitutions and whether it substantively alters the identities of the unions that were selected by employees as their bargaining agents (Chaison, 1986). The Canadian labour boards have taken a similar approach, although they have forced a merger when bargaining units were consolidated in the postal system in 1988. In Britain, government officials scrutinize merger petitions and ballots but only to ensure that they are freely approved by an informed membership (Chaison, 1997). In contrast, Australian merger procedures are designed to control form and frequency. Legislative amendments in 1972 discouraged mergers, particularly among large unions, by requiring majority turnouts in merger votes. But this was revised in 1983 and 1990 to encourage amalgamations of unions in similar jurisdictions and absorptions of small unions into much larger ones. A reduced voter turnout is permitted when unions share a community of interest. Members of large unions do not have to vote when very small unions are being absorbed (Creighton, Ford and Mitchell, 1993). In addition, by the raising of minimum size of federally registered unions, the Australian government coerced small unions to merge by sending the unambiguous signal that they must grow, merge, or perish, unless exempted from the rule.

Although legislation can produce planned structural change, it remains unclear how far the state can and should go in modifying union structure. The relevant questions are obvious but seldom asked. When are high levels of union fragmentation (too many small unions) or concentration (too many large unions or too many members in the top unions) contrary to the public interest? Should a compact labour movement be a policy objective? The creation of larger unions might reduce inter-union disputes and increase administrative efficiency. But does it also reduce the ability of union members to influence union policy? Is competition between unions contrary to the public interest because it wastes union resources and leads to jurisdictional disputes? Might it also improve the quality of union services and the responsiveness of union officers? Is the public interest best served or protected when a labour movement has some particular mix of large and small unions, or regional and national unions, or industrial and occupational unions?

Advocates of structural reform claim that 'unions must be regarded as the sources and not the objects of reform' (Gill and Griffin, 1981, p. 362), but this seems unlikely if reform is closely tied to the public interest. Governments unfriendly to unions could argue that the greater good is served by having, for example, more small unions to carry out state-sponsored enterprise bargaining, or unions confined to industries to reduce jurisdictional disputes. The real purpose might be to limit union size, financial resources and political clout. It is noteworthy that the public interest, expressed in terms of national competitiveness, has been used to justify legislation, promoted as reforms, that weakened unions in Britain and decollectivized labour relations in New Zealand (Chaison, 1997).

The definition of the public interest in union structure is far more than a theoretical matter. Before it is too late and poor policies are accepted and good ones rejected, we need an informed debate about the societal impact of union structure and the appropriate role of the state in the reform and rationalization.

## What is the future of the small union in restructured labour movements?

Proponents of structural reform usually assume that small unions are ineffective. As I noted earlier, critics point to the apparent lack of economies of scale in operations; there are too few members to financially support or utilize specialized union departments, a wide array of union services, and expert staff. Small unions cannot afford organizing, strike benefits, and labour education programs. Nor can they lobby effectively or maintain the legal staff necessary to contest unfair labour practices and prepare wage and grievance cases for tribunals (ACTU/TDC Mission to Western Europe, 1987).

The size at which unions achieve economies of scale is rising because it has become more expensive to pay officers and staff and maintain headquarters. Also, members of smaller unions now have greater expectations about the quantity and quality of services that their unions should provide. This is because large unions now commonly recruit members outside of their traditional jurisdictions and, in this competition, small unions are being compared by members as well as non-union workers with these 'full-service unions' (Chaison, 1986).

It has been argued elsewhere (e.g., Chaison, 1980, 1986) that small size may not be problematic to unions that negotiate only a few collective agreements, or that represent specialized groups or workers in narrow geographic areas. These would include national unions of professional athletes, airline pilots and performing artists, regional unions of public employees, and enterprise unions at large companies.

Also, there might be advantages to small size. Officers of small unions answer their many critics by arguing that they are able to maintain close contact with members and are responsive to their needs. For example, the general secretary of the Rossendale Union of Boot, Shoe and Slipper Operatives (2,000 members in 20 factories in Lancashire, Britain) claimed: 'Our structure is firmly based on the shop floor and in the local community. We know all of our members and employers and understand what's going on in the factories and the communities' ('Small unions happy to fight on', 1992, p. 15). Moreover, small unions that are limited to narrow geographic areas can facilitate much-needed job mobility among workers by providing continuity of earnings and encouraging the upgrading of skills. In this way, they could be crucial to regional industrial development. Thus, community-based unions might provide a new sense of purpose and legitimacy to labour movements (Piore, 1991).

We should not assume that the size-effectiveness relationship is simple or direct. Strauss (1993, p. 11) noted that 'minimum and optimum size of a union may depend on a variety of factors: labor and product market size, the variability of employment, employers' attitudes, average income per member, the availability of legal protections, among others'. Size effects may also be moderated by the geographic dispersion and homogeneity of the membership and whether the small union is growing or declining (Strauss, 1993).

Despite the complexity of size effects, reform proposals nevertheless conclude that bigger is better for unions, their members, and their labour movements. Although it may be too late for small unions in Australia and New Zealand where minimum size requirements created a rush to merge, some questions about small unions must be answered before their fate is sealed elsewhere. What is the relationship between union size and representational effectiveness, financial solvency, and membership satisfaction, participation and commitment? And how can these relationships be altered? For instance, can large unions somehow maintain the same level of membership participation as smaller ones? Can small unions increase their variety and quality of membership services without expanding or merging?

More specifically, can large unions gain some benefits of smallness by chartering homogeneous locals or regional divisions? Can small unions attain economies of scale in operations by forming alliances with each other or becoming autonomous sections of national unions after mergers?

**Is it too late to rationalize union jurisdiction?**

The rationalization of union jurisdiction entails reducing the overlap between unions' memberships, usually by creating industrial unions. A Special Review Body of the British Trades Union Congress observed that industrial unions have greater strength in collective bargaining because of the common interests of members. They can establish coherent wage policies, lower the incidence of jurisdictional disputes, create uniform policies towards industry development, reduce conflicts between local branches, operate with fewer full-time union staff, and provide a higher level of membership services (Trades Union Congress, 1988).

Jurisdictional boundaries can be realigned by law or federation policy, through transfers of members or the promotion of mergers. But the debates over jurisdiction are often so old and intense that we fail to notice that jurisdictions are now so muddled and union membership so diverse that any appreciable degree of rationalization is impossible.

In the United States, union jurisdiction as a statement of organizing accomplishment or intent is nearly meaningless. A study of the scope of organizing in the mid-1970s and 1980s found that;

> statements of union jurisdiction have lost their force and authority as restraints in the selection of organizing targets. As a result, organizing is opportunistic in the sense that unions can recruit members where they believe they have the greatest chances of winning [certification] elections even if they must venture beyond the industries that are considered to be within their primary or traditional jurisdiction (Chaison and Dhavale, 1990, p. 307).

Major unions recruited outside their traditional jurisdictions; nearly all organized in wholesale and retail trade, health services, and food and kindred products, and about half were in textiles and printing and publishing. In the mid-1980s, 13 unions organized in at least 40 of the 84 industry classifications.

Union mergers in the United States have blurred the boundaries of jurisdiction beyond recognition. The Steelworkers absorbed the Upholsterers (1985) and the Electronic Workers took in the Furniture Workers (1986). The Communications Workers created a media division from the Typographical Union (1987). The National Writers Union became part of the Auto Workers (1991), the Garment Workers joined the Food and Commercial Workers (1994), the Firemen and Oilers went into the Service Employees (1994) and, in a particularly odd match, a nurses' association in New Jersey affiliated with the Operating Engineers (1992) (Williamson, 1995). In the early 1980s, the Communications Workers absorbed a large local of state police in Texas, while the United Food and Commercial Workers' new affiliates included locals of leather workers in New York City and baseball players in Puerto Rico ('Independent joins CWA', 1992; United Food and Commercial Workers, 1993). Finally, the Service Employees absorbed 47 local independent unions and 7 state employee associations between 1980 and 1993; among the new members were social workers and prison guards, school crossing guards and watchmakers (Service Employees International Unions, 1994).

Strauss (1993, p. 16) observed:

> For years, American unions organized at the fringes of their core jurisdictions... But now, desperate to stem the loss of membership in their traditional jurisdictions, many unions seek to grab every prospect they can find, regardless of jurisdictional lines, doing so through either organizing campaigns or mergers. Unions losing membership in their traditional core are the ones most likely to ignore their outer jurisdictional constraints and turn themselves into general unions.

In Canada, jurisdictional boundaries are so broad that rationalization is out of the question. One of the largest and most militant unions, the Canadian Auto Workers, has absorbed unions of fishermen and seafood workers, textile workers, electrical workers, machinists, chemical workers and railway and transport workers. Perhaps the most dramatic illustration of diversity by design was the three-union amalgamation forming the Communications, Energy and Paperworkers Union (CEP) in 1992. This is the fourth largest private sector union in Canada. Prior to the merger, the officers of the three unions (the Communications Workers, the Energy and Chemical Workers and the Paperworkers) believed that their organizations were financially unstable and at a disadvantage in bargaining because their membership was homogeneous. Diversification ensured against having many members on strike at the same time or suffering destabilizing membership losses because of new production technologies or increased competition in product markets. At the time of the merger, the CEP officers proudly proclaimed that their union was:

> one of the most diverse organizations in the Canadian labour movement, cutting across the resource and service sectors of the national economy and spanning several major industries — paper, forestry, communications, natural gas, oil, manufacturing, mining and transportation, electronics and chemical (Communications, Energy and Paperworkers Union, 1992, p. 16).

In Great Britain, one still finds many occupational unions and industrial unions that recruit and represent workers regionally (e.g., the Fire Brigades Union, the Northern Carpet Trades Union, the Scottish Union of Power Loom Overlookers, and the National Union of Insurance Workers). But the largest unions have exceptionally diverse memberships. A recent union directory lists the main trades and industries of the General, Municipal, Boilermakers and Allied Trades Union (863,000 members) as local authorities, health services, food, leisure and clothing, while those of the Manufacturing, Science and Finance Union (552,000 members) are skilled and professional workers in all industries, financial services, health, universities and the voluntary sector. The Amalgamated Engineering and Electrical Union (835,000 members) covers manufacturing, engineering, electrical supply, electronics, construction, plumbing and foundries. The Transport and General Workers (1,037,000 members) simply covers all industries (*New Statesman and Society Guide*, 1995).

Membership diversity is common because organizing is opportunistic and mergers are guided by officers' and members' self-interests. The rationalization of jurisdictions by creating industry-wide unions would require membership transfers, and the undoing of some mergers and the inducement of others. This is far beyond the powers of labour federations and, if compelled by law, would constitute unprecedented denials of employees' freedom of association. Even in Australia, where mergers were strongly encouraged by law and the federation, specific combinations were not forced and the 18 national affiliated unions at the end of 1993 had mixed jurisdictions. For example, there was a union for building, construction, mining and timber, another for distribution, warehousing and manufacturing, and another for rural industries, infrastructure and manufacturing (Australian Council of Trade Unions, 1994).

Not only is membership diversity irreversible, but it has unintended consequences that are seldom recognized. A heterogeneous membership creates pressures for the establishment of semi-autonomous industrial divisions or sections with their own officers, staff and funds. These structures attract merger partners by allaying officers' and members' fears that their interests will be submerged after merger into a large union. Additional mergers expand or form new industrial divisions, as do members gained from organizing outside the union's core jurisdictions. This results in federated governing structures with decentralized decision-making, which may be perpetuated by separate conventions, headquarters and newspapers. Officers of these federated unions have to develop skills in resolving conflicts among the diverse membership groups. Election to national office becomes an exercise in building and maintaining coalitions. New officers positions are added to represent divisions and at-large officer positions are reduced in number. Union patronage increasingly occurs at divisional levels. Conflicts may arise as national officers try to retain power through centralized financial control while divisional officers appeal to industrial or occupational interests.

Federated structures used to manage membership diversity could lead to factionalism, particularly disputes about the apportionment of delegates at union conventions, seats on governing councils and the allocation of dues income. We might find greater membership commitment and loyalty to divisions than to the national organization (Chaison and Dhavale, 1990). An officer of a recently merged Australian union may have been expressing a common concern when he asked: 'Is it possible for us to develop the appropriate horizontal links across a divisional structure that will enable the union to hang together in a cohesive fashion?' ('Union vows to defend wages', 1990, p. 2).

The implications of membership diversity in terms of union governance are only briefly discussed in this chapter. The point is that these are unintended consequences of the blurring of jurisdictional boundaries and membership diversity; they must be addressed now because in most countries we are well beyond the stage at which jurisdiction can be rationalized.

## Conclusions

Proposals for the reform and rationalization of union structure link macro-level changes with micro-level outcomes. They assume that fewer and larger unions and the reduction of jurisdictional overlap, often through industrial unionism, leads to greater effectiveness in organizing, representation, governance and administration. These assumptions seem quite reasonable, but some fundamental questions remain unanswered.

The public interest in union structure is poorly defined, yet it can justify sweeping structural changes. How is reduction of inter-union competition in the public interest? Are there optimal mixes of small and large unions in labour movements? Even the unions' role as the source of reform could be questioned. If structural reform can be linked to greater productivity, lower labour costs, improved worker representation, and national competitiveness, how then does one justify leaving the task of reform to the unions themselves? Should federations preempt the restructuring programs of hostile governments by imposing reform on affiliates (e.g., by transferring members or forcing mergers), even if this restricts members' free choice of bargaining agents and conflicts with the federations' role as a voluntary association?[5]

Small unions are dismissed as ineffective representatives that linger on because of the personal ambitions and obstinacy of their officers or the provincialism of their members. There seems to be no place for small unions in reformed labour movements unless they represent highly specialized groups of workers or if reform entails shifting bargaining to the enterprise level. The limitations of small unions seem obvious and have certainly been repeated often enough, but the size-effectiveness relation has received scant research attention. We should look beyond the direct effects of size and ask how large unions can alter their structures to simulate smaller ones, and how small unions can achieve economies of scale while retaining independence.[6]

Finally, in countries where workers choose their unions and unions choose their organizing targets and merger partners, it is too late to rationalize jurisdiction. Jurisdictional boundaries have been obscured beyond the point of realignment into industrial unions, but the implications of membership diversity are largely unexplored. How does diversity affect members' satisfaction, loyalty, commitment and participation? Can diversity be both a source of strength and weakness — stabilizing union finances and allowing continued growth while producing internal factionalism and indecisive leadership? Will membership diversity lead to factionalism and schisms or to apathy?[7]

This chapter raises some difficult and controversial questions about structural reform and rationalization because too often assumptions are left unchallenged, conclusions are reached with little or no support, and legislators and union officers are not benefiting from a body of neutral, academic research. The questions presented here form a research agenda that can be intellectually challenging and socially relevant, while also dealing with the practical problems of amending laws and building or rebuilding unions and labour movements. Hopefully, as research progresses, our work will aid in the development of new proposals, and not just demonstrate their shortcomings.

## Notes

1. For example, in Australia, where reform proposals seem to flourish, particularly noteworthy are the reports of the Committee of Review into Australian Industrial Relations, the Hancock Committee (*Australian Industrial Relations Law and Systems*, 1985), the Australian Council of Trade Unions (*Future Strategies for the Trade Union Movement*, 1987), the Australian Council of Trade Unions and Trade Development Council (*Australia Reconstructed*, 1987), and John Niland (*Transforming Industrial Relations in New South Wales*, or the *Green Paper on NSW Industrial Relations*, 1989).

   There are two reviews of national industrial relations systems that have served as models for later commission and task force reports: the British *Report of the Royal Commission on Trade Unions and Employers Associations, 1965-1968* (the Donovan Commission) and *Canadian Industrial Relations: The*

*Report of the Task Force on Labour Relations* (the Woods Commission, 1968). Both reports are critical of multi-unionism, union fragmentation and the incidence of jurisdictional disputes.

2. In 1992, 88 percent of the 297 Canadian unions had fewer than 30,000 members (Labour Canada, 1992).
3. In 1991, 76 percent of Australian unions had fewer than 10,000 members (Creighton et al., 1993).
4. This union officer was apparently thinking of the German labour movement.
5. See Davis (1992) for a description of the ACTU Congress at which its secretary, Bill Kelty, justified restricting union members' choice of representative to further industrial unionism, more effective representation and a stronger labour movement. As a guide to union mergers and a way to reduce multi-unionism, the federation proposed three categories of unions.

   'Principal' unions were granted the right to recruit all employees in a given industry or, in certain cases, occupational categories. 'Significant' unions were recognized as having substantial numbers of members in the industry or occupation and they were obliged to form a single bargaining unit with the principal union. 'Other' unions, lacking significant membership, were entitled to maintain their membership if they agreed to be part of the single bargaining unit (Davis, 1992, p. 88).
6. Chaison (1987) surveyed officers of small unions in the United States (i.e., those with less than 50,000 members) and found a lack of support for a federation of small unions. He concluded:

   > Underlying the responses may be a widely held view that small unions, even in combination, lack the financial resources to build a strong federation capable of quickly or completely resolving their problems. While the concept of a small union federation may be attractive in an abstract sense, pragmatic union officers may consider it to be a risky structural experiment with little chance of immediate benefit (Chaison, 1987, p. 7).
7. Strauss (1993) suggests the possibility that membership diversity will lead to apathy.

## References


ACTU/TDC Mission to Western Europe (1987), *Australia reconstructed*. Australia Government Publishing Service, Canberra, Australia.

Australian Council of Trade Unions (1987), *Future strategies for the trade union movement*, Australian Council of Trade Unions, Melbourne, Australia.

Australian Council of Trade Unions (1994), *Union amalgamations (federally registered unions)*, Australian Council of Trade Unions, Melbourne, Australia.

'British unions divided on mergers' (1989), *The Worklife Report*, vol. 6, no. 5.

Chaison, G. N. (1980), 'Union mergers, union fragmentation and international unionism in Canada', Paper presented at the Annual Conference of the Canadian Industrial Relations Associations, Montreal, Quebec.

Chaison, G. N. (1986), *When unions merge*, Lexington Books, Lexington, Massachusetts.

Chaison, G. N. (1987), 'The evaluation of a federation of small unions', Working Paper No. 87-103, Clark University, Graduate School of Management, Worcester, Massachusetts.

Chaison, G. N. (1997), *Union mergers in hard times: The view from five countries*, Cornell University Press, Ithaca, New York.

Chaison, G. N. and Dhavale, D. (1990), 'The changing scope of union organizing', *Journal of Labor Research*, vol. XI, Summer.

Committee of Review into Australian Industrial Relations (1985), *Australian industrial relations law and systems*, Australian Government Printing Service, Melbourne, Australia.

Communications, Energy and Paperworkers Union (1992), *Final merger report*, Communications, Energy and Paperworkers, Ottawa, Canada.

Creighton, W. B., Ford, W. J. and Mitchell, R. J. (1993), *Labour law: Text and materials*, second edition, The Law Book Company Ltd., Sydney, Australia.

Davis, E. (1992), 'The 1991 ACTU Congress: Together for tomorrow', *Journal of Industrial Relations*, vol. 34, March.

Fiorito, J., Gramm, C. and Hendricks, W. E. (1991), 'Union structural choices', in Strauss, G., Gallagher, D. G. and Fiorito, J. (eds.), *The state of the unions*, Industrial Relations Research Association, Madison, Wisconsin.

Gill, H. and Griffin, V. (1981), 'The fetish of order: Reform of Australian union structure', *Journal of Industrial Relations*, vol. 23, September.

'Independent joins CWA', (1990), *Compensation and Working Conditions*, vol. 44, May.

Katz, H. (1993), 'The decentralization of collective bargaining: A literature review and comparative analysis', *Industrial and Labor Relations Review*, vol. 47, October.

'Labor Letter', (1993), *Wall Street Journal*, October 19.

Labour Canada (1992), *Directory of labour organizations in Canada, 1991-1992*, Supply and Services Canada, Ottawa, Canada.

Lover, J. (1980), 'Why unions won't reform', *Management Today*, September.

*New Statesman and Society Guide to Trade Unions and the Labour Movement*, 1995 (1995), New Statesman and Society, London.

Niland, J. (1989), *Transforming industrial relations in New South Wales, Volume 1*, NSW Printer, Sydney, Australia.

Niland, J. (1994), 'Change and the international exchange of ideas', in Niland, J., Lansbury, R. and Verevi, C. (eds.), *The future of industrial relations: Global change and challenges*, Sage, Thousand Oaks, California.

Niland, J. and Spooner, K. (1992), 'Structural change and industrial relations: Australia', in Gladstone, A. et al. (eds.), *Labour relations in a changing environment*, deGruyter, New York.

Noble, K. (1986), 'Once mighty U.M.W. is seeking more muscle', *New York Times*, November 2.

Piore, M. (1991), 'The future of unions', in Strauss, G., Gallagher, D. G. and Fiorito, J. (eds.), *The state of the unions*, Industrial Relations Research Association, Madison, Wisconsin.

*Report of the Royal Commission on Trade Unions and Employers Associations*, 1965-1968 (1968), HMSO, London.

Service Employees International Union (1994), *SEIU: Putting the power of diversity to work*, Service Employees International Union, Washington, D.C.

Shabecoff, P. (1980), 'Big labor, little labor', *New York Times*, May 11.

'Small unions happy to fight on', (1992), *Labour Research*, vol. 81, May.

Stewart, A. (1989), 'The Industrial Relations Act 1988: The more things change...', *Australian Business Law Review*, vol. 17, April.

Strauss, G. (1993), 'Issues in union structure', in Bacharach, S., Seeber, R. and Walsh, D. (eds.), *Research in the sociology of organizations*, JAI Press, Greenwich, Connecticut.

Task Force on Labour Relations (1968), *Canadian labour relations: The Report of the Task Force on Labour Relations*, Information Canada, Ottawa, Canada.

Trades Union Congress (1988), *First Report of the Special Review Body*, Trades Union Congress, London.

'Union vows to defend wages', (1990), *Metal Workers*, vol. 11, August.

United Food and Commercial Workers (1993), 'Independent union affiliations with UFCW, 1985-1993', United Food and Commercial Workers, Washington, D.C.

Williamson, L. (1995), 'Union mergers: 1985-94 update', *Monthly Labor Review*, vol. 118, February.

# Part II

## THREATS AND CHALLENGES TO CONTEMPORARY TRADE UNIONISM

# 3 Swedish trade unionism: Threats and challenges

*Rudolf Meidner*

Swedish trade unionism has for a long time been exceptionally strong because of its high degree of unionization (at present approximately 85 percent) and through its close cooperation with the Social-Democratic Party. Although specific circumstances and historic traditions have played an important role in making Swedish unions powerful institutions, the fact that full employment prevailed in Sweden up to the beginning of the 1990s may have been the decisive factor for union strength.

The Swedish TUC (LO)[1] stands out as the prototype of 'political unionism' and has made large contributions to the construction of the Swedish Model with full employment and general welfare as the highest prioritized goals and active manpower policy, centralized wage policy and the wage policy of solidarity as fundamental elements (Hedborg and Meidner, 1984).

This picture would be correct as a description of Sweden in the post-war period up to the 1980s, and many of these elements are preserved. The degree of unionization is constantly high and by international comparison at a record level. Unlike in practically all other countries, unionization in Sweden has not decreased in the latest international crisis. The wage policy of solidarity is still the guiding star for the union movement, and Sweden has the most egalitarian wage structure of all industrialized countries. The system of general welfare is mainly intact and the public sector share of the total workforce is still 30 percent — again an exceptional figure compared to other countries. But in two respects decisive changes have occurred which have led many observers to talk about the end of the Swedish model.

---

Rudolf Meidner, National Institute for Working Life, S-171 84 Solna, Sweden.

*Rudolf Meidner*

## The breakdown of the Swedish model

Since the beginning of the 1990s full employment has been replaced by mass unemployment, near the average level of unemployment in the EU countries. The increase in unemployment in Sweden was abrupt, something which can only be explained by a combination of various factors: a deep international crisis which hit Swedish export heavily, cuts in the public sector, a collapse in the building and construction industry and, not least, higher priority to price stabilization at the expense of the traditional full employment goal.

In the mid-1980s the employers' association (SAF) withdrew from the central bargaining system, a system which many observers considered the nucleus of the Swedish Model. The employers wanted to replace central bargaining by branch and local wage negotiations. The LO lost its counterpart. It goes without saying that these two changes on the labour scene have affected the role which the union movement has played in Sweden and have weakened the unions' position, both as 'political unions' and in the area of wage setting.

Does the breakdown of the Swedish Model imply the end for political unionism in Sweden, a degradation of the union movement to the limited influence on the country's social and economic development which is the normal situation in most industrialized countries?

Full employment is a social goal per se, but for the trade union movement it is a necessary condition for union strength and vitality. The debilitation of the trade unions in Western Europe coincided with the emergence of mass unemployment in the latter part of the 1970s. Full employment is for the unions both a question of ideology and of their bargaining power.

The wage policy of solidarity — equal pay for equal work — is based on the government's willingness and ability to avert the negative consequences of this wage policy in economically weak branches and firms. Abundant labour in firms which are unable to pay fair wages should be assisted in their efforts to find new and hopefully better paid jobs. Active labour market policy is, from a union point of view, a necessary complement to the wage policy of solidarity. Not accidentally has the Swedish union movement been the warmest promotor of active manpower policy measures.

The union leadership early realized that a conflict could emerge between full employment and price stability. The LO has consequently recommended a strong anti-inflationary policy, carried out by a combination of general fiscal and monetary measures and selective labour market policy (Turvey, 1952; *Trade Unions and Full Employment*, 1952). The politicians' inability to make these two goals compatible has contributed to undermining the industry's competitiveness and thereby also full employment.

Incomes policy is a poor and inefficient substitute for a determined non-inflationary policy. It means that the unions take over the responsibility for economic stability which the membership does not perceive as the unions' mission. Unions are fighting organizations and should not be the government's extended arm. This perversion of responsibility between the government and the unions — a frequent phenomenon in many developed countries — creates a credibility gap between the union leadership and rank and file.

It is the loss of full employment which in my view poses a deadly threat to the union movement. Since the mid-1950s the Swedish bargaining system has been based on central negotiations between the peak organizations LO and SAF. This system has been an important condition for the wage policy of solidarity: it has meant support to the weak groups and wage restraint for the well-paid. For many decades this policy was acceptable also to the employers, who found it advantageous for the profitable and expansive firms. There is little doubt that the wage policy of solidarity has contributed to the rapid growth of Swedish multinational companies in the 1960s and 1970s. But, in the wake of the intense process of internationalization the large companies — which dominate the employers' organization — lost their interest in the solidaristic wage policy and preferred a decentralized market-oriented wage setting to central bargaining. In the early 1980s, the SAF withdrew formally from the peak bargaining system although in reality central bargaining was not totally abandoned (Pontusson and Swensson, 1996).

It is obvious that SAF's exit from the bargaining arena was a setback for the unions who lost their common counterpart. The LO had to rely on its own ability to coordinate the wage claims of the affiliated member unions.

So far we have dealt with factors outside the union movement which created difficulties for the unions to act along traditional lines: the government's tendency to burden the unions with the responsibility for economic stability, and the employer-induced breakdown of the centralistic bargaining system. In addition to that a number of internal developments weakened the union movement.

The share of workers in the manufacturing industry, the hard core of the union movement, is shrinking continuously. The service trades, public and private, make up the majority of LO's membership. Tensions between unions in the private and public sectors have arisen which have further undermined the LO's authority. The principle of equal wage increases for employees in branches with high productivity growth, for example the engineering industry, and employees in labour-intensive branches in the service sector with low productivity gains, was called into question. A central point of the solidaristic wage policy was no longer accepted in the union movement.

Further, LO — the blue-collar workers' confederation — is no longer the dominating organization on the Swedish labour market, which is now much more fragmented than earlier. Cartels of white-collar unions are increasingly participants at the bargaining table. Although the demarcation line between LO and TCO (the central organization of salaried employees) is almost clear-cut and not subject to organizational dispute, the LO-affiliated unions have to look carefully after the interests of their own members, with an eye on the TCO groups. There are inceptions of joint action between blue- and white-collar unions in a few cases, but a common strategy for the two parts of the Swedish labour force seems far away. Most serious, however, is the fact that the LO never has been able to find norms for fair wage differentials. We have to recall that the concept of solidaristic wage policy is comprised of two equally important parts: equal pay for equal work is the operationally easier part of the concept. It is much more difficult to identify and to achieve the second part, which claims that wage differentials should be motivated by differences in the kind and nature of work.

The LO has been surprisingly successful in compressing the Swedish wage structure, which is more egalitarian than in other highly developed countries (Hibbs and Locking, 1990). But the LO failed to accomplish the second part of the concept of the solidaristic wage policy: to construct a generally acceptable job evaluation system as a basis for rational and fair wage differentials. There are indications that the equalizing process has passed the point where skill and experience should have motivated wage differentials — fully in line with the original concept of solidaristic wage policy. Misdirected egalitarianism has resulted in internal tensions and has, in few and exceptional cases, led to open conflicts.

I have now listed a number of developments which threaten the Swedish union movement, its leading role as a wage-setter and its traditionally central role in the Swedish society. The unions are under hard pressure and they have to find strategies which are adjusted to new conditions. If they want to survive as offensive and mobilizing bodies, they have to face these threats and remove them, one by one, by new and well-founded strategies. Below follows a discussion of such strategies.

## New union strategies needed

Not surprisingly, the arguments for new union strategies are reversals of facts and developments which I have labelled as threats against the unions. Briefly summarized: full employment must be restored, the wage policy of solidarity must be reconsidered, new forms of workers' financial participation must be developed, and closer cooperation between the blue- and the white-collar unions is needed. Let me develop my arguments in more detail.

### *Return to full employment*

I shall risk repeating myself by saying that the return to full employment is a matter of the first importance. There simply is no room for union strategies in an economy with mass unemployment. It is fashionable in Western Europe, and especially in Brussels, to make the issue of unemployment a matter of international cooperation and joint action. White books, solemn statements and conferences like the EU's Essen conference in 1995, give the impression that Western Europe can solve its unemployment misery through EU initiatives and policies. I am in open disagreement with this optimistic view. The Maastricht Treaty and its convergence rules say nothing about full employment but they are very verbose on the subject of price stability. A policy for full employment is mainly a task for the national governments and their political resolution.

Sweden can build on its long experience of full employment, especially in the period after the oil crisis of the 1970s when Sweden did not experience the mass unemployment which existed in Western Europe and which decreased only slightly in the booming 1980s.

It is not sufficient to combat unemployment with active manpower policy. Economic policy as a whole must aim at creating high employment using labour market policy as a complement rather than a substitute. Keynes may be antiquated but he was not totally wrong in pointing to the need for sufficiently high domestic demand.

The unions can only act as a lobbying group even in a country with close links to the labour government. At present the government sees the reduction of the large budget deficit as the main objective and seems willing to tolerate high unemployment for a foreseeable future. The electoral support for this policy is weak and will force the government to retreat. The Swedish people's commitment to full employment has strong traditions and an unemployment rate of ten percent will oust every government from office.

### *Vitalization of the wage policy of solidarity*

The trade union movement has important tasks also after the return to a full employment economy if it wants to regain its former position. The wage policy of solidarity must be readjusted and vitalized. The employers' intention was to make central negotiations impossible. This strategy was supposed to give free scope to market forces, increasing wage differentials and, finally, result in a segregated labour market. The LO can block such a development by coordinating the wage claims of its affiliated unions — unions in the manufacturing industry and in private and public service. The latter groups need central union support because they face the risk of being outdistanced, not only in respect of wages but also concerning work conditions and social security.

LO's authority, which obviously has weakened in the last years, must be reestablished. The experiences of the last wage rounds carried out by the national unions are encouraging: the negotiations have resulted in wage increases close to the figures which are recommended by the central organizations. To regain its authority vis-à-vis the member unions, the LO must make new efforts to find norms for wage differentiation, which, in fact, implies a return to the original concept of solidaristic wage policy. All earlier attempts to find such norms for wage differentials which are motivated by differences in the kind of work, skill, experience, etc., have become rigid and the way has been open to an employer offensive for decentralized bargaining and market-adjusted wages.

New initiatives have emanated from some unions, especially the Metal Workers' Union. In a number of reports, the union has suggested to extend the wage policy of solidarity to a 'solidaristic work policy', thereby combining wage setting and work organization. Instead of accepting individual wages which can be used as instruments of management's control, the union proposes that wages should follow clearly defined steps of competence and upgraded skills.

It is obvious that these ladders of competence and skill have to be based on the specific conditions of each branch and each company. The idea of an all-embracing job evaluation system has been abandoned. However, a fair and robust system for wage setting requires a balance between central and local wage negotiations, in which the central organization has the responsibility for the overall principles and guidelines whilst the local union, together with management, assumes responsibility for the internal 'career' within the firm, i.e. for wage increases which are motivated by higher competence and skill. Maintaining the concept of solidaristic wage policy therefore calls for a considerably better and more sophisticated union strategy than the present one, which is aimed mainly at levelling out the wage structure.

### *New forms of financial participation*

Signs of such a strategy can be observed and discussions in the trade union movement have started. In another area of great importance the Swedish unions are without strategies, leaving all initiatives to the employers. What I have in mind is the fact that the solidaristic wage policy postulates wage restraint for well-paid groups in profitable firms. This implies forfeited wages and corresponding profits for the companies and their owners. The LO has tried to solve this dilemma by the proposal to introduce wage-earner funds financed by excess profits, i.e. socializing profits that result from the wage policy of solidarity (Meidner, 1978).

The proposal failed to gain approval in the political branch of the labour movement and was heavily diluted. Five small regional wage-earner funds, in reality traditional unit trusts, were established in 1984 but dissolved seven years later. The unions were back to the starting point, with the distributional dilemma of their wage policy unsolved.

In the meantime the Swedish employers launched a larger number of company-based profit-sharing schemes which undermined the wage policy of solidarity by favouring already well-paid groups. Warnings from the LO headquarters and from national union centers did not stop local unions from accepting, without scruples, the employers' offer of making additional payments related to the profitability of the company.

What is needed is a firm union position and a strategy how to handle the problem of employer initiated, non-negotiated profit-sharing schemes, especially since Sweden as an EU member state has to promote various forms of 'financial participation', according to an EU Council recommendation of 1992. By obeying this recommendation the Swedish government would contribute to further eroding the traditional Swedish wage policy of solidarity.

### *Cooperation between blue- and white-collar unions*

It is not sufficient that the LO finds new methods of coordination in the area of wage policy, that a balance can be achieved between central guidelines and local application, and, finally, that profit sharing can be integrated into the union strategy. In the long term it is also necessary to coordinate the wage policy for the stagnant LO and the expanding TCO. On the firm level we can already see examples of coordinated wage negotiations between LO, TCO and the confederation of employees with academic qualifications, SACO. In the engineering industry, this cooperation can expand to other branches and eventually develop into cooperation between cartels of blue- and white-collar unions. On the horizon a united wage-earner front can be discerned, a natural development for organizations with joint interests.

Paradoxically enough, such a merger would not necessarily imply a more centralized bargaining system. On the contrary: a 'wage-earner collectivity' can make it easier to find a fair balance between the need for coordination and the inexorable trend towards decentralization in the process of wage setting.

## Swedish unions after the entrance into the EU

Let me conclude with some remarks on the new situation for Sweden and Swedish unionism after Sweden's joining the EU. The crucial question is whether a single country with a population of less than ten million is able to restore and maintain full employment whilst practically all other member states have tolerated mass unemployment for decades.

There are indications that unemployment has become a central issue for the EU commission and the EU parliament. Popular discontent with the present situation of Western European labour markets can be a serious threat to the EU as such. The new member states, and Sweden foremost, are determined to play an active role in focusing EU efforts on employment issues.

In my view the hope that EU will change its priorities is illusive. The 1996 EU conference will hardly change the convergence rules and add high employment as a fifth eligibility criterion for membership of the Monetary Union. The conference will be dominated by governments who in their own countries give the highest priority to price stability.

It remains for Sweden to find its own ways to restore full employment, a mission which is difficult but not totally unrealistic. The best argument for optimism is that Sweden maintained high employment up to the beginning of the 1990s while the rest of Western Europe was plagued by mass unemployment. That fact can hardly be explained by mere fortune but is mainly the result of a deliberate policy. The Swedes have discussed the dilemma of combining full employment and price stability for a long time and have based their policy on the conviction that these two goals are compatible. Sweden may be successful where other countries have failed. A failure to restore full employment would mark the end of the Swedish labour movement as a political force.

Once the threat of permanent mass unemployment is averted, the way is open to union vitalizing and restructuring. This process must be the Swedish unions' own work. Cross-border labour cooperation has its main focus on balancing the forceful expansion of the transnational companies but will, in the foreseeable future, have little influence on national wage policy. The best contribution which national unions can make towards strengthening unionism internationally is achievements on the home front. Strong, successful unions can encourage weak organizations in other member states and stand out as examples worth following.

## Concluding remarks

Swedish trade unionism has a proud and impressive history. It has made valuable contributions to the development of Sweden as a progressive welfare state. Full employment and close cooperation between the unions and the Social-Democratic Party, which has dominated the political life of the country for the major part of the post-war period, have been the main factors behind the success story of Swedish unionism.

Until the mid-1970s the conflict between high employment and price stability could be solved without state intervention in the traditional bargaining process. The ideology of solidarity has been the guideline in Swedish wage policy which was carried out through centralized negotiations between LO and the employers' peak organization (SAF). The result was a remarkably egalitarian wage structure.

The deep international crisis, increasing unemployment and the employers' retreat from the centralized negotiations have weakened Swedish trade unionism. Only a return to full employment can create a basis for renewed union strength. But there is also an obvious need for restructuring union policy in the areas of wage policy and work organization. The slogan 'Solidary wage policy must be broadened into a solidary workplace policy' indicates new union strategies.

## Note

1. This article refers mainly to the LO. The two white-collar confederations (TCO and SACO) do not have the historical connection with the Social-Democratic Party and are not part of the 'labour movement' in the traditional sense.

## References

Hedborg, A. and Meidner, R. (1984), *Folkhemsmodellen*, Rabén & Sjögren, Stockholm.

Hibbs, D. A. and Locking, H. (1990), *Wage compression under solidarity bargaining in Sweden*, Trade Union Institute for Economic Research, Stockholm.

Meidner, R. (1978), *Employee investment funds*, Allen & Unwin, London.

Pontusson, J. and Swenson, P. (1996), 'Labor markets, production strategies and wage bargaining institutions: The Swedish employer offensive in comparative perspective', *Comparative Political Studies*, vol. 29, no. 2, April.

*Trade Unions and Full Employment* (1952). Report delivered to the 1951 Congress of Swedish Trade Unions, Stockholm.

Turvey, R. (ed.) (1952), *Wages policy under full employment*, William Hodge, London.

# 4 Political exchange in Austria's collective bargaining system: The role of the nationalized industries

*Wolfgang Pollan*

Through much of the postwar period industrial countries have experienced a tendency for wage increases to exceed the room provided by productivity increases. In many countries policymakers have resorted to incomes policies to combat inflation without depressing employment. Some of these policies were successful, others not. The search for the forms of institutional underpinnings which might favor successful incomes policies has identified a number of features, some of which have been bundled together as corporatism. Centralized bargaining, or the coordination of wage claims through a central authority within the union federation, is considered an essential feature of the link between the structure of the labour market and economic performance. A high degree of unionization, weak plant-level worker representation, and a high degree of organization on the employers' side are further key elements of corporatism. Other socio-economic features which have been suggested as supporting successful incomes policies are the sense of vulnerability to international markets, a strong social democratic tradition, the acceptance of the unions as 'social partners', as well as certain characteristics of the legal system (Dore, 1994). A discussion of the issue of private versus public ownership, however, has been lacking in these accounts.

Austria's system of Social Partnership, with its heavy emphasis on wage restraint, seems to have endured for almost four decades, while in other countries attempts at incomes policy have failed repeatedly. This chapter draws attention to the role played by the nationalized industries in Austria's incomes policies and shows that this feature, in combination with the strong position

Wolfgang Pollan, Austrian Institute of Economic Research, P.O. Box 91, A-1103 Vienna, Austria.

of works councils, is crucial in solving the puzzle of the durability of Austria's concertative arrangements.

Sections 2 and 3 sketch the main institutions of social corporatism in Austria and review the structure of collective bargaining. The nationalizations of 1946 and 1947, which greatly expanded the power resources of the labour unions and of the Socialist Party and provided the basis for wage moderation as practiced by the trade union federation, are dealt with in section 4. Section 5 raises the question of why strong bargaining units or work place organizations are willing to accept peak level bargaining, and examines the sources of Austria's high wage disparity. The chapter ends with a discussion of the prospects of continued wage restraint in the face of drastic changes in the economic environment: the erosion of the state-owned sector and Austria's membership in the EU.

## A sketch of the trade union organization and the other institutions of Social Partnership

The organizations constituting the Social Partnership are the trade unions, the Chambers of Labour, the Economic Chambers and the Chambers of Agriculture.

### *The trade unions*

The trade unions were given the present organizational structure at the end of World War II when the new Trade Union Federation *(Österreichischer Gewerkschaftsbund, ÖGB)* was formed. The reorganization centralized bargaining, finances, and authority within the Trade Union Federation. In contrast to the fragmentation of the trade union movement along craft and political lines characteristic of the pre-war period, the new federation consisted of 16 (now 14) unions organized along industrial lines. The one important exception is the Union of Salaried Workers representing all white-collar workers in the private sector. There are separate party caucuses within the national unions and the Federation, the far most important faction being the Socialist.

According to the statutes of the ÖGB, the concentration of authority in the Federation probably surpasses that of any other democratic trade union movement. In principle, the ÖGB is in a position to exercise strong leadership over the affiliated unions. The ÖGB controls the finances of the fifteen unions, and has veto power over the employment of the secretary of each. The centralization of authority within the Federation and the individual unions is ensured through an indirect system of electing union officials: the elections of representatives to works councils serve de facto as union elections at the lowest echelon.

### *The Chambers of Labour*

The Chambers of Labour were established in February 1920, at a time when the revolutionary worker council movement in Austria and the model character of the worker council governments in Munich and in Budapest pressured the bourgeoisie to major concessions in an attempt to defuse the revolutionary spirit after World War I. At the same time, the Works Council Law was enacted. Both bodies of law, which were reenacted in almost identical form after 1945, have been considered fundamental preconditions for the establishment of Social Partnership. The provincial Chambers of Labour are public-law entities in which all wage and salary earners (with the exception of civil servants, senior management staff in enterprises, and employees in agriculture and forestry) are ex officio members. They were given the same legal status as the Economic Chambers in 1921 and were charged with the task of consulting over government bills and of representing employees on advisory and administrative committees. The top organization of the regional Chambers of Labour has been the Austrian Congress of Chambers of Labour. The Chambers of Labour have worked in close cooperation with of the unions, with most of the top offices in both organizations being held by the same people concurrently.

### *The Economic Chambers*

The unions are more encompassing regarding wage bargaining than the employers' bargaining units. At the provincial level, the Economic Chambers are public-law entities with compulsory membership; at the federal level the corresponding organization is the Federal Economic Chamber. At both levels, the Economic Chambers are subdivided into six sections, which in turn are subdivided into more than 100 branch organizations which have the status of a public-law body and have the right to negotiate collective agreements. In fact, many insist on exercising this prerogative; hence the large number of collective agreements in force in Austria. Many wage contracts, though, adopt the settlement terms of other larger employment groups.

*Wolfgang Pollan*

## The structure of wage bargaining in Austria

### *Collective agreements*

In Austria, unlike e.g. in Sweden where bargaining at the national level took place until 1983 (Calmfors and Forslund, 1990, p. 83), there is no 'national wage round'. The individual unions instead bargain their own settlements, but wage bargaining is coordinated informally through inter-union preparatory talks and later on through the wage leadership of certain major unions. This process has evolved slowly and seems to have culminated around 1980. Since the second half of the eighties wage settlements have been more differentiated (Pollan, 1991). There is also the machinery of the Social Partnership, the Parity Commission and the Subcommittee on Wages, in particular, to ensure wage control (Flanagan, Soskice and Ulman, 1983; Pollan, 1992); these institutions, however, have been no more than a (useful) façade in the wage and price setting process over the last three decades.

In 1993, 428 collective agreements were concluded. Nonetheless, wage bargaining is highly concentrated. Grouping those bargaining units together that form a joint bargaining committee, or usually adopt the wage settlement of another bargaining unit, reveals that the three largest wage bargains cover about 45 percent, the five largest wage bargains about 63 percent of the dependent labour force in Austria.

According to Austrian law, collective agreements are binding for all employers within the scope of an agreement and for all employees whether unionized or not. Provisions of a workplace arrangement or an individual agreement will prevail if they are more beneficial to the employee. About two percent of wage and salary earners are not covered by any collective agreements, mostly in areas where there is no employers' organization which could negotiate a collective agreement (such as in domestic services and non-profit institutions).

### *A second level of wage bargaining*

Collective agreements that cover a wide range of economic activity may not be appropriate for individual enterprises which are bound by the provisions of the wage settlement. They may need to be adjusted at local levels. In Austria, negotiated wages and salaries are minimum rates which set a floor for the wage and salary rates that are actually paid (effective wages and salaries). They also provide a reference point for time rates and for fringe benefits.

Many employees are remunerated above the minimum wage and salary rates negotiated by the unions for the industry in question.

As mentioned above, the Works Council Law was enacted after World War I as a concession by the bourgeoisie to the revolutionary spirit of the time. After a series of minor revisions, this body of law was amended in the Collective Labour Relations Act of 1973. The power of the works councils is very extensive, with provisions very similar to those in force in West Germany. The works councils have the right to participate in social and personnel questions. In economic affairs, the councils are above all entitled to be informed and consulted. On certain economic issues that would result in major organizational or structural changes in the enterprise to the disadvantage of workers, the works council may object to certain plans and suggest a 'social plan' which may be referred to an arbitration board.

Another central feature of the Austrian system of codetermination in the realm of economic affairs is the provision that one third of the members of the supervisory boards of public limited companies be representatives of the employees. This board appoints the members of the board of directors and is also concerned with major decisions of the enterprise.

One of the works councils' prerogatives is to negotiate 'workplace arrangements' with the employer on many issues. With regard to wages and salaries, the works agreements may only cover procedural aspects, but not the level of wages and salaries (including bonuses and allowances). Compensation issues are the exclusive prerogative of collective agreements. Nonetheless, agreements between employers and works councils on pay raises are common practice. In many firms, particularly large ones, the works councils open negotiations with management over further wage increases, subsequent to the conclusion of collective agreements. Plant level negotiations usually aim at raising the level of effective wages by at least the same percentage as that negotiated for minimum wages. In good business years this standard is exceeded; the difference, wage drift, has been viewed as a great threat by the trade unions since the late fifties, for it undermines their control over wage raises received by workers, and forces them to press for wage increases even if wage increases are generally judged undesirable from an overall economic point of view (Kienzl, 1971, p. 40).

## The role of nationalized industries in political exchange

Since 1945 the ÖGB has been a leading advocate and defender of the nationalization of Austria's large firms. The nationalization program drawn up in the fall of 1945 was based on a plan worked out by the ÖGB and provided for the socialization of a large number of firms. Even though the full program was not implemented, the nationalization of 1946 included the largest enterprises in the basic goods industries, large firms in other manufacturing branches, and the three largest banks. In 1947 all utility companies were also nationalized. These two phases of nationalization fulfilled the dreams of the Socialist Party, of the unions, and of the labour wing of the Conservative Party (ÖVP). The ÖVP as a whole did not oppose the nationalization of the pared down list of enterprises, most of which were so-called 'German property', because this measure helped to keep these firms out of reach of the Soviet Union (März and Weber, 1978, p. 129).

The nationalized industries in manufacturing have had varying organizational forms, but all were characterized by the great influence exercised by the two main political parties (the Socialist Party [SPÖ] and the ÖVP) in the management of the nationalized industries. As Goldmann (1986, p. 14) from the Federal Chamber of Labour writes: 'The parties considered the nationalized industries as their property and treated them accordingly. The primacy of politics dominated economic concerns.' Because of its economic importance, questions concerning the management and, in the nineties, those of privatization of the nationalized industries have long dominated the discussion in Austria on industrial policy and on economic policy in general.

For 1978, a year in which the nationalized industries were still intact, a detailed breakdown of ownership in the Austrian economy is available. Firms owned by the federal government, the provinces, and the communes, directly or indirectly, employed about 9 percent of all wage and salary earners. If employment in the postal service and the Federal Austrian Railways is included, the employment share rises to 13.7 percent. Employment in the federal government as well as in provincial and local governments brings the figure up to 28.2 percent. In an international comparison, this puts Austria among the countries with a high share of employment in the public sector and in nationalized industries. In the manufacturing sector, a key sector in any country, the employment share of the nationalized industries was about 20 percent. If employment in the enterprises owned by the nationalized banks is included, the percentage rises to at least 25 (Arbeiterkammer, 1991).

The socialists and the unions regarded the socialization of core manufacturing industries, utilities, and the three largest banks as the key to a radical change in the working of the Austrian economy. The socialist vice-chancellor, Adolf Schärf, called the act of nationalization 'the ax at the roots of the economic and political power of the bourgeoisie' (cited in März and Weber, 1978, p. 135).

There is broad consensus on the importance of nationalization for Austria's economic and social structure. By weakening capital and expanding the power resources of the unions the nationalizations of 1946 and 1947 vastly widened the influence of the labour unions and constituted the most important structural reform which Austria has experienced over the last fifty years. 'Only a bourgeoisie emaciated by nationalization could be forced to engage in a continuous compromise with labor as organized by the Socialist Party and a socialist-dominated union federation.' (März and Weber, 1978, p. 136). Katzenstein (1984, pp. 136-7) takes a similar view: 'The nationalization of most of the large industrial and financial corporations has shifted power away from Austria's business community toward a trade union eager to share in the exercise of power. This shift provides the economic foundation for a balance of power between the two major parties, the SPÖ and the ÖVP, as well as their ancillary organizations representing the interests of labor and business.'

The involvement of labour in policy making extends from the management of the nationalized industries to the whole socio-economic sphere. Within the so-called Social Partnership, the ÖGB and the Federal Chamber of Labour, together with the Federal Economic Chamber and the Chambers of Agriculture, play a decisive role in formulating economic and social policies.

> The activity of the Social Partners covers all areas of economic and social life in Austria. Negotiations involve every and any aspect: the price of milk, the price of gasoline, the tariff of each position, preferential loans to individual enterprises, the interest rate of the savings pass book, and, at the community level, even the setting up of dog toilets in public parks; exceptions are only in such general areas as education, science, culture, the penal and judicial system. In these areas there are open social conflicts, whose solution does not belong to the traditional tasks of the union movement. (Margulies, Moser and Rosner-Valter, 1980, p. 89)

With labour fully integrated into the policy-making process, the labour unions find it easier than in other countries to make wage restraint palatable to the rank and file, by pointing to the deep involvement in practically all areas relevant for union members. Such encompassing tradeoffs and the wide scope of bargaining make labour, interested in real wage increases and full employment, feel compelled to take account of inflation, productivity, and high investment rates; employers, seeking a high and stable profit rate, are forced to pay attention to improvements in social policy.

The elite awareness of the interdependence of public policies is further enhanced by the fact that Austria is ruled by a 'cartel of elites', i.e. a handful of officials who hold several positions at the same time, positions that are not clearly distinct in the public's eye. Experts from the labour side, especially from the Chambers of Labour, have frequently moved into important government posts and management positions in the nationalized industries and banks.

## Wage restraint

In a discussion of the Austrian variant of wage restraint it is useful to clearly distinguish between two levels: successful cooperation between peak organizations, and the collective action problem at the intra-organizational level.

### *Cooperation between peak level organizations*

Incomes policies as an integral part of any corporatist arrangement involve wage restraint on the part of unions, the under-utilization of their labour market power. The ÖGB soon accepted that wage moderation would produce benefits for the labour side. The overall macroeconomic orientation of the ÖGB is reflected in its general guidelines for wage increases as expressed by Kienzl (1973, p. 227) during the early seventies: The ÖGB 'pursues a wage policy which is oriented towards economic growth. Such a policy, which is in the self-interest of wage earners, should support a sufficiently high growth rate; i.e. wage increases should be low enough to leave enough room for profits conducive to economic growth'.

In Austria, insights into the working of the economy have been complemented by elite awareness of the interdependence of public policies, and the location of policy makers and their advisors in national bargaining structures where a wide range of issues are connected and longer-range effects are sometimes considered. But there was an additional factor which helped introduce and maintain wage restraint. The massive socialization in the years after 1945, by creating a power base for labour in the Social Partnership, not only enabled the labour movement to participate in policy making, it also directly affected the willingness of the peak organization of labour, of individual unions, and of union members to agree to accommodating wage policies.

As Lange (1984, p. 114) points out, the peak labour organization is less likely to agree to wage moderation if it can expect that the 'excess' profits produced by wage regulation will not go into investment but will instead end up as dividends or speculative spending, or will be invested outside the national economy. In a country where the labour movement has in effect gained control over the core sectors of the economy and has a strong say in the investment process of the overall economy, such worries are inappropriate, and wage militancy directed against the unions' own creation would be counter-productive. Rather, the union federation and the unions involved can expect that a reduction in wage costs due to wage moderation can contribute to higher investment which in turn would improve the competitiveness of the economy. This feature of Austria's economy also explains the extremely low strike rate in Austria and the absence of serious discussions of the idea of a wage earners' fund.

### *Cooperation between bargaining groups*

In Austria, it has been accepted by and large that wage regulation produces real benefits for labour. But what makes individual unions or bargaining groups participate in agreements with capital? Wage restraint is a public good but it may not be produced, because it may be irrational on the part of individual workers or groups of workers to contribute to it. This is the problem of collective action. Proposals for wage moderation create a prisoner's dilemma: any group of workers consenting to wage restraint takes the risk of losing out because others can be expected to 'free ride'. The rational strategy therefore is one of non-cooperation (Dore, 1994).

In an iterated game this result can be reversed. This section applies the logic of collective action to wage restraint and follows Lange (1984, p. 102-106) in considering incomes policy as a way of bringing about cooperation among bargaining groups with conflicting interests. This view allows us to highlight some of the factors that have contributed to the apparent long-term success of incomes policies in Austria. Within the theoretical framework of an intertemporal non-cooperative game, workers, even if they are assumed to be wholly self-interested, 'can rationally consent to wage regulation under certain conditions, given that they have some minimal normatively-based extensive group identity' (Lange, 1984, p. 106). Players must not be myopic; i.e. the time discount rate must not be too large. The immediate benefits of noncooperation (of defecting) must be more than offset by the punishment in future periods for failing to cooperate. Another crucial requirement for the implementation of rules is that the actions of all players can be observed or monitored, and that, if a deviation from cooperation occurs, credible retaliatory strategies are available. The management of incomes policy thus requires mechanisms of self-policing or of policing by some external authority.

The problem of the 'free rider' which obstructs cooperative behaviour is obscured in wage bargaining in Austria. All bargaining groups appear to cooperate by adhering more or less to the current wage norms; increases in negotiated wage rates have been clustered closely together. These are the wage settlements that are reported in the national media and form the basis of pattern bargaining. But the 'officially' negotiated wage increases hide the actual higher wage increases in some sectors.

Strongly organized bargaining groups, i.e. those most capable of breaking away from the guidelines, do not oppose peak-level bargaining (which takes into consideration the survival of marginal firms): once the official bargaining results are on the table, works councils in favored industries set out to negotiate supplemental agreements, which raise wage increases and improve working conditions beyond those agreed upon in the publicized settlements. These supplemental agreements — transgressions in terms of the iterated n-person game — are kept from public scrutiny, so as not to induce others who followed the pace-setting wage settlements to transgress (or defect, in the language of the prisoner's dilemma). The prevalent practice of distributing these wage increases over a myriad of fringe benefits inhibits comparisons across firms or professions. Examples of supplemental agreements can be found in the private as well as public sector.

In a series of games, a stable cooperative outcome requires a certain number of players to cooperate in each play. This condition is easily satisfied in a setting where there are two groups of players: one group of players is in a privileged position; they well understand the rules of the game, are keen to benefit from the public good 'wage moderation', and are able to play a double game: cooperating ostensibly, but cheating in secrecy. The second group, operating in a more or less competitive market, has little maneuvering room for pushing through wage increases in excess of the market wage, and cannot 'defect'.

The existence of large wage differentials, the segmentation of the economy into a high-wage and a low-wage sector in turn strengthens compliance with wage moderation. High wages in the privileged sector tend to reduce employment in this sector and force labour to seek employment in the low-wage sector, further depressing wages (Solow and McDonald, 1985). In Austria this secondary sector consists of the huge tourism sector, other private service industries (with the exception of the banking and insurance sector), major parts of the relatively large construction industry, the typically low-wage branches of manufacturing and of the small business sector, and accounts for more than 50 percent of dependent employment. Wages in these sectors are determined by the vagaries of demand and supply. This is one source of the relatively high wage flexibility that has been found for Austria (Biffl, Guger and Pollan, 1987).

## *Large wage differentials*

If overall wage guidelines regarding negotiated wage increases are basically adhered to, but some bargaining groups are able to supplement their wage increases, wage dispersion is bound to widen over time. Though in each year the additional wage increase accruing to a particular bargaining group in defiance of the wage norm may seem small, over the course of one or two decades the accumulated sums may be quite large.

A prime example is the development of wages in the petroleum industry in comparison to the textile industry: while from 1966 to 1990 negotiated wage rates in the petroleum industry rose only moderately faster than in the textile industry (7.6 percent versus 7.0 percent per annum), effective wages in the petroleum industry advanced much faster than those in the textile industry: 9.2 percent versus 7.2 percent (Bundeswirtschaftskammer; Österreichisches Statistisches Zentralamt). This example well illustrates the wage development in an industry that is government-owned and protected against competition.

Wide wage differentials can also be documented for the manufacturing sector as a whole. Hedström and Swedberg (1985), investigating the hypothesis that the organizational strength of left parties and trade unions tend to decrease wage dispersion while constant or increased wage dispersion are expected in countries with weak labour movements, found that Austria had the lowest inter-industrial wage dispersion in the late 1950s, but that dispersion increased rapidly during the 1960s and 1970s; in 1979 Austria was the European country with the highest level of inter-industry pay differentials, even though this country scored high on the three indicators of the strength of labour: parliamentary strength of left parties, degree of unionization, and degree of centralization of trade union confederations.

Table 4.1 presents an international comparison of wage costs (including fringe benefits) per hour in manufacturing for later years; it also reveals a relatively high degree of wage dispersion in Austria: the variation coefficient is exceeded only by that of the United States and Japan, is similar in value to West Germany, Great Britain, and Belgium, is lower in the Netherlands and France, and is considerably lower in the Scandinavian countries. An OECD study also puts Austria in the group of countries with high and rising wage differentials (OECD, 1993).

**Table 4.1**
**Dispersion of hourly labour costs in manufacturing in OECD countries**

| Country | Coefficient of variation* 1984 | 1988 |
|---|---|---|
| Austria | 18.8 | 20.3 |
| West Germany | 19.1 | 18.0 |
| Italy | 10.2 | 13.0 |
| Great Britain | 18.1 | 18.9 |
| France | 17.3 | 14.5 |
| Netherlands | 16.9 | 16.7 |
| Belgium | 17.4 | 18.7 |
| Denmark | 8.2 | 9.1 |
| Sweden | 10.2 | 10.3 |
| USA | 27.9 | 28.9 |
| Japan | 27.6 | 27.5 |

* Standard deviation divided by the mean in percent.

*Source*: Guger (1991), own calculations.

## Concluding remarks and outlook

In the literature on corporatism (Bruno and Sachs, 1985; Calmfors and Driffil, 1988; Lijphart and Crepaz, 1991) Austria has been considered to have one of the most corporatist structures in the OECD area, but this categorization and its interpretation, particularly in cross-country studies which attempt to correlate the degree of corporatism with economic performance, has suffered from two defects: the focus on the formal structures of consensual negotiations (Marin, 1982) and the neglect of the historical factors, the nationalization after 1945 in particular.

Consideration of the historical roots cautions against characterizing Austria's Social Partnership as a socio-political system that is 'exportable' or as a tripartite institution. There has been no actor called the 'state' with a long-term 'strategic design', which has served as architect of the socio-political order. Rather, the evolution of the Social Partnership should be seen as a path-dependent process, with several factors contributing to the emergence of a corporatist structure over time: first came the establishment of the Chambers of Labour and the passage of the law on works councils in 1920;

these were historical accidents. The centralized ÖGB, as founded in 1945, was a response to catastrophic events (Maier, 1984, p. 50-52); the Chambers of Commerce were already in place after the war and were given their final form in 1946. The massive nationalization program pushed through by the unions and the Socialist Party in 1946 and 1947 was another momentous change, which tilted the balance of power in favor of the labour movement. At the plant level, the labor movement was able to rely on the socialist-dominated works councils. Even with these favorable starting positions, it took a long time for the organizations representing labour and capital to develop concertation patterns and to coalesce into the Social Partnership.

Incomes policies as an integral part of any corporatist arrangement involve union wage restraint. The massive nationalization in Austria not only weakened capital but has also directly affected the willingness of the peak organization of labour and of individual unions to agree to accommodating wage policies: having in effect gained control over the core sectors of the economy, the labour movement has been able to make sure that 'excess' profits would go into productive investment rather than end up as dividends or in speculative spending. Since bargaining groups in the core sectors are natural wage leaders in the economy, an overall moderate wage policy must follow.

Wage restraint is only the macroeconomic aspect of unions' wage policy; the other is wage equity, a major driving force of any union organization. While the labour movement has had considerable success in dealing with macroeconomic issues, it has failed on the equity front. The ÖGB and the unions have not been able to sanction individual bargaining groups or work place organizations. Nor have they had much power in forcing various business sectors to agree to 'normal' wage increases. As a result, some labour groups have seriously lagged behind in the development of wages and working conditions.

The nationalizations provided the main foundation for Austria's Social Partnership and wage bargaining system. This base has been eroding for some time now. In the mid-seventies the nationalized industries in manufacturing, as organized under the umbrella of the *Österreichische Industrieverwaltungs AG (ÖIAG)*, employed some 120.000 workers. Employment has been falling since then. The drastic losses in the years 1983 to 1986, centering on a loss of several billion schillings in oil speculation, set in motion a reorganization which broke the ÖIAG into several small holdings. After the reorganization, job losses accelerated markedly. Through redundancies, early retirement, closures, sales, and privatizations, the labor force in the nationalized industries in manufacturing was drastically slimmed down. By 1994 the number of those employed in present or former nationalized industries had dropped to a low of 60,000. By the end of 1996 the state is scheduled to give up majority interests in all firms. Privatization is also reducing the number of enterprises under government control in other sectors of the economy.

Does the retrenchment of public ownership mean the end of Social Partnership and of wage moderation? Not necessarily. True, the institutions of Social Partnership are under great pressure to prove their merits to an increasingly skeptical public; with the federal government and EU institutions taking over a large part of the agenda in the social and economic sphere, most observers foresee a sharply reduced role for the social partners.

With regard to incomes policies, it may be a coincidence that at a time when the flaws of the Austrian version of wage moderation — rising inequality — become increasingly visible, Austria's entry into the European Union imposes a harsh discipline on those sectors of the economy which had been protected from outside competition or pampered with subsidies. The leeway of workers in these sectors to secure above-average wage increases has diminished greatly in this new era of liberalization. Even the federal and local governments, under pressure to meet the fiscal criteria of the Maastricht treaty, have begun a consolidation drive and, despite the vociferous protest of the public sector unions, have taken the lead in curbing wage growth. Wage moderation may continue, but under different auspices, those of the market. Industrialists, ready to exploit the weakness and disarray of the unions, are pushing hard for an increase in labour market flexibility, for decentralized wage bargaining, and, alarmed by competition from Eastern Europe, for reductions in overall labour costs. On all fronts, unions and works councils are on the defensive.

In several sectors the problems of coping with the new economic challenges are plainly visible: wage negotiations have become more difficult and drawn out, and the number of strike threats and of strikes has risen over the last few years. It seems as if Austria may well be on its way to a more discordant system of industrial relations. And yet, there is hope that, in view of the good overall experience with consensus policies in the past and the threat of global competition, the worst forms of industrial strife can be avoided.

## References

Arbeiterkammer (1991), *Wem gehört Österreichs Wirtschaft wirklich? Studie der Kammer für Arbeiter und Angestellte für Wien*, Orac Verlag, Wien.

Biffl, G., Guger, A. and Pollan, W. (1987), *The causes of low unemployment in Austria*, The Employment Research Centre, Occasional Papers in Employment Studies No. 7, The University of Buckingham, Buckingham.

Bruno, M. and Sachs, J. B. (1985), *The economics of worldwide stagflation*, Harvard University Press, Cambridge, Mass.

Bundeswirtschaftskammer, *Die arbeitskosten in der industrie Österreichs*, various issues, Vienna.

Calmfors, L. and Driffil, J. (1988), 'Bargaining structure, corporatism and macroeconomic performance', *Economic Policy*, no. 6, April.

Calmfors, L. and Forslund, A. (1990), 'Wage formation in Sweden', in Calmfors, L. (ed.), *Wage formation and macroeconomic policy in the Nordic countries*, SNS Förlag and Oxford University Press, Oxford.

Dore, R. (1994), 'Introduction: Incomes policy: Why now?', in Dore, R., Boyer, R. and Mars, Z. (eds), *The return to incomes policy*, Pinter Publishers, London.

Flanagan, R. J., Soskice, D. W. and Ulman, L. (1983), *Unionism, economic stabilization, and incomes policies: European experience*, Brookings Institution, Washington, D. C.

Goldmann, W. (1986), 'Verstaatlichte industrie heute', *Arbeit & Wirtschaft*, vol. 40, no. 11.

Guger, A. (1991), 'Arbeitskostensituation nach branchen deutlich verschieden', *Monatsberichte*, Austrian Institute of Economic Research, vol. 64, no. 10.

Hedström, P. and Swedberg, R. (1985), 'The power of working-class organizations and the inter-industry wage structure', *International Journal of Comparative Sociology*, vol. 26, March-June.

Katzenstein, P. J. (1984), *Corporatism and change: Austria, Switzerland, and the politics of industry*, Cornell University Press, Ithaca and London.

Kienzl, H. (1971), 'Wirtschaftspartnerschaft, stabilität und wachstum', in Schmitz, W. (ed.), *Geldwertstabilität und wirtschaftswachstum, Festschrift für Andreas Korp*, Springer Verlag, Vienna.

Kienzl, H. (1973), 'Gewerkschaftliche lohnpolitik und stabilität', in *Sozialismus, Geschichte und Wirtschaft, Festschrift für Eduard März*, Europaverlag, Vienna.

Lange, P. (1984), 'Unions, workers and wage regulation: The rational bases of consent', in Goldthorpe, J. H. (ed.), *Order and conflict in contemporary capitalism*, Oxford University Press, Oxford.

Lijphart, A. and Crepaz, M. (1991), 'Corporatism and consensus democracy in eigtheen countries: Conceptual and empirical linkages', *British Journal of Political Science*, vol. 21.

Maier, C. S. (1984), 'Preconditions for corporatism', in Goldthorpe, J. H. (ed.), *Order and conflict in contemporary capitalism*, Oxford University Press, Oxford.

Margulies, H., Moser, U. and Rosner-Valter, S. (1980), 'Der verwaiste klassenkampf: Gewerkschaften in Österreich', in Hellmann, M. F., Oesterheld, W. and Olle, W. (eds), *Europäische gewerkschaften*, Olle and Wolter, Berlin.

Marin, B. (1982), *Die Paritätische Kommission: Aufgeklärter technokorporatismus in Österreich*, Internationale Publikationen, Vienna.

März, E. and Weber, F. (1978), 'Verstaatlichung und sozialisierung nach dem Ersten und Zweiten Weltkrieg: Eine vergleichende studie', *Wirtschaft & Gesellschaft*, vol. 4, no. 2.

OECD (1993), 'Earnings inequality: Changes in the 1980s', *Employment Outlook*, OECD, Paris.

Pollan, W. (1991), 'Die verlangsamung der lohninflation seit 1985', *Monatsberichte*, Austrian Institute of Economic Research, vol. 64, no. 3.

Pollan, W. (1992), 'Preisregelung in Österreich', *Wirtschaftspolitische Blätter*, vol. 39, no. 1.

Solow, R. and McDonald, I. (1985), 'Wages and employment in a segmented labor market', *Quarterly Journal of Economics*, vol. 100, no. 4, November.

Österreichisches Statistisches Zentralamt, *Statistische nachrichten*, various issues, Vienna.

# 5 Formal and informal representativeness in Italy: Members and voters of the confederal trade unions

*Patrizio Di Nicola*

What is happening to the Italian trade union movement? For a long time both Italian social scientists and union leaders themselves regarded the decline of the organized labour movement as a consequence of the loss of appeal of unions, contrary to other European countries. According to Visser (1993, p. 17) while unionism has been the largest and probably the most influential social movement of the twentieth century, as we approach the end of the century it seems to have lost its importance. After a large growth in membership during the 1970s, at the end of the 1980s most European unions lost members and unionization rates declined. This happened in Austria, Italy, Holland, France, Switzerland, Germany, United Kingdom, Ireland and even in some Scandinavian countries.

Many explanations have been given for this negative trend. Visser identified seven main reasons for the process of de-unionization: from unemployment and inflation to social and cultural changes (a turn toward identity politics, rather than collective movements) — even if in practice it is quite difficult to disentangle the role of different variables in different countries (Visser, 1993, p. 28). Others have provided different explanations for national differences in unionization (in particular, for the lack of negative trends in some countries).

---

This chapter was originally written as part of a report on membership trends presented at a meeting of top-level Italian trade unionists. The research behind it was founded by Cgil, and the study benefited from long, interesting discussions with many colleagues at Ires, the research Institute of Cgil. Aris Accornero, Jelle Visser and Paul Smith commented on a first version of the paper. I am particularly indebted to Roberto Franzosi. Address correspondence to Patrizio Di Nicola, Work & Technology Research Association, Via Yambo 8, 00159 Rome, Italy.

Hanckè (1993) saw the existence of a large network of works councils as the main explanation of good union performance even during the critical years. Fosh (1993) perceived workplace unionism as allowing the possibility of union renewal (at least in the British context).

Is the Italian case really similar to others in Europe? After all, even in Italy union membership has fallen in the past fifteen years. Yet, in spite of the loss of members, the density rate at the end of the 1980s was better than at the beginning of the 1970s. Could the parabola of Italian unionism, to use the title of Accornero's book (1992), be explained by works councils, inflation, or, in Accornero's view, by broader cultural changes? According to Accornero, the rise in unionization in Italy during the 1970s was related to a 'proletarian model' offered by the unions to the people.

'The proletarian model' refers to a set of claims involving not only the bargaining process on wages or the rights of workers and unions, but also a package of keywords with a strong social appeal. During the 1970s Italian unions fought against inequality in the workplace using attractive arguments: the right to low-rent housing, wage increases equal for everyone, regardless of skill level ('everybody has a mouth under his nose' was a powerful unionists' argument). This bargaining policy, pursued at both macro and micro levels, promoted egalitarianism. Unions were able to hold together different segments of the working class: blue- and white-collar workers, pensioners, and members of the petty bourgeoisie. According to Accornero's analysis, egalitarianism became the key reason for union decline during the 1980s. Wage differences being so small, the structure of the Italian working class became *flat.* Unions were held responsible for this situation and the reason for union growth during the 1970s became, in the next decade, the reason for their decline.

This explanation, based on one central argument, is quite appealing. But could egalitarianism justify the 'end of the Italian model of unionization'? In our opinion, the Italian affaire is more complex: many workers changed their attitude toward unionization, as they shifted from *formal* union affiliations (joining through membership) toward a *selective kind of support* of unions. We think that Italian workers moved from being members of a union to be voters for a union, from formal to informal representation. To argue this view, we will first look at membership trends of peak unions; then, we will look at the results of recent elections for the renewal of worker councils (the first since the 1970s). The analyses will show that while membership is decreasing, electoral support for unions is still very high. Finally, we will consider the outcome of recent surveys on unionization. Again, survey data show that union membership, participation, and support to unions can only marginally be influenced by different work and cultural contexts.

## Historical account of Italian industrial relations

### *The Italian landscape*

To put the analysis in historical perspective, let us first briefly sketch the recent history of Italian unions. After the end of fascism the political parties that participated in the Resistance and Liberation War reached an agreement for the reconstruction of a single trade union, Cgil. Cgil was organized in accordance to the traditions of the pre-fascist unions: under its umbrella came many vertical unions that represented workers from the same industries and that coexisted with a network of Chambers of Labour. Workers were free to join or not to join. There were no provisions for a union shop system. The benefits of national labour contracts extended to all workers, regardless of union membership. Workplace representation was granted to the workers via the *Commissioni Interne,* a plant based committee 'different from the unions, and not entitled to enter into collective bargaining or to call a strike', mainly based on work-capital co-operation (Regalia, 1995, p. 218).

The *united* Cgil (as it is referred to) survived the bitterly fought election of 1948 between the Popular Front and the Christian Democrats (Bedani, 1995, part 2). But soon after that the union split into two parts, with the Catholics forming Cisl. After a few years republicans, social democrats, and other parties created a third union, Uil.[1] For the workers the decision of joining a union was therefore more an ideological choice than a strategy for improving working conditions: up to the late 1960s the unions, particularly Cgil, the largest one, refused to enter into plant-level bargaining. Union leaders, being often members of Parliament, represented workers' interests at the institutional level.

### *Unionization, de-unionization*

During the 1950s Cgil membership declined, partly due to internal divisions, but mostly because its members and militants, many communist activists, were repressed in the workplace (Accornero, 1959). Cisl, although less subject to repression, did not expand its membership. The curve began to rise at the end of the 1960s, during the 'hot autumn'. Cgil membership increased by 1.2 million between 1970 and 1975; Cisl gained close to 800,000 new members in the same period, and the three main confederations made an agreement to achieve reunification and created an intermediate body (the United Federation Cgil-Cisl-Uil) that would be a 'bridge' toward real unification. At the beginning of 1970s, the Parliament produced a new legislation on workers' rights (the *Workers' Statute* of 1970), allowing the unions to set up new bodies for workplace representation. In the same years the Union Federation took an important decision: union leaders should not serve in Parliament. This way, the unions severed their link with political parties.

Union membership rose until 1980. But thereafter the Italian landscape changed again. The number of active workers in the unions fell rapidly as workers retired in a process well-known in Italy as the *substitution effect* (Di Nicola, 1991a) whereby the pensioners' unions became the largest ones (see Figure 5.1).

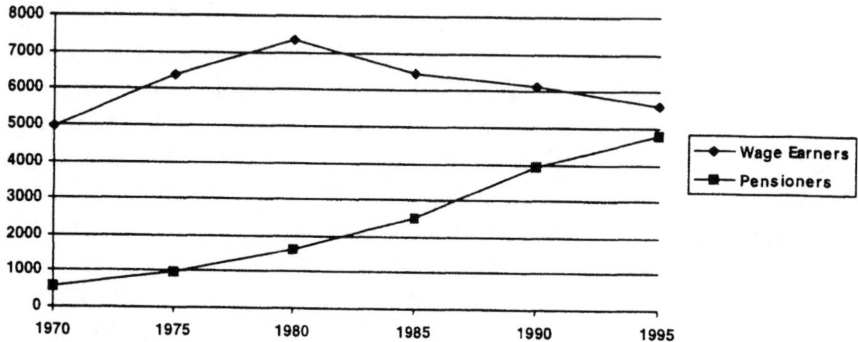


**Figure 5.1 Union membership in Italy, 1970 - 1995 (in thousands)**

Labour conflicts as well have changed significantly in recent years. Since 1985, many unions not affiliated with the main confederations have emerged (the so-called autonomous unions) and have been very militant. These unions were particularly strong in the public service sectors (mainly education, transport, and health) and they conducted strikes in a distinctive way: against the service users instead of the service owners (Accornero, 1985; Pipan, 1989). The militancy of the new unions was facilitated by the weakness of the traditional unions following the end of the united Federation, which had collapsed in 1984 over policy differences on the reduction of the inflation rate.

Along with the decline in membership, the major Italian unions suffered a severe decline in density rates. Contrary to the opinion of many trade union leaders, this was only minimally due to the reduction of salaried work in traditional sectors (see Table 5.1). The main reason may be found in the increased number of workers (white collar, professional, highly skilled, highly educated, young and female) employed in small tertiary firms or those in traditional branches, performing non-traditional jobs, such as design and marketing. The traditional, blue-collar dominated unions were not successful in attracting these emergent groups of workers.

**Table 5.1**
**Membership and density rate in Italy, 1981-1990**

| Sector | Number of members | | Difference | Density rate | |
|---|---|---|---|---|---|
| | 1981 | 1990 | 1981-1990 | 1981 | 1990 |
| Agriculture | 1,020,491 | 708,875 | -311,616 | 99.9 | 84.3 |
| Industry | 3,216,579 | 2,464,481 | -752,098 | 48.2 | 41.8 |
| Services (private sector) | 1,280,136 | 1,263,036 | -17,100 | 31.3 | 24.1 |
| Services (public sector) | 1,387,618 | 1,436,115 | +48,497 | 51.0 | 48.1 |

*Source*: Our elaboration on Cgil-Cisl-Uil data and National Statistical Bureau figures

In summary, at the beginning of the 1990s, Italy still had three strong and representative unions, holding more than ten million members. But the 'key members' in these unions were the pensioners: they comprised more than 40 percent of total membership. The solidarity within the working class was more difficult to manage, mainly because a large proportion of workers did not join the unions and when they went on strike, they often supported the 'autonomous' unions. Among union leaders there was the sensation of having lost the appeal and the representation 'power' they had held just fifteen years before (Carrieri, 1995). In spite of this situation (fall in membership, fall in density rates, difficulties in attracting emergent groups of workers, etc.), micro-bargaining activity at the factory level increased in the 1980s as revealed by surveys conducted by Ires Lombardia and Cesos (Regalia, 1990; Baglioni and Milani, 1990).[2]

## When the workers vote

In 1991, under the pressure from the 'loss of representation power', the main unions decided to create a new kind of works councils in the Italian factories and offices. The old councils, the CdF, *Consigli di Fabbrica,* emerged at the end of the 1960s riding on the wave of the blue collar 'revolt' against the capitalist work organization (Rogers and Streeck, 1994, p. 136; Regalia, 1995; Franzosi, 1995). Twenty years later these organizations were no longer capable of articulating the demands of the new workers. At the base of the representation of the *Consigli di Fabbrica* there was de facto the idea of *homogeneity* of workers: working at the same plant, on the same assembly line or department, the blue and white collar workers develop common interests and goals. In practice the members of CdF did not represent all the workers, but the interests of their specific work group. They were elected (and very often nominated) to the CdF by their comrades in a single 'union list' that took into account the necessity to achieve a balance between Cgil, Cisl and Uil delegates. The CdFs, therefore, were at the same time factory councils (in charge of bargaining) and the basic building block of the Union Federation in the plant, as they were the expression of a single channel of representation (Accornero, 1992).

Twenty years later, new technologies, new forms of organization of production, the decline in the numbers of blue-collar workers (even in centrality of the 'mass workers'), and the social composition of unions, changed the face of factory life; the differences between workers became greater than the similarities between them. Moreover, the end of the so-called *pact of unity of action* between unions generated competition in many CdFs, and also, in absence of new elections, a forced stability.

In 1991 union leaders decided to create new councils called RSU *(Rappresentanza sindacale unitaria)*. The new councils were not to be 'informal' as in the past. RSUs were to be elected by all the workers from lists of candidates presented by *individual and competing* unions and all union rights in the factory were to belong to the RSU. In practice, nothing happened; the sector unions supported with enthusiasm the idea of creating new councils, but they avoided the elections. The matter was raised again during the trilateral macro-bargaining held in July 1993. On that occasion, it was decided to establish a new pattern for the Italian industrial relations panorama.

Employers' representatives and union leaders agreed to split bargaining into two levels. The parties were to sign agreements every four years at the national level on general matters such as cost of labour, inflation, etc. At the factory level, the parties were to bargain every two years on specific issues previously not directly addressed, such as organization of labour, technological innovation, the anchoring of salaries to the economic performance of the plant, and productivity objectives. In the 'July protocol' it was agreed to facilitate the creation of the new factory councils network. Few people[3] thought that the three confederations could triumph in the electoral results, especially after a ten-year decline in unionization and after the establishment of rank and file committees and grass-root organizations *(auto convocati)*. At most, the optimists thought that electoral de-legitimization (in terms of both a small number of votes in favour of the traditional unions and a large number of non-voters), could 'shake' the union bureaucracies and therefore lead to a change. But the story turned in a different way. At the elections over 75 percent of the work-force participated in the ballot and the three peak unions gained more than 90 percent of the valid votes.

This result, even if analyzed by sectors and geographical areas, shows that blue-collar workers from factories in the North and employees from the advanced tertiary industry voted in equal measure for the confederal trade unions. How can this situation be explained? Did the fall in representativeness in the 1980s and at the beginning of the 1990s reveal the workers' search for a new relationship with the unions?

## Why do workers join unions?

While many studies have focused on why workers join unions (Bain and Elsheikh, 1976; Kelly and Kelly, 1994; Sverke and Abrahamsson, 1994; van Rij, 1994; and, specifically for Italy, Romagnoli, 1980, and La Valle, 1989), there are no final answers. Perhaps, there are a plurality of reasons behind workers' attitudes toward unions. From previous surveys we know that commitment to unions can depend on the business cycle, on political attitudes (left wing workers join the unions more often than people oriented toward the right wing, the 'red' areas have a density rate higher than other areas), on the sector of activity (in Italy the density rate in primary and secondary sectors is higher than in the private services), on gender (males are more often members of a union) and on many other variables. For the above reasons the development of country-specific models of union commitment is rather important. The results of two surveys conducted in different environments characterized by high union density rates can help us do this.

The first sample (Di Nicola, 1994) is composed of 3,920 workers of the 10,000 employees at the Bank of Italy. These workers are highly educated; the union density rate is close to 80 percent; a total of seven unions operate in the Bank and non-confederal organizations hold the majority of the members. The second sample (see Carrieri et al., 1995) is far smaller and very different: 599 workers, representing a universe of ten thousand textile blue collar workers in a 'red' area of Italy, where the progressive parties obtained 48 percent of the votes at the March 1994 general election and over 50 percent in April 1996. Cgil is the most representative union in these regions, with a density rate close to 72 percent. Politically the workers are more 'left wing' than the population; the union members voted for a left wing party at the general elections in 79 percent of the cases. And some 55 percent of the non members voted for the Progressive party.

Participation in union activities (factory-wide meetings, union meetings and strikes) is high in both samples. The reasons for being members of a union are different in the two samples, but not as different as one would expect: the 'pure ideological' workers (the ones who declare that they join unions because 'they are working class organizations') are close to 11 percent at the Bank and close to 15 percent in the red area.

If we build a model using membership/participation variables (Figure 5.2), the workers can be considered as being members of one of four different groups: *activists* (they are union members and have a high participation index); *followers* (they actually join a union, but they rarely participate in union activities); *supporters* (even without being members, they have a high participation index); *indifferent* (they do not join a union and do not participate in any union activity).[4]

| | | **PARTICIPATION IN UNION ACTIVITIES** | |
|---|---|---|---|
| | | **High** | **Low** |
| **MEMBERSHIP** | **Yes** | *Activists*<br>Red Area: **49.1%**<br>Bank of Italy: **39.9%** | *Followers*<br>Red Area: **31.7%**<br>Bank of Italy: **34.0%** |
| | **No** | *Supporters*<br>Red Area: **4.8%**<br>Bank of Italy: **7.2%** | *Indifferent*<br>Red Area: **13.7%**<br>Bank of Italy: **18.9%** |

**Figure 5.2 Union commitment typology**

What can be ascertained from the figure? Mainly that even in largely different contexts some aspects of the commitment towards unions are very similar. In fact: a) over 25 percent of non-members support union actions. They are the kind of workers that help the unions *through participation instead of through membership;* b) on the other hand, there is a large part (over 40 percent) of union members that have only a 'formal' approach to labour organization. They join the unions, and this is enough: they 'fulfil' any obligations toward the unions by paying the membership fee; c) the majority of workers (activists plus supporters) are, regardless of membership, 'coherent' union-members and not mainly for 'ideological' reasons. They bring their contribution (in terms of fees, and participation) to unions and they expect a positive, measurable result from union action: being members, it is possible to defend their own rights in a better way, and how unions are evaluated is strongly related to the 'effectiveness' of union actions and performances. This is quite obvious in many countries (Freeman and Medoff, 1984) but not in Italy, where unions have been regarded for a long time as 'transmission belts' of the political parties.

## Conclusion

The largest Italian unions are experiencing a strong contradiction: while membership and density rates have fallen, they have had very good results in the election of the works councils. The elections have shown that Italian workers did not call into question the existence of strong confederal trade unions, but rather the forms of representation. Those forms of representation need revising. The criteria to measure the proximity-distance between workers and unions also need revising: the Italian experience indicates that there were many trade union members who, when it came to their involvement in union activities rather acted as non-members, whereas there were non-members who displayed levels of participation similar to those of activists. The lack of representativeness in the 1980s and at the beginning of 1990s concealed therefore more than just a distrust of unionism and the workers' mania of 'protecting one's own rights'. Workers rejected formal adhesion (mainly membership and militancy) based on 'great ideologies'.

Are Italian workers shifting from being members of unions to being voters for a union? It is still too early to tell. In 1995, a third of all workers belonged to one of the three main unions, but in the future we may see a greater number of workers leaving unions, giving only *selective adhesion* to them. We do not think that Italy in the future will have 'memberless unions', as some social scientists are arguing for France (Rosanvallon, 1988). But the changes will mark a new era of the Italian unionism, as the *informal adhesion* will emerge as a new form of support for the unions. As a consequence, unions will have to undergo a process of reorganization, closer to the workplaces, *become leaner*, and with greater decentralization of the decision making processes. But a further reduction in membership will imply another major change: the members' fees will cease to be the most important way for financing union activities. Italian unions will have to think of providing new services (Olson, 1965, would call them *selective incentives*) for the members, a process which may transform Italian 'inclusive unionism' into less encompassing organizations.

## Notes

1. Cgil stands for "Confederazione Generale Italiana del Lavoro", while Cisl is the acronym for "Confederazione Italiana Sindacati dei Lavoratori". Uil is the "Unione Italiana del Lavoro".
2. Ires Lombardia and Cesos are two Italian research institutes, belonging respectively to Cgil and Cisl. Over the years they produced many interesting studies on micro bargaining at plant level.
3. And not only in the unions. The industrialists, for instance, hardly pushed for having a clause to grant a minimum level of representation to the traditional unions. They were really fearful for a clamorous of Cgil, Cisl and Uil. In their opinion this would generate an uncontrolled I.R. scenario in the firm, possibly dominated by "wild" worker councils.
4. The figure was built by crossing the membership status of the interviewees (3920 at the Bank and 599 in the textile workers sample) with the participation index calculated in both samples. The latter index was developed by averaging the answers to three questions on participation in various union activities (workplace meetings, strikes for labour contracts, strikes for political reasons). Each question allowed three possible answers (always, sometimes, never), scored from 1 to 3. The participation was then operationalized (low, high) using the average as break point.

## References

Accornero, A. (1959), *Fiat confino. Storia della O.S.R.*, Edizioni Avanti!, Milano.

Accornero, A. (1985), 'La "terziarizzazione" del conflitto e i suoi effetti', in Cella, G. P. and Regini, M. (eds.), *Il conflitto industriale in Italia,* Il Mulino, Bologna.

Accornero, A. (1992) *La parabola del sindacato,* Il Mulino, Bologna.

Baglioni, G. and Milani R. (1990), *La contrattazione collettiva nelle aziende industriali in Italia,* Franco Angeli, Milano.

Bain, G. S. and Elsheikh, F. (1976), *Union growth and the business cycle,* Basil Blackwell, Oxford.

Bedani, G. (1995), *Politics and ideology in the Italian workers' movement,* Berg, Oxford.

Carrieri, M., Di Nicola, P., Feltrin, P. and Palumbo, S. (1995), *Tra locale e generale. Lavoro, sindacato e politica tra gli addetti del settore tessile di Pistoia,* Chamber of Labour, Pistoia.

Carrieri, M. (1995), *L'incerta rappresentanza,* Il Mulino, Bologna.

Di Nicola, P. (1991a), 'Sindacalizzazione e rappresentanza negli anni ottanta', *Ires Materiali,* no. 3.

Di Nicola, P. (1991b), 'Confederali, autonomi, cobas: La sindacalizzazione nel terziario', *Politica ed economia,* no. 2, February.

Di Nicola, P. (1994), 'Lavoro e sindacato in Banca Centrale', *Ires Materiali,* no. 1.

Fosh, P. (1993) 'Membership participation in work-place unionism: The possibility of union renewal', *British Journal of Industrial Relations,* vol. 31, no. 4.

Franzosi, R. (1995), *The puzzle of strikes. Class and state strategies in postwar Italy,* Cambridge University Press, Cambridge.

Freeman, R. B. and Medoff, J. L. (1984), *What do unions do?,* Basic Books, New York.

Hancké, B. (1993) 'Trade union membership in Europe, 1960-1990: Rediscovering local unions', *British Journal of Industrial Relations,* vol. 31, no. 4.

Kelly, C. and Kelly, J. (1994), 'Who gets involved in collective action?: Social psychological determinants of individual participation in trade unions', *Human Relations,* vol. 47, no. 1

Istat (1990), *Rilevazione delle forze di lavoro. Media 1989,* Collana d'informazione, no. 20, Roma.

La Valle, D. (1989), 'Esiste un ciclo della partecipazione sindacale? Osservazioni sulla esperienza italiana', *Quaderni di sociologia,* no. 12.

Olson, M. (1965), *The logic of collective action,* Harvard University Press, Cambridge, Mass.

Pipan, T. (1989), *Sciopero contro l'utente,* Bollati Boringhieri, Torino.

Regalia, I. (1990), 'La contrattazione articolata in Lombardia nel 1987-88. Un'analisi alla luce delle relazioni industriali', *Ires Papers,* collana Ricerche, no. 28.

Regalia, I. (1995), 'Italy: The costs and benefits of informality', in Rogers, J. and Streeck, W. (eds.), *Works councils: Consultation, representation and co-operation in industrial relations,* University of Chicago Press, Chicago.

Rogers, J. and Streeck, W. (1994) 'Workplace representation overseas: The works councils story', in Freeman, R. B. (ed.), *Working under different rules,* Russel Sage Foundation, New York.

Romagnoli, G. (1980), *La sindacalizzazione tra ideologia e pratica,* Ed. Lavoro, Roma.

Rosanvallon, P. (1988), *La question syndical: Histoire e avenir d'une forme social,* Calman-Lévy, Paris.

Sverke, M. and Abrahamsson, B. (1994), *Union commitment: A conceptualization based on instrumental and value rationality,* Arbetslivscentrum, Stockholm, mimeo.

Van Rij, C. (1994), *To join or not to join,* Nimmo, Amsterdam [dissertation].

Visser, J. (1990), *In search of inclusive unionism,* Kluwer, Deventer

Visser, J. (1993) 'Syndicalisme et désyndicalization', *Le Mouvement Social,* no. 162.

# 6 Legitimizing union structures: Trends in New Zealand

*Raymond Harbridge and Anthony Honeybone*

Fundamental change aptly describes the shift in the legislative framework of industrial relations in New Zealand. Since 1984 the New Zealand economy had been subject to a 'deregulation frenzy' guided by a powerful cadre of New Right bureaucrats within Treasury (Jesson, 1989). Until 1991 the industrial relations system, however, had remained largely unchanged. Certainly the reform that had occurred was not to the extent or pace of reform in the wider economy. In 1991 the industrial relations system abandoned its historical roots of collectivism and state involvement with the implementation of the Employment Contracts Act 1991 (the Act). This legislation was underpinned by a 'New Right' ideology, founded on neo-classical economics, and involved a radical redefinition of the state's role.

The deregulation of the labour market had a dramatic effect on unionization. For unions, deregulation effectively meant the removal of all forms of external legitimacy. The state, operating within the confines of an ideology premised on individualism, laissez-faire economics, and the free market withdrew all statutes that legitimized the role of unions in the economy. Consequently the Act does not include a single reference to the notion of trade unions or trade unionism. This represented a fundamental change in the ideology that had

---

Associate Professor and former Research Fellow, respectively, Industrial Relations Centre, Victoria University of Wellington, P.O. Box 600, Wellington, New Zealand.
Research grants: Public Good Science Fund (FRST Contract: VUW F503); Victoria University's Internal Grants Committee; Research Committee of the Faculty of Commerce and Administration. A longer version of this chapter has appeared in the *Journal of Labor Research*, XVII, 3, (Summer, 1996) pp. 425 - 444, and we are most grateful to the Journal for allowing this version to be published.

underpinned the industrial relations system in New Zealand for the past 100 years.

We analyze the effect of this shift by utilizing a framework established by Visser (1991) for reversing the decline of unionism in any given country. Visser proposes that unions need a legitimate role in the labour market. Legitimation for Visser entails that unions can negotiate multi-employer contracts, have a secure non-contested workplace presence, and can engage in inclusive bargaining whilst avoiding the problems of 'free-loaders'. In New Zealand, the Act has made it extremely difficult for unions to have a legitimate role. There are no mechanisms in place to enhance any form of multi-employer collective bargaining. Employers have no obligation to bargain with unions and other bargaining agents. The previous system of compulsory unionism, which created inclusive coverage, has been abolished, and the outlawing of the traditional 'closed shop', has raised the issue of free-loading. New Zealand's recent experiment with labour market deregulation will provide our laboratory in which we test international hypotheses regarding union decline.

## Collective bargaining and unionism

Internationally there has been considerable debate over the causes of union decline and five determinants are identified in the literature (Visser, 1991). While there is general agreement over these determinants there is considerable dispute as to the relative impact. These five key determinants are: The changing structure of the labour market (Chaison and Rose, 1987; Moore and Newman, 1988; Visser, 1990); Public policy and the legitimization of unionism (Weiler, 1990; Freeman and Pelletier, 1990; Beaumont, 1991); Public opinion and societal values (Lipset, 1990; Schmidt, 1993); Employer resistance and union avoidance strategies (Freeman and Medoff, 1984; Kochan et al., 1986); and Union organizing strategies (Freeman and Rebick, 1989; Reshef, 1990).

To determine the prospective position of industrial relations in New Zealand, it is necessary to review the historical context of New Zealand unionism. Howard (1977) and Hince (1993) propose that the industrial relations system in New Zealand does not conform to traditional Euro-American theories of the union movement. Such theories are premised on competition in the labour market, the class struggle between labour and capital, and structural effects of the capitalist system. In New Zealand, however, a theory of trade unionism needs to incorporate a deterministic role for the state (Hince, 1993).

The state in New Zealand has played a pervasive and dominant role in determining the characteristics of the industrial relations system by forming the nucleus for explaining the origin, growth, purpose, and (we argue) the decline of trade unions. Whilst we do not attempt to develop a general theory of industrial relations, we want to reinforce this notion of the determinate role of the state.

For almost 100 years, from 1894 to 1991, the state legislatively legitimated the role of unions in society. This philosophy was effected by a combination of legislative recognition of both employee and employer unions and a legislative base of compulsory conciliation and arbitration which underpinned collective relations between the participants.

Prior to 1991, official registration of unions regulated the membership coverage of organizations and established an acceptable level of financial accountability and democratic operation in their internal affairs. Bargaining rights and access to the state-supported mechanism of conciliation and arbitration, with resultant 'blanket' or 'common rule' coverage of minimum terms and conditions of employment contained in awards and agreements, were conferred on registered organizations. State-provided enforcement mechanisms underpinned the established standards. A system of preference for unionists evolved into a legislative basis of compulsory unionism. This system continued throughout the twentieth century without any fundamental change in philosophy or structure.

Within this legislative cocoon unionism flourished, at least in terms of numerical size and collective bargaining spread. In 1985 some 223 registered unions and 26 state sector service organizations had a combined membership of 683,006 within a full-time work force of slightly more than 1,000,000 (Harbridge et al., 1995). Collective bargaining coverage was (marginally) in excess of this proportion of the work force. In parts of the public sector (e.g. teaching, police, firefighters, post-office and railways) union membership was close to 100 percent (Hince and Harbridge, 1995).

The legislation had a distinct effect on the nature of unionism which emerged under the arbitration system. The dominant type of union was typically small and lacked sufficient resources to be effective in their own right. The term 'arbitration unions' (Holt, 1986; Roth, 1973) reflects their reliance on the protections afforded by the arbitration system; unqualified preference, compulsory unionism, and most importantly the requirement to settle disputes through arbitration in preference to protracted industrial action. Thus, while the system allowed these unions to develop it also shaped the form this development took, as unions organized themselves around the principles of the state-sponsored system. Undeniably unions were a product of the arbitration system itself, 'shaped by the structure of the system [and] by the complex network of rules and procedures which governed its operation' (Nolan and Walsh, 1994, p. 9) and were characterized by a preoccupation with procedural issues rather than participation in traditional areas of 'grass-roots' union activism (Hince and Harbridge, 1995, p. 3).

Unionism prospered under these conditions and the needs of the state for regulation and control of industrial affairs were satisfied. Such unions were also frequently referred to as 'paper unions' - unions created by, and operating because of and within the constraints of, a legislative base. Whilst there are, from time to time, clear exceptions to this model, and some variations in terms of 'grass-roots' organization and activism, the 'arbitration' union was the dominant strand of unionism that developed and functioned in New Zealand. Such unions were ill-prepared to meet the challenge of the massive shift in the legislative base embodied in the Act 1991.

## New Zealand in deregulatory mode

The Act of 1991 brought labour law matters in line with other deregulatory changes that had taken place since the election of a Labour Government in 1984. Labour's pro-market reform was designed first to reorientate firms and enterprises towards being international rather than domestic businesses, and second to reform the public service (Hawke, 1994, p. 549). Although industrial relations practices were specifically altered with the abolition of compulsory union membership, and various legislative amendments to alter wage-fixing processes, Labour did little to deregulate the labour market itself.

### *The Employment Contracts Act*

Following its landslide election to government in 1990, the National Party continued with these deregulatory policies but tackled the labour market. Compared with the Labour Relations Act, the Act has little to say about the issue of collective bargaining. Part One of the Act simply provides for freedom of association and gives employees the right to associate or not to associate with other employees for the purpose of advancing their collective employment interests. Membership of any employees' organization is entirely voluntary, and discrimination in employment matters on the grounds of membership or non-membership of an employees' organization is prohibited.

Part Two of the Act deals with representation and bargaining arrangements. There are two principles involved. First, employers and employees are free to choose who will represent them in bargaining. Second, two types of bargaining outcomes are available: individual or collective employment contracts. The type of contract and its contents are a matter for negotiation. Individual employment contracts may be negotiated at any time but may not be inconsistent with any applicable collective employment contract. Collective employment contracts may be negotiated between one or more employers and any or all of the employees engaged by those employers. An employer may negotiate with the employees themselves or their authorized representatives.

There is no longer any provision for the exclusive registration of union coverage for any specific occupational or industry-based group. Employers and employees can represent themselves or be represented by a bargaining agent who can be any other person, group, or organization they choose.

The change in direction is most clearly demonstrated by reference to the objectives of the new legislation and its predecessor (Kiely and Caisley, 1993). The purpose of the Labour Relations Act 1987 was: To facilitate the formation of effective and accountable unions and effective and accountable employers organizations; to provide procedures for the orderly conduct of relations between workers and employers; and to provide a framework to enable agreements to be reached between workers and employers. By contrast, the purpose of the 1991 Act is: To promote an efficient labour market and to provide for freedom of association and to allow employees to determine who should represent their interests in relation to employment issues.

### *The decline of New Zealand unions*

Historically New Zealand unions enjoyed a privileged position and by international standards had high levels of density and membership. At the height of their success, in the period 1989 to 1991, unions negotiated collective bargains covering over 720,000 employees and were successful in persuading some 603,000 of these employees to become members (Harbridge and McCaw, 1991). The Act has radically altered that as can be seen in Table 6.1.

Union membership fell by over one third in the first four years of the new system — from 603,000 to 376,000 members at December 1994. The overall number of unions remaining in existence declined to around 80; a number of unions have become insolvent and have filed for liquidation; staff retrenchments within unions has been widely reported and in some cases this has led to a reduction in services and capacity (Harbridge and Hince, 1994).

The combined impact of recent legislative change on the number and size of registered unions in the period 1985 - 1991 is dramatic. There was an effective decline in the number of registered unions from 223 in 1985 to 80 in 1991. Total membership steadily declined after reaching a peak of 683,006 in December 1985. Union density peaked at 44.7 percent in 1989, chiefly as a result of the fall in the wage and salary earner component of the full-time labour force to a twenty-year low of 892,800. The decline since 1991 has been more dramatic. Union density has fallen to an all time low of 23.4 percent as union membership has declined despite increases in work force participation. In 1994 the full-time and part-time work force grew to 1,600,000 while union membership declined to 376,000. The dramatic changes between 1985 and 1991 are a direct result of the legislative change as are the changes from 1991 - 1994.

**Table 6.1**
**Unions, membership and density, 1985 - 1994 ***

| | Unions | Membership | Density |
|---|---|---|---|
| December 1985 | 259 | 683,006 | 43.5% |
| September 1989 | 112 | 648,825 | 44.7% |
| May 1991 | 80 | 603,118 | 41.5% |
| December 1991 | 66 | 514,325 | 35.4% |
| December 1992 | 58 | 428,160 | 28.8% |
| December 1993 | 67 | 409,112 | 26.8% |
| December 1994 | 82 | 375,906 | 23.4% |

*Union membership is reported as full-time-equivalent union members. Density is total union membership as a percentage of the full-time employed work force reported as by the Household Labour Force Survey. Thus density reported understates actual density.
*Source:* Harbridge et al., 1995.

## Reversing the decline: Four hypotheses

Notwithstanding the indisputable impact of the Act on unions, union decline in New Zealand may already have been taking place. Certainly that has been the international experience. Visser (1991) reports that virtually all OECD countries have experienced negative or reduced union growth and that throughout the 1980s union density fell in all OECD countries except Finland, Iceland, and Sweden.

Visser (1991) presents four hypotheses for reversing the decline of unionism. If, internationally, these are the necessary and sufficient conditions for unions to prosper, then what are the prospects for unions in New Zealand? Each hypothesis is examined in the New Zealand context.

### *Hypothesis 1: Industry wide, multi-employer bargaining*

New Zealand's industrial conciliation and arbitration system enabled and encouraged a compulsory multi-employer bargaining system. The blanket coverage provision in the Act ensured that an award prescribed employment conditions for all 'employers in the occupation or industry in the industrial district concerned, regardless of whether they had taken part in the negotiations or were even aware of them' (Nolan and Walsh, 1994, p. 14). The state not only required the universal application of the award, but it also took responsibility for the enforcement of awards and agreements. The result by 1989/1990 was that multi-employer bargaining accounted for 77 percent of all employees covered by registered awards or agreements. The sector analysis of this coverage presented in Table 6.2 identifies that multi-employer bargaining was particularly prevalent in the private sector — with 93 percent of all private sector coverage being in multi-employer bargains.

**Table 6.2**
**The decline of collective bargaining coverage by type of settlement and sector (1989/1990 – 1994/1995)**

| | Private sector | | Public sector | | All sectors | |
|---|---|---|---|---|---|---|
| Type of settlement | 1989/ 1990 | 1994/ 1995 | 1989/ 1990 | 1994/ 1995 | 1989/ 1990 | 1994/ 1995 |
| % employees in multi-employer agreements | 93% | 14% | 55% | 27% | 77% | 20% |
| % employees in single employer agreements | 7% | 86% | 45% | 73% | 23% | 80% |
| Total coverage (thousands of employees) | 413.6 | 209.1 | 307.8 | 156.4 | 721.4 | 365.5 |
| % decline in bargaining coverage | | 49% | | 49% | | 49% |

*Sources:* Harbridge (1991) for 1989/1990 data and Harbridge unpublished data for 1994/1995.

The data in Table 6.2 identifies the extent of the collapse of collective bargaining coverage in New Zealand in the period 1989/1990 - 1994/1995. There has been a 50 percent collapse of collective bargaining. While the collapse is in both the public and private sectors, the primary effects of it have been in the private sector. This collapse has been brought about by the failure of multi-employer settlements which have forced large numbers of employees into individual contracts. In the public sector, job (in)security has played a significant role. The impact of corporatization and then privatization in many government spheres led to a significant reduction in employment and to many large scale redundancies (Walsh and Wetzel, 1993).

The data confirm the reliance of private sector unions on multi-employer bargaining under New Zealand's traditional bargaining system. Public sector unions were in a somewhat different position. They had comparatively few employers (the state in its various forms) to deal with and had been weaned from occupational bargaining and onto enterprise bargaining as a result of public sector reforms in 1988. As a result, public sector unions were already far less dependent on multi-employer bargaining than were their private sector counterparts.

The new bargaining regime under the Act presents unions with a very different scenario. The Act actively discourages multi-employer bargaining and provides no specific mechanism for 'extending' any settlement to employers. The discouragement comes through provisions making it illegal for unions and workers to strike in support of a multi-employer contract. That in itself is more indicative of attitude than an actual impediment. The American V. S. Clark, writing in 1906, observed that unions in New Zealand were 'litigious rather than militant organizations' (Clark quoted in Roth, 1973, p25). This tradition of litigious behavior was maintained throughout the century with unions rarely relying on strike action to secure a bargaining position. The legal restriction on strikes imposed under the Act is, however, no aid to gaining multi-employer bargains.

In the five years since the enactment of the Act, multi-employer bargaining has largely collapsed. In a nation where multi-employer bargaining was the norm for nearly 100 years, where all but seven percent of the unionized private sector work force were covered by a multi-employer bargain, just 73,000 workers (20 percent of all workers covered by a collective bargain) are covered by multi-employer arrangements. As has been well-documented, single-employer, enterprise bargaining has become the dominant form (McAndrew, 1993).

In terms of Visser's hypothesis about the need for industry-wide, multi-employer bargaining, close analysis of the multi-employer contracts held reveals that very few are industry wide. Most are extensions of an enterprise agreement to other enterprises owned or franchised within a particular corporate structure. Accordingly the extent of genuine industry wide, multi-employer bargaining is even more limited than the data suggest.

While the decline of multi-employer bargaining was expected by many unionists when the legislation was enacted, the extent of the decline has been a surprise. The collapse has come about largely because of employer opposition to multi-employer settlements. The negotiation of multi-employer bargains requires the existence and co-operation of an appropriate employers organization. The tradition in New Zealand has been that one central organization of employers, the New Zealand Employers Federation, has coordinated multi-employer bargaining through the award system. Industry associations played a minimal role in such negotiations. With the change in the legislation, the New Zealand Employers Federation encouraged employers away from multi-employer arrangements and proposed enterprise settlements in their place. Industry associations were poorly placed to step in and fill the breech as a coordinator of multi-employer deals. Accordingly, unions were largely unable to find authorized employer organizations prepared to cooperate with multi-employer bargaining arrangements. The result, predictably, has been the collapse of multi-employer settlements which has had a major impact on unionization levels and is certain in New Zealand to be a key cause of falling union density.

### *Hypothesis 2: A secure non-contested instutionalized workplace presence*

Until 1991 unions in New Zealand had, through an historical process of registration, gained exclusive non-contestable rights to bargain collectively for workers in occupations or industries that the Registrar of Unions had included in the union's membership rule. The effect of registration was to prevent any other union or employees' group accessing the process of conciliation and arbitration on behalf of that group — effectively prohibiting competition between unions. Through this process the state guaranteed the existence of individual unions by providing a protected membership pool. Unions were similarly protected against employer opposition. Once registered, access to conciliation and arbitration ensured a right not only to the bargaining process but also to a secured (albeit minimalist) bargaining outcome.

Under the Act three effects have become apparent as a direct result of open contestability for coverage and the outlawing of compulsory union membership. First, the patterns of amalgamation and merger that had commenced under the Labour Relations Act 1987 have continued. There is little evidence that a proliferation of small enterprise based unions has resulted from the non-contestability provisions of the Act. A clutch of new small unions have appeared but in most cases these are simply effective small unions that had been forced to amalgamate under the Labour Relations Act '1,000 member' rule that have reconstituted to their original membership base.

Second, there is remarkably little evidence of unions 'poaching' members from other unions. The New Zealand Council of Trade Unions (NZCTU) has a non-raiding policy between unions. While there is little public evidence of 'poaching', a media report in late 1993 quoted the Trade Union Federation (12 non-NZCTU unions) as stating that they had begun a campaign against unions taking members from each other. Trade Union Federation Secretary, Maxine Gay, had described an offer to members of the Engineers Union for free installation of 'Sky' television on presentation of a new membership card as 'poaching' (*Evening Post*, 14 December 1993, p. 1). No substantive evidence of 'poaching' was identified throughout the debate but the debate itself identifies that 'poaching' is an issue of concern.

Third, there is little evidence of any widespread development of 'staff associations' or employer-sponsored groups that might not meet the test of employer independence. To date, 35 collective employment contracts covering 10,400 employees have been identified as being negotiated by staff associations. One of these staff associations is in fact a traditional (though never registered) 'union' — the New Zealand Police Association — and their contract covers some 6,250 employees. Another staff association, the Firestone Rubber Workers, is one of the reconstituted unions referred to earlier, and should probably be treated as a 'union' rather than a staff association. The lack of 'staff associations' comes as no real surprise. There is simply no necessity for employers to promote such organizations — the usual pattern of their development. Under the Act, the employer is required to recognize the bargaining representative selected by each employee, but, unlike North American requirements, there is no obligation to bargain with that representative at all, let alone in 'good faith'. Employers that take a strong de-unionization position need not sponsor their own in-house union; they can simply refuse to bargain with the union or representative appointed by their employees. Unions in New Zealand no longer operate in a secure, non-contested environment. Employers can 'contest' union representation simply by refusing to negotiate and this is the most important means of destabilizing unions in New Zealand.

*Hypothesis 3: Inclusive bargaining*

Inclusive bargaining requires that unions negotiate for members and non-members alike. A collective agreement applying to all employees, irrespective of union membership, ensures that an employer will not deliberately seek to engage non-unionists because they are less expensive than unionists. Previously, bargaining in New Zealand was inclusive: Awards and collective agreements registered with the Commission applied to all employees irrespective of union membership and it was not possible for employers to contract out of award conditions and payments. Under the Act there is no automatic extension mechanism which enables the employment contract to cover new employees. The very notion of a contract is that it applies to the parties who sign it; the employer(s) and their *existing* staff, not necessarily those new employees who will be engaged in the future. This makes it possible for employers to undercut the existing contract by engaging new staff at lower rates. Many unions have sought to negotiate a clause requiring the employer to offer any new employee the right to become party to the existing collective employment contract. But frequently employers are not agreeing to a 'new employees' clause and are agreeing instead to a provision stating that new employees would only be covered by the existing contract with the employer's consent.

Approximately 50 percent of employees covered by collective contracts are under contracts which are automatically extended to new employees. A smaller number of employees, nine percent of the sample, are covered by contracts with no provision for extension, but over 40 percent are on contracts where the extension to new employees is discretionary (Harbridge and Honeybone, 1995). Some contracts explicitly exclude the addition of new employees to the contract. Two forms of this discretionary extension are common. The most common simply states that, where the parties agree, new employees may be added to the contract. The second type states that the consent of the employer is required for new employees to be added.

It is clear from some union leaders' claims that employers are hiring new workers at lower pay and conditions than other staff and that some (if not many) employers have not exercised their discretion and have refused to engage new staff on the existing contract. New employees, in the public service for example, are being engaged on individual contracts which omit many conditions (including overtime, redundancy entitlements, and other allowances) contained in the collective contract. The development of 'tiered' employment systems for staff based on their date of engagement is extensively reviewed in the literature (e.g. Heetderks and Martin, 1991) and has both advantages and disadvantages for firms. For unions it has only disadvantages. New hires engaged on an inferior employment contract are unlikely to unionize as the union is very much caught between a rock and a hard place: If the union is to settle an inclusive contract covering all employees then it is dealing with an employer who is most unlikely to want to raise the cost of benefits for new hires. Accordingly, the union either has to reduce the benefits available to existing employees (an unpopular move guaranteed to lead to de-unionization) or to accept a tiered contract with different conditions applying to staff undertaking the same functions (sure to be unpopular with new hires as they receive nothing more than the employer was offering anyway). The failure of legislation in New Zealand to provide for inclusive bargaining is certain to be a major determinant in any second wave of de-unionization.

### *Hypothesis 4: The 'Free-Loader' problem*

The free-loader problem is a simple one. Employers who decide against the 'tiered' employment strategy, apply the union-negotiated collective employment contract to all their employees. Unions then bargain inclusively; their contracts apply to all employees irrespective of union membership and accordingly non-unionists get the benefits of being a unionist without paying a union fee. Unionists feel disgruntled about the inequity of this situation and see little point in continuing with their union membership as the so-called benefits of unionism are free anyway.

It is difficult to know to what extent free-loading is a problem for New Zealand unions and it is certainly not a new problem. Compulsory unionism was rarely enforced under the previous system and many thousands of employees who were obliged to join the appropriate union were either never requested to join in the first place or were rarely successfully pursued if they failed to join after being requested. It is impossible to know the extent of under-recruitment under the old system of compulsory unionism but in some industries it was very large indeed. In the 1989/1990 bargaining round, we had estimated that under-recruitment ran well in excess of 100,000 potential members. Unions traditionally placed little importance on recruitment techniques and training in recruitment matters was given little prominence. Until a 1976 amendment to the Industrial Relations Act 1973, unions were able to give lists of recalcitrant nonmembers to officials of the Department of

Labour who were then required to prosecute these 'offenders' for a breach of the Act — prosecution was avoidable by the non-member joining.

Historically, New Zealand unions had a poorly developed approach to recruitment strategy, mounted few public union organizing drives, relied extensively on the law of compulsory unionism as their primary recruitment technique, and undertook little (if any) training in recruitment matters for union officials.

Under the Act, with compulsory membership gone and multi-employer bargaining largely dissipated, unions have been poorly prepared to recruit members. It is unclear to what extent free-loading is now a difficulty. The data we have been gathering on collective bargaining coverage report the numbers of employees covered by the contract, *not* the number of union members. Curiously, union membership now exceeds collective bargaining coverage by more than 100,000 employees — a reflection of unionists (particularly in the public sector) retaining their membership even though a new collective contract has not been put in place, not any suggestion that free-loading is no difficulty. Many union officials spoken to in the course of our research dismiss the free-loader issue as of little significance. Others see it as important, and in fact critical, if they are to successfully survive.

## Conclusion

New Zealand presents an interesting test for the various theories about union decline. The causes of decline held in the international literature are relevant in New Zealand, but they do not explicitly capture the deterministic role of the state. The changed structure of the labour market has had its impact since 1988, but we argue that impact has been limited. Public opinion and societal values may be more individualistic than those previously held by society at large, but there is no evidence of any significant 'anti-union' backlash. We have shown that historically, union organizing strategies have been weak as a result of the system within which they developed. The majority of New Zealand unions have yet to develop the proactive organizing and recruitment strategies required in order for them to prosper in the new environment.

There is no doubt, however, from our evidence that the removal of external legitimization of unions through legislative mechanisms has been the dominant factor in the decline of New Zealand unions. This conclusion fits neatly with the theories developed by Howard (1977) and Hince (1993) that Euro-American theories about unionization have limited applicability in Australia and New Zealand. Employers at the 'shop floor' level did not drive the deregulatory changes. Those changes developed from the ideological approach of the central organizations of employers, business groups, and, in turn, the state. The state shaped the industrial relations environment which led to the decline in unionization. This environment was one in which the state failed to provide for or acknowledge any rights or privileges for trade unionism.

This marked a fundamental change from the previous legislative grant of union privileges which effectively embodied the criteria of legitimation established by Visser (1991), resulting in high levels of union density. We have demonstrated the effect of the removal of external legitimation by the state in 1991 with the introduction of the Act. Unions so far have been unable to meet the conditions for the first hypothesis as they have been unable to secure industry-wide, multi-employer bargaining. Unions have had limited success in securing a non-contested and institutionalized workplace presence, the condition required by the second of Visser's hypotheses. The last two hypotheses, inclusive bargaining and free-loading, place irreconcilable demands on unions. A limited form of compulsory unionism or traditional 'closed shop' is the usual method of resolving this contradiction, but this is specifically outlawed by the Act.

The fundamental change from 100 years of state-sponsored unionism to a situation revoking all form of external legitimacy for unions sends out clear signals to employers and employees of the role of unionism in society. It seems highly unlikely that, under the present legislative system, unionism in New Zealand will prosper.

## References

Beaumont, P. B. (1991), 'Human resource management and international joint ventures: Some evidence from Britain'. *Human Resource Management Journal* , vol. 1, pp. 90-101.

Chaison, G. N. and Rose, J. B. (1987), 'The state of the unions revisited: The United States and Canada', in Jain, H. (ed.), *Emerging trends in Canadian industrial relations: Proceedings of the 24th Annual Meeting of the Canadian Industrial Relations Association,* McMaster University, June 4-6, Hamilton, Ontario, pp. 576-594.

Freeman, R. B. and Medoff, J. L. (1984), *What do unions do?* Basic Books, New York.

Freeman, R. B. and Pelletier, J. (1990), 'The impact of industrial relations legislation on union density', *British Journal of Industrial Relations*, vol. 28, pp.141-164.

Freeman, R. B. and Rebick, M. (1989), *Crumbling pillar? Declining union density in Japan,* National Bureau of Economic Research, Working Paper 2963. National Bureau of Economic Research, Cambridge, MA.

Harbridge, R. (1991), 'Collective bargaining coverage in New Zealand: The impact of the Employment Contracts Bill'. *Australian Bulletin of Labour* , vol. 17, pp. 310-324.

Harbridge, R. and Hince, K. W. (1994), 'Bargaining and worker representation under New Zealand's employment contracts legislation: A review after two years', *Relations Industrielles* , vol. 49, pp. 561-581.

Harbridge, R., Hince, K. W. and Honeybone, A. (1995), 'Unions and union membership in New Zealand: Annual review for 1994', *New Zealand Journal of Industrial Relations*, vol. 20, pp. 163-170.

Harbridge, R. and McCaw, S. (1991), 'The Employment Contracts Act 1991: New bargaining arrangements in New Zealand', *Asia Pacific HRM* , vol. 29, pp. 5-26.

Harbridge, R. and Moulder, J. (1993), 'Collective bargaining and the Employment Contracts Act: One year on', *Journal of Industrial Relations*, vol. 35, pp. 62-83.

Hawke, G. (1994), 'The economy', in *New Zealand Official Year Book*, Government Printer, Wellington, pp 543-551.

Heetderks, T. and Martin, J. (1991), 'Employee perceptions of the effects of a two-tier wage structure', *Journal of Labour Studies* , vol. XII, pp. 279-295.

Hince, K. W. (1993), 'Is Euro-American union theory universally applicable?: An Australasian perspective', in Adams, R. J. and Meltz, N. M. (eds.), *Industrial relations theory: Its nature, scope, and pedagogy*, The Scarecrow Press, London, pp. 81-102.

Hince, K. and Harbridge, R. (1995), *What the law gives the law can take away: Lessons from New Zealand for grassroots organizing*. Paper presented to the 21st Annual Conference of the Southwest Labor Studies Association, May 4 - 6, University of California, Los Angeles.

Holt, J. (1986), *Compulsory arbitration in New Zealand: The first forty years*. Auckland University Press, Auckland, New Zealand.

Howard, W. A. (1977), 'Australian trade unions in the context of union theory, *Journal of Industrial Relations*, vol. 19, pp. 255-273.

Jesson, B. (1989), *Fragments of labour: The story behind the labour government.*. Penguin, Auckland, New Zealand.

Kiely, P. and Caisley, A. (1993), 'The legal status of bargaining under the Employment Contracts Act 1991: A review of recent cases', in Harbridge, R. (ed.), *Employment contracts: New Zealand experiences*, Victoria University Press, Wellington, New Zealand, pp. 53-69.

Kochan, T. A., McKersie, R. B. and Chalykoff, J. (1986), 'The effects of corporate strategy and workplace innovations on union representation', *Industrial and Labour Relations Review* , vol. 39, pp. 487-501.

Lipset, S. M. (1990), *Continental divide: The values and institutions of the United States and Canada*, Routledge, New York.

Marshall, R. (1991), 'Labor in a global economy', in Hecker, S. and Hallock, M. (eds.), *Labor in a global economy*, University of Oregon Books, Eugene, OR, pp. 10-24.

McAndrew, I. (1993), 'The process of developing employment contracts: A management perspective', in Harbridge, R. (ed.) *Employment contracts: New Zealand experiences*, Victoria University Press, Wellington, New Zealand, pp. 165-184.

Moore, W. J. and Newman, R. J. (1988), 'A cross-sectional analysis of the post-war decline in American trade union membership', *Journal of Labor Research*, vol. 9, pp. 111-126.

Nolan, M., and Walsh, P. (1994), 'Labour's leg iron? Assessing trade unions and arbitration in New Zealand', in Walsh, P. (ed.), *Trade unions, work and society: The century of the Arbitration System*, The Dunmore Press, Palmerston North, New Zealand, pp. 9-37.

Reshef, Y. (1990), 'Union decline: A view from Canada', *Journal of Labor Research*, vol. 11, pp. 25-39.

Roth, H. (1973), *Trade unions in New Zealand: Past and present.*, A. H. and A. W. Reed, Wellington, New Zealand.

Schmidt, D. E. (1993), 'Public opinion and media coverage of unions', *Journal of Labor Research* , vol. 14, pp. 151-164.

Visser, J. (1990), 'In search of inclusive unionism', *Bulletin of Comparative Labour Relations*, vol. 18 (whole issue).

Visser, J. (1991), 'Trends in trade union membership', in OECD *Employment outlook*, OECD, Paris, pp 97-134.

Walsh, P., and Wetzel, K. (1993), 'Preparing for privatization: Corporate strategy and industrial relations in New Zealand's state owned enterprises', *British Journal of Industrial Relations*, vol. 31, pp. 57-74.

Weiler, P. C. (1990), *Governing the workplace: The future of labour and employment law*, Harvard University Press, Cambridge, MA.

# 7 Union responses to the restructuring of the pulp and paper industry in Quebec

*Reynald Bourque and Claude Rioux*

This chapter examines the impact of the changes in the economic environment of Quebec's pulp and paper industry on sectoral and local union strategies and structures. Pulp and paper manufacturing is the main industry in Canada, the world's most important producer of market pulp and newsprint. Nearly 40 percent of the jobs and mills in the industry are located in Quebec, where newsprint production is concentrated, while the market pulp comes mainly from the western province of British Colombia. The deterioration of the commercial and financial situation of the pulp and paper industry in Quebec during the early nineties has led to numerous job losses. Management demands for increased work flexibility in order to reduce production costs were first rejected by labour organizations, but the deepening of the crisis at the end of the 1980's has compelled some local unions affiliated to the Quebec-based Fédération des travailleurs du papier et de la forêt (FTPF) to negotiate flexibility agreements to insure the survival of their mills and, in so doing, to improve job security. From 1989 to 1994, a growing number of local agreements were negotiated to introduce various measures of job flexibility in maintenance and production; in some cases major organizational changes, including semi-autonomous teams, were implemented.

These changes were accompanied by a review of union strategies and structures at both the sectoral and local levels. At the sectoral level, the traditional role of the FTPF — that is, defining the main bargaining agenda

---

Reynald Bourque, Professor, School of Industrial Relations, University of Montreal, C. P. 6128, Succ. A, Montréal, Quebec, Canada, H3C 3J7. Claude Rioux, Coordinator, Fédération des travailleurs du papier et de la forêt (FTPF-CSN), 155 E. Charest, Québec, Quebec, Canada, G1K 3G6.

and coordinating local negotiations — was weakened by two factors: the decentralization of the bargaining structure and the emphasis placed on local issues, particularly in older mills threatened by corporate downsizing plans. Consequently, the services required from the FTPF by its local unions increasingly shifted to more technical expertise, such as financial analysis, production and human resources management. The FTPF structure for the coordination of local negotiations that had existed over the last two decades was dropped during the 1993 negotiations at the request of local unions, a move that challenged industry-wide union solidarity. Another problem faced by the FTPF was the differentiation process emerging from local agreements in some older mills; by comparison, changes introduced through collective agreements in recently modernized plants were more limited in scope.

Our purpose here is to analyse the changes in FTPF strategies and structures in a context of increased competition in the global pulp and paper market. We begin by reviewing the literature on union responses to economic restructuring in industrialized countries since the end of the 1970s. We then turn to the economic trends in the Canadian pulp and paper industry over the last two decades. In the third section, we focus on unions and bargaining structures particular to the pulp and paper industry in Canada and Quebec. Next, we review the main changes in collective bargaining and labour-management relations in pulp and paper mills represented by FTPF affiliates and the new relations that these changes have engendered between FTPF and its local affiliates. Finally, we will discuss the major challenges entailed by the ongoing process of industrial restructuring on unions' strategies and structures.

## Unions and industrial restructuring

Increased international competition, as well as changes in industrial structures and the distribution of employment in advanced industrial societies, are challenging the role of labour unions as collective actors in the employment relationship. The prevailing strategy of job control unionism, institutionalized in the labour organizations of the North American manufacturing sector during the post-war period and deeply embedded in union structures and practices, is currently under pressure to adapt to those changes (Piore, 1986).

Labour unions must face a number of major problems at different levels as a consequence of ongoing economic restructuring. At the plant level, the organizational and technological changes currently being introduced are significantly challenging local unions to adapt their strategies and practices to this more competitive environment. Unions must take positions concerning new forms of work organization while fulfilling their responsibilities, such as the protection of working conditions and the quality of worklife. Often, unions have to rethink the role of the collective agreement as the primary instrument of job regulation in the workplace and review certain rules regarded as basic mechanisms of job control unionism. At the industry level, economic restructuring is characterized by a movement towards the decentralization of collective bargaining, a movement that reduces the unions' ability to take wages out of competition and to standardize working conditions in the unionized sector. At the national level, in the context of the so-called globalization of economies, union influence on national economic and industrial policies is generally considered to be weaker than before. Thus, labour organizations have to adjust their strategies and structures in order to respond to the new challenges at all three levels.

Recent research suggests that three distinct strategies have been followed by North-American firms to adapt to a more competitive economic environment in the 1970's and 1980's. The first strategy characterized employers who openly oppose the unionization of their employees, encourage decertification of unionized employees, transfer production from unionized to non-unionized plants, or open greensites while closing old, unionized plants (Kochan, Katz and McKersie, 1986). The second strategy is to promote an active Human Resource Management policy to increase job satisfaction and direct participation in order to reduce the demand for unionization (Kochan et al., 1986). The third strategy is to cooperate with unions in implementing more flexible work systems in exchange for more job security (Kochan et al., 1986; Voos, 1994). This last strategy has been observed mainly in highly unionized sectors, where the union avoidance approach was discouraged by the existence of strong and well organized unions (Kochan et al., 1986). This strategy is also more frequent in industries where competition is based on quality and the competence of the workforce rather than on the sheer cost advantage of standardized production (Kochan and Osterman, 1994; Piore, 1986; Voos, 1994). North-American pulp and paper is one such industry: it is capital intensive rather than labour intensive, and union density is very high (Birecree, 1993; Bourque and Rioux, 1994; Eaton and Kriesky, 1994).

Labour-management cooperation in highly unionized and capital intensive industries is often seen as instrumental for the achievement of increased productivity, and in many cases a joint process of labour-management cooperation in which unions agree to support the productivity effort has been implemented in the workplace (Eaton and Voos, 1992; Voos, 1994). Union support in these cases usually involves agreement to major changes in work rules, pay incentives and work reorganization intended to achieve the continuous improvement of productivity (Cappelli and McKersie, 1987; Voos,

1994). These productivity agreements often involve programs that give employees a chance to acquire new skills and to exercise a degree of self-supervision (Eaton and Voos, 1992; Kochan and Osterman, 1994). There is some evidence that these participation programs enhance union influence over traditional management rights in the area of work organization and can increase member satisfaction due to a greater involvement in their work (Eaton and Voos, 1992; Kochan et al., 1986). There is also some evidence that a participation program in a unionized firm tends to be more extensive and lasts longer than one in a non-union firm because unions, as representative institutions, can communicate the views of employees on the program's operation (Cooke, 1990; Eaton and Voos, 1992; Voos, 1994).

The issue of participative programs was strongly debated within North-American labour organizations in the 1980's (Katz, 1988). Industrial relations literature points to distinct labour policies towards participative programs. According to one policy, to enhance the mill's productivity in an increasingly competitive global economy, labour unions must support participatory schemes (Kochan and Osterman, 1994). A second policy opposes participative programs, which are seen both as an instrument designed to increase managerial control over work organization and as a way to reduce the union's bargaining power (Parker and Slaughter, 1988; Wells, 1993). Another policy is to support participative programs enhancing the voice of the employees in the workplace and designed to improve productivity (Eaton and Voos, 1992; Voos, 1994). This last policy was favoured by FTPF and its local unions in the pulp and paper industry in Quebec.

## The pulp and paper industry in Canada and Quebec

The Canadian pulp and paper industry is one of the most important contributors to the country's merchandise trade balance, ahead of other major sectors of the Canadian and Quebec economies. Since the 1950s, four Canadian companies have a dominant role in newsprint and mechanical printing papers. Their combined capacity represents about 28 percent of the North American total, so that they continue to be important players in the market place. More than 75 percent of Canadian pulp and paper output is exported throughout the world. About one third of this output comes from Quebec, mostly in the form of newsprint.

During the last fifteen years, the growth of demand for paper, paperboard and wood pulp in the industrialized countries has meant that new capacities have had to be developed. This is especially true of newsprint, where traditional export markets, mainly in the U.S.A., have changed substantially. In fact, between 1980 and 1992, more than two million tonnes were added to the U.S. capacity, whereas demand increased by about one million tonnes. The subsequent action taken by the Canadian industry has been to reduce its newsprint capacity. To achieve this, no fewer than twenty old newsprint machines were shut down and some other machines were converted from newsprint production to specialized writing and printing papers. Producers in the Nordic countries, however, followed also this last strategy. Between 1985 and 1992, the capacities for printing and writing papers were increased by 87 percent in Canada and 62 percent in the Nordic countries, whereas consumer demand increased by only 26 percent in the U.S. and 47 percent in Western Europe. Stiff competition and lower prices ensued. Even if there was fairly interesting growth in Western European markets, the supply came from either domestic producers or the Nordic countries.

This obviously does not leave much room for Canadian exports in those markets. Furthermore, only low-cost producers will be able to compete in this very mature market and they will have to also comply with more stringent environmental regulations (Ministère des Forêts du Québec 1992). Newsprint will be increasingly made on high-speed machines in order to get low unit operating costs, meaning that slower machines will be diverted to speciality paper only if they are competitive in terms of operational flexibility and cost.

At the outset of the current period of change, the fundamentals of the pulp and paper industry in Canada and in Quebec are very different from what they were in the past. The U.S. market share of Canadian mills has shrunk from 80 percent in 1950, to 60 percent in 1980, and to 50 percent today. In other words, the Canadian share of this market is back to where it was in the mid 1920's (Hay-Roe, 1995). These findings are important for an understanding of the changes in union strategies and labour-management relations that have occurred in recent years in Quebec's paper industry.

## Bargaining structures in the pulp and paper industry

Pulp and paper is one of the most highly unionized industries in Canada. In 1992, the estimated union density was 82 percent for Canada as a whole and 83 percent for Quebec (Price Waterhouse, 1994). Unions and management have a strong and enduring tradition of centralized collective bargaining. Until 1994, two collective bargaining structures were to be found in the Canadian pulp and paper industry, one in Western Canada and one in Eastern Canada, each reflecting differences in industrial structures.

In Western Canada, mainly British Columbia, where the industry is specialized in market pulp, the bargaining structure is highly centralized. Until recently, negotiations were industry-wide, with the two major unions — the Communication, Energy and Paperworkers Union (CEP) and the Pulp, Paper and Woodworkers of Canada (PPWC) — negotiating together while the Pulp and Paper Industrial Relations Bureau acted as agent for its member companies.

In Eastern Canada, collective bargaining structures are more decentralized. This is due in part to diversification: notwithstanding the importance of the newsprint segment, the industry also produces writing and printing papers as well as paperboard. Most of the workers in Eastern Canada are represented by local unions belonging to the CEP. Unlike the situation in Ontario and Atlantic Canada, where the CEP is in a hegemonic position, there are two central labour organizations in Quebec. These are the CEP and the FTPF, which is affiliated to the Quebec-based Confédération des syndicats nationaux (CSN). The CSN is Canada's second largest national labour organization, the largest being the Canadian Labour Congress (CLC), to which the CEP is affiliated. The FTPF's current membership in the pulp and paper mills of Quebec is about 5,500 workers, whereas the CEP represents close to 15,000 members in the pulp and paper industry in Quebec.

The CEP and the FTPF are substantially different in their internal structures. Local unions in the CEP are chartered by their national body to which they belong, as provided by its bylaws, whereas local unions in the FTPF structure are voluntarily affiliated to their federation. Voluntary affiliation gives the FTPF's local unions a wider degree of autonomy; they can disaffiliate at any time, regardless of the legal period and the Quebec Labour Code provisions for union disaffiliation. Another characteristic of the FTPF affiliates is that they are organized along industrial lines without any reference to craft or specific jobs, whereas the historical development of CEP local unions often proceeded from craft or job structures. Thus, CEP members in any given mill are usually organized in two separate unions: the papermakers local union and another union representing production and maintenance workers.

These distinctive internal affiliation procedures largely account for the different collective bargaining practices in the CEP and the FTPF. The CEP has an institutionalized and well- entrenched practice of pattern bargaining in Eastern Canada. Before negotiations CEP national officers call a conference where the bargaining agenda is defined with local unions representatives. Usually, one of the four big newsprint companies is then picked as the pattern setter. Once the CEP reaches an agreement on issues such as wages, improvements to fringe benefits, vacations, holidays and shift differentials, that becomes the pattern for all local unions and their employers. As a minority union in Eastern Canada's pulp and paper industry, the FTPF has not been a party to the foregoing process, but, ordinarily, the employers followed the standard agreement provisions as negotiated by the CEP and integrated them in the agreements reached with the FTPF local unions.

## Union responses to industrial restructuring: the experience of the FTPF and its local unions

As noted in the previous section, certification in the CSN structure is vested exclusively in the local union, and the federations play essentially an advisory role for local unions with a high degree of formal autonomy. However, basic industry characteristics, such as its relative homogeneity, common technology, the similarity of products, and the labour relations traditions impel the local unions to link up through the federation in order to share information and establish a common agenda on major issues (Bourque and Rioux, 1994). This is central to the collective bargaining process and practices in an organization where trade-offs between local autonomy and sectoral linkages have to be realized. It is achieved to some extent through the coordination of bargaining objectives, strategies and tactics. Basically, the coordination model in FTPF-CSN is as shown in Table 7.1.

This model reflects a particular situation where sectoral issues are subject to the control and approval of the local unions. The federation brings to the local unions experience and expertise. Every local union has to reconcile its own priorities with those of the other locals, and it is the federation's responsibility to facilitate choices and to communicate a sense of direction in order to achieve the objectives set at the early stage of negotiations. With union solidarity at stake, it is a process in which checks and balances have to be strictly maintained. Moreover, this model requires the homogeneity or at least the similarity of the basic economic situation that prevails in each mill where local FTPF unions are present.

In 1990, negotiations for FTPF local unions started within the framework already described, with a session where sectoral priorities were determined. Local unions' priorities were set on wages and job security. However, from the very start of the formal bargaining talks, a large majority of employers argued that they needed greater flexibility in work organization to improve their competitive position within the North American pulp and paper industry, particularly in relation to U.S. companies that had successfully implemented the team concept and eliminated production and maintenance work restrictions (Birecree, 1993; Eaton and Kriesky, 1994). Flexibility language in one form or another spread to all CEP and FTPF contracts in 1990, even though some CEP locals struck over this issue. The employers' demand to eliminate mandatory shut-downs on two of the four or five holidays was also strongly opposed by the local unions in both labour organizations, but it was ultimately integrated into the negotiated pattern.

**Table 7.1**
**Coordination of collective bargaining process and structures, FTPF-CSN**

| Stage | Issues | Level | Responsibilities and roles |
|---|---|---|---|
| 1. Preliminary | Local problems | L.U. | Proposal and negotiation |
| | Enforcement of contract | L.U. | Review of existing contract, proposal and negotiation |
| | Wages | F | Technical studies and recommendation to local unions |
| | Fringe benefits | F | Technical studies and recommendation to local unions |
| | Sectoral problems (job security, technological changes, health and safety) | F | Technical studies and recommendation |
| 2. Barganing | Structure | F | Proposal, recommendation |
| | | F | Implementation |
| | | L.U. | Approval |
| | Information | L.U. | Forwarded to structure |
| | | F | Transmission to local unions |
| | Negotiation | L.U. | Local and sectoral issues approval |
| | | F | Sectórial issues |
| | | F | Stategy/control of results |

*Notes:* L.U. = local union; F = federation

The issue of changes in work organization persisted during the life of the 1990-1993 contracts. As the world pulp and paper markets collapsed in the beginning of the 1990s due to over-capacity, employers implemented cost reduction measures and downsized their workforce. This situation put strong pressure on FTPF local unions. They had to manage the consequences of job losses, which in some cases affected close to 20 percent of their total membership. At worst, the future of some mills was thought to be at stake. The focus shifted from sectoral problems to local ones. In this environment of economic hardship, there was an increasing development of flexible work arrangements as well as other emerging bargaining issues and practices. Various experiments in union-management cooperation were developed at the local mills level to improve productivity and job security (Bourque and Rioux, 1994). Many innovations were included in collective agreements, such as union participation in semi-autonomous work teams, training and early-retirement programs, and ISO 9000 certification process. By 1993, a majority of the FTPF contracts included such features.

In 1993, a new round of bargaining began, and the FTPF again implemented coordination structures similar to those of 1990. However, unlike the 1990 negotiation process, most of the work involving the planning of priorities was quite irrelevant, because many substantive and local issues had been resolved during the term of the 1990-1993 agreements. Low inflation and corporate financial losses (Price-Waterhouse, 1994) softened the wage demands of the unions, which were not expecting much in this area. As in 1990, the employers raised a new issue. This time it was the matter of long-term collective agreements, a prevalent feature in the U.S. industry (Birecree, 1993; Eaton and Kriesky, 1994). At the end of 1993, two employers initiated informal talks on the local level with their union counterparts in order to explore so-called mutual gains bargaining as a new way to negotiate the coming contracts and concluded in each case a six years agreement ensuring an extended period of labour peace. Following these two collective agreements, several long-term agreements were concluded by FTPF affiliated unions in 1994 and 1995.

In the recent years, the increased attention to work organization, joint management of training, different pay systems, and the implementation of employee involvement programs at the mill sites have confronted the FTPF and its local unions with a new reality where diversity prevails. As a consequence, local unions representatives and shop stewards must learn new skills, especially the so-called 'soft skills,' such as those related to financial analysis, knowledge of industrial processes, conflict resolution, and problem solving (Bourque and Rioux, 1994). Even at the local level, the union's structures, roles, responsibilities, and relationships with its members are under stress. This raises new issues, such as the respective roles and responsibilities of the local union and a semi-autonomous team in matters of discipline. Such conditions make communication with the members critical.

There are also implications at the sectoral level. Traditionally, the coordination of bargaining on wages and benefit issues has been central to the FTPF's activities. Basically, between negotiations periods, local unions deal with the enforcement of their local labour agreements. Thus, the main day-to-day responsibility of the FTPF is to provide its affiliated unions with professional expertise and a staff with experience in contract interpretation and with bargaining skills. The FTPF is also responsible for the training of the local union officers and stewards in bargaining techniques, grievance procedures, and health and safety prevention. This traditional set of services is still important, but innovations have been introduced in response to the shifts already discussed, particularly in the FTPF's training program. This program now includes topics such as financial analysis, work organization theory and practice, communication, and conflict resolution. Experiments and workplace innovations are widely discussed at FTPF bi-annual meeting and at the FTPF biennial convention, where cases are presented by the local union officers involved. Due to these innovations, the FTPF staff's traditional role of technician is shifting to that of a facilitator, striving to inject critical analysis and a sense of direction into the local union's activities.

## Conclusion

The loosening of pattern bargaining and the increased tendency of collective agreements to be 'tailored' to the economic situation of each industrial plant were recently noted in the United States, even in industries, including paper, where a long-standing tradition of centralized or coordinated bargaining practices existed (Voos, 1994). The case of the FTPF in the pulp and paper industry in Quebec is particular because of the high degree of autonomy at the local union level that has fostered the move toward greater decentralization of collective bargaining and agreements. In the last three years, the FTPF was less involved than before in policy-making. At the outset local unions are the major players, and in 1993, FTPF attempts to bring in tight bargaining coordination structures and practices were largely failures. However, the FTPF has demonstrated the adaptability of its services in the face of changing conditions. The FTPF also made improvements in the transmission of workplace experiments and the interaction among its affiliated local unions.

Work reorganization in mills represented by FTPF affiliated unions has in some cases engendered more cooperative labour-management relations, particularly where jobs were threatened by a depressed economic situation. Critics of the union policy that supports participation programs point mainly to the eventual weakening of union solidarity and the risk of unions and employees being absorbed into the management agenda (Parker and Slaughter, 1988; Wells, 1993). Thus, to conciliate employee participation and work flexibility, the strategy proposed by FTPF is to take into account market imperatives as well as the objective of increased control over work organization. It is of prime importance that unions negotiate their participation in productivity improvement plans without being subsumed in the managerial logic of competition.

The decentralization of collective bargaining structures that is concomitant with changes in work organization constitutes an important challenge for union strategies. Labour unions are generally opposed to the dilution of centralized bargaining structures, because such erosion is seen as a threat to the principle of keeping wages out of competition and to standardized contract provisions (Katz, 1993). Bargaining structures do condition in many ways the range of possible union strategies. It is not surprising, therefore, that in a context of industrial restructuring unions are currently engaged in a review of their existing structures. The movement towards more decentralized union structures suggests the emergence of a new representational model, one entailing a 'strategic' alliance between the local union and the employer. This raises a number of questions as to the most appropriate kinds of intermediary structures and services, the weakening of national federations like the FTPF, and the possible development of individualized servicing of the type developed in a few union federations in the UK (Murray, 1994). One major challenge that economic restructuring poses for labour organizations is the achievement of a new equilibrium between increased local union autonomy and the need for external structures to maintain labour solidarity and social unionism.

The decentralization of bargaining structures generally entails a change in relations between local unions and their sectoral and central structures. This decentralization process means new challenges for labour organizations. The first is the increasing isolation of local unions from their sectoral and central structures and their absorption into a micro-corporatist universe, defined by the employer's logic of competitiveness. A second challenge is the need to change the role of federal and central union structures and services so as to accommodate local unions seeking specialized resources. Another major challenge for central and sectoral union organization is to create coordination structures for local unions in order to compensate for the dilution of the pattern bargaining which had previously been the norm. These problems have created centrifugal tensions within labour organizations and are central to the reorientation of union strategies and structures.

## References

Birecree, A. (1993), 'Corporate development, structural change and strategic choice: Bargaining at International Paper Company in the 1980s', *Industrial Relations*, vol. 32, pp. 343-366.

Bourque, R. and Rioux, C. (1994), 'Tendances récentes de la négociation collective dans le secteur du papier au Québec', *Relations industrielles-Industrial Relations*, vol. 49, pp. 730-749.

Cappelli, P. and McKersie, R. B. (1987), 'Management strategy and the redesign of workrules', Journal of Management Studies, vol 24, pp. 441- 462.

Cooke, W. (1990), *Labor-management cooperation: New partership or going in circles?*, Upjohn Institute for Employment Research, Kalamazoo.

Eaton, A. and Voos, P. (1992), 'Unions and contemporary innovations in work organization, compensation, and employee participation', in Mishel, L. and Voos, P. B. (eds.), *Unions and economic competitiveness*, M. E. Sharpe Inc., Armonk, pp. 173-216.

Eaton, A. and Kriesky, J. (1994), 'Collective bargaining in the paper industry: Developments since 1979', in: Voos, P. B. (ed.), *Contemporary Collective Bargaining in the Private Sector*, IRRA Series, Madison, pp. 25-62.

Hay-Roe, R. (1995), 'The restructuring of the Canadian pulp and paper industry'. *Papertree Letter*, March.

Katz, H. (1993), 'The decentralization of collective bargaining: A literature review and comparative analysis', *Industrial and Labor Relations Review*, vol. 47, pp. 3-22.

Katz, H. (1988), 'Policy debate over work reorganization in North American unions', in: Hyman, R. and Streek, W. (eds.), *New technology and industrial relations*, Basil Blackwell, London, pp. 220-232.

Kochan, T. A., Katz, H. C. and McKersie, R. B. (1986), *The transformation of American industrial relations*, Basic Books, New York.

Kochan, T. A. and Osterman, P. (1994), *The mutual gains enterprise: Human resource strategy and national policy*, Harvard Business School Press, Boston.

Ministère des Forêts (1992), *L'industrie des pâtes et papiers: situation et perspectives d'avenir*, Direction du développement industriel, Service des études économiques et commerciales, Gouvernement du Québec, Québec.

Murray, G. (1994), 'Structure and identity: The impact of union structure in comparative perspective', *Employee Relations*, vol. 6, pp. 24-40.

Parker, M. and Slaughter, J. (1988), *Choosing side: Unions and the team concept*, South End Press, Boston.

Piore, M. J. (1986), 'Perspectives on labor market flexibility', *Industrial Relations*, vol. 25, pp. 146-166.

Price Waterhouse (1994), *Canadian forest industry*, Price Waterhouse, Vancouver.

Voos, P. B. (1994), 'An economic perspective on contemporary trends in collectve bargaining', in Voos, P. B. (ed.), *Contemporary collective bargaining in the private sector*, IRRA Series, Madison, pp. 1-23.

Wells, D. (1993), 'Are strong unions compatible with the new model of human resource management?', *Relations industrielles-Industrial Relations*, vol. 48, pp. 56-85.

# 8 Renewal and crisis in Russian unionism

*Boris Kagarlitsky*

In Russia, the times are troubled. In the seven years since Mikhail Gorbachev proclaimed his *glasnost*, countless aspects of Russian life and society have changed beyond recognition. The Soviet Union has disintegrated. The Communist Party, after expiring, has been reincarnated; after being banned, it has been restored. Only one structure remains solid, holding out against all odds. That structure is the trade unions.

## Old and new unions in Russia after 1989

The traditional Soviet trade unions played an important role in society, but one which rarely attracted much attention. They concerned themselves with questions of social welfare; organized workers' leisure-time activities and facilities for children; helped provide workers with consumer goods; and at times, consulted with enterprise managements on questions related to industrial safety. The leader of the trade union at an enterprise was in effect an unofficial deputy director with responsibility for social matters. During the *perestroika* period the trade unions remained virtually untouched by the reforms. It was only in 1990 and 1991 that serious changes began in the union structures.

The miners' strikes of the summer of 1989 showed that the old trade union structures were unable to cope with the challenges presented by the new conditions. In most cases, the strikes were not accompanied by a mass exodus of members from the official union, or by attempts to form new union bodies. The miners in most cases continued to regard the existing union as a useful

Boris Kagarlitsky, Institute of Political and Labour Studies, Kolpachniy per. 9A, 101831 Moscow, Russia.

organ of distribution — worth belonging to, but quite irrelevant to labour conflicts. Workers' struggles were seen as the province of strike committees, which in the course of 1989 and 1990 arose in all the coal mining regions of the USSR. But as the months passed, the leaders of the strike committees came to understand the potential of the trade union as an organizational form. A section of the activists in the miners' movement took leading posts in the traditional union bodies. Eventually, other activists began establishing a new union.

The first generation of activists in the independent labour movement held numerous hopes that turned eventually into cruel disappointments. The leaders of the workers' committees took a suspicious attitude to the intelligentsia, but were readily coopted by government *apparatchiks* and local populist leaders who used the miners to further their own intrigues. Within a few years many leaders of the strike committees became prosperous business entrepreneurs and state officials. The slogan 'The workers' movement should stay out of politics!' was used to justify a refusal to pursue an independent working-class political course, and later, to bind the workers' committees to the policies put forward by Yeltsin and his neo-liberal associates — policies that were anti-worker in their very essence.

The emergence of alternative trade unions represented the first serious challenge to the traditional structures. Large numbers of 'alternative' unions arose after 1989 and attracted worker activists who were dissatisfied with the bureaucratism and inactivity of the official organizations. The largest of the new structures was the Independent Union of Miners (NPG). Somewhat earlier, the Association of Socialist Trade Unions (SOTSPROF) had been formed. The word 'socialist' in this name was later tactfully changed to 'social', and then dropped entirely. This reflected the organization's political evolution.

Socialists and anarcho-syndicalists who had been active in SOTSPROF during its early days were purged from the leadership. The new trade unions immediately launched a furious struggle against their traditional counterparts, which they saw as their main adversaries. Before long the alternative union leaders, who had originally acted as oppositionists criticizing the old unions for their links with the state, themselves began appealing to the government in hopes of winning support against their rivals. The anti-communism of most of the alternative union federations drove them into the embraces of extreme neo-liberals. After the collapse of the USSR, when the Russian government set its sights openly on broad privatization and the construction of capitalism, the leaders of the alternative unions gave their backing to any decision made by the Russian authorities. They ignored the fact that many of these decisions were openly hostile to workers' interests.

It is not surprising that the new trade unions failed to win the majority of workers to their side. Even where a significant exodus from the old unions took place, people were in no hurry to join the new ones. Political purges, splits and financial scandals in the alternative unions began attracting publicity. Press reports spoke of the NPG having received money from the Russian government for the purpose of organizing the anti-Gorbachev strike in the spring of 1991. Members publicly accused their leaders of corruption and of misappropriating money. Analogous scandals took place in SOTSPROF and smaller organizations.

As the conflict grew between the Russian authorities and the leadership of the traditional trade unions, the alternative unions began to enjoy increasing government support. In the Russian Trilateral Commission on Labour Relations, the number of places allotted to the alternative unions was out of all proportion to their membership. The leadership bodies of SOTSPROF were provided with office space in state buildings (for example, in the Moscow Soviet), and the state-owned mass media gave these unions generous publicity. The alternative unions also received substantial support from the American trade union federation, the AFL-CIO.

During the 1992 strike by teachers and health workers, representatives of SOTSPROF appealed to workers in these sectors — admittedly, without success — to refrain from joining the stoppage. After two years, the 'old' and 'new' unions had effectively swapped roles. The alternative union organizations merged increasingly with the authorities, while the traditional unions took on the role of an independent opposition force.

## Traditional unionism changes

1990 was the year when changes started in the traditional unions. The All-Union Central Council of Trade Unions was abolished, and the General Confederation of Trade Unions was established to take its place. After the collapse of the USSR, it was transformed into an 'international association'. The Russian unions set up the Federation of Independent Trade Unions of Russia (FNPR) headed by Igor Klochkov. It continued to play the role of a safety net, helping their members solve everyday problems that ranged from buying cheap sugar to finding places for children in summer camps; in conditions of acute economic crisis, these functions of the traditional unions were valued more and more highly. At the same time, the unions took on new and unfamiliar tasks. New people, many of whom had never been part of the old bureaucracy, appeared in the leadership of the branch and territorial organizations. Some of them had been active in the strikes of 1989 and 1990.

This recovery of traditional unionism in Russia was similar to the processes that happened in most Post-Communist countries, where old union organizations turned out to be better equipped to face the changes than the new unions which called for these changes. The evolution of the traditional trade unions followed a contradictory course, but for millions of people who were suffering from the economic crisis and from the government's policies, the FNPR remained the sole all-Russian structure through which something might be achieved. The most radical renewal took place in the Moscow Federation of Trade Unions (MFP). The MFP's new chairperson, Mikhail Shmakov, announced that he intended to turn the federation into an influential force, capable of defending its positions both against the authorities and the leadership of the FNPR.

Shmakov, who turned 45 in 1993, is a typical representative of the new generation of union leaders who took up their posts between 1989 and 1992. As these people came to prominence, rapid changes began to occur. The new leaders sought to break as rapidly as possible with the past of the 'official' trade unions. They brought with them a new style and new ideas. Shmakov was the first person in the Russian trade union movement to enter into dialogue with the young radicals of the 'informal' left-wing organizations that had arisen during the perestroika years. Radical left activists who earlier had been making furious attacks on the old trade union bureaucracy were soon to be found among the consultants and officials of the trade unions. Many of these people not only learnt to wear ties, but also proved unexpectedly effective in their new roles. The dominant ideology of the union leaders and activists during that time could be described as left conservatism. As later events proved, it was also in line with the moods of the masses. In meetings and demonstrations, people were condemning the destruction of the country's productive potential, and speaking of the need to save the social and productive infrastructure.

After August 1991, when the Communist Party was suspended and the structures of the USSR collapsed, the trade unions remained almost the only mass organizations in the country. More than 80 percent of union members remained faithful to their organizations despite the changes that had taken place (Buketov, 1996, p. 142). The FNPR and the regional federations retained their property and incomes. Compared with the chaos and corruption prevailing in Russia, the trade union bureaucracy, which was accustomed to precisely observing traditional norms, seemed a model of honesty and efficiency. However, the trade union leadership lacked both a clear strategy and a full understanding of its own strength.

## Unions and corporatist labour relations

It is important to mention that different types of unionism in Russia corresponded to different types of problems and conflicts. While 'old' unions were good in acting at the national level, in most cases they remained totally unable to become a militant force at the level of an enterprise. Here they cooperated closely with the managers as a sort of social section of the administration. It is worth mentioning, however, that this cooperation often brought very good results for the workers. In the cases when real conflicts emerged at this level it was mostly the alternative union which was active mobilizing the protest potential. Thus old unions tended to be 'nice' with the managers of individual enterprises but tough with the government and alternative unions acted the opposite way.

Labour relations in Russia are still very corporatist in the sense that administration not only represents the owner against the workers but also represents the 'labour collective' against the state or the owners. Even in privatized enterprises the state is not only a participant in the joint-stock company but also the main source of subsidies and the only real source of investment. Studies of Russian and Western economists in 1992-94 proved that during this period of privatization, marketization and 'de-statization' dependence of individual enterprises on the State increased dramatically and now it is stronger than ever since the 1965 economic reform (Buzgalin, 1992, pp. 4-6; Kotz and Weir, 1996, p. 173-180). That explains why with the economy being almost totally privatized, all serious problems are still resolved on the level of the national government.[1]

At first the FNPR leaders were ready to give critical support to the Russian government, while the MFP leadership called for a more radical and independent course. But as the social costs of the reforms became obvious, the FNPR officialdom underwent a radicalization. The trade unions fought for the indexation of wages, and for the setting of the minimum wage at a level equal to the subsistence minimum income. Privatization, accompanied by job losses and, often, by the shutting down of enterprise union organizations, aroused acute dissatisfaction among unionists. Within the FNPR, the conviction grew that the social interests of workers were being defended far better in state sector enterprises than in privatized ones (Kagarlitsky and Clarke, 1994, p. 24).

The authorities held talks with the trade unions, and made various concessions on matters that were not crucial to the government's strategies. However, the wage indexation law adopted in 1991 was not observed.

Moreover, the Finance Ministry made a deliberate practice of refusing to provide state-owned enterprises, and even other government departments, with the funds they needed to pay wages on time. This could not fail to radicalize the trade union movement.

While striving to end the dominance of communist ideology in the trade union movement, the FNPR leaders constantly stressed that the unions needed to stay out of politics and to keep their distance from political parties. Nevertheless, the heightened conflict with the government showed that trade unions could not remain apart from the political process. At a mass meeting of MFP activists in October 1992 they called for 'a new course and new reforms', which the trade unions needed to advance in place of 'the failed reforms of the liberal Gaidar team' (Kagarlitsky and Clarke, 1994, p. 24). The concept which labour radicals put forward involved a mixed economy with a strong state sector capable of becoming the 'locomotive of development' (Pronin, 1994). A further element was an agreement between the government, enterprise managements and the trade unions to ensure control over prices and wages.

The FNPR leadership faced the problem of finding political allies willing to aid its struggle for a new course. Klochkov and a number of other trade union leaders spoke out in support of the initiatives of the centrist Civic Union. Meanwhile, many trade union activists were involved in moves to establish the Party of Labour. The trade unions joined with the Civic Union in campaigning to preserve functioning industries and economic links between regions of the country, and in calling for the development of the internal market. However, the Civic Union rested above all on enterprise managers, while the task of the FNPR was to defend the interests of hired workers.

## Unions vs. the government of 1993

The conflict between the government and the unions, which was getting worse during 1992, reached its peak in the summer of 1993. In the Urals region factory whistles sounded and defence plant workers gathered for mass meetings, while in Rostov Province in the south coal miners held a one-day warning stoppage. In the Maritime District in the far east, a general strike took place on August 10. Ships that had not been unloaded lay in the ports and sounded their sirens. The crews of foreign ships replied with their own sirens, expressing solidarity with the strikers.

The main issue behind these struggles was the violation by the government of the general wage agreement that had been negotiated with the FNPR. At the meetings, workers demanded not just the observance of this document, but that the government should resign. In the first ten days, one and a half million people took part in collective actions.

Unlike earlier waves of strikes and demonstrations, the struggles during the summer of 1993 were led by the trade unions and took place on the scale of the country as a whole. For the first time since 1905, workers were mounting protest actions simultaneously in the most diverse sectors and regions, advancing general, all-Russian demands.

The success of the traditional unions in drawing millions of their members into action took the government by surprise. The FNPR had earlier showed its ability to conduct tough, effective negotiations on general, regional and sectorial wage agreements designed to defend workers' jobs and incomes. But the union federation's weak spot had been its inability to mobilize workers in active struggle. The authorities consciously exploited this weakness. Making concessions during talks, they then refused to fulfil the obligations they had accepted.

In 1992 the FNPR had been powerless to counteract this policy. As a result, the authorities did not expect that the trade unions would be able to mount serious resistance in 1993 either. However, the situation had changed dramatically. Two years of liberal reforms had not only resulted in a catastrophic decline in production, the collapse of the internal market, falling living standards and hyperinflation, people had also become more conscious of their interests.

In 1993 the authorities received a rude shock. Still, the fact remained that the union leaders and activists were operating without a clear strategy and program of action. However much the FNPR suffered as a result of 'trade union bureaucracy', its most dangerous malady was arguably spontaneity. The demands which the trade unions were putting forward in mid-1993 were ones which had arisen spontaneously from below; the higher echelons of the union leadership simply recorded these demands, summarized them, and presented them to the government. The strength of the collective protests was in large measure the result of this responsiveness to rank and file sentiment. But the failure to develop a consistent analysis, and the lack of a coherent project, represented crucial weaknesses.

Relying largely on trial and error, the unions consistently lagged behind the development of events. The FNPR let almost a year go by without declaring its opposition to the government's course. While the MFP immediately found a niche in constructive opposition, the all-Russian union federation tried to maintain a line of critical support for the reforms. This was while Gaidar and his team were implementing a program which had been dictated by the

International Monetary Fund, and which required the smashing of the trade unions as effective organs of workers' self-defence.

In the course of 1993 the FNPR repeated the path which the Moscow unions had traversed in 1992. Meanwhile, the MFP had become far less radical. The MFP leaders had become hostages of their own success. In 1991 and 1992 they had won concessions from the city government, but now they were having to concentrate on preserving their gains and on not rocking the boat.

The collective actions in August had to a significant degree unfolded spontaneously, and in September they began just as spontaneously to abate. In August it had been possible to foresee two scenarios: an optimistic one, in which the unions mastered the situation and became an important social force, and a pessimistic one in which the unions lost control over events and became incapable of effective action. Everything developed according to the pessimistic scenario. After Yeltsin's Decree no. 1400, which declared the parliament dissolved, Klochkov was faced with a choice. If the trade unions failed to threaten strikes in favour of the constitution, no-one would take their declarations seriously. But if the unions called for strikes, they would not be able to organize them successfully. The result was the adoption of an ambiguous call for protest actions 'up to the use of strikes'; this failed to bind anyone to a concrete course of action, and frightened nobody. Seeing that the FNPR was helpless, the authorities launched their next onslaught, stripping the unions of control over the social welfare funds and threatening the FNPR with dissolution (Patrushev, 1994).

The Russian government does not appear to want the complete abolition of the FNPR, since there are numerous everyday problems which the authorities are simply unable to solve without the help of the trade union apparatus. However, the government succeeded in intimidating the trade union leaders. After the bombardment of the 'White House', panic broke out among the union officialdom. A congress of the FNPR was held, and a new leadership was elected. MFP leader Shmakov became chairperson of the all-Russian federation. A new stage was proclaimed in the trade union reforms. However, Shmakov took the helm at a time when prospects for the trade unions were far from promising. The new leadership was forced to make concessions, and to try to avoid head-on confrontations with the authorities. Shmakov said that collective actions belong to the past (Vesty FNPR, 1993, N 11, p. 12). New leadership stressed the need for moderation, while at the same time striving to bring the situation under their control.

FNPR unions are faced with a complex of interlocking necessities: the need for labour movement struggle if the rights of Russian workers are to be defended; the need for broad rank and file involvement if this struggle is to triumph; and the need for union structures to be open, accessible and democratic if involvement is to be a reality. There can be no confident predictions as to the outcome. The only certainty is that Yeltsin and his ministers will bitterly resist attempts by the unions to maintain jobs and living standards. If the Moscow authorities and the MFP have managed a degree of 'social partnership', this will not be repeated on the level of Russia as a whole. The Russian government simply does not have the resources which the Moscow authorities have been able to throw into the solving of social problems.

While Shmakov spoke about the need to reform the unions, inside FNPR bureaucracy became even worse. The leadership was for some time paralyzed by its own apparatus and the lack of strategy. At the very moment when FNPR was discussing the new moderation, union members got radicalized and frustrated. Many of them voted in December 1993 for the CP, others didn't vote, some even supported Zhirinovsky's Liberal Democrats just to create problems for Yeltsin. Klochkov was elected to the new parliament as a member of the Agrarian List, while the centrist Civic Union which was supported by right wing labour failed to get the necessary 5 percent of the national vote.

Even before the elections of December 1993, the likely nature of Russian labour relations during the next period was beginning to emerge. During November energy sector workers fought and won two important battles against the government. Ironically, the labour movement bodies involved included the Independent Union of Miners, whose leadership has increasingly been forced by government attacks on the coal industry to abandon its pro-Yeltsin stance. Few Russian trade unionists have the strategic power of the energy sector workers, and in many cases the government would be quite happy to see workers shut down production in loss-making plants. But falling real wages, swiftly deteriorating social welfare benefits and the prospect of catastrophic levels of unemployment are nevertheless forcing workers to look toward collective action to secure their self-defence.

### Unions turn to electoral politics

After the 1993 elections, in which the trade unions failed to participate as an organized and independent force, the majority of trade union leaders declared that this omission would not be repeated in the elections due for 1995. Electoral successes were seen as a necessary way to overcome the consequences of the defeats of collective actions in 1993 and the lack of a clear strategy in 1993-95. The FNPR has been preparing to take part in elections for a considerable period. But the federation's own inconsistency has repeatedly forced it to abandon existing gains and to start again from the beginning. After dropping the idea of establishing a Party of Labour, union leadership discussed a proposal to found a 'Union of Labour', but again there were no positive results. Some of the participants in the original Union of Labour project eventually joined in forming the Russian Social Democratic Union (RSDS), but the FNPR was not among these forces. A number of trade union officials appeared on the RSDS electoral slate, but only in secondary positions. In the spring of 1995 FNPR chairperson Mikhail Shmakov made a fresh attempt to form a political bloc around the trade unions; on the basis of the FNPR, the movement 'Trade Unions of Russia to the Elections' was established. In launching this movement, the FNPR declared its readiness to go to the polls independently, but the federation's leaders meanwhile held talks with a number of political groups.

Here, the internal contradictions of the FNPR made themselves felt. Many sectorial trade unions were gravitating toward their corresponding ministries. The trade unions of the fuel and energy complex in particular showed a readiness to set up their own bloc together with management. When this alliance failed to materialize, leaders of these unions preferred to collaborate with the bloc 'Our Home is Russia' than with the opposition. This course, however, met with opposition from the trade union rank and file.

The Independent Coal Employees Union formed its own organization with the name 'Miners of Russia'; this also received support from the coal industry management. In similar fashion, the trade unions of road transport workers also drew up their own list of candidates. The Union of Workers of the Agro-Industrial Complex remained faithful to the Agrarian Party of Russia, something which is not surprising if one reflects that the party bodies are two-thirds identical to those of the union. Meanwhile, the territorial trade union federations have been inclined to collaborate either with the Communists, or with the Federation of Manufacturers of Russia, headed by Yuri Skokov. When Skokov came to head the Congress of Russian Communities (KRO), many local trade union leaders promptly began supporting this organization.

Shmakov, however, was categorically opposed to collaborating either with the KRO or with the Communist Party (KPRF). The possibility of a bloc with the KPRF was ruled out by the importance for the FNPR of convincing the government of its moderation. The conference of the 'Trade Unions of Russia - to the Elections' decided to establish a bloc with the Industrial Party, representing industrial management. This alliance of the trade unions and industrialists also received the name 'Union of Labour'.[2]

All blocs supported by trade unions suffered a crushing defeat. The notion of an alliance between trade union officials and enterprise directors who were failing to pay wages to their employees was obviously not impressive to voters. Neither the directorial nor the trade union wing of the 'Union of Labour' had a clear political ideology, or any grasp of how to operate politically. The bloc scored only 1.7 percent of the vote. This outcome is being cited by enemies of the FNPR as convincing proof that for the great majority of people who belong to trade unions this membership is something purely formal. The refusal by the FNPR leaders to accept responsibility for this failure and to recognize the problems with which they are faced represents an additional moral defeat. Speaking at the second congress of the oil and gas construction workers' union on 20 December, FNPR Chairperson Mikhail Shmakov characterized the results of the elections as a success.[3] His opponents inside FNPR, meanwhile, had also suffered a defeat after linking themselves to KRO. The new trade unions also went down to defeat, though this was less apparent, since their candidates were hidden in various lists. So, there was no clear alternative to FNPR leadership within the labour movement.

The only lesson learned by FNPR leadership after all these defeats was that it would be safer to have close relations with the government. In 1996 presidential elections FNPR and MFP were in Yeltsin camp, though Shmakov didn't declare it officially.

This new friendship between FNPR and the government brings us back to pre-perestroika years. FNPR unions are becoming again more and more like their Soviet predecessors. That can lead to the gradual weakening and perhaps extinction of traditional union structures, which are likely to concentrate their energies increasingly on a single task: managing their property. Although the alternative unions are not in a condition to exploit the crisis of FNPR, it is quite probable that a flow of activists and entire organizations to the 'alternatives' will occur, and that direct links, by-passing FNPR, will arise between traditional and new unions.

This process will acquire particular strength if the alternative unions, overcoming their original ideology, prove better able than the FNPR *nomenklatura* to join in the general shift of society to the left.

## Notes

1. A big debate on 'new corporatism' was launched in Russia by Pavel Kudyukin and Valentin Rupets in 1994-95. While Rupets sees corporatism as a specific Russian system of labour relations which should be accepted but transformed in a democratic way, Kudyukin sees it more as an obstacle to the development of more modern labour relations (Kirichenko and Kudyukin, 1993; Kudyukin, 1994; Rupets, 1994).

2. After the elections 'The Unions of Russia - to the Elections' was transformed into a political organization called 'The Union of Labour', not to be confused with the electoral bloc, which desintegrated after 1995 elections.
3. While the polls show in 1995 and 1996 that a considerable part of the union members voted for KPRF, the party didn't try to use that to regain any amount of real influence in the unions.

## References

Buketov, K. (1996), 'Kollektivniye deystviya profsoyusov i stachechnoye dvizheniye v Rossii v 1995 g.' (Collective actions of trade unions in Russia in 1995), *Alternativy* (Alternatives), no. 1, pp. 20-27.

Buzgalin, A. V. (1992), *Differentia cpecifica otchestvennoy economiki* (Differential characteristics of our economy), Economicheskaya Demokratiya Publishers, Moscow.

Kagarlitsky, B. and Clarke, R. (1994), 'Russia's trade union movement', *Links*, no. 1, pp. 19-28.

Kirichenko, O., Kudyukin, P. (1993), 'Perviye shagy sotsialnogo partnerstva v Rossie' (First steps of social partnership in Russia), *Politicheskie issledovaniya* (Political studies), no.1, pp. 20-31.

Kotz, D. and Weir, F. (1996), *Revolution from above: The demise of the Soviet system*, Routledge, London.

Kudyukin, P. (1994), 'Sotsialnoye partnerstvo ili korporativism?' (Social partnership or corporatism?), *Voprosy ekonomiky* (Problems of economy), no. 5, pp. 34-45.

Patrushev, S. (1994), *Rabochee dvizhenie v Rossii posle oktiabria 1993 goda* (Russian labour movement after 1993), Doklady i soobsheniya ISPRAN (Institute of Comparative Political and Labour Studies), Moscow.

Pronin, S. V. (1994), *Usloviya formirovaniya rossiyskogo rabochego i profsoyusnogo dvizheniya 90-kh godov i ego zadachi* (Conditions for the development of Russian labour movement and its tasks), Doklady i soobshenia ISPRAN (Institute of Comparative Political and Labour Studies), Moscow.

Rupets, V. (1994), 'Ob osobom napravlenii rossiyskogo profsoyusnogo dvizheniya' (On a specific trend in Russian trade unions), *Profsoyusnoye obozrenie* (Trade union review), no. 7, pp. 16-18.

Vtoroy s'ezd FNPR (FNPR second congress), (1993), *Vesty FNPR* (FNPR News), 1993, no. 11, pp. 1-20.

# 9 Against the flow? Issues of growth and structure in the South African trade union movement, 1979-1995

*Ian Macun*

Since the legal recognition of trade unionism for black workers in 1979, the number of workers joining trade unions in South Africa has grown dramatically. This growth has occurred despite harsh and conflictual realities of South African industrial relations and also despite increasing unemployment and poor economic performance during much of the 1980s and early 1990s — factors which have mitigated against union growth in other countries. Union growth is closely related to the issue of structure — the organizational form that unions assume and the boundaries within which they operate. In this area, developments in the South African union movement also differ in significant respects from trends in other countries. Unlike the trend toward a reduction in the number of unions, particularly smaller unions, the number of unions in South Africa has grown and while there has been considerable rationalization, many unions still exhibit jurisdictional overlap and adhere to a decentralized model of union organization.

This divergence between developments in the South African union movement and its international counterparts raises questions both about explanations of international trends and about the likely role of trade unions in South Africa's process of social and economic change. Will the South African unions, for instance, begin to experience a decline as the economy opens up to international competition? Will rationalization of union structure and greater centralization within the union movement be necessary for unions to cater for members' interests and play a part in macroeconomic management?

---

Ian Macun is Deputy Director and Research Officer in the Sociology of Work Unit, Department of Sociology, University of Witwatersrand, Private Bag 3, WITS, 2050 South Africa.

This chapter will take a step back to focus on the relatively basic issues of the nature of growth amongst South African unions and the evolution of union structure. An underlying assumption of the chapter is that the role of unions in social change is affected quite fundamentally by their coverage, by their form of organization and, therefore, by the way in which they are able to articulate the interests of their members. In other words, there is a relationship between union growth, union structure and union strength and power. The relationship is not a straightforward one and there will be variation with respect to particular sections of the union movement. Moreover, one cannot assume any simple equation between numbers, structure and strength, and any assessment of national union movements has to take into account a range of historical, organizational, political and social factors.

The following will thus offer a tentative and limited outline of the main contours of union growth in South Africa and the structure that characterizes the union movement at present. A second aim will be to offer some explanation of the nature of union growth and the structure of the union movement. Such explanations are necessary in order to gain insights into what future trajectories are likely for South African unions and, indeed, to assess whether the South African experience may hold lessons for explaining the trajectory of unions internationally.

## Growth

What has been the pattern of union growth in South Africa historically? What have been the most important factors affecting growth? These may be key questions of concern, but finding adequate answers is complicated by the lack of proper data and, although there is a substantial body of literature on the history of labour in South Africa, the growth of the union movement has not been a significant focus in the literature. It is possible, however, to sketch a rough trajectory of union growth and to provide greater detail for the contemporary period.

As was the case in many colonial situations, trade unionism was brought to South African industry by mainly white, skilled workers. Unionism took root early on in the emerging industrial centres, with unions being formed by printers, engineers, iron moulders and other skilled workers from 1881 onwards (Simons and Simons, 1983). The largest number of trade unions and union members were concentrated around the mining industry which developed rapidly on the Witwatersrand from 1886. Although some of the early unions for skilled workers and artisans did include coloured and Indian workers, African workers were largely excluded from unions.

The first significant attempt at organizing African workers occurred with the formation of the Industrial and Commercial Workers Union in 1919, which claimed over 100 000 members at its height in the mid-1920s. Other waves of unionization amongst African workers followed. During the 1930s and 1940s, important attempts at organizing black workers took place in the context of a rapidly expanding manufacturing industry. By 1945, it is estimated that roughly 40 percent of Africans employed in commerce and industry were unionized in 119 unions (Fine with Davis, 1990). After the war years, unionism of black workers declined and only revived with a third wave of black unionism occurring from 1955. The impetus for black unionism in this period lay in the formation of the South African Congress of Trade Unions (SACTU) which was closely allied to the broader Congress Movement of the time.[1] With the repression of the political opposition movement by the National Party government in the early 1960s and, with SACTU's close alliance to this movement, it went into a rapid decline.

Throughout this period, unions organizing primarily white workers or those unions representing artisan and skilled workers, continued to exist. Their growth was slow and always limited by the smaller number of potential members among the strata they sought to represent. Growth was further affected by persistent political and ideological divisions amongst these workers and their organizations. Overall then, the growth of unions up to the 1970s was gradual and uneven. Moreover, it was severely restricted by legislation, by state action and by the failure of unions organizing black workers to establish any permanence in the face of these political constraints.

It was in the early 1970s that unions with a quite different organizational style emerged and rapidly established themselves amongst black workers. Abandoning the style of mass recruiting that had characterized many of the earlier phases of unionization amongst black workers, the new union leaders targeted a smaller number of factories within particular industries and areas. Such an organizational style did not deliver large numbers, but established a clear presence for the new unions in a slowly expanding circle of plants. Union membership and density thus remained low during the 1970s, but unionized plants 'projected a powerful demonstration effect in key sectors, such as the motor, metal, clothing, textile, and chemical industries' (Thompson,1994, p. 352).

The permanence of these unions was guaranteed, partly through their organizational style, but also due to the amendments to the industrial relations legislative framework which occurred in the wake of the Wiehahn Commission Report of 1979 and which extended recognition to unions representing African workers. Prior to the legislative amendments, the emerging, black trade unions were unable to register and gain access to the industrial relations machinery provided for by the Industrial Conciliation Act (renamed the Labour Relations Act in 1981) — hence the terms distinguishing between registered and unregistered, or independent trade unions.

After 1979, South Africa experienced an explosion in union growth, with more than 2 million workers joining unions in the period 1979 to 1993 and union density increasing by roughly 43 percent! (See Table 9.1). The most rapidly growing unions during this period were those organizing mainly black workers and, in particular, the unions which have been affiliated to the Congress of South African Trade Unions (COSATU) which was formed in 1985. Throughout the 1990s, the membership of COSATU affiliated unions have comprised over 40 percent of total union membership.

**Table 9.1**
**Employment, union membership, density, and number of unions, 1979-94**

| Year | Employment (non-agricultural) | Trade union membership | Density (%) | Number of unions |
|---|---|---|---|---|
| 1979 | 4 579 900 | 701 758 | 15.32 | 167 |
| 1980 | 4 812 968 | 808 053 | 16.78 | 188 |
| 1981 | 5 026 935 | 1 054 405 | 20.97 | 200 |
| 1982 | 5 132 001 | 1 225 454 | 23.87 | 199 |
| 1983 | 5 056 366 | 1 273 890 | 25.19 | 194 |
| 1984 | 5 117 321 | 1 406 302 | 27.48 | 193 |
| 1985 | 5 036 935 | 1 391 423 | 27.62 | 196 |
| 1986 | 5 066 287 | 1 698 157 | 33.51 | 195 |
| 1987 | 5 141 993 | 1 879 400 | 36.55 | 205 |
| 1988 | 5 225 950 | 2 084 323 | 39.88 | 209 |
| 1989 | 5 261 531 | 2 130 117 | 40.48 | 212 |
| 1990 | 5 282 552 | 2 458 712 | 46.54 | 198 |
| 1991 | 5 137 849 | 2 718 970 | 52.92 | 195 |
| 1992 | 5 038 358 | 2 905 735 | 57.67 | 195 |
| 1993 | 4 984 088 | 2 890 174 | 57.98 | 201 |
| 1994 | 4 957 665 | 2 470 481 | 49.83 | 213 |

*Note:* The figures are based on reporting to the Department of Labour (previously Department of Manpower) in terms of the old Labour Relations Act. The act excludes the public service, the military and police, agriculture and domestic workers.

Despite being the fastest growing, the COSATU unions have not been the only unions that have grown. The second largest grouping of unions, those affiliated to the National Council of Trade Unions (NACTU) have also reported growth. There has also been a gradual expansion in membership of certain unions organizing primarily non-manual or white collar workers, for example, the South African Society of Bank Officials (SASBO) as well as growth in union membership in the public service. The federation of unions representing primarily non-manual workers, the Federation of South African Labour (FEDSAL), has grown by over 100 000 members over the past five years.

During the 1980s and 1990s, artisan unions have been confronted by a number of challenges which have been dealt with in different ways and which complicate generalization about growth amongst these unions. Some of the old racially 'mixed unions' responded to the legislative changes of 1979 by revising their constitutions and opening their organizations to the possibility of expansion amongst black workers. Other unions, albeit a minority, have retained a racially exclusive character and thereby accepted limits to increases in membership. Although there is a problem of evidence regarding trends amongst the artisan unions, it would seem as though there has been a general decline in membership of these unions.

Racially exclusive unions, at least those representing white workers only, have shown a clear decline in both the number of unions and in their membership. The South African Confederation of Labour (SACOL), the main white labour federation, claimed 200 000 members in 10 affiliated unions in 1986 and presently has in the region of 50 000 members in 4 affiliates.

The basic pattern during the 1980s and 1990s has, thus, been one of sustained growth in unionization among black workers across all sectors of the economy (excluding agriculture), a more gradual, but clear increase in unionization among white collar and public sector workers and a variable, but general decline in the rate of unionization among mainly white, skilled workers.

### *Explaining union growth*

How might one account for the dramatic, overall growth of South African unions? In the context of South Africa's particular social and political history, a multi-causal approach is appropriate given the diversity within the SA union movement and the likely significance of qualitative change in explaining union growth (Macun and Frost, 1994). Economic factors, such as change in prices and wages, have shown a marked correspondence with union growth, at least for black workers, throughout the 1980s and early 1990s. Organizational factors, especially those of leadership and union mergers, have also been influential in causing growth of black unions. Given that the most substantial membership increases have been amongst the black trade unions, organizational factors that have contributed to rapid growth have been primarily those of leadership and union mergers or consolidation. With regard to leadership, it has been usefully argued that the quality of union leadership in the post-1973 period has 'proved capable of holding unions together and of evolving strategies which were successful in resisting employer and state repression' (Erwin and Morris, 1988, p. 289). If one examines the pattern of union growth amongst the progressive unions in the early part of the 1980s, it is evident that it occurred in spurts and spread from sector to sector, rather than advancing in all sectors simultaneously and at a similar pace. Such a pattern of growth is determined to a significant extent by union leadership.

Leadership as a factor in union growth could apply at both national and local levels. In South Africa, the development of a shop steward structure, which acted as a local level leadership, has been particularly significant in ensuring union growth during the 1980s. Shop stewards have, in many cases, provided the key to effective recognition battles and, by offering a democratic alternative to the established, registered union movement, attracted workers to the black unions. On the other hand, the different leadership style of the artisan and skilled worker unions and the relatively high degree of fragmentation amongst these unions, may well have contributed to their general decline. A crucial issue affecting artisan unions and racially exclusive unions, is that of the closed shop. The use of the closed shop has been central to the growth of certain racially mixed artisan unions in the early to mid 1980s and its more recent demise in a number of industries is likely to have contributed to the decline of these same unions.

Labour market factors which have been so important in affecting union decline in a number of the advanced industrial countries, have been relatively less important in South Africa. Union growth has increased throughout the 1980s and 1990s despite a continuing high rate of unemployment. Changing patterns of employment have, however, been more significant in affecting union growth. Firstly, growth in employment in the tertiary sector throughout the 1980s corresponds to the trend toward higher unionization within this sector. Secondly, the lack of growth in the number of whites as a proportion of total employment is related to the decline of unions organizing these workers. The decline in membership of artisan unions, due largely to retrenchments, may also reflect a contraction of employment in skilled work. Finally, the rate of increase in unionization in manufacturing slowed during the first half of the 1990s due to the decline in employment in this sector.

Political factors have clearly also contributed to union growth during this period. The legislative reforms of 1979 certainly facilitated union growth for a short period, but legal reform is not useful in explaining longer term growth. More important is the social context within which individual workers choose to join a union in South Africa. The social context has itself varied over time and, more importantly, has assumed a different meaning for different workers. For the predominantly white skilled and semi-skilled workers, the economic benefits of unionization have historically been inextricably linked to the maintenance of racial advantage in the division of labour. As capitalism gradually began to abandon its racial character from the 1970s, and as unions have become less successful in defending racially based job demarcation, so membership of racially exclusive unions has become less attractive.

For black workers, on the other hand, the economic attractions of union membership have been linked to the role of unions in providing a 'voice' (Webster,1988). The 'voice' effect of unions can, however, be conceived of in different ways. One aspect to union 'voice' in South Africa has to do with the lack of citizenship up to the democratic elections of 1994. In this sense, unions have provided a voice for black workers by articulating common political interests which, until the unbanning of political parties in 1990, had little alternative means of expression. Establishing the importance of unions political voice in attracting members is not, however, a straight forward matter. Union membership does not, for example, show any noticeable increase or decrease in relation to significant political moments during the 1980s and 1990s: The rate of change in union density does not increase markedly with the heightened labour militancy which occurred during 1984, the state campaign of repression in 1986 and the unbanning of black political parties in 1990.

To suggest that political factors have not been central to union growth is not to suggest that unions in South Africa are not political in character. The growth of unions and their nature or character, while related, are not one and the same. The political character of many South African unions is primarily related to their strategy of pursuing broad working class interests and to the close alliance between certain unions and political groupings. While these features may attract workers to unions, they do not automatically do so and the connections between union growth and political activity is often more tenuous than assumed and confounded by a range of other factors.

A more significant 'voice' effect of unions for black workers has been that related to the sphere of production where unions have been able to provide representation for black workers vis a vis employers. The importance of this representational voice lies in the social fabric of the employment relationship in South Africa, one characterized by authoritarianism reinforced by a hierarchical and racial division of labour. Within such a social context, union organization has inevitably had to act as a protective shield against racial authoritarianism and had to represent members interests in daily struggles between management and individual workers.

Although there is not adequate evidence on the micro history of unionization in firms during the 1970s and 1980s, it could be assumed that unionization often put down roots around individual grievance and disciplinary issues or around cases of dismissal, particularly of workers trying to introduce unionization in a plant. In certain cases, employers were also willing to deal with union organizers around individual grievance and disciplinary issues, prior to having formally recognized the union for bargaining purposes.

The role of unions in providing a representational voice has undoubtedly been an important factor in influencing workers to join unions. While this social context in not unique insofar as many countries, developing countries in particular, can be characterized as having highly authoritarian employment relations, the interconnection between authoritarianism and racism in the South African workplace may contribute to the extremely rapid process of unionization amongst black workers. Racial authoritarianism may also be important in explaining why black unions tended to take root in larger companies where the social and emotional distance between workers and employers is greater and where the costs to workers of joining a union (in the form of employer retaliation, for instance) would probably be less than in smaller companies (Visser, 1994).

The key factors which can be identified as explaining union growth are, therefore, economic, organizational and the micro political role of unions — that is, their representational role in the context of racial authoritarianism within the workplace. Legal reform and the macro political role of unions in relation to the Apartheid state could be said to have facilitated union growth, but did not determine it. Finally, the representational role of unions could be seen as equally important for workers of different racial groups insofar as unions will operate to protect their members and advance their interests in the context of a racially structured employment relation.

The consolidation of trade unions during the 1980s, principally through the formation of COSATU and NACTU, has ensured an added spurt to union growth. Within COSATU, the federations merger policy created unions 'which were stronger numerically and organizationally, and better able to make rational use of their resources and personnel. Strong, nationally-organized industrial unions were the foundation for both a quantitative and qualitative growth in membership' (Baskin,1991, p. 448). This aspect of union organizational development leads to the issue of structure and its significance both for growth and for the challenges facing South African unions.

## Structure

While South Africa is clearly in the process of becoming a highly unionized society, the structure of the union movement still carries with it a significant imprint of the past. The first and most striking aspect of union structure in South Africa is the large number of unions and union federations that exist. Unlike many other countries, where the number of unions have decreased throughout the 20th century through mergers and transfers, the number of unions in South Africa has remained relatively unchanged (see Table 9.1). Indeed, from the 1950s to the early 1990s, the number of unions has increased slightly. In 1960 there were 185 unions, in 1970 there were 182 unions and this number has increased to over 200 in the early 1990s. The majority of unions are relatively small and remain unaffiliated to any of the main federations. They are widely spread across the different sectors of the economy and represent workers from a range of different occupational groupings. Many seem to have remained in existence for a considerable period of time, despite the fact that the costs of servicing union members have been increasing and the optimal size for financially viable and effective unions has also increased as a general trend.

Parallel to the continued existence of smaller unions, for which union organization may not have changed much, there has been a dramatic process of rationalization within the unions affiliated to the major federations and, in particular, the Congress of South African Trade Unions (COSATU). At its formation in 1985, COSATU had 33 affiliates and, through a rapid series of mergers, it presently concentrates 1.3 million workers in 15 affiliates. The average size of COSATU affiliates is around 80 000 members, which may allow for financial viability, but not necessarily effective union organization. Many unions affiliated to COSATU have grown extremely rapidly and have experienced increased strain on their organizational resources.

A second aspect of union structure is that, although there are a large number of unions, the majority of unionized workers are concentrated within relatively few unions and union federations (see Table 9.2). The existence of a large number of unions within the South African union structure does not, therefore, necessarily imply a high degree of competition between unions. Rather what one finds is an island of large unions, dominating within particular sectors of the economy, within a sea of many, smaller unions.

**Table 9.2**
**Union federations, number of affiliates and membership, 1994**

| Federation | Affiliates | Membership[a] | |
|---|---|---|---|
| Congress of SA Trade Unions (COSATU) | 15 | 1 317 496 | (45%) |
| National Council of Trade Unions (NACTU) | 18 | 334 733 | (12%) |
| Federation of SA Labour (FEDSAL) | 16 | 257 258 | (10%) |
| Federation of Independent Trade Unions (FITU) | 24 | 236 000 | (8%) |
| SA Confederation of Labour (SACOL) | 4 | 54 290 | (2%) |
| United Workers Union of SA (UWUSA)[b] | | | |

*Notes:* There were a total of 9 federations registered with South Arica's Department of Labour in 1994, but the ones contained in the table represent the overwhelming majority of organized workers and are the most influential.

[a] The percentage in the membership column reflects the federation's membership as a proportion of total membership.

[b] Estimates of UWUSA membership fluctuate between 30 000 and 100 000, but reliable figures are not available.

Thirdly, South Africa's union structure can be described as having evolved, much like the British tradition, from a predominance of craft unions in the early part of the century to a situation of multi-unionism in the latter part of the century. The concepts which can be used to analyze the broad contours of multi-unionism are those of; artisan unions, industrial unions (open and exclusive) and non-manual or white collar unions. These concepts can be usefully applied to analyze union structure in South Africa, provided that they are used as concepts against which unions can be analyzed, rather than categories into which unions have to be fitted. Despite the relatively large number of unions in South Africa, the majority assume the characteristics of either artisan unions, industrial unions (primarily open industrial unions) and non-manual unions.

It should be noted that the open industrial unions,which have shown the most rapid growth and which concentrate the largest proportion of union membership, are not true industrial unions. They do not encompass the entire organizational hierarchy within industry, but remain primarily representative of black workers in the lower level of skill. Moreover, the potential for the establishment of genuine industrial unions is, of course, closely related to the ability of artisan unions to adapt their internal structure and to open themselves to a racially mixed membership during the 1980s and 1990s.

## *Changes in union structure*

The pattern of union growth from the 1970s and the legal reforms of this period have introduced significant rationalization into the structure of the union movement. This process has begun to reverse the state of fragmentation that characterized the union movement up until the late 1970s, a fragmentation that had reached a peak in 1951 already, after the political and legislative onslaught on the union movement by the Nationalist Party government (see, inter alia, Lewis, 1981 and Williams, 1979). The formation of more effective union federations during the 1980s has also contributed to a higher degree of coordination amongst unions.

Despite the move toward greater rationalization, it cannot be suggested that the union movement displays greater organizational unity. Examining the above features, it is evident that the number of unions and federations representing and coordinating the interests of relatively few workers, still leaves the union movement fragmented organizationally. It also remains politically fragmented. COSATU and NACTU represent the left of the union movement, FEDSAL and FITU the centre or moderate axis and SACOL and UWUSA, the right wing. The more significant division now lies between the left and the centre, unlike the situation prior to the 1970s. Most importantly, the structure of the union movement remains fragmented by an organizational structure which mirrors the division of labour — a division still expressed significantly in racial terms.

A crucial issue raised by an examination of union structure is that of the relationship between federations and their constituent unions. In the South African union movement, this relationship exhibits a high degree of decentralization with the common model being one of affiliate driven federations. The majority of federations have limited administrative resources and decision making power in the internal structure of federations lies with representatives of affiliates. No federation plays any significant role in collective bargaining, none have any veto rights over negotiated settlements and there is no tradition of federations administering strike funds for unions. NACTU has, at times, tended towards a greater degree of centralization by resourcing affiliated unions and playing a role in bargaining activity, but this is changing toward greater decentralization.

To suggest that federations are decentralized does not mean that leaders cannot exercise substantial influence over the affairs of affiliates or that federations do not exercise political influence. A decentralized model does, however, pose questions about the capacity of federations to either mobilize workers or exercise constraint over members demands. A corollary of decentralized union structure may also be that it becomes more difficult to coordinate and articulate a coherent set of relatively common interests.

The current structure of the union movement in South Africa has a certain inevitability about it, given the way that unions have grown according to certain sectors and along occupational and racial lines. The consequences of this structure may be a weaker union movement and a more difficult transition in the country. During the past decade there has been a growing emphasis in the literature on the correspondence between high centralization and unity within union movements, on the one hand, and improved economic performance, effective centralization of collective bargaining and more stable transitions, on the other hand (cf. Cameron, 1984; Visser, 1992; Valenzuela, 1989.).

Some of the key conclusions of this literature are, simply put, that countries with powerful, centralized union movements have maintained higher rates of employment, that in countries with fragmented union movements, the search for 'responsible wage policies' has been more difficult, and, that where union leadership is divided politically and ideologically, a rise in labour mobilization and conflict, which may destabilise transitions, is more likely. Taken at face value, the current structure and character of the union movement in South Africa, would appear to suggest detrimental outcomes on all these points. To anticipate such problems could neglect the salience of the mix of factors which have shaped the specific trajectory of the South African union movement and should, therefore, not be treated as a given in the future.

## Conclusion

This chapter has sought to highlight a set of features characterizing union growth and structure in South Africa, primarily from the late 1970s to the present. It has been suggested that the growth of trade unions has been concentrated among black workers and among white collar workers, with artisan unions and racially exclusive unions declining. Explanations for this growth can be found in economic and organizational factors, which have been used to explain union growth in many other countries. But union growth has also been determined by the social context in which the employment relationship is embedded, one characterized by racial difference and racist practices in the workplace. As long as these features characterize the employment relationship, so are they likely to feed unionization.

The ability to exercise direct, oppositional power at the micro level does not mean that unions are necessarily powerful at the industry and national level. In interaction with political parties and employer organizations, union power is affected more by strategic and institutional factors, one of which is related to the structure of the union movement. The chapter has tried to portray the structure of the union movement in relation to three major categories; non-manual unions, artisan unions and industrial unions, mainly open industrial unions. It is, thus, a multi-union structure with a large number of small, unaffiliated unions and a smaller proportion of larger unions affiliated to either one of six federations. This structure reflects the rapid growth of the union movement and reflects the major lines of cleavage within the union movement — along lines of race, division of labour and political orientation.

Although the South African union movement is less fragmented today than it has been historically, it is still characterized by a marked lack of unity and cohesion as a movement. It is, however, important to point to countervailing trends which have emerged during the past few years and which will undoubtedly have a significant impact on the union movement. These include: the formation of tripartite forums in which the larger federations have played an important role around policy formation regarding labour legislation, industrial strategy and macroeconomic management; the development of industry wide bargaining arrangements in certain sectors of the economy, and; the beginnings of a possible realignment within the union movement, with certain unions reassessing their affiliations and others realigning and regrouping themselves. Although in their early stages, it is possible that these trends could provide an impetus towards greater cohesion within the union movement during the second half of the decade.

Whether greater unity and cohesion is attained or not will be particularly significant in the current period of transition and economic restructuring, one in which the power of the union movement is likely to depend increasingly on its ability to shape and influence macroeconomic management and the political process. Its ability to do so effectively will require not only greater cooperation between federations, but also centralization within federations. Such cooperation and centralization can, however, be achieved in different ways and, in the context of the historical legacy of the union movement in this country, is likely to be most easily achieved through inter-organizational coordination, rather than a drive for unification within the union movement.

While a unitary, encompassing organization may provide the most powerful organizational expression of working class interests, a more 'federative', less-encompassing form of inter-organizational coordination is a more likely outcome where the working class remains relatively heterogenous. Whatever the outcome in South Africa, it would appear that while growth was the most phenomenal feature of the union movement during the past decade, the move toward greater centralization and a more encompassing form of interest representation, will be the key issue for the present decade.

Finally, developments in the South African union movement emphasize the importance of taking seriously the social, political and historical determinants of collective action. Overreliance on economic factors in the explanation of trade union developments is likely to foreclose the possibility of understanding contrasting trajectories amongst union movements and the lessons that these hold for the future of unions in diverse national contexts.

## Note

1. The Congress Movement comprised the African National Congress (ANC), the South African Indian Congress (SAIC), the SA Coloured Peoples Congress (SACPO) and the Congress of Democrats (COD).

## References

Baskin, J. (1991), *Striking back: A history of COSATU*, Ravan Press, Johannesburg.

Erwin, A. and Morris, M. (1988), 'Trade unionization in South Africa' in Nattrass J. (ed.), *The South African economy - its growth and change*, Oxford University Press, Cape Town.

Cameron, D. (1984), 'Social democracy, corporatism, labour quiescence and the representation of economic interest in advanced capitalist society', in Goldthorpe, J. (ed), *Order and conflict in contemporary capitalism*, Clarendon, Oxford.

Fine, R. with Davis, D. (1990), *Beyond Apartheid: Labour and liberation in South Africa*, Ravan Press, Johannesburg.

Lewis, D. (1981), 'The South African state and African trade unions: 1947-1953', *Africa Perspective*, no.18.

Macun, I. and Frost, A. (1994), 'Living like there's no tomorrow: Trade union growth in South Africa, 1979-1991', *Social Dynamics*, vol.20.

Simons, J. and Simons, R. (1983), *Class and colour in South Africa 1850-1950*, International Defence and Aid Fund, London.

Thompson, C. (1994), 'Strategy and opportunism: Trade unions as agents for change in South Africa', in Niland, J., Lansbury, R. and Verevis, C.(eds.), *The future of industrial relations*, Sage, London.

Valenzuela, J. S. (1989), Labour movements in transition to democracy: A framework for analysis, *Comparative Politics*, July.

Visser, J. (1992), 'The strength of union movements in advanced capital democracies: Social and organizational variations', in Regini, M. (ed.), *The future of labour movements*, Sage, London.

Webster, E. (1988), 'The rise of social-movement unionism: The two faces of the black trade union movement in South Africa', in Frankel, P., Pines, N. and Swilling, M. (eds.), *State, resistance and change in South Africa*, Croom Helm, London.

Williams, K. (1979), 'Trade unionism in South African history', in Jubber, K. (ed.), *South Africa: Industrial relations and industrial sociology*, Juta, Cape Town.

# Part III

## UNION STRATEGICAL AND STRUCTURAL CHANGE

# 10 Changing strategic capacities: Union amalgamations in Canada and Australia

*Charlotte Yates and Peter Ewer*

Over the last 15 years, capital has become more mobile and competition has intensified. Governments have reduced their size and role in regulating the economy. For workers, the result has been job loss, declining real wages, and a change in the nature of work and those who are employed. Organized labour has been displaced from the privileged economic and policy position accorded to it by Keynesian economic management. For unions, the consequences of this economic and societal restructuring have been declining memberships and resources. In Australia, union density has dropped from 51 percent in 1976 to 35 percent in 1994 (ABS Cat. No.6325). While union density in Canada has remained quite steady, ranging from 37 to 39 percent of the non-agricultural workforce between 1976 and 1994, wide fluctuations in union membership can be seen across economic sectors and between individual unions. For example, union density in the mining sector dropped from approximately 51 percent in 1968 to 29 percent in 1992 (CALURA, Catalogue 71-202).

As foreign-dominated, 'branch-plant' economies which rely heavily upon raw material exports for foreign exchange earnings, Australia and Canada

---

Charlotte Yates is Associate Professor of Labour Studies and Political Science, McMaster University, Canada; Peter Ewer is Research Associate, Union Research Centre on Organization and Technology (URCOT), Melbourne, Australia. A special thanks to all the labour leaders and activists who spent time talking with us and providing documentation about amalgamations. The interpretation of that information is ours alone. Thanks to SSHRC and the McMaster Arts Research Board which provided the funding necessary for the research on Canada contained within this paper. Address correspondence to Charlotte Yates, Labour Studies/Political Science, McMaster University, 1280 Main Street West, Hamilton, Ontario L8S 4M4, Canada.

have been especially vulnerable to international economic realignments that began in the 1970s (Ewer, Higgins and Stephens, 1987; Wolfe, 1984). The most significant effect of international competitive pressures has been the opening up of the two economies, with Australia undertaking a radical dismantling of its high tariff regime and Canada entering into free trade agreements with the United States and Mexico. This new openness has made labour and state more vulnerable to the demands of business and has accelerated the loss of jobs in the industrial sector (Drache and Glasbeek, 1992). Such job loss strikes at the heart of union membership which in both countries has been heavily concentrated in heavy industry, transportation and raw material extraction. Further weakening unions are the moves by governments and corporations either to decentralize industrial relations by encouraging enterprise unionism or to avoid unions altogether by engaging in union-busting or avoidance campaigns. Although Canadian unions have not experienced the national collapse in union membership seen in Australia, unions in both countries have had to grapple with these threats to their membership and their established industrial relations practices.

While reeling from these attacks, unions have been squeezed between demands from management on one side and from a more diverse workforce on the other. Whether under the guise of Human Resource Management (HRM) or of a more brutal neo-conservative ideology, managements have begun to compete with unions for employee loyalty, often promising workers self realization and personal fulfilment in exchange for their embrace of a corporate culture and practice (Willmott, 1993, p. 517).Where collective practice does appear in this economic liberal universe, as for example in team work, it is tightly contained within the boundaries of the corporation, uncontaminated by association with other social actors, such as unions (Ewer 1995; Robertson, Rinehart, Huxley and the CAW Reserch Group on CAMI, 1992). This cultural attack on unionism is a phenomenon common to both Australia and Canada, although it takes significantly different forms in the two countries.

Meeting this challenge for workers' loyalty is made more difficult for unions by the tough economic times which prevent delivery of improved wages and working conditions. Meanwhile, the workers who are or might be union members have also changed. The paid labour force in both Australia and Canada is increasingly multi-cultural, multi-racial and feminized; standard full-time work has declined and employment in the service sector has risen markedly. To appeal to this new workforce, unions must re-examine the age-old questions of 'working class identity' and union strategy.

This chapter studies how unions in Australia and Canada have pursued amalgamations as a response to economic restructuring and associated union membership decline. Amalgamations are seen as a way of increasing membership size and resources, which can be translated by unions into greater industrial and political power. Amalgamations or mergers involve the joining together of two or more unions either to expand an existing union or form a totally new one. This chapter argues that increased size is not easily translated into more power. Joining together two or more unions puts pressure on unions to adapt their organizational and cultural practices in order to meet the needs of their growing and often more diverse membership. Amalgamations may also result in a rearticulation of union relations with management and government. We argue that these organizational and cultural changes alter labour's capacity to intervene strategically in the workplace, society and politics, the result of which is alterations in union capacity to mobilize membership support and engage in effective action.

## Union amalgamations

Below, we will discuss in some detail the experiences of union amalgamations in Australia and Canada. The argument will be made that although amalgamations offer solutions to some of the challenges faced by unions, they pose new problems like increased union rivalry, more diverse memberships with conflicting claims and the tendency towards bureaucratization.

The material presented comes from a variety of original and secondary sources, including interviews and informal conversations with various union officials in both Australia and Canada. Union newspapers and internal documents along with observations of many union meetings, conferences and debates provided the authors with a deeper understanding of the dynamics of change set in motion by the amalgamation process.

### *Union amalgamations in Australia*

Despite several attempts prior to the 1980s to promote industry unionism, the Australian labour movement has displayed a remarkable atttachment to occupational or craft unionism. In 1986, Australia had 326 unions, ranging from small occupational unions, to larger craft unions with a membership coverage across different industries, and large 'general' unions which enrolled so-called 'unskilled' or production-grade workers (ABS Cat No. 6323.0). To complicate matters still further, Australia's federal system of government gave rise to a federal system of industrial relations, which in turn resulted in the creation of a large number of unions confined to particular States.

Union amalgamations as an internal organizational strategy of the union movement was revived in the 1980s by a sense of crisis, driven by the decline in union membership as a proportion of the workforce. In response to this trend, the peak national federation, the Australian Council of Trade Unions (ACTU), unveiled in 1987 a program to restructure Australian unionism along industry lines. This document, entitled *Future Strategies for the Trade Union Movement*, went through a number of drafts, principally because definitions of industry unions proved so contentious in a movement historically organized by occupation. The Future Strategies document laid out the ACTU's plans for rationalization of union structures along industry lines, offering a blueprint for union amalgamations that saw craft unions all but eliminated. At its core however, the ACTU put the argument for amalgamation in blunt structural terms: 'it is obvious that Australia has too many unions', most of whom were 'not capable of providing the level of service for their members that is needed' (ACTU, 1987, p. 12).

In short, amalgamation between unions was conceived by the Australian labour movement as a necessary response to what was held to be essentially a structural, rather than ideological or cultural, problem: 'the solution seems obvious: unions need to amalgamate to form larger, more efficient, units' (ACTU, 1987, p. 13). This argument would later be buttressed by another ACTU strategy document, which claimed that larger union groupings were needed for effective union participation in economic and social policy debates (ACTU-TDC, 1987, p. 169). This line of argument had particular significance because between 1983 and 1996, the ACTU was involved in a social contract with the Federal Labor Government. Known as the 'Accord', this social contract involved union wage restraint in exchange for access to public policy making. Other contributors to the debate located the labour movement's membership crisis in its inability to adjust to a rapidly changing labour market, including the rising rate of female participation in the labour force (Berry and Kitchener, 1989). Peetz (1990) estimated that half the fall in the proportion of unionists in the workforce could be attributed to the failure of unions to keep pace with these changes in the composition of the labour force.

The Australian unions' commitment to internal reorganization combined with the Labor Government's commitment to economic liberalization to provide the Business Council of Australia (BCA), Australia's most strategic employer group, an unexpected entry point into the debate on union and workplace reform. The BCA put its own agenda on the table with its 1989 report entitled *Enterprise-based Bargaining Units: A Better Way of Working* (BCA, 1989a). This report characterized trade unions and industrial tribunals as 'external' to the workplace. Specifically, the BCA identified the key problems in Australia's industrial relations system as 'the craft and occupational nature of Australia's unions, the nature of the award structure to which that gives rise and the lack of enterprise focus which results'.[1] The BCA was taking aim at the very heart of Australian union organization (BCA, 1989b, p. 35). In programmatic terms, the BCA argued that the ACTU's amalgamation program would leave the occupational definition of Australian unionism relatively unaltered. The BCA called instead for a process of union 'rationalization' designed to cut back the number of unions in any given workplace with the ideal of single union coverage (BCA, 1989b; Frenkel and Peetz, 1990). The BCA further recommended the substitution of the arbitrated award system with enterprise bargaining, a development it anticipated would displace unions from their pivotal role in the workplace and enable managers and employees to develop a 'new workplace culture' compatible with the competitive needs of their enterprise (BCA, 1989a, p. 96).

The Labor Government's approach to these issues reflected the tension between the Party's traditional union constituency and the government's commitment to economic rationalization. Over the five years from 1988, successive pieces of legislation marginalised the traditional multi-employer award system in favour of enterprise bargaining agreements. By way of compensation for the union movement, these same legislative changes eased the requirements governing union amalgamations.

The ensuing wide ranging union organizational reform was driven by a number of competing forces. In 1989 the ACTU Congress adopted a program of organizational reform that included a typology for union rationalization. This typology moved the ACTU beyond amalgamation as its primary organizational strategy and tacitly acknowledged the BCA's agenda for union 'rationalization' at the workplace. Under the scheme developed by the ACTU, unions were deemed as 'principal', 'significant' and 'other'. To each category was attached different rights to recruit and service members, whereby unions designated as 'significant' or 'other' lost membership and resources (Dabscheck, 1995).

Throughout the early 1990s, meetings convened by the ACTU along industry lines conferred the status of 'principal, significant and other' on affiliated unions, albeit amid rumblings of discontent. Coupled with the powers of industrial tribunals to regulate union coverage, the ACTU-led rationalization process gave amalgamations a significant momentum. Only through mergers could unions extend their status as 'principal' unions, in compensation for those industries where the ACTU deemed them to be in the other, less privileged categories. This 'negative' motivation to amalgamation was complemented in the ACTU strategy by more positive inducements. In particular, ACTU negotiations with the Federal Labor Government resulted in a publicly funded assistance program, under which unions received financial support to promote amalgamation proposals to their members. As a result of ACTU pressures and legislative interventions, the amalgamation process rapidly gathered pace. By 1994 the ACTU's blueprint had been largely put in place, albeit with some substantial amendments.

Some of the organizational amendments were driven by rivalries over recruiting zones, that the ACTU mediated at a central level. Another issue that complicated the implementation of the ACTU's industry model involved the ideological alignments within the movement. Although the Australian union movement is not split in a *structural* way between a 'left' with socialist credentials, and a 'right' loyal to a capitalist, market economy, nevertheless this dichotomy is a significant informal factor in local industrial politics. This fissure helps explain why successive drafts of the ACTU's *Future Strategies* revised the industrial groupings designed to guide amalgamation, and why the final outcomes of that process differed so substantially from the original model. For example, the metal industry unions never seriously contemplated amalgamation, preferring instead to divide along factional lines, each ideological camp collecting smaller, like-minded unions along the way.

These factional differences gave rise to a tendency toward 'general', rather than strictly industry, unions. This pattern is discernible in manufacturing industry in particular. The other significant divergence from the ACTU blueprint lies in the survival of craft unionism. Those craft unions seemingly most at risk from the industry model (the Electrical Trades Union and the Plumbers and Gasfitters Employees' Union), neatly met this challenge by amalgamating together. They accommodated their different occupational cultures - and among their State branches, different factional positions - by adopting a divisional structure which maximised the autonomy groups enjoyed in this new 'super' craft union. And as if to symbolise the interplay between factional loyalties and occupational culture, the amalgamated electrical and plumbing union then merged with the telecommunications and postal workers union, which itself contained a craft union base among technicians, and branches with conflicting factional loyalties.

Between 1991 and 1993, 98 amalgamations were completed in Australia (Dabscheck, 1995). Although 188 unions remain, membership is overwhelmingly concentrated in 19 'super unions'. The trend toward general, conglomerate unions arising from factional accommodations is the most noticeable structural outcome of the amalgamation process. Another less obvious outcome has been the marginalization of regional union bodies. These 'labour councils' exist at both state and provincial level, and served an obvious role as coordinating bodies among the myriad of occupational unions that affiliated to them. Officials from these labour councils have been among the more vocal union critics of ACTU strategy (Costa and Duffy, 1991), but the centralization of power in the 'super' unions and the ACTU has served to reduce their prominence in union affairs.

Conversely, some union activities that were previously centralised have been broken up by the amalgamation process. Trade union education, for example, was previously resourced and conducted by a publicly funded agency, the Trade Union Training Authority (TUTA). Again, this centralised arrangement had a logic in the fragmentation of the movement, such that individual unions were often too small to mount their own education programs for members. With the advent of super unions however, the resources previously devoted to TUTA have been distributed to these larger organizations.

The logic of larger size giving greater resources with which to 'service' the membership has been confirmed only by the ability of the super unions to deliver a new range of consumer services and products. Here we see at work the current orthodox assumption in union circles that unionism can be sold as a product, rather than as an industrial benefit and/or philosophical allegiance. Market-based prescriptions for union renewal are now commonplace, particularly on the 'right-wing' of the movement (Costa and Duffy, 1991; Costa, 1992). In this, the Australian union movement appears to be reinforcing the managerial rhetoric of the self-realization through the free market, and its explicitly anti-collectivist nostrums. In so doing, the union movement unconsciously buttresses the BCA's cultural project, the corner stone of which are employer efforts to 'win the "hearts and minds"' of their employees (Hilmer, McLauchlin, Macfarlane and Rose, 1991, p. 7).

In terms of industrial capability, super unions in the mining and maritime industries have recently fought to a standstill the union-busting activities of Conzinc Riotinto Australia (CRA), a major resources corporation, using a combination of traditional militancy and such arbitral powers left to the national industrial tribunal. But both the ACTU and the business community agree this is only one stage in a longer battle, the balance of which continues to favour the new corporate aggressiveness. Significantly, the CRA offensive has been mounted under the industrial relations legislation enacted by the Labor Party. This is ironic as the union movement dutifully mobilized its members in the 1993 election, and helped return a Labor Government by the narrowest of margins, only to see that Government pass legislative amendments which gave non-unionists access to the arbitration and conciliation system for the first time.

Moreover, the emergence of the super unions does not yet appear to have significantly increased the capacity of Australian unionism to organise the 'new' working class. Australian unions have been notoriously patriarchal (O'Donnell and Hall, 1988), and organized migrant workers only on distinctly assimilationist lines (Nicolaou, 1991; Bertone and Griffin, 1992). Although the ACTU has put in place affirmative action strategies for female union *leaders*, it has simultaneously embraced enterprise bargaining, which is likely to disadvantage women workers (Yates, 1996). The ACTU claims its own research shows women workers are not being disadvantaged in monetary terms by enterprise bargaining (LIN, 1994); independent research suggests the contrary (Hall and Fruin, 1994; Smith and Ewer, 1995). The wages question aside, Probert (1995) has been particularly critical of union strategies in enterprise bargaining that trade-off the interests of part time workers (mostly women), to preserve the position of full-time, permanent employees.

Yet, these conclusions may be premature as the ACTU (yet again supported by public funding) has in 1995 placed young recruiting organizers in the super-unions. These organizers are not necessarily selected from the ranks of the industries in which they are expected to recruit, but come from a variety of backgrounds (including direct from university). This strategy of employing the 'best and the brightest' has not yet been evaluated with any rigour. While some argue that these young organizers offer hope by reflecting more accurately the complexion of the new working class, cynics ask 'could such highly motivated and talented people perceive their jobs as recruiters as being an initial step in establishing careers as labour *apparatchiks*?' (Dabscheck, 1995, p. 136).

Overall, the process of union amalgamation and rationalization has, in the words of Dabscheck (1995, p. 135), 'involved unions turning in on themselves at a time when wages and working conditions have been subjected to seemingly incessant attack by employers'. There is at least anecdotal evidence for this assertion. Local union activists interviewed for this research are bitterly critical of the energy and resources spent rationalizing the union movement while they faced job losses, attacks on working conditions and community services, and the privatization of public utilities. Semi-official 'think tanks' within the labour movement are now suggesting the super unions need to be 'democratized' (Evatt Foundation, 1995), which raises questions not only about the legalistic way in which the reform of union structures has been conducted in Australia, but whether wholesale union amalgamation might have been the wrong solution to the wrong problem.

## Union amalgamations in Canada

In contast to Australia and most other western countries, Canada's rate of unionization since 1976 has remained quite steady, ranging from 37-39 per cent of the non-agricultural workforce. Gross numbers of union members have also increased quite steadily between 1976 and 1993, registering actual declines only in two years — 1983 and 1993 — both of which were the final years in deep recessions. This growth has slowed since 1990.

Even the number of unions operating in Canada has increased between 1983 and 1994, although this is largely a statistical artefact resulting from changing reporting procedures by Statistics Canada. Yet, this aggregate picture masks the fluctuations in individual union membership that have characterized the experience of most unions operating in Canada. Declines in union membership have often been met by increased organizing activity and in many cases, mergers with other unions. Whereas there were 55 mergers affecting Canadian unions between 1956 and 1984, the majority of which were initiated by U.S.-based International Unions, there were 73 mergers between 1984 and 1993, most of which were initiated by Canadian unions (Chaison, 1986; CALURA, Catalogue 71-202, 1992). A handful of unions have been disproportionately involved in amalgamations, including the Canadian Autoworkers' Union (CAW), the United Steelworkers of America (USWA), the United Food and Commercial Workers (UFCW) and the Canadian Union of Public Employees (CUPE). The Communication, Energy and Pulp and Paper Workers (CEP) union is an entirely new union formed in 1992 out of a merger principally involving three unions.

In Canada, union amalgamations have not been driven by a peak labour organization or a clearly articulated central agenda, whether of union reform or workplace restructuring. The Canadian labour movement is organizationally and programmatically too fragmented to launch such an undertaking. In 1992, there were 498 labour organizations operating in Canada with 15,179 union locals. Because of Canada's enterprise bargaining system, union locals most often play the primary role in negotiating collective agreements, the result of which is 27,328 collective agreements in Canada in 1992 (CALURA, Catalogue 71-202, 1992). There are several competing union centrals as well as hundreds of stand alone unions unaffiliated with any central labour body. The Canadian Labour Congress (CLC), the main union central, represents only about 60 percent of unions in Canada. The CLC has declining influence within the labour movement and has been increasingly ineffective in fulfilling its responsibility of adjudicating jurisdictional conflicts between unions, a role potentially vital in sorting out the problems arising out of union amalgamations.

Canadian unions have been driven to amalgamations by the rapidly changing economic environment of Canada, which includes significant job loss as a result of plant closures and business downsizing, more aggressive employers determined to rewrite collective agreements and right-wing governments which have dismantled the social welfare system and rewritten labour laws to strengthen the hand of employers and impede union certification and negotiation of contracts (Panitch and Swartz, 1993; Grinspun and Kreklewich, 1994). Mergers between unions became in the 1990s a quick means of arresting membership decline while also offering the possibility of continued union influence with employers, governments and within the labour movement itself. For small unions joining with bigger ones there are the added anticipated advantages of gaining access to lucrative strike funds, better service and extensive union education and research facilities.

Although the industrial union model is usually held out as the exemplar for union reorganization, ideological politics within the Canadian labour movement have militated against the emergence of industrial unions in favour of general unions. Ideological politics have split the labour movement on two axes — radicalism versus moderate unionism and nationalism versus continentalism. In turn, these have reinforced organizational divisions between national and international and, with a couple of exceptions, between private and public sector unions. Thus unions look for merger partners based on ideology as much as on an occupational or industrial basis.

The ideological and strategic politics of amalgamations have been kept alive and well by the CAW. The CAW is more explicit than other unions in its conception of amalgamations as both a solution to immediate problems of membership decline as well as part of a broader political strategy. Canadian Autoworkers had long taken a critical stance towards social democratic politics, arguing in favour of a concerted union movement that would use its industrial muscle and combined resources to shape industrial policy and national development (Yates, 1993, chapter 6). After an abortive attempt in the early 1980s to form a Canadian Metalworkers' Federation and the separation of the Canadian Autoworkers' from their parent body, the U.S.-based International Union of Automobile Workers (UAW), Canadian autoworkers were faced with a smaller membership, fewer resources and reduced political-economic influence. The Canadian Autoworkers' responded with a strategy to build 'one big union' that would safeguard the CAW's position in the labour movement and mobilize support for an alternative to the corporate agenda. Amalgamations offered the fastest and most effective route to this goal.

Between 1985 and 1996, the CAW amalgamated with 23 unions involving 98,695 workers including fishworkers, railway and garment workers and a good portion of the airline employees (Yates, 1995).

The final driving force behind amalgamations has been demands by either unions or employers for consolidation of unions and industrial relations structures. This imperative has been most important for public sector workplaces and those with multiple unions on site. Government cutbacks and legislative attacks on public sector unions have driven many of these unions to band together so they can consolidate their organizational and financial resources. For example, the merger between the 35,000-strong Health Employees Union in British Columbia with the Canadian Union of Public Employees was driven largely by HEU's desire to gain access to CUPE's national Defence Fund, a pool of money designated for fighting back against government cutbacks, and to rejoin the CLC (CUPE, 1994, p. 1).

For employers, the goal of rationalization is similar to that advanced by the BCA in Australia of having one union in one workplace. Single union coverage reduces the costs of maintaining multiple collective agreements and facilitates the negotiation of a 'flexible' labour process, especially multi-tasking. Employers in the Canadian postal service and the railways, which had multiple unions on site, have both rationalized union structures, using the Canada labour code to force amalgamations between unions. This phenomenon is likely to grow as governments drive for cost efficiency by amalgamating municipalities, hospitals and school boards, the process of which will require parallel amalgamations by unions present in these workplaces. The result is often growing hostility between unions which once respected each others jurisdictions and differences and now are forced into competition for their own survival.

Amalgamations succeeded in arresting membership decline for many unions. Smaller unions which joined with these and other larger unions have certainly gained access to more resources, although the extent of control these previously independent unions exert over the allocation of central resources varies according to the structure of integration by merging unions (Chaison, 1986) and the outcomes of internal political struggles. The process of pooling resources has been fraught with difficulties as merging unions seek to hang onto their own staff, disagree over what constitutes adequate servicing of members and, in some cases, struggle against moves to centralize control over resources. Nonetheless, anecdotal evidence suggests that workers previously represented by small stand-alone unions have fared better in the collective bargaining process, even though their union headquarters may be in disarray.

In both Canada and Australia, amalgamations are seen as a way of consolidating organizational structures, both internal to the union and in collective bargaining. This consolidation is expected to allow more efficient use of resources, improved service to members and more effective coordination of union activities. One indicator of organizational consolidation is a decline in the number of unions, locals and agreements operating on a national scene. Fewer unions and locals can arguably pool resources and expertise, thus allowing for greater efficiency and better service to members. It is difficult to assess whether amalgamations have had much impact on these numbers in Canada, owing to changes in the mid 1980s to Statistics Canada reporting procedures. An examination of individual unions produces a more complex story. The Canadian Union of Public Employees, the single largest union in Canada with 409,810 members and 2321 locals in 1994 (CALURA, Catalogue 71-202), has been stymied in its efforts at internal reorganization by internal political struggles around issues of local versus national control. Even successes in reorganization, such as the USWA's consolidation of 36 union locals in lower mainland British Columbia into four locals, has taken months of politicking and careful negotiation. The benefits for members lie in the capacity of the four locals to afford the salary of one full-time elected chairman whose sole job is to service the members and the collective agreement. In other cases, employer pressure to devolve collective bargaining and industrial relations to the workplace level counters union efforts to organize newly amalgamated locals into concerted collective bargaining arrangements or coordinated strike activity.

General unions are more prevalent in Canada as a result of amalgamations. They pose their own obstacles to achieving the benefits of union consolidation. Whereas industrial unions can achieve economies of scale, due to the homogeneity of their membership and the similar types of work done by their members, general unions experience more demands on their resources arising out of the need to represent a diverse, often previously unknown, group of workers. General unions must therefore spend greater resources in understanding the needs of new groups of workers, and negotiating and servicing a diverse range of collective agreements.

With the move towards general unionism, union protocol that once upheld jurisdictional integrity in Canada and disciplined unions that poached in other's territory has been cast aside. Unions now cross over jurisdictional boundaries and vie openly with one another for membership. This competition for members has a number of negative consequences for Canadian unions. Union centrals such as the CLC and the provincial federations of labour have been pushed to the side of union affairs at the very time when coordination is most needed. Federations have also been proven ineffective in resolving jurisdictional disputes and mending the necessary fences to build labour unity. Competition between unions also undermines membership commitment by encouraging unionists to behave as consumers, shopping for the best union deal in town. In Ontario and elsewhere in Canada, governments have encouraged this behaviour with changes to labour laws that facilitate decertification of unions and ease the legal pursuit of complaints against one's union.

In this period of merger mania, the Canadian labour movement has never been so internally divided. While much of the conflict grows out of sharpening ideological and political differences which in turn grow out of difficult economic times, rivalries over amalgamations and union size exaggerate and complicate these conflicts. Unions have yet to achieve the benefits of rationalized organizations as a result of amalgamations and are unlikely to achieve financial efficiencies owing to the nature of general unions. Yet, not all is lost from the amalgamation drive. Many unions such as USWA and CAW have been internally changed by their amalgamation with more diverse groups of workers and the need to reassess union goals and strategies accordingly. These changes, combined with their significant resources, could make them a potent force in organizing the growing number of precariously employed workers, most of whom are women and youth. Finally, under political pressures from increasingly right-wing governments the union movement shows signs of putting its differences aside to fight a common foe. Recent mass rallies organized by Ontario unions in alliance with a cross-section of social groups to protest current government policies provide a basis for hope about labour's future. The rally held in Hamilton on February 24, 1996 brought together 100,000 people, the largest single demonstration in Canadian history, who retraced the steps of workers from over 100 years ago in their march for the nine-hour day. There are also signs of some union successes in organizing new workplaces including sports retail outlets and fast food chains. Amalgamations are janus-faced. Whether Canadian unions can reap the benefits and dispel the hazards of this reorganization strategy remains to be seen.

## Conclusion: The remaking of union identities and practices

The fate of unionism is now a subject of international research attention. In this debate, the relationship between union identity and organizational structure is a key field of inquiry, to which Hyman (1994) has contributed a typology of union strategy and organizational types (Table 10.1). As with any framework of this kind, Hyman's typology is highly generalized, and obscures important organizational choices (e.g. between occupational or industry models of recruitment). Nevertheless, it does help locate developments in Canada and Australia within a wider debate, and we use it here to conclude our review of union amalgamations.

**Table 10.1**
**A typology of union identities**

| Focus of action | Key function | Ideal type |
| --- | --- | --- |
| Indivdual worker | Services | Friendly society |
| Management | Productivity coalition | Company union |
| Government | Political exchange | Social partner |
| Mass support | Campaigning | Social movement |

*Source:* Hyman (1994).

In Australia, the union movement has opted to combine centralized national structures, designed to support the social-contract politics of the Accord, with a recruitment and retention strategy based on the provision of 'services', of both an industrial and consumer type. With respect to employers, unions have offered their co-operation with management-led restructuring of the workplace, in exchange for continued union recognition. As such, Australian unions exhibit Hyman's key functions of services, productivity coalition and political exchange, and pay comparatively less attention to the campaigning function of a mass social movement. This combination arises from the particular political and institutional circumstances facing unionism in Australia. Long protected by a judicial system that afforded legal recognition to unions, the Australian movement is seeing its privileged position eroded as public policy facilitates the globalization of the domestic economy. The strategic response of the ACTU has been to ask the business community to exchange continuing union recognition for workplace cooperation. The ACTU has used social contract politics to ward off the overt threat of a conservative government and based its recruitment strategy on the provision of new consumer services. Thus, Australian unionism has chosen to encourage the market discourse, hoping that the commodification of union services will find a place in the industrial relations 'marketplace'. Having taken a route signposted by managerialism, the union movement now finds itself faced by a new conservative government, which is openly supportive of further legislative change to weaken union organizing rights.

In Canada, by contrast, the absence of a strong peak union council is reflected in a wider range of organizational strategies, from a cooperative stance vis-à-vis management, to assertive rejection of modern managerialism. This diversity is reflected in the experiments by Canadian unions with quite different types of activity to attract workers. As such some unions have paid more attention to Hyman's category of the social movement. Community organizing has shifted the role once played by the 'professional' and seasoned union organizer in many unions. Community leaders and local labour activists broaden the appeal of labour through community activism and set up the initial contacts and confidence in a union during an organizing campaign. This strategy articulates the role of unions in terms appreciable to local workers, and is a step toward re-establishing the roots of unions within communities and new social groupings. The International Ladies and Garment Workers Union in Toronto has devised several innovative techniques for contacting homeworkers in a bid to build ties between them and the union, with the long-term hope of establishing a homeworkers' union local. Unfortunately, a recent amalgamation between the ILGWU and the more conservative Amalgamated Clothing & Textile Workers Union may undercut this strategy. Nonetheless, both these examples illustrate union attempts to devise strategies that meet the challenges for unions of shifts toward hard-to-organize small and 'hidden' workplaces. These strategies begin to address the cultural challenges emanating from within these unions and prepare a possible groundwork for initiating union alternatives to the corporate agenda.

As we have seen, unions in both Canada and Australia have seen the complexion of their membership change. One factor contributing to this transformation is the union amalgamation process. Whereas both labour movements envisioned the creation through amalgamation of truly industrial unions along the lines of those in Europe, this model did not emerge. Instead, there have developed a number of large general unions whose memberships are heterogeneous. Many unions, such as the USWA and CAW in Canada and the Australian Manufacturing Workers Union have experienced an increase in the numbers of women and/or visible minorities in their ranks. These workers bring with them different concerns and demands. Women workers often vary in their approach to industrial action and in their strategizing, drawing from experiences in groups from the women's movement (Briskin and McDermott, 1993; Adamson and Briskin, 1988). Other new members bring unique cultural and organizational practices from their previous union which may not be readily consistent with the dominant union culture and practices of their new union, resulting in conflict and pressure for organizational and cultural change. The sheer size of many of the emerging general unions pose problems of bureaucracy versus democracy and efficiency versus representation. At the root of these problems lie the questions of how best to build workers' commitment to their union and structure union activities and decision-making processes so that tactical unity is achieved and mobilizational capacity is sustained.

In attempting this, unions must also deconstruct the exclusive identities and practices of the older industrial, social democratic unions. They must wrestle with the collapse of socialist ideas and the capturing of social democratic parties by economic rationalism, a situation that has opened an intellectual and ideological space which unions are having difficulty filling. To start, unions must construct new identities that make sense of the diverse work and life experiences of their memberships and of currently non-union labour. In so doing, unions must recast themselves as agents of change in workers' lives and build new ties that will bind workers to unions. This task becomes ever more urgent as the openings for alternative solutions to competitiveness and flexible specialization begin to close as HRM's corporate discourse becomes hegemonic.

While amalgamation is a common theme in the response of Australian and Canadian unions to national climates that are increasingly inhospitable, significant differences emerge between the two movements which go to fundamental choices of strategy. We might say that organized labour in Australia has conceptualized its members as actors in the marketplace, and in consequence offered them a 'market of services'. It now finds itself facing an overtly hostile government equipped with a centralized organizational structure designed to support this marketing, and a social contract politics forged with a party of labour. The Canadian union movement, whether by design or default, instead provides a 'market of ideas', that reflects differences between unions over the nature and purpose of trade unionism. The organizational practices adopted by each movement flow from these differences in outlook. While Australian unionism turns to market relationships as a recruitment tool, Canadian unions are strategically more diverse, including some who favour market unionism and others who seek to locate themselves within their local communities. Whether each model is an appropriate response to the problems faced by unionists in Australia and Canada, or whether one proves an organizational dead-end, must remain questions for the future.

## Note

1. The award system referred to here, and subsequently, is a product of Australia's judicial-based system of arbitration and conciliation. Within this system industrial tribunals resolve disputes by handing down awards which legally bind employers and unions to the wages and conditions proscribed in them.

## References

ABS Catalogue 6325.0, *Trade union members Australia.*

ACTU (1987), Australian Council of Trade Unions, *Future strategies*, ACTU, Melbourne.

ACTU-TDC (1987), Australian Council of Trade Unions and the Trade Development Council Secretariat, *Australia reconstructed*, AGPS, Canberra.

Adamson, N. and Briskin, L. (eds.) (1988), *Feminist organizing for change: The contemporary women's movement*, Oxford University Press, DonMills, Ontario.

BCA (1989a), Business Council of Australia, *Enterprise-based bargaining units: A better way of working*, Volume 1, BCA, Melbourne.

BCA (1989b), Business Council of Australia, 'Rationalising union coverage at the workplace' in *Business Council Bulletin*, September, pp. 34-38.

Berry, P. and Kitchener, G. (1989), *Can unions survive?* Building Workers Industrial Union, Canberra.

Bertone, S. and Griffin, G. (1992), *Immigrant workers and trade unions*, AGPS, Canberra.

Briskin, L. and McDermott, P. (eds) (1993), *Challenging unions: Feminism, democracy and militancy*, University of Toronto, Toronto.

CALURA (Corporations and Labour Unions Returns Act - Statistics Canada), Part II-*Labour Unions*, Catalogue 71-202, selected years.

Chaison, G. (1986), *When unions merge*, Lexington Books, Lexington, Mass.

Costa, M. (1992), 'Mythology, marketing and competition: A heretical view of the future of unions', in Crosby, M. and Easson, M., *What should unions do?*, Pluto Press, Sydney.

Costa, M. and Duffy, M. (1991), *Labor, prosperity and the nineties: Beyond the Bonsai economy*, The Federation Press, Sydney.

CUPE (1994), Canadian Union of Public Employees, *The Leader*, vol. 9, Nov.-Dec.

Dabscheck, B. (1995), *The struggle for Australian industrial relations*, Oxford University Press, Melbourne.

Drache, D. and Glasbeck, H. (1992), *The changing workplace*, James Lorimer & Co, Toronto.

Evatt Foundation (1995), *Unions 2001: A blueprint for trade unions activism*, Evatt Foundation, Sydney.

Ewer, P. (1995), 'Union busting, and what to do about it', *Frontline*, April.

Ewer, P., Higgins, W. and Stephens, A. (1987), *Unions and the future of Australian manufacturing*, Pluto Press, Sydney.

Frenkel, S. and Peetz, D. (1990), 'Enterprise bargaining: The BCA's report on industrial relations reform', *Journal of Industrial Relations*, vol. 32, No 1, pp. 69-99.

Grinspun, R. and Kreklewich, R. (1994), 'Consolidating neoliberal reforms: "Free trade" as a conditioning framework', *Studies in Political Economy*, Spring, pp. 33-61.

Hall, P. and Fruin, D. (1994), 'Gender aspects of enterprise bargaining: The good, the bad and the ugly', in Morgan, D. (ed), *Dimensions of enterprise bargaining and organizational relations*, USW Studies in Australian Industrial Relations, Monograph No 36, Industrial Relations Research Centre, Kensington.

Hilmer, F., McLauchlin, P., Macfarlane, D. and Rose, J. (1991), Employee Relations Study Commission of the Business Council of Australia, *Avoiding industrial action: A better way of working*, Allen and Unwin, North Sydney.

Hyman, R. (1994), 'Changing trade union identities and strategies', in Hyman, R. and Ferner, A. (eds.), *New frontiers in European industrial relations*, Basil Blackwell, Oxford.

LIN (1994), Labour Information Network, *Update on enterprise bargaining*, December.

Nicolaou, L. (1991), *Australian unions and immigrant workers*, Allen and Unwin, Sydney.

O'Donnell, C. and Hall, P. (1988), *Getting equal*, Allen and Unwin, Sydney.

Panitch, L. and Swartz, D. (1993), *The assault on trade union freedoms*, Garamond Press, Toronto.

Peetz, D. (1990), 'Declining union density', *Journal of Industrial Relations*, vol. 32, No 2, pp. 197-223.

Probert, B. (1995), *Part-time work and managerial strategy: 'Flexibility' in the new industrial relations framework*, AGPS, Canberra.

Robertson, D., Rinehart, J., Huxley, C. and the CAW Reserch Group on CAMI (1992), 'Team concept and Kaizan: Japanese production management in a unionized Canadian auto plant', *Studies in Political Economy*, vol. 39, pp. 77-107.

Smith, M. and Ewer, P. (1995), *The position of women in enterprise bargaining and the national training reform agenda*, AGPS, Canberra.

Willmott, H. (1993), 'Strength is ignorance; Slavery is freedom: Managing culture in modern organizations', *Journal of Management Studies*, vol. 30.

Wolfe, D. (1984), 'The rise and demise of the Keynesian era in Canada', in Cross, M. and Kealey, G. (eds), *Modern Canada: 1930-1980s readings in Canadian social history*, Volume 5, McClelland and Stewart, Toronto.

Yates, C. (1993), *From plant to politics: The Autoworkers Union in postwar Canada*, Temple University Press, Philadelphia.

Yates, C. (1995), 'Mergers and organizing: CAW responses to challenges of the 1990s', in Steedman, M. Suschnigg, P. and Buse, D. (eds), *Hard labour lessons: The Mine Mill Centennial Conference 1993*, Dundurn Press, Toronto.

Yates, C. (1996), 'Neo-liberalism and the working girl: The dilemmas of women and the Australian union movement', *Economic and Industrial Democracy*, November.

# 11 The degree of autonomy of Canadian local unions of national and international unions

*Diane Veilleux and Renaud Paquet*

This chapter seeks to determine the degree of autonomy of local unions with respect to decisions pertaining to internal management as well as to the protection of employee interests. Although not particular to the American or Canadian organized labour movement, the problem of relations between local and parent unions in North America is unique in light of the social role of American unionism and the legal framework in which this role is carried out. In fact, unlike in some European countries, North American unions concentrate their efforts at the company level. While their efforts focus primarily on the company, the American and Canadian labour movements have distinguishing characteristics in that the latter has greater sociopolitical ramifications (Kumar, 1993). The primary role of unions is to negotiate a collective agreement with the company and then ensure that the work rules contained in the agreement are respected (Rankin, 1990). Union activity thus takes place mainly at the local level and is closely linked to the legal framework that defines the parameters of collective bargaining in Canada. The various labour laws provide that once it has obtained the support or votes from the majority of the employees involved or a specific group of employees, a union gains the exclusive right to negotiate on behalf of all those employees or specific groups (Carter, 1995).

Given the local orientation and legal framework of union activity, it may seem surprising that the question of local union autonomy is raised. This

---

This research was made possible by a grant from the HRCC research fund of the Université de Montréal. The researchers would like to thank Marie-Hélène Jetté and Nathalie Beaudet for their assistance on this project. Address correspondence to Diane Veilleux, École de relations industrielles, Université de Montréal, C.P. 6128, succursale Centre-ville, Montréal (Quebec), H3C 3J7, Canada.

issue, however, is central to the relationship between local and parent unions (Freeman and Medoff, 1984; Estey, 1981). National and international unions[1] do not arise from an amalgamation of locals. Rather, it is the central authority that issues charters to newly created local unions. How much latitude, then, do locals have in their internal management and bargaining with company management? This question becomes all the more significant given that pattern bargaining, practised by traditional industrial unionism, is being challenged. In fact, the emergence of a negotiation model, dubbed 'the model of enterprise unionism' by Paul Weiler (1990, p. 204), promotes flexibility in the management of companies and active employee participation, thus requiring that locals be vested with greater autonomy when negotiating new collective agreements.

This question raises two issues: the extent to which a collective agreement corresponds to the objectives of the company and its employees, and industrial democracy. The more control a local exercises in determining the specific content of negotiated work rules, the more likely these will conform to local needs (Katz, 1993). In contrast, unions with centralized decision-making powers provide employees with little opportunity to actively participate in decisions that affect them, thereby tainting the democratic nature of organized labour (Strauss, 1990). At a time when the credibility and *raison d'être* of some social institutions are being challenged, and company survival hinges on work rules better suited to new flexible production methods (Katz and Kochan, 1992), the problem of local decision-making autonomy becomes of paramount importance.

All national and international unions, hereinafter referred to as 'ramified unions' (Verge and Murray, 1991, p.146), are responsible for the creation of local unions and must issue charters to the locals before these can be officially recognized. Locals may unite one or several bargaining units. For example, a local union may have only one certification and represent the employees of one employer, or it may have several certifications and represent the employees of several employers. Moreover, some locals, as we will see, do not have certification; instead their ramified union is certified. In Canada these unions represent employees of the federal public service. Despite their specific nature, these national unions that operate in the federal public service have been included in this analysis for two reasons: they represent a large number of Canadian employees, and they allow us to analyse to what extent certification influences the degree of local autonomy, not only in the representation of employees during the negotiation and administration of collective agreements but also in local internal management.

National or international unions exercise varying degrees of control over the internal management of their local unions as well as over the locals role as employee representative. The degree of local autonomy appears to be determined by one of two opposing links — contractual or organic. When the link is contractual, the local is quasi-independent of its ramified union, that is, somewhat like a 'franchisee' of the union milieu. In order to operate under the banner of a well-structured organization and benefit from the services and advantages it provides, locals must submit to the rules of the ramified union. When the link is organic, locals are not considered separate from their ramified union but are rather like administrative divisions. In this case, the ramified union is directly involved in the internal management of the local as well as in the protection of professional rights.

Other possible scenarios exist between these two extremes. For example, local unions may exercise a large measure of autonomy with respect to their internal management but retain little control over activities pertaining to collective bargaining or the referral of grievances to arbitration. In some cases, local unions and the central authority share power regarding the two aforementioned areas of activities. For example, local unions are vested with decision-making powers that they exercise jointly with the central authority. Our goal is to propose a categorization of the national and international unions that will lead to a better understanding of the various degrees of autonomy they grant to their locals.

## Methodology

Several approaches exist to evaluate degrees of local autonomy. Just as Anderson (1978) did in a study of union democracy, we have identified three approaches. The first involves studying the legal dimension of the relationship between the different components of the union structure. The other two focus on analysing the attitudes and behaviour of the parties concerned as well as the actual use of their vested powers. Accordingly, the researcher studies the central authorities and the local unions by means of interviews with the parties concerned. We opted for the first approach, favouring an analysis of the ramified unions constitutions. We analysed the bylaws applicable in April 1995. Although such an approach has its limitations, in that there may exist a discrepancy between the formal written rules and their actual application, it nonetheless allows for a better understanding of the legal ties that characterize the relationship between ramified unions and their local entities.

As previously mentioned, according to the Canadian and North American model, the primary role of unions is to negotiate a collective labour agreement and, once it is ratified, control its administration. The degree of local union autonomy in activities relating to the protection of professional interests constitutes the first aspect of the relationship between locals and ramified unions. In order to better understand this relationship, the distribution of decision-making powers between the two levels will be analysed in relation to the following activities that are the heart of the representative role of organized labour and the collective bargaining process (Hébert, 1992): (p1) approval of bargaining demands, (p2) ratification and signature of the collective agreement, (p3) strike authorization, (p4) authorization to draw on strike funds and (p5) submission of grievances to arbitration.

The second aspect of the relationship between locals and ramified unions pertains to the degree of autonomy exercised by the local union in its internal management. Whether the management of locals is controlled by members or by the ramified union has a significant impact on the degree of union democracy. The following indicators will provide a better understanding of the relationship between the two levels of organized labour: (m1) frequency of general membership meetings, (m2) term of office for officers, (m3) designation of executive board positions, (m4) duties of office, (m5) selection of convention delegates, (m6) setting union dues, (m7) local union merger, (m8) local union dissolution, (m9) drafting and adopting of local bylaws, (m10) disciplinary measures for members, and (m11) disciplinary measures for local officers.

The degree of autonomy for each indicator is measured on a scale from 1 to 5, with 5 representing the highest degree of autonomy. The varying degrees are as follows: (1) outside decision, (2) outside decision following consultation with local union, (3) joint decision, (4) internal decision subject to external parameters, and (5) internal decision not subject to external parameters.

Our analysis focused on 13 of the largest and the most representative unions of various sectors of activities, with members in Québec and in other provinces of Canada. We excluded from our study the unions in the construction industry, because the collective bargaining in this sector is governed by special rules, complicating comparison with other unions. All the unions studied but two[2] are affiliated with the Canadian Labour Congress (CLC), a central labour organization that unites 60 percent of the 4,000,000 unionized workers in Canada (HRD, 1995). Of these 13 unions, seven are national and six international.

*National unions* The Canadian Union of Public Employees (CUPE) is the largest union in Canada, with a membership of 410,000 employees in 2,400 locals. It represents employees who work predominantly for Crown corporations, in the municipal public sector and in education. The Public Service Alliance of Canada (PSAC) has 159,000 members in 1,400 locals. They are employed mostly by the federal government in blue-collar and administrative support positions, and in jobs relating to programme administration. The Professional Institute of the Public Service of Canada (PIPS) has a membership of 31,000 professionals employed by the federal government of Canada. The Canadian Union of Postal Workers (CUPW) has 51,000 members working for the Canadian postal service; most are employed by Canada Post, a wholly owned Crown corporation. The Canadian Communications, Energy and Paper Workers Union (CEPW) has a membership of 160,000 in 645 locals. One of the largest industrial unions in Canada, the CEPW represents members in such diverse industries as communications, electrical, electronics, paper and forestry products, energy as well as in chemical and petrochemical. The Canadian Brotherhood of Railway, Transport and General Workers (CBRT&GW)[3] represents employees mostly in the transport industry and, more specifically, in railway transport. Many of its 33,000 members work for corporations owned by the Canadian federal government. The National Automobile, Aerospace and Agricultural Implement Workers Union of Canada (CAW)[4] has members working mostly in the automobile, implement and transportation equipment manufacturing, and fishing industries. Before the merger with the CBRT&GW, the union represented 170,000 members in 131 locals.

*International unions* Uniting 175,000 Canadian employees in 138 locals, the United Food and Commercial Workers International Union (UFCW) is the largest international union in Canada. It represents employees in the retail, manufacturing and service sectors. Among international unions, the United Steelworkers of America (USWA) ranks second in Canadian membership. With 25 districts throughout North America, its three Canadian districts consist of 875 locals representing 161,000 workers in various sectors: metallurgy, electronics, banking, hotel and safety. The International Brotherhood of Teamsters, Chauffeurs, Warehousemen and Helpers of America (IBT) is composed of 41 locals in Canada, uniting 95,000 workers in the public sector as well as the food, brewery, milk products, construction, chemical products, energy, air transport and trucking industries. Uniting some 80,000 employees from 23 locals, the Service Employees International Union (SEIU) represents members in e.g. the public, health and building maintenance sectors. In Canada, the International Brotherhood of Electrical Workers (IBEW) comprises 119 locals and represents 67,000 employees working in the construction, telecommunications, railway and aeronautics sectors.

International Association of Machinists and Aerospace Workers (IAM) represents 148 locals and unites 55,000 Canadian employees mainly in the aeronautics, railway, aerospace, pulp and paper manufacturing equipment and heavy machinery manufacturing equipment sectors.

## The two-poles analysis

In light of the indicators and degrees of autonomy previously established, the analysis of 13 union constitutions reveals the degrees of autonomy held by locals in the protection of employees' professional interests and internal management.

### *Degree of autonomy in the protection of employees' professional interests*

It should be noted that collective bargaining within PSAC, PIPS and CUPW takes place at the national level. As such, the locals are administrative divisions with no autonomy regarding the protection of their members professional interests. In the other ramified unions in this study, bargaining may also extend beyond the local level; several bargaining units may unite on a voluntary basis to negotiate with employers. However, for the purposes of this study and with the exception of nationally certified unions, we quantified the indicators pertaining to the protection of professional interests on the basis of local negotiations, although the central bylaws of some unions specify particular methods for more wide-ranging negotiations.

As Table 11.1 indicates, the overall degree of local autonomy regarding the protection of employees' professional interests is as follows: CUPE and SEIU are very autonomous (5-4); CEPW, UFCW, IAM, IBT, CAW, IBEW are autonomous (4-3); CBRT&GW and USWA are semi-autonomous (3-2); and PSAC, PIPS, CUPW are non-autonomous (2-1).

The very autonomous locals have complete authority over almost all the indicators pertaining to the protection of professional interests. Only the use of strike funds is subject to the parameters outlined in the provisions stipulated in central bylaws. Although more varied in nature, the locals identified as autonomous have three common characteristics; whereas almost all of them have complete authority to approve contract demands and submit grievances to arbitration, they must obtain central authorization to use strike funds. Because of their generally autonomous nature, IBT, IBEW and CAW locals are classified as autonomous; however, it must be pointed out that their ramified unions are party to the collective bargaining process — a factor that somewhat reduces their overall autonomy. Also of interest is the fact that among locals in the same category, UFCW unions generally enjoy a wider range of autonomy than their counterparts. In order to ensure union democracy among UFCW locals, the central constitution establishes parameters regarding collective bargaining and strike decisions. Consequently, regarding the protection of employees professional interests, these locals are classified as somewhat autonomous, rather than very autonomous. At UFCW, therefore, respect for union democracy is tempered with respect for local union autonomy.

**Table 11.1**
**Protection of professional interests: Overall degree of local union autonomy**

| | Indicator[a] | | | | | |
|---|---|---|---|---|---|---|
| Union | P1 | P2 | P3 | P4 | P5 | Mean[b] |
| CUPE | 5 | 5 | 5 | 4 | 5 | 4.8 |
| PSAC | 1 | 1 | 1 | 1 | 1 | 1.0 |
| PIPS | 1 | 1 | 1 | 1 | 1 | 1.0 |
| CUPW | 1 | 1 | 1 | 1 | 1 | 1.0 |
| CEPW | 5 | 5 | 2 | 2 | 3 | 3.4 |
| CBRT | 4 | 4 | 2 | 2 | 1 | 2.6 |
| CAW | 5 | 3 | 2 | 1 | 5 | 3.2 |
| UFCW | 4 | 4 | 4 | 2 | 5 | 3.8 |
| USWA | 5 | 2 | 2 | 2 | 3 | 2.8 |
| IBT | 5 | 2 | 4 | 2 | 5 | 3.6 |
| SEIU | 5 | 5 | 5 | 4 | 5 | 4.8 |
| IBEW | 5 | 2 | 2 | 2 | 5 | 3.2 |
| IAM | 5 | 5 | 2 | 2 | 5 | 3.8 |

[a] P1 = approval of bargaining demands, P2 = ratification and signature of collective agreement, P3 = strike authorization, P4 = authorization to draw on strike funds, P5= submission of grievances to arbitration.
[b] Degree of autonomy: 1 = outside decision, 2 = outside decision following consultation with local, 3 = joint decision, 4 =internal decision subject to external parameters, 5 = internal decision not subject to external parameters.

The CBRT&GW and USWA locals are considered semi-autonomous and are subject to the central power's decision-making control regarding the call to strike, the use of strike funds, and the submission of grievances to arbitration. Moreover, the international union is party to the collective bargaining process of USWA unions. PSAC, PIPS and CUPW locals are completely under central control in all important aspects pertaining to the protection of employees professional interests. This confirms that local unions lose all discretionary power regarding the protection of professional interests when certification is held by the ramified union rather than by the locals. One would then expect that a certified local union would be wholly autonomous in the negotiation and administration of collective agreements; however, this is not the case. Ramified unions still maintain more or less extensive control over their certified locals. This control could arguably be lessened when collective bargaining is confined to one local, but when it affects more than one local within the same ramified union, the latter then would likely seek to tighten its control.

*Degree of autonomy in the internal management of the local unions*

Eleven indicators were used to determine the degree of autonomy in the internal management of local unions. Table 11.2 indicates the overall degree of autonomy in the internal management of ramified union locals. Based on the results in the table, the following classification of degrees of autonomy in the internal management of union locals may be established: SEIU, CEPW, CUPE, IAM are autonomous (4-3); PIPS, UFCW, IBT, IBEW, USWA, CUPW are semi-autonomous (3-2); and PSAC, CAW, CBRT&GW are non-autonomous (2-1).

None of the locals of the unions studied can be classified as very autonomous in matters of internal management. Moreover, whether or not locals are certified is not a deciding factor in issues of internal management. The opposite is true in the area of protecting employees professional interests. While Table 2 demonstrates that in this area no clear typology emerges among unions in the same category, a few more or less common characteristics may be noted. Thus, in matters of internal management, the locals characterized as autonomous must generally conform to certain parameters set out in central bylaws but have more or less variable discretionary power in the decision-making process. In this way, international and national ramified unions alike ensure that although their locals manage their internal affairs, they all abide by certain fundamental rules. Still, some aspects of management are subject to stricter control by ramified unions; accordingly, the central authority controls the designation of local executive board positions (CEPW, CUPE, IAM), description of officers duties (CUPE, IAM), drafting and approval of local bylaws (SEIU, IAM), and discipline of officers (CEPW). Notwithstanding their classification as autonomous, the constitutions of the SEIU and CEPW unions point to a preference for an institutional approach that grants their locals far-reaching autonomy.

Six ramified unions' locals are semi-autonomous and are subject to central authority control on between five and seven indicators; the central power makes decisions regarding local union mergers and, except for PIPS, also makes decisions regarding the designation of local executive board positions as well as the description of the duties of officers. Other aspects also fall within central authority jurisdiction, notably the approval of local bylaws (UFCW, IBT, IBEW, USWA), frequency of meetings (IBT, IBEW, CUPW), officers term of office (IBT, CUPW, USWA), union dues (CUPW, USWA, PIPS), delegate selection (UFCW), dissolution (PIPS, CUPW, USWA) and the discipline of members and officers (PIPS).

**Table 11.2**
**Internal management: Overall degree of local union autonomy**

| | Indicator[a] | | | | | | | | | | | |
|---|---|---|---|---|---|---|---|---|---|---|---|---|
| Union | M1 | M2 | M3 | M4 | M5 | M6 | M7 | M8 | M9 | M10 | M11 | Mean[b] |
| CUPE | 5 | 4 | 1 | 1 | 4 | 4 | 4 | 4 | 1 | 4 | 4 | 3.3 |
| PSAC | 4 | 1 | 1 | 1 | 2 | 4 | 1 | 1 | 1 | 2 | 4 | 2.0 |
| PIPS | 4 | 5 | 5 | 5 | 4 | 1 | 1 | 1 | 4 | 1 | 1 | 2.9 |
| CUPW | 1 | 4 | 1 | 1 | 4 | 1 | 1 | 1 | 4 | 4 | 4 | 2.4 |
| CEPW | 4 | 4 | 1 | 5 | 4 | 4 | 4 | 4 | 4 | 4 | 1 | 3.5 |
| CBRT | 1 | 1 | 1 | 1 | 4 | 1 | 1 | 1 | 1 | 4 | 4 | 1.8 |
| CAW | 1 | 1 | 1 | 1 | 4 | 1 | 1 | 1 | 2 | 4 | 4 | 1.9 |
| UFCW | 4 | 4 | 1 | 1 | 1 | 4 | 2 | 4 | 2 | 4 | 4 | 2.8 |
| USWA | 4 | 1 | 1 | 1 | 4 | 1 | 2 | 2 | 2 | 4 | 4 | 2.4 |
| IBT | 1 | 1 | 1 | 1 | 4 | 4 | 1 | 4 | 2 | 4 | 4 | 2.5 |
| SEIU | 4 | 5 | 5 | 5 | 4 | 4 | 2 | 4 | 2 | 4 | 4 | 3.9 |
| IBEW | 1 | 1 | 1 | 1 | 4 | 4 | 1 | 4 | 2 | 4 | 4 | 2.5 |
| IAM | 4 | 4 | 1 | 1 | 4 | 4 | 2 | 5 | 2 | 4 | 4 | 3.2 |

[a] M1 = frequency of general membership meetings, M2 = term of office for officers, M3 = designation of executive board positions, M4 = duties of office, M5 = selection of convention delegates, M6 = setting of union dues, M7 = local union merger, M8 = local union dissolution, M9 = drafting and adopting of local bylaws, M10 = disciplinary measures for members, M11 = disciplinary measures for local officers.

[b] Degree of autonomy: 1 = outside decision, 2 = outside decision following consultation with local, 3 = joint decision, 4 = internal decision subject to external parameters, 5 = internal decision not subject to external parameters.

The locals classified as non-autonomous are under the central authority control of PSAC, CBRT&GW and CAW unions regarding eight indicators. Six indicators fall within the control of the three previously mentioned unions: the term of office of officers, designation of executive positions, description of officers' duties, mergers, dissolution of locals and approval of local bylaws.

The following aspects also fall within central authority control: union dues (CBRT&GW, CAW), frequency of meetings (CBRT&GW, CAW), delegate selection (PSAC) and discipline of members (PSAC).

## Conclusion

In this chapter, we studied the degree of autonomy of Canadian locals chartered by national and international unions. In the North American context, the local constitutes a basic cell, but also the hard core of union organization. In fact, member recruitment is done through the local for purposes of certification that gives it the right to impose the collective bargaining of employees' working conditions on an employer. Once certification is achieved, the members of the local, as well as other employees who are not members of the local but are included in the certified bargaining unit, are subject to a compulsory check-off of union dues and must count on the local for all matters concerning negotiation and the administration of the collective agreement. Consequently, in the eyes of the bargaining unit employees, whether or not they are members of the local, it plays a role of paramount importance in protecting their professional interests. However, the autonomy of the local with regard to the national or international union which created it is not necessarily proportional to the major role that the local is required to play in local collective bargaining. In fact, national and international unions, in particular those in industrial sectors, have adopted centralizing collective bargaining practices, furthering union solidarity in order to increase their bargaining power. Although collective bargaining prevails on a local basis, i.e. employer by employer, the industrial unions have succeeded, with the collective bargaining pattern, in imposing similar working conditions in major industrial sectors. This centralizing approach to collective bargaining translates into control, to varying degrees, over the locals of national and international unions.

Our purpose was to examine the degree of autonomy of the locals of national and international unions because we consider this subject an important issue in the present socio-economic context, and one that requires unions to rethink their whole operating structures. The question of decentralization of union structures is the subject of considerable discussion in the North American and European literature, although the details of the issue differ from one continent to the other. In the North American context, the degree of autonomy granted to locals by national or international unions is one of the important elements that must be taken into account in the debate concerning the reorganization of union structures. It would be preferable for locals to exercise greater decision-making power in matters directly concerning them in order to deal with new local questions, for instance renewed militancy and member solidarity, or flexibility in the organization of labour. Do the bylaws of international unions providing for the existing formal structures give locals the right to redefine their roles in the union's structure, or do they maintain the control of the national or international unions in this area? Determining the degree of autonomy of locals, as provided in unions' bylaws, offers some clues.

Consequently, we have proposed a categorization of national and international unions according to the degree of autonomy they grant to their locals. This categorization is based on various indicators that we do not claim to be exhaustive. The indicators are significant factors, nevertheless, whether in the protection of professional interests or in internal management. This categorization shows that locals' autonomy does not automatically depend on whether they are chartered by a national or an international union, except for nationally certified unions in the federal public service. Although the national and international unions in industrial sectors have a reputation of centralizing control, our categorization tends to prove that this reputation is not necessarily founded in every case. Most unions in this study could be classified as industrial unions. Some are very decentralized, others not at all.

As the results demonstrate, the nationally certified unions (PSAC, CUPW, PIPS) in the federal public service are at one end of the spectrum. Overall, they give very little autonomy to their locals, which essentially constitute administrative divisions of the unions that created them. In this way, the certified national unions can maintain a permanent and direct link at the local level, without granting any significant decision-making power at this level. At the other end of the spectrum, some national and international unions (SEIU, CUPE) give great autonomy to their locals. These unions, in the services sector, constitute a good example of what we referred to before as 'franchisees' of the parent union. These locals cannot be considered only administrative divisions of the parent unions. According to the bylaws, at least, they have their own identity. The degree of autonomy of other locals falls somewhere between these two extremes. However, some major industrial unions (USWA, CAW) grant their locals a degree of autonomy that leads us to consider the latter to be basically administrative divisions rather than 'franchisees' of the parent union.

Is it better for a national or international union to go with a decentralized structure? Our aim was not to answer this question, but rather to demonstrate that some locals are in a better position to handle this question themselves than others, depending on the bylaws governing their links with the ramified unions. Whether locals actually want decentralization and how that could be achieved while preserving union solidarity remains to be seen.

## Notes

1. National unions are Canadian unions with an exclusively Canadian membership. They represent 66 percent of the unionized employees in Canada (HDR, 1995). International unions have their head office in the United States and have members in Canada as well as in the U.S. They represent 30 percent of the unionized employees in Canada.
2. The Professional Institute of the Public Service of Canada (PIPS) is independent. The International Brotherhood of Electrical Workers (IBEW) is affiliated with the Canadian Federation of Labour.
3. The CBRT&GW ceased to exist as a union in August 1994; it was merged with the CAW. At the time of this study (April 1995) the bylaws governing the new organization had not yet been printed.
4. Following the merger of the CAW and the CBRT&GW (August 1994) and at the time of this study (April 1995), the new version of the union's bylaws had not yet been printed. The merged union has 205,000 members (HRD, 1995). The analysis was done based on the bylaws in effect at the time of the merger.

## References

Anderson, J. (1978), 'A comparative analysis of local union democracy', *Industrial Relations*, vol. 17, no. 3.

Carter, D. (1995), 'Collective bargaining legislation', in Gunderson, M. and Ponak, A. (eds.), *Union-management relations in Canada*, Addison-Wesley, Don Mills.

Estey, M. (1981), *The Unions: Structure, development and management*, McGraw-Hill, New York.

Freeman, R. B. and Medoff, J. L. (1984), *What do unions do?*, Basic Books, New York.

Hébert, G. (1992), *Traité de négociation collective*, Gaétan Morin éditeur, Boucherville.

HRD, Human Resources Development Canada (1995), *Directory of labour organizations in Canada*, Bureau of Labour Information, Ottawa, Canada.

Katz, H. C. (1993), The decentralization of collective bargaining', *Industrial and Labor Relations Review*, vol. 47, no. 1.

Katz, H. C. and Kochan, T. A. (1992), *An introduction to collective bargaining and industrial relations*, McGraw-Hill, New York.

Kumar, P. (1993), *From uniformity to divergence: Industrial relations in Canada and the United States*, Queen's University, IRC Press, Kingston.

Rankin, T. (1990), *New forms of work organization: The challenge for North American unions*, University of Toronto Press, Toronto.

Strauss, G. (1990), 'Union Democracy', in Strauss, G., Gallagher, D. G. and Fioroto, J. (eds.), *The state of the unions*, IRRA Series, Washington.

Verge, P. and Murray, G. (1991), *Le droit et les syndicats*, Les Presses de l'Université Laval, Québec city.

Weiler, P. (1990), *Governing the workplace, The future of employment law*, Harvard University Press, Cambridge.

# 12 Decentralization in the Danish public sector: The emergence of local pay bargaining strategies

*Torben Andersen*

Since 1987, as a result of efforts to improve public sector performance, pay bargaining in the Danish public sector has been decentralized. Successive governments and public sector employers have long argued for the necessity for major changes if they are to be able to continue to provide services and develop new ones. In this process the focus is mainly on a rationalization of the system of collective agreements (cf. *Udvalget om større fleksibilitet i det offentlige aftale- og overenskomstsystem,* 1988, p. 15). The demand for long-term structural adjustments was accompanied by demands for increased short-term flexibility, which focused attention on the pay system. Barriers to renewal, such as automatic mechanisms for pay increases and the lack of flexibility in pay structures introduced decades ago, have been identified as key problems in the change process. Employers would like to be able to encourage employees doing a particularly valuable job, and this has mainly resulted in demands for increasing the individualization of the pay system. Commentators have interpreted this as part of the general attack on (public sector) trade unionism, describing the new initiatives as a sign of *ideological instability.* Employers' pressure and increasingly tighter public budgets make shared norms and the social order more difficult to maintain, and the potential undermining of responsible attitudes which have hitherto characterized pay bargaining could create scope for new conflicts in the sector. The risk of *Balkanization* and

---

Thanks to Dorthe Pedersen, Centre for Public Organization & Management, Copenhagen Business School, for useful comments. Address correspondence on this chapter to Torben Andersen, Institute for Organization & Management, Aarhus School of Business, Haslegaardsvej 10, 8210 Aarhus V, Denmark.

possible trade union rivalry, similar to that described by Jonsson (1992, p. 200) in the Swedish case, could in this respect appear as a negative scenario.

The demand for decentralization in the Danish public sector seems in large measure to come from the private sector. The pressure on the industrial relations system, and, in particular, emphasis on the reform of structural aspects, such as organizational structures, the bargaining machinery, and the pay system, is reflected in international literature (Baglioni and Crouch, 1990, pp. 11ff; Ferner and Hyman, 1992, p. 9). The demand for increasing flexibility through reorganization and decentralization in corporate life are features which are easily recognizable in most European countries during the 1980s (Ferner, 1991; Beaumont, 1992; Beadle, 1993), the US and Canada (Beaumont, 1992), and Australia (Niland et al., 1991; Brown, 1993).

The Swedish and Danish public sectors have much in common in this respect: The doctrine of new public management has largely been presented in proposals from the Ministry of Finance and by several committees reviewing, in particular, the pay system (Sjölund, 1995, p. 3; Elvander, 1988, pp. 312ff). Private sector developments thus act as inspiration for changes in the public sector pay systems; they are not an attack on ideology, as has been the case in Britain. The changes in the Swedish pay system started in 1985, where the individualization of pay and payment by result were implemented in order to avoid personnel problems. Elvander (1988, p. 246) mentions one of the problems: *the double imbalance*, i.e. highly skilled employees are difficult to recruit at the same time as lesser skilled workers are paid higher wages than in the private sector. In Sweden, individualization challenged the former solidary wage policies, leading to the emergence of trade union rivalry. This leads to the question of what happens when another Nordic model of collective bargaining takes the first step towards decentralization.

Besides being of current interest as regards global developments in industrial relations, the reason for studying the process of decentralization is to understand the outcome of the processes and the mechanisms by which the public sector changes. Changes in management strategies and the implications for industrial relations have, among others, been studied by Sandberg (1984), Fox (1974), Friedman (1977), and Purcell and Ahlstrand (1994). These have all tried to relate types of management strategies to work relations or industrial relations in the workplace, albeit often without addressing the pay issue and the outcome of the bargaining processes. The aim of the present study was to identify similar types of categories in the public sector management and trade union response.

The traditional high level of trade union presence in bureaucratic (public sector) organizations and complex bargaining machineries could result in a more solid trade union response to the new management initiatives (compared with private sector developments, where management prerogative seems to prevail). Similarly, the presence of several highly educated groups of employees (technical, professional and functional experts) provide a basis for less management-dominated processes, perhaps with participation and involvement as central aspects. In addition, the lack of competitive pressure for many public jobs could make it easier for trade unions to maintain the national pay structure and resist the spread of individualization.

## The historical basis

Since the 1960s, pay determination has been highly centralized in Denmark, both in the public and private sector. Synchronized collective bargaining rounds every second year, and a high degree of coordination between the public and private sector bargaining arenas, has produced rather similar pay increases. However, the decentralization of the late 1980s has meant a change back to the model which characterized the 1940s and 1950s (Scheuer, 1988). Decentralization in Denmark is so far of a limited vertical kind, from the confederations to trade unions or cartels and to employers' associations in specific industries (Scheuer, 1991, p. 18).

Centralization prevailed in public sector pay bargaining until the mid-1980s primarily for political reasons, first and foremost incomes policy. Other political aims, e.g. equal pay and improved conditions for low-wage income groups, were also pursued to some extent. In practice, the main aim of wage control was to ensure that public sector pay increases matched those in the private sector. However, conditions changed from the mid-1980s, when incomes policy became less important and the focus shifted towards the growth in the public sector.

The emergence of a low inflation society meant, furthermore, that many problems with personnel policies (including pay policies) had to be solved within the framework of much lower pay increases. The exception was the collective bargaining round in 1987, where the government boosted the economy prior to the general election, and where public sector employees won a pay rise of 6-7 percent (Due and Madsen, 1988, p. 245; Due et al., 1993, pp. 364ff). In return, employers demanded an increase in productivity, to be achieved through reorganization and the introduction of new technology, providing a larger degree of customer-designed services. This required a well-organized personnel policy, including favourable conditions for recruiting and keeping employees, which led to demands for more decentralized personnel policies and pay negotiations. Recruiting and retaining personnel in key areas was therefore one of the central aims of public sector employers' attempts to increase flexibility in the pay system.

From the mid-1980s, personnel policies (including pay) were in turn decentralized at state, county and municipal level. The Ministry of Finance issued a large number of recommendations on pay and personnel issues, and the possibilities for developing local policies increased. Local initiatives, greatly inspired by 'suggestions' from central level, increased gradually during the late 1980s, resulting in more diversified employment conditions.

## Decentralization in the private sector

In order to fully understand the decentralization in the public sector, it is necessary to look at the development in parts of the private sector. The main argument for the decentralization of collective bargaining in the mid-1980s came from central level actors in the metal industry. Increasing internationalization, together with new competitive pressures, weakened the protection which the home market had given many Danish companies. In the steel and metal industry, about 60 percent of the companies are mainly subcontractors, and many of these were now experiencing international competition for the first time (Ibsen and Stamhus, 1993, p. 49). Firms were competing mainly on quality and deliverance guarantee, and Danish subcontractors in the metal industry had to depend on their high level of flexibility and ability to reorganize quickly in order to survive. This led to demands for greater freedom in pay policies at company level.

### *The three phases of decentralization*

In the late 1980s, there were three coherent and partly overlapping phases of decentralization, which had a rather profound effect on pay issues (Ibsen et al., 1995, pp. 28ff): First came the decentralization of competencies in the bargaining process through an adjustment of organizational structure; second, a change in the collective agreements structure (an extension of the area covered by minimum wages); and third, a change in pay systems, the introduction of payment by qualifications and results, and the individualization of wage determination.

In the first phase, diverging preferences among employers created a pressure for decentralization. Basically, employers in the iron and metal industry demanded major changes, which the collective agreement between the Danish Confederation of Trade Unions (LO) and The Confederation of Employers

(DA) was not able to deliver. As a result, metal industry employers and trade unions negotiated their own collective agreement.

The second phase of the decentralization process consisted of a reorganization and adaptation of the more company-specific pay bargaining model. The employers, who once again took the initiative, succeeded in reconstructing the various wage agreements, combining six major agreements into one overall industry level agreement. The balance between pay increases negotiated at local versus central level was now changed in favour of the former. However, before the local bargaining could begin, new payment systems had to be implemented in companies which had agreements with unions affiliated to CO-Industri (the Danish Industry Workers Union). Whereas companies in the metal industry used the minimum wage agreement (pay bargaining taking place at both central and local level), employers in the other industries used normal wage agreements (pay bargaining taking place at central level only, during the bargaining rounds). The necessity for harmonization of the two types of wage agreements was obvious: the increase in the normal pay rates was acting as a norm for wage demands under the minimum wage agreement, i.e. pay increases in some sectors gave employees in other sectors almost automatic pay increases. The employers wanted to depart from this *mechanism*, which meant a decentralized bargaining structure, a necessary condition of which was a farewell to solidarity in the LO's pay policy.

The third phase of decentralization marked the introduction of new market-oriented pay systems and the end of traditional collective bargaining routines. This phase is now proceeding more rapidly, with new models of pay systems being tested or implemented in many companies (Ibsen and Stamhus, 1993, pp. 77ff). Many of the initiatives have been introduced by both sides, i.e. CO-Industri seems to be an active partner to a much larger extent than before. However, while employers emphasize the individual aspects of payment by result and payment by qualifications, the union is more concerned with collective and objectively measurable aspects. Both sides seem however to agree that pay should reflect the results and profit of the individual company.

## Local pay bargaining in the public sector

The historical account above is important for understanding the decentralization of pay bargaining in the public sector. First of all, the rationalization of the bargaining structure has taken rather similar directions in the two sectors. Two large employee bargaining cartels have been formed: The bargaining committee of the central organizations, covering the unions of state employees and civil servants (CFU), and the bargaining committee for civil servants and salaried employees in local administration and institutions (KTO) (Due and Madsen, 1988, p. 100 and 1990, pp. 157ff). Employers have likewise rationalized their structure of representation, resulting in two bargaining arenas (for the state and the counties/municipalities) for coordinating demands and outcomes on more general employment issues.

At the same time, the union cartels have been able to overcome the border problems between the confederations. At present, the two cartels in the public sector, CFU and KTO, cover employees in the three large confederations (which also organize private sector employees). However, this has not resulted in a transition from normal to minimum wage agreements. Instead, local wage pools have been set aside since 1987. Local pay increases are now, as in the private sector, negotiated between the central level bargaining rounds every second year, and the pools represent a substantial innovation, since part of the pay increase can now include individual pay increases. The local wage pools increased in size at the 1989 bargaining round, and again in 1991. Since 1993 they have amounted to just under 1 percent (0.7 percent in counties and municipalities, and 0.9 percent in the state) of the total wage settlement, which commentators have described as a rather modest result after six years of negotiations between the parties (Ibsen et al., 1995, p. 13).

## Method

The wage pools in 37 workplaces in state, counties and municipalities have been studied. However, because of the different degree of decentralization in the three sectors, the workplace concept has had to be defined rather broadly. At the time of the interviews, some of the workplaces already had a pool they could bargain over, while in other cases workplaces shared a pool (due to management preferences to keep the power of discretion in the bargaining process at higher organizational levels). The term *workplace* was therefore defined as a physical entity, which could range from an office in a larger department, e.g. an institute at a university, to a whole institution, e.g. a municipality (Ibsen et al., 1995, p. 25). Due to this broad definition, the analysis contains both a vertical dimension, i.e. the identification of *paths of decentralization* or lack of decentralization, and a horizontal dimension, i.e. in the comparisons between workplaces and across sectors (Ibsen et al., 1995, pp. 13ff). Individual workplaces are thus both small case studies, interesting in their own right, and entities used to identify different paths within each sector. The focus is both on the particularities of the individual case studies and on indicators of mechanisms across cases. The variations and similarities between the two could indicate the possibility of convergence over time.

One of the key issues in localizing the paths of decentralization was to find the factors which acted as barriers. In other words, why did the implementation stop, or why did it cause so many difficulties and conflicts in some areas? To try to answer this, we found it important to identify management strategies at higher levels and the strategies of the local trade union branches. Identifying the paths thus also involved analyzing the two sets of strategies at several organizational levels and how the two parties seemed to work internally.

The data collected included interviews with managers (often personnel managers) and shop stewards (or trade union representatives), more than 200 in-depth interviews in all (an average of 5 to 6 interviews per workplace). Parallel to this 4,046 questionnaires were distributed among public sector employees, of which 1,912 were returned, (47 percent answered) (Andersen et al., 1994, p. 13). The reason for including employees' attitudes to the wage pools is that the study aimed at uncovering a larger variety of barriers, and, in particular, to illuminate rank-and-file members' and employees' attitudes to top-level trade union representatives and public sector managers.

The workplaces were randomly selected across sectors, size, geography and groups of employees, and the study therefore included actors with a broad range of political opinions on local wage pools. In some places, trade unions opposed to wage pools dominated (e.g. nurses at hospitals), while in other workplaces neutral or positive trade unions outnumbered the critical groups (e.g. economists and lawyers at ministries). It was similarly anticipated that management preferences would be characterized by a large variation, i.e. those further down the hierarchy would depart from official policy, particularly considering local managers' preconditions for a satisfactory and fair distribution of the pay increases. The interview schedule and the questionnaire mainly focused on the period 1993-95 , i.e. events during the latest bargaining round.

## Local strategies of pay bargaining

The local wage pools have first and foremost meant an increasing diversity in pay bargaining practices. The traditions of bureaucratic wage systems and centralized pay bargaining, resulting in a highly homogeneous way of distributing pay and pay increases, have in this respect been replaced by a variety of practices. Due to the lack of common traditions in this area and the large variety of possible ways of using wage pools, no best practice has emerged. It is possible to identify similarities across the cases, however, i.e. the behaviour of local actors can be systematized, and common patterns of development seem to emerge over time.

*Management and trade union strategies*

Since 1987, personnel and line managers, trade union representatives and shop stewards at many public workplaces have faced the task of implementing local wage pools. Table 12.1 presents management and trade union strategies, and also tries to identify the main outcomes of the interaction of these. By focusing both on process and outcome aspects (in practice it is difficult to separate the two), we hope to illustrate the often very vague link between strategies and outcome. With the risk of exaggerating the behavioural consistency of the parties, it is possible to identify at least three main patterns of behaviour in the pay bargaining process, to which the term strategy has been applied. However, the majority of the workplaces are characterized by aspects of all three models, in different time periods. An important distinction in the table is the level of activity (whether the parties are passive or active in the process).

With the first strategy, where shop stewards act in the interests of the union (in a more radical manner), local wage pools often seem to produce conflict, especially if management insists on deciding who should receive pay increases. Some managers regard this as the first step towards reforming a rather old-fashioned pay system based on seniority. Decentralization is seen by the unions as a problem, because it can mean that pay increases are being individualized (decentralization is transformed into individualization). In the first bargaining round, the result was that no resources were distributed at all in these workplaces. More recently, different types of agreements have been reached, after mediation at central level. If local management express a more collectivist attitude, compromises emerge when unions change towards a more pragmatic strategy. One way of reaching a compromise is to split the pay increases, with half the money being distributed by management and the other half by the shop stewards. Whereas management often prefer to spread the pay increases over several departments in order to help line managers increase employee motivation, the unions often distribute their part evenly between groups. In situations where local management is passive, trade unions have to work for the pay increases themselves, apply for the money at a higher organizational level, and they also have to make sure it is distributed fairly. This seems to be the outcome of the passive by passive combination, i.e. the unions ignore the local wage pools for political reasons, but when they realise that other groups or workplaces have received the pay increases instead, they start to apply themselves, due to pressure from members.

**Table 12.1**
**The distribution of local wage pools under different combinations of management and trade union strategies**

| | Management strategy | | |
|---|---|---|---|
| Stop steward strategy | Individualistic (active) | Collectivistic (active) | Passive |
| Radical or solidary (active) | Few resources are distributed; conflict common. | Compromise between management preferences (often distributed to departments) and trade union demands (equal distribution between groups). | Similar to centralized collective bargaining (pay increases, if any, are distributed equally between the groups). |
| Cooperative (active) | Compromise: management preferences for individual increases are merged with trade union demands for general principles. | Principles for distribution are formulated with regard to development of work-places and individuals. | Trade unions try to develop principles and maximize the number of employees receiving pay increases. |
| Passive | Management prerogative rules. General principles for pay increases are seldom developed. | Management decides primarily, but ensures that no groups lose out. | Few resources are distributed, mainly due to lack of interest. |

When shop stewards are more cooperative and management has more individualistic preferences, the union will often use general principles to determine who receives the pay increases, whereas management is guided by the behaviour of individual employees. This seems to be the case most often, i.e. management wants to change the individual incentive structure, while the unions want to apply objective and functional criteria. These two approaches are only rarely in conflict, because the two parties often end up choosing the same employees. In other words, those expressing the 'right' attitudes are often fulfilling objective criteria on qualifications, type of tasks performed, etc. The bargaining ends up as a compromise which management is able to accept, since it gives them the possibility of rewarding a few hand-picked employees. Similarly, if both sides have the same cooperative attitude, the process of joint regulation will include close cooperation before the bargaining round (the actual bargaining process runs very smoothly, and only includes the formal confirmation). Here, both parties develop new criteria for distributing pay increases and correcting the imbalances produced by the bureaucratic pay system. Fairness seems to dominate, i.e. the groups who lost out in the last bargaining rounds have better chances of receiving pay increases. In other words, norms of fairness are maintained, even though it has become more difficult for the actors to keep an overall view of the process at the same time as new criteria are developed. In the last situation, shop stewards have a cooperative attitude while management is basically passive. Here, the union often tries to maximize local pay increases and distribute them equally between the groups, i.e. no group must lose out, especially the smallest. Management's motive for remaining passive can be lack of interest due to the size of the wage pools (they are considered too small), or a lack of interest in ensuring that employees receive the increases.

Finally, local union representatives can avoid the bargaining process for ideological reasons, lack of interest (because of the limited scale of the pay increases or because there is no chance of getting them), or because there is no shop steward present. Where local management is individualistic, the local wage pools appear as a management tool, giving individual managers the power to decide how many and who will receive a pay increase. In this case, management disregards formal criteria, which seems to produce some of the discontent with local wage pools, inasmuch as employees feel they have no chance of getting a pay increase unless they belong to the group of employees management prefers. In the situation where management has collective preferences, one of its main jobs is to distribute the pay increases while at the same time making sure that no individual (who deserves a pay increase) or group is ignored. The last situation, where both management and trade unions are passive, results in very few pay increases, even though individual employees themselves can apply at higher levels.

While the first union strategy was characteristic of the majority of workplaces, the cooperative strategy has become more common. Several of the shop stewards stressed the difficulty of cooperating with managers who do not do all they can to ensure their employees' rights. Shop stewards are seldom able to obtain pay increases without management agreeing. The strategies used by the parties are thus often determined by the strategy of the other side. The other side's bargaining strength is also an important factor, though not necessarily in the classical sense that weakness on the other side is considered an advantage. The case studies show that trade unions prefer an active management group ready to negotiate over pay increases; they also prefer management to have a cooperative attitude in matters affecting both workplace and employees. The cooperative strategy can, however, be of limited success, especially in cases where the bargaining process takes place centrally, at levels above the workplace. If, in such cases, the parties ignore workers recommended by both managers and shop stewards, and instead give pay increases to other employees in their attempt to reach a compromise, it will result in discontent both from local management, shop stewards, and particularly those employees who had expected to get a raise.

Even though the unions have regarded local wage pools as problematic, due to the lack of solidarity involved, the different strategies used by local managers in the 37 workplaces surveyed do not point to any deliberate trend to bypass trade unions. In all the cases, shop stewards were considered to be parties in the bargaining process as long as they had an active attitude. Notwithstanding, it is still possible to find workplaces where management prerogative prevails, and where the participation of shop stewards mainly has a legitimizing effect (the bargaining process is only a formal briefing). By contrast, in some cases, unions took the initiative to build up local clubs (often including 2-3 unions). Here, competencies in pre- and post-bargaining issues, i.e. coordinating demands beforehand and communicating the results to members, had a very positive effect on the outcome and on members' attitudes to the trade union role. In this way, local pay bargaining made the unions more visible, i.e. members were able to see shop stewards 'fighting' for their pay increases, and at the same time illustrated the difficulties the shop stewards were facing.

## Conclusion

In contrast to the period before 1987, pay is now a central employment issue in the public sector. Even though only marginal resources have been distributed according to new principles, i.e. local wage pools still represent less than one percent of the total wage sum, they seem to have a much more profound impact on the behaviour of local management and shop stewards. In other words, the symbolic value is much larger than the actual (measurable) outcome.

The stereotype of the highly collectivistic public sector manager has to some extent been undermined. In some workplaces, management still employs a highly individualistic strategy, mainly distributing pay increases to staff they favour, and this didn't seem to cause any problems where trade unions were passive. Other managers tried to distribute the pools without creating too many conflicts, especially at the beginning of the period. Pedersen (1996, p. 15) has called this a state of *cease-fire* between management and market-oriented principles on the one hand and traditional principles of equal distribution between groups on the other. Pluralistic perspectives were therefore present, i.e. in some workplaces the interests of the parties seems to a large extent to be shared — where managers and employees are in the same union, for example. However, it is also possible to identify classical conflicts due to a low level of trust, created by management as well as by the union. Here, both parties seem to favour a more adversarial relationship. This did however not include management attempts to negotiate pay increases directly with employees, thereby bypassing the union. In this case, managers were mainly emphasizing their ability to manoeuvre, i.e. insisting on the necessity for more individual ways of rewarding employees who excelled.

In some workplaces, management distributed pay increases according to the logic of a zero-sum game, i.e. distributing a fixed sum of money among different trade unions. Unsurprisingly, this led to union rivalry. In other workplaces, the two sides were more interested in working together to increase the total pay sum. Local wage pools often seem to reinforce existing patterns of relations between management and employees. In some workplaces, wage pools were an opportunity for employees to express their dissatisfaction with employment conditions. In other workplaces, management regarded local wage pools as an additional opportunity to cooperate with experienced shop stewards. Local wage pools do not result in negative attitudes to local managers being reversed. On the contrary, the views of the shop stewards seemed to be reinforced by management actions, i.e. an unpopular manager became even more unpopular when pay increases were considered to be distributed unfairly. In this light, management's ability to 'buy' change was rather limited.

At the beginning of the period, both shop stewards and local managers faced several (collective) problems in building up the bargaining 'machinery' and individual strategies. In this respect, central level employers have been much more successful, inasmuch as the bargaining arenas are now in place and the parties at local level have sorted out the practicalities. In workplaces with a more paternalistic management attitude, the unions have been unable to distribute pay increases fairly (according to trade union values), though they still have to participate in legitimizing an 'unfair' distribution. Since the wage pools are the subject of bargaining between the parties, both the trade unions and the employers are contributing to some extent to the legitimacy of the system — in the union's case by providing a sort of democratic control over the system. Even though the participation of weak trade unions leads to the legitimization of management decisions (Sandberg 1984, p. 115), the strategy of obstructing local bargaining showed no success in the long run. Management's possibility for distributing pay increases to other groups of employees has made even the most resistant trade union accept local wage pools. In many cases, this has just as much a pragmatic as a normative basis. This conclusion seems to be in line with the argument presented by Sandberg (1984, p. 116), who observed that the combination of participation and mobilization is problematic.

The strategy of building up competencies seems much more promising; the first step towards building new trade union strategies therefore includes the production of information and training of shop stewards in the *technicalities* of wage pools, i.e. how to act before, during, and after the bargaining process. Only in very few cases does this change into more active trade union policies for developing the workplace, however. The mutual need for managers and trade unions to make staff participate and emphasize the possibility of developing people both in relation to work and participation in trade union activities (Sandberg, 1984, p. 114) has been neglected in many cases. Trade union strategies which have emphasized both participation and bargaining, and served to develop competencies *through* these processes, could easily be taken a step further, by developing skills in work organization and production issues. Many of the future problems facing public workplaces seem to cross the traditional border between management and employees, and between different groups of employees.

## References

Andersen, T., Helmer, J., Ibsen, F., Pedersen, D. and Stamhus, J. (1994), *Medarbejdere og lokalløn - en spørgeskemaundersøgelse,* Forlaget Kommuneinformation, København.

Baglioni, G. and Crouch, C. (eds.) (1990), *European industrial relations: The challenge of flexibility*, Sage, London.

Beadle, R. (1993), *Public sector pay: In search of sanity*, The Social Market Foundation, London.

Beaumont, P.B. (1992), *Public sector industrial relations*, Routledge, London.

Brown, W. (1993), *Enterprise bargaining systems. International case studies*, Background Paper No. 33, Economic Planning Advisory Council, Australia.

Due, J. and Madsen. J. S. (1988), *Når der slås søm i, overenskomstforhandlinger og organisationskultur,* DJØFs Forlag, København.

Due, J. and Madsen, J. S. (1990), 'Centraliseret decentralisering', i *Årbog for arbejderbevegelsens historie*, Selskabet til Forskning i Arbejderbevegelsens Historie, København.

Due, J., Madsen. J. S. and Jensen, C. S. (1993), *Den danske model*, DJØFs Forlag, København.

Elvander, N. (1988), *Den svenska modellen: Löneförhandlingar och inkomstpolitik 1982-1986*, Allmänna Förlaget, Stockholm.

Ferner, A. (1991), *Changing public sector industrial relations in Europe*, Warwick Papers in Industrial Relations, No. 37, University of Warwick, Industrial Relations Unit, Coventry.

Ferner, A. and Hyman, R. (eds.) (1992), *Industrial relations in the new Europe*, Basil Blackwell, Oxford.

Fox, A, (1974), *Beyond contract: work: Power and trust relations,* Faber & Faber, London.

Friedman, A. L. (1977), *Industry and labour: Class struggle at work and monopoly capitalism*, MacMillan, London.

Ibsen, F. and Stamhus, J. (1993), *Fra central til decentral lønfastsættelse,* DJØFs Forlag, København.

Ibsen, F. and DELFA-gruppen (1995), *Lokalløn i den offentlige sektor,* Forlaget Kommuneinformation, København.

Jonsson, E. (ed.) (1992), *Belöningar och effektivitet i offentlig förvaltning,* Studenterlitteratur, Lund.

Niland, J., Brown, W. and Hughes, B. (1991), *Breaking new ground: Enterprise bargaining and agency agreements for the Australian public service,* Report for the Australian Minister for Industrial Relations.

Pedersen, D. (1996), Lokalløn i Danmark, in Lægreid, P. and Pedersen, O. K. (eds.), *Forvaltningspolitik og personaleorganisationer*, DJØFs Forlag, København (forthcoming).

Purcell, J. and Ahlstrand, B. (1994), *Human resource management in the multi-divisional company*, University Press, Oxford.

Sandberg, Å. (ed.) (1984), *Framtidsfrågor på arbetsplatsen,* Arbetslivscentrum, Varia rapport nr. 45, Stockholm.

Scheuer, S. (1988), Struktur og forhandling, in *Årbog for arbejderbevægelsens historie 1990*, SFAH, København.

Scheuer, S. (1991), *Leaders and laggards: Who goes first in bargaining rounds?*, University of Warwick, Industrial Relations Research Unit, Public Leverhulme Lecture, Coventry.

Sjölund, M. (1995), *Transition in government policies. The problem of legitimacy,* Unpublished manuscript, University of Örebro, Novemus School of Public Affairs, Örebro.

Udvalget om større fleksibilitet i det offentlige aftale- og overenskomstsystem (1988), *90'ernes aftaler og overenskomster. Betænkning 1150*, Statens Information, København.

# 13 A new political unionism: Welfare workers and union feminism in Sweden

*Winton Higgins*

The Swedish union movement has often been taken as the archetype of political unionism, that is, of a union tradition that goes well beyond the ambit of unions' conventionally limited socio-economic role, and that abandons western union movements' normal political deference towards their affiliated political parties. Political unionism can also entail transcending sectional interest in favour of universalistic values, such as the pursuit of equality and a democratic associational life in all spheres of social practice. As early as the late 1940s the Swedish Trade Union Confederation (LO) broke away from the tutelage of the Social Democratic Party, that originally spawned it six decades earlier, when it began to incubate the Rehn-Meidner Model (Higgins, 1985). That model not only lay the basis for the whole labour movement's subsequent approach to public economic management; it was the core element of 'the Swedish model' for postwar economic development up to the early 1980s, and the social priorities, institutions and mobilizing rhetoric of labour that it fostered remain highly visible today. Swedish unionism has maintained a direct and independent role in public policy formation ever since. Without political unionism, the internationally impressive facade of Swedish social democracy would have been little more than that — a mere façade.

---

I would like to thank Annika Baude, Åsa Nelander and Lennart Svensson for their invaluable help in this research. I would also like to thank them, Geoff Dow and Cecilia Åse for their insightful comments on an earlier version of this chapter. My 'The Swedish Municipal Workers' Union — A Study in the New Political Unionism', *Economic and Industrial Democracy* Vol. 17 no. 2 (1996) presents some of the material herein in more expanded form. Address correspondence to Winton Higgins, School of History, Philosophy and Politics, Macquarie University, NSW 2109, Australia.

In hindsight, however, the reform tradition so created bore a deep equivocation. As Acker (1992, p. 283) has suggested, two 'discourses of reform' formed around this development. The first dealt with the economy, growth, productivity, wage-labour and class; the second with women, children, the family and the welfare state's caring services. Both were essential to social democracy's modernizing project, but the relationship between them was bedevilled by opposing priorities and the tendency of the first discourse to overshadow and distort the second. And while LO's political unionism articulated the first discourse, this priority frustrated the aspirations expressed in the second and served its female constituency — not least those employed in the caring services of the welfare state — poorly.

Yet LO's largest union, the Swedish Municipal Workers' Union (Svenska Kommunalarbetareförbundet — hereafter Kommunal), which for at least the last decade has had an 80 percent female membership representing roughly half LO's women members, organized the workers in precisely this sector. The latter exemplified the gross gender inequities in the workplace and labour market, and women's effective exclusion from union affairs, that the first discourse of reform colluded in. A revolt against the gender order in worklife, and the version of modernization it represented, were already brewing in Kommunal at the beginning of the 1990s, when gender relations in Swedish society at large suddenly erupted over conservative attacks on the welfare services that women relied upon to free them for paid work, and in many instances, that provided them with their jobs as well. Union feminism played a prominent part in a resurgence of the women's movement, which was now inspired by a third-wave feminism strongly critical of the limitations of the official reformist approach to fostering gender equality. Kommunal, whose membership bore the brunt of the conservative attack on welfare, was thus well placed to exhibit the new union feminist politics, and its recent development demonstrates that its agenda has farreaching implications for both a wider ambit for political unionism and for the democratic renewal of worklife.

## Women, paid work and the caring services of the state

Recent feminist theory (for instance Pateman, 1988 and Jónasdóttir, 1992) emphasizes the specifically *modern* sources — especially enshrined in the canon of liberal individualism and in the ascendancy of instrumental rationality — of women's subordination in western societies today. This insight radically contradicts the basic premise in the social democratic approach to fostering gender equality. According to it, gender inequality points to the survival of 'old-fashioned' prejudices and practices that 'progress' in the form of its own modernizing mission will naturally erode, with a little help from consensual anti-discrimination of the type prescribed by second wave feminism. For its adherents this basic premise rules out the possibility that a modernization process itself can actually reproduce women's subordination, and that its bearers can actively collude in the latter. The two discourses of reform appear in this view as simply the two sides of the same coin.

Given the power of the modernization myth one can understand the enthusiasm expressed by supporters of gender equality (above all in Dahlström, 1962) when, in the late fifties and early sixties, Swedish women began their wholesale entry into paid employment. Like other western European countries undergoing rapid industrial expansion, Sweden had to choose between women and guest workers as the source of a new labour supply, and the choice by and large fell on women. They were thereupon seen to be breaking out of their confinement to the private, domestic sphere — the locus of their subordination, dependence and exclusion from the power and privileges of the public, economic sphere — to enter upon a new, public world of equal empowerment, opportunity and personal autonomy. Women were at last to gain entry into postwar 'employment society', in which substantive citizenship depends on paid work.

A necessary precondition to women — including carers of small children and of other dependents such as the frail aged and the handicapped — taking paid work was the welfare state assuming responsibility for a significant part of their caring functions. The caring activities of the welfare state, located in the municipalities and counties, in turn became a vital labour market for women; for some time now, around two thirds of the female workforce in Sweden works in the public sector.

Over three decades later, there can be no doubt about the success of the drive to recruit women into the paid workforce. Their participation rate in it trails men's by a slim margin (81 percent as against 85 percent); their comparative hourly wage rates are impressive on international standards (90 percent of the male rate in the private sector and 84 percent in the public sector); and they are actually more unionized than men (87.1 percent as against the male rate of 84 percent in the blue-collar sector) (NORD, 1994:3, pp. 83, 92; LO, 1994a, table 2). Results like these, together with Swedish women's unique political representation — they occupy 42 percent of the seats in parliament and half the ministerial posts in the present social democratic government — seem to confirm the gender equalizing triumph of the modernizing project.

A closer look at women's worklife and its outcomes, however, soon dispels any illusions that it has represented the royal road out of subordination to equal socio-economic citizenship. Nearly half of all women employees under 25 years of age work part time, and in the blue-collar sector 53 percent of all women do so, many involuntarily. Women's jobs have been particularly subject to casualization, and 'permanent temporary status' is now widespread. The benefits of female wage *rates* comparable to men's hardly translates into equal incomes in this environment, especially given the effect of wage differentials and interrupted and parttime status on post-retirement incomes under the national superannuation scheme. These factors leave the average adult woman with just 66.1 percent of the income of her male counterpart (NORD, 1994:3, pp. 88 and 92; *LO granskar*, 1995, p. 2). In Kommunal's own area of the labour market, this inequity is particularly striking. As late as 1992 the ten most common male occupations enjoyed average monthly fulltime wages over 12,000 kronor, while average fulltime wages for the ten most common female wages all fell below that mark. To this should be added the fact that 60 percent of Kommunal's women work part time, and 37 percent do so involuntarily (Kommunal, 1994a).

Pronounced gender segregation on the Swedish labour market incubates inequities of this kind, and arguably even more dispiriting aspects of women's experience of work. Their incidence of high occupational health and safety risks, of inconvenient working hours and split shifts, lack of freedom and discretion on the job, lack of training and career development opportunities all demonstrably — and often drastically — exceed men's (LO, 1993/4:3, diagrams 10 and 15 to 18, and table 5; LO 1993/4:5, table 5).

When Kyle (1979) published the first major study of women's experience of paid work she entitled it *Female Guest Worker in Male Society*. She thus put her finger precisely on the role women were unwittingly recruited to in the Swedish economy — as the cheap, expendable and peripheral workforce. But unlike actual guest workers, their role was made permanent by what Hirdman (1987) theorized — for the purposes of a landmark public inquiry into the distribution of power in Swedish society — as 'the gender system,' a constitutive element of organizational life. Two props or 'logics' support it in worklife in particular: gender segregation by occupation, and the male norm — that is, the common implicit assumption that the 'normal' worker is a man, and women on the labour market constitute a special, anomalous case (Hirdman, 1987, pp. 197-8). The gender system as the harbinger of women's subordination had simply followed them as they moved from the domestic sphere to the labour market, and it had thereby bitterly frustrated the feminist optimism that had originally accompanied that move. The highly modern gender system appears unfazed by gender-neutral anti-discrimination measures as the latter enjoyed no leverage on the logics of a segregated labour market and the male norm implicit in work organization (see in general Acker et al., 1994; Baude, 1992; and Wikander, 1992).

The union movement, as a main bearer of the first discourse of reform referred to above, has been deeply implicated in the gender system. It has stood out in Swedish society as a conspicuous laggard in according women adequate representation in leadership, delegate and negotiating positions, despite recurring and spirited criticism from Qvist's survey of 1974 to the public inquiry into women's underrepresentation in Swedish associational life of 1987 (SOU 1987:19; and see Bergkvist, 1994, pp. 126-45). Qvist pointed to the obvious but crucial link between the absence of women from the decisionmaking and negotiating functions of the union movement and the poor outcomes for women workers that the unions have achieved (Qvist, 1974, pp. 96 and 127). Kommunal was a glaring case in point: as late as the mid-eighties around 80 percent of its leadership and functionaries were men while 80 percent of its membership were women (Svensson, Aronsson and Höglund, 1990, p. 136).

Two factors perpetuated this underrepresentation. First, the labour movement traditionally ruled out separate women's caucuses on the oft-quoted dictum from the founding father of Swedish social democracy, Hjalmar Branting, that 'class comes before sex' (Karlsson, 1981, p. 16). The sex of the class' representatives was thus deemed irrelevant, and anyway working women were said to have more interests in common with their class brothers than with other women. Second, the unions' organizational culture is markedly masculine — demands on functionaries and meeting times usually assume freedom from domestic responsibility; meeting format and procedure are typically impersonal, bureaucratic and turgid; and women activists meet forms of male resistance that render them inaudible, invisible and objects of harassment (Hermansson, 1993; Thorgren, 1994; Eriksson, 1995).

From the early 1980s women's worklife increasingly came under the added threat of withdrawal of resources from the caring services of the welfare state as social democratic economic policy fell under the influence of 'the Treasury right' — a withdrawal that affected Kommunal's membership above all. The government covered this withdrawal with the internationally conventional rhetoric that it was part of a 'reform' of the sector that would deliver greater efficiency and 'choice' to the users/'consumers' by commercializing the services and introducing 'market solutions,' especially in the forms of a buyer and seller relationship between funding authority and care provider and unit costing. And as is *de rigueur* with traditional economic liberal projects of this sort, the mode of implementation was highly technocratic. As municipal notables fell into the fashion of 'playing private enterprise' (Hedlund, 1994, p. 103) they spawned a veritable army of consultants personifying 'abstract and elitist trendiness' (von Otter and Svensson, 1995, p. 10) to plan the top-down reorganization of the services as part of their corporatization and commercialization.

To the extent that these changes went ahead they were usually highly regressive for community, users and workers alike (see for example Socialstyrelsen, 1994; Svärd, 1994a and 1994b). In being demoted to the role of 'consumers' the citizens of local government areas — actual and potential users of the services in question — lost the right of both insight into, and 'voice' about, how these public services were organized; they were left with the mere choice between prepackaged, commodified services whose nature and quality they had no input into. Even more disempowered were the care workers, as their jobs disappeared altogether (100,000 did so by the early nineties) or were reorganized by self-styled experts along Taylorist lines without consultation, and their new terms of employment left them open to casualization, the stress and other occupational risks attendant upon understaffing, and the 'flexibility' of inconvenient and unpredictable working hours. In a slack labour market, degradation of working and employment conditions became the key to cost advantage.

Kommunal, LO's and Sweden's biggest union with 665,000 members representing the most disadvantaged workers in the country's labour market, thus faced a formidable — and political — challenge in simultaneously defending women's working conditions and the welfare state against an unholy alliance of the gender system and the economic fundamentalism of a resurgent right in both government and opposition (Boréus, 1994). Let us now turn to how it met this challenge.

## Worklife reform

What made Kommunal's response to the challenge markedly political was that, far from trying to defend a status quo, it went on the offensive in aid of a democratic associational life in both service provision and in its own organization.

The union's first modest experiments in reorganizing services in the early 1980s distanced themselves from the older, bureaucratic disempowerment of both user and worker as much as it would later fend off corporatized versions of this disempowerment. The first of these experiments was the initiative of a local organizer in the small municipal of Ljusnarsberg. In order to head off threatened lay-offs and a slide in working conditions in the homecare service for the aged and handicapped, the local branch of the union undertook a consultative process with both care workers and users of the service to reorganize it in the interests of greater cost efficiency, but also to make the work itself more rewarding and to minimise occupational health and safety risks (Svensson et al., 1990, pp. 146-7).

The success of this small project pointed to a viable democratic alternative to the traditional rationalizers' top down approach to reorganization. Projects with the same twin goals of cost efficiency and greater job and service quality thus began in the much larger municipalities of Örebro and Norrköping. They proved an even more convincing argument for a distinctively democratic, bottom-up and from-within reforming process involving both workers and users.

Lennart Svensson, who would play a major role in inspiring and diffusing this approach, especially in homecare, gleaned the lessons from these projects in a book length report (Svensson, 1986). He pointed to the need to empower the worker collectives in each case, especially in setting up autonomous work groups, and located the problems in the existing care services in the hierarchical chains of command and compartmentalized administrative units. The book lay heavy emphasis on the democratic *process* that produced the reforms and the crucial role of the union in facilitating it. But, he argued, traditional union structures and routines obstructed this role. They were male-dominated, and so highly unrepresentative and off-putting for the women in the services concerned. Retention of these structures and routines was also self-defeating: the rank and file enthusiasm and activism that the reorganization process stimulated did not carry over into greater involvement in the union's own affairs (Svensson, 1986, ch. 9).

The union centrally then took the decision to generalize the democratic approach to worklife renewal, and in 1988 it launched its training programme *Kom vidare i vården* ('Come further in care'), which was designed to prepare workers to play an independent role in the democratic reorganization of the caring services. The programme took its inspiration from both Kommunal's earlier experiences and from 'the Växjö model' that two psychiatric nurses had developed in residential psychiatric care in that city (Lindroth, 1994, p. 11). The union allocated 20 million kronor to the programme, and drew into it members of associated unions that were affected by changes in the sector. In so doing it helped pioneer an initiative that would later affect much wider groups on the Swedish labour market — collaboration between blue- and white-collar groups. Around 150,000 Kommunal members underwent training under the auspices of this programme, which has ensured a wide diffusion throughout the care sector. Its prescription for a democratic reform process ('bottom up' and 'from within') and its formula of autonomous work groups now define the standard approach to effectivizing care services (see Lindroth, 1994 for an extensive evaluation).

In 1991 in Malung municipality Kommunal pioneered a new programme, *Kom an då* ('Come on then' — later shortened to *Kom an*) which was even more focussed on preempting private consultants and other traditional rationalizers in achieving financial savings. The pilot scheme this time was roadmaking and maintenance, a typical male-dominated service. The municipality had demanded a 10 percent cost saving over three years, and Kommunal's project — which put in place a flatter work organization, autonomous work groups and better working conditions without redundancies — returned a 10.5 percent saving in the first year (Kommunal, 1993, pp. 48-9). After this success the union heavily promoted *Kom an* so that it complemented and partly replaced its predecessor. It took the further significant step of incorporating its own consultancy firm, Komanco, with its own budget and housed in the union's head office in Stockholm. Komanco now operates in close co-operation with Kommunal's energetic educational programmes. Its main architect, Lars-Åke Almqvist, co-ordinates this enterprise, which has overseen projects in a quarter of Sweden's municipalities as well as several county administrations and private corporations (*Kommunal-Nytt*, 17/94). Around 50,000 local government employees have participated in its training programmes, and like its predecessor, it stimulated co-operation between Kommunal's blue-collar workers and the white-collar colleagues in the municipal sector, especially those in the local government clerical union, SKTF.

Kommunal's worklife reform strategy offers municipalities a self-sustaining process of everyday rationalization — to adopt the parlance of industrial management — through tapping the 'silent knowledge' of the working collectivity with intimate hands-on experience of each specific work situation as to how cost and quality gains can be achieved in their arena (Utbult, 1995). It initiates a continuous, interactive process between the work team, responsible organs of local government, personnel from allied services and other care providers, users and the local community whose needs the caring services have to respond to and whose resources they have to call upon. We see here a comprehensive alternative to the traditional rationalizers' reactive and one-off quick fixes that abstract from the concrete nature of welfare services and do not take stock of local needs and resources (above all those unique to each work team). In a highly unionized labour market like Sweden's, Kommunal's modus operandi also enjoys the advantage that employees take a leading role in, rather than resist, the reform effort. The latter in turn offers workers and their union a vehicle for pursuing many of its longterm policies on pay and conditions, such as the demand for fulltime status and a shorter working week across the board, and equalization of women's and men's wage rates through, among other ways, skill development and job evaluation. (See in general Svensson et al., 1990; von Otter and Svensson, 1995; and Kommunal, 1994b. For similar experiences in the democratization of home care under the auspices of the Worklife Fund see Aronsson et al., 1995.)

Lennart Svensson and his collaborators in the eighties distilled ten theses for democratic effectivization of welfare services (Svensson et al, 1990, pp. 22-35 and 178-92; von Otter and Svensson, 1995, pp. 36-7), and these constitute the basis of Komanco's method today. They may be summarized as follows:

1 Reorganization takes time. It is a process rather than a single event, and one that continues to sustain itself on the basis of the employees' enthusiasm, sense of responsibility and rising job satisfaction.

2 The impetus in the reform process should come from below and within, from care workers and service users — even if the support of responsible authorities is also vital to provide resources and continuity.

3 Equals learn from equals — the horizontal exchange of information, experience and support between colleagues and with those working in adjacent functions are the most important learning tools and social resources in renewal.

4 Practice rather than theory is the starting point for reform. Welfare workers must learn to value their own experience and competence rather than being overridden and feeling inhibited by outsiders' self-styled 'expertise.' Theory has a role to play later in contextualizing proposals and providing critical distance.

5 A vital resource in renewal work is 'live wires' who generate new ideas and above all galvanise their workmates as a collectivity. The gelling of worker collectives brings the greatest gains in efficiency and quality.

6 The union has a key role to play in renewal work — through various forms of material and intellectual support, co-ordination, education programmes, mobilization and programmatic direction, as with Kommunal's two training programmes referred to above.

7 Instead of being put through an often counterproductive and expensive standard educational programme, the worker groups can learn collectively

by using the study circle, which is the traditional form of educational activity in the Swedish union movement. Conventional training certainly has its contribution to make, but should not displace the collective learning process.

8 Reforms usually only succeed when they bring real benefits to the workers themselves — in job security, more freedom and influence in the way work is carried out, and better general working conditions.

9 A serious reform-minded employer should be prepared to commit money and other resources to the developmental process and understand that the benefits will accrue over time.

10 To participate in the renewal process is personally developing and enlarges the individual's competence and ability to meet new situations and constantly rising demands on skill in the wider labour market.

## The politics of worklife reform: The defence of the welfare state

Kommunal's approach to the renewal and defence of the welfare state builds on a pointed, macro-social critique of the inapposite micro-economic criteria deployed by welfare opponents and traditional rationalizers. At the same time it is a democratic approach consciously opposing the ascendant technocratic (neomanagerialist) one. It empowers welfare workers individually and collectively, as well as the users whom they meet daily and can consult in group discussions. Kommunal's strategy also employs forms of organization and learning that are traditional to popular movements — above all in the study circle and, as we shall see, in the networking of the women's movement. Lennart Svensson and his colleagues express its ultimate logic as 'the transformation of the public bureaucracy into a popular movement' (Svensson et al, 1990, p.188).

To bolster its macro-social critique of economic fundamentalism, Kommunal has shown that if a care worker is laid off this may appear a substantial saving of a wage in accounting terms, but she or he does not thereby cease to receive an income from the public purse. After one calculates what various public authorities then have to pay out in unemployment and other benefits, only 12,000 a year has been saved and 200,000 kronor in services has been lost (Kommunal, 1994a, pp. 8-9) — to say nothing of the possible human loss and public expense if the individual concerned joins the longterm unemployed, and if the remaining members of the work group sustain a higher level of occupational injury and illness through being overtaxed on the job.

Another common form of micro-economic blindness is to miss the crucial link between well functioning homecare and minimizing the institutionalization of the frail aged and handicapped. To skimp on homecare is to invite massive increases in the residential care budget, as institutionalization is much more expensive than homecare.

## Union feminism and the renewal of union organization

From the end of the 1980s gender relations in Sweden reached something of a crisis point (Åström and Hirdman, 1992) in ways that directly affected Kommunal. The economic liberal revival, visible both in social democratic economic policy and the rightward swing of the 'bourgeois' opposition parties, directly threatened the ambit of quality of welfare services, and thus not only women's job opportunities but also their very ability to free themselves of domestic responsibilities sufficiently to go to work. This threat, and increasing frustration with gender inequities in worklife and union nonchalance towards them, stimulated the first signs of revival of the women's movement, with union feminism to the fore. In September 1991 a conservative government took office after an election in which women's representation in parliament sank from 37.5 to 33.4 percent. The women's movement now became highly visible (Curtin and Higgins, 1995). LO came under considerable pressure to be much more responsive to its one million women members — 46 percent of its membership — and start acting like the 'women's organization of some significance' (Waldemarsson, 1992, p. 105) that its membership in fact made it.

Changes in Kommunal anticipated and contributed to the feminization of LO. In 1989 Lillemor Arvidsson, a nurse's aid from provincial Uddevalla, assumed the leadership of the union, and so became the first chairwoman of any blue-collar union in the country and only the second woman to sit on the LO executive. As the leader of the country's largest union she also took her place on the social democratic party executive. She quickly became a formidable presence in the leadership of the labour movement. Her deep roots in the movement — her mother was a Kommunal member at the time of her birth! — were unassailable, while her plain speaking and fierce loyalty to her female constituency made her a loose cannon on the slippery, polished deck of the social democratic establishment. She quickly became a favourite with the media, and her resignation from the party executive a year after she had joined it in protest at the government's 'crisis package' — she was the only union leader to protest against its wage freeze and strike ban — made her a focus for the women's movement's and other radical opposition to the direction of economic policy.

Under Arvidsson's leadership the structure and routines of Kommunal began to change. There was a steep increase in women's representation. They gained a majority on the union executive, and of the 13 leadership and delegate categories women have constituted a majority in eight since 1993 (Kommunal, 1994a, p. 22). Experiments were initiated in new meeting formats and procedures to encourage women's activism, using smaller meetings based on personal acquaintance from the workplace, simpler procedures and informal language. Making the union organization more 'woman-friendly' in this way has allowed it benefit from the activism generated in the worklife reforms it sponsors. Women's networks, mentor schemes and training programmes within the union are part of the resources it is now mobilizing to this end. As Kommunal's gender equality programme makes clear, women's under-representation is still a problem, and it recommends that the 1997 congress adopt a quota of a minimum 40 percent female representation for all elected union positions (Kommunal, 1994a, pp. 47 and 55). In another clear break with tradition, Kommunal also explicitly identifies itself with the feminist cause (Kommunal, 1994b, p. 10).

Kommunal's initiatives in worklife renewal and feminization of its own organizational life — to say nothing of Lillemor Arvidsson as a role model for women union activists — have made a major contribution to worklife reform strategies and the rise of union feminism in LO. In the mid-eighties the metalworkers' union had taken the lead in proposing a 'solidarity work policy' to in effect displace LO's traditional solidarity wage policy. The nub of the proposal was that new manufacturing systems and work practices demanded rapid changes in skills and more flexible work organization, which were incompatible with insistence on an egalitarian wage structure; in the new circumstances unions should seek to equalize career opportunities instead. Metall's version of worklife reform leaves the process entirely at the gift of management, and as Rianne Mahon (1994) has pointed out, acceptance of management's call for a more dedicated and 'flexible' workforce contains gendered assumptions about freedom from domestic responsibilities that are likely to lock women out of the new career structures for core workers (see also Baude, 1992). The advantage of Kommunal's model is that it puts organized labour in control of the reform agenda and thus in a position to eliminate any jeopardy to women's participation.

The resurgent women's movement in Sweden has organized itself around informal single-sex networks, and many of these have sprung up in Kommunal and the union movement in general. As Maud Eduards (1992) has argued, breaking the taboo against women's separate organizations is a precondition to ending their subordination. Twenty women in LO formed one, Tjejligan ('the women's gang'), in the lead-up to the 1991 election — in clear contravention of the traditional ban on women's caucusing. Surprisingly, the LO leadership not only decided to condone it, but to back it as well with its own financial and organizational resources. Along with Kommunal itself, Tjejligan has become a spectacular expression of union feminism with a membership of 14,000 in 1995 and a politically hardhitting, glossy magazine, *Clara*, sold at news stands throughout the country. Initially formed to highlight women's issues in the 1991 election campaign, Tjejligan's main ongoing role — as with the other networks in the union movement — is to act as a meeting place for women unionists, to support women activists seeking elected office and to act as a reference group for those who are elected. Its entry onto the scene has prompted a new saliency for women's worklife issues in LO's reports and policy documents, and a determination by LO staffers to lift women's representation throughout LO's own organization and those of its affiliates (Quick, 1994; Curtin and Higgins, 1995).

Kommunal itself took a vital step in 1995 to raise its political profile by establishing its own social policy unit, with 21 analysts and publicists, to promote the interests of its members *as citizens* in a properly resourced and well maintained welfare state. This reinforces a familiar pattern in the institutional development of political unionism, whereby higher levels of ambition to articulate and pursue the political interests of organized labour stimulate activism and institutional growth to render union structures adequate to their enhanced role.

## A gender perspective on worklife

A key theme in the new Swedish women's movement is the critique of the gender neutral character of the official approach to gender equality (Eduards, 1991). As I have indicated above, this approach has done little to remove the props or 'logics' of the gender system in worklife — labour market segregation and the male norm. The gender composition of Kommunal's own membership points to the extent of this segregation in welfare services. On the Swedish labour market as a whole, 41 percent of women employees work in occupations that are between 90 and 100 percent female, and another 35 percent work in ones that are between 60 and 90 percent female (NORD, 1994:3, pp. 88 and 92-3; *LO granskar*, 1995, p. 2). For its part, the male norm expresses itself mainly in the skewed social definition of skill that devalues the skills that women in fact exercise in many of their occupations — not least caring ones — and consequently diminishes the economic rewards to women's work (see Jenson, 1989). But the typical failure of work organization to build in allowance for the interface between work and family life (including childbearing) is another expression of the norm which tends to exclude women from more rewarding jobs. Kommunal's bargaining stance and more recent experiences in worklife reform have introduced a gender perspective that concentrates on the specifics of women's pay rates, occupational skills and life patterns to redress gender inequities at work. It thus models the new, 'third-wave' feminist line on gender reform.

In 1993 Kommunal managed to have LO accept the principle of special increases to women's wage rates (*kvinnopotter)* for the purposes of co-ordinated wage negotiations — a triumph in itself, even if its implementation at this level of the wage-fixing process has at least temporarily been thwarted by the LO unions' failing in the 1995 wage round to reach agreement on a common bargaining stance, which has left the unions to negotiate individually. But the mechanism remains on the agenda for Kommunal's own negotiating stance. The second prong in the strategy to raise women's wages is integrated into Kommunal's own adaptation of solidarity work policy with its emphasis on work development and the worker's constant acquisition of new skills (Kommunal, 1993 and 1995a). This adaptation dovetails with the union's commitment to the organizational renewal of municipal services which I reviewed above, and which I will return to briefly below. Training was one of two main issue for the union's 1995 congress (the other being work evaluation — Kommunal, 1995a and 1995b).

Work evaluation is thematically related to the emphasis on skill development, and complements the connection between competence and wage development. But it has a somewhat more radical edge in that it problematizes the social construction of skill and the comparative gendered evaluation of existing work content. As Jane Jenson (1989) has argued, a notion of skill is conventionally read into most male occupations, whereas the competence women bring to their typical occupations is ascribed to a natural talent. Skills are thus achievements and attract economic rewards, whereas natural talents can make no such claims. When men take over women's work (such as cooking) it suddenly becomes an achievement — a skilled and well paid profession. When women take over men's occupations (such as typing) they are correspondingly downgraded. Because job evaluation actually examines the content of work, it carries the possibility of exposing the male norm behind the traditional definitions of skill and the differential rewards that attach to them.

The municipalities of Sundsvall, Örebro, Växjö, Sundsvall and Gävle have hosted projects on work evaluation in the context of a general local government initiative known as KOM (*Kvinnor och män tillsammans* — men and women together) which the Work Environment Fund (*Arbetsmiljöfonden*) funded. Of these the Gävle projects are possibly the most ambitious. They employ much the same methods as those applied in the democratic renewal of welfare services, including the study circle format (and even a much appreciated theatrical revue, 'Helga Wrede,' produced for the KOM programme), and also comes to grips with how gendered wage differentials arose historically (Sandgren and Baude, 1993). The projects thus serve a double purpose — to distil a fairer and more rational basis for comparative wage rates, and to expose for a wide circle of participants gendered assumptions about the content and value of women's and men's work.

Kommunal's mission to tackle gender issues in the organization and evaluation of work attracted a useful ally in 1992 in the Work Life Fund (*Arbetslivsfonden*). It was planned to function for five years from 1990 and was intended to finance projects in workplaces throughout the country, the main aim of which was to reorganise them in order to improve the working environment, especially to eliminate physical and psychological risk factors. The government made much of its aim to thereby abolish the 400,000 worst jobs in the country. A 1.5 percent levy on employers' wage costs provided 11,000 million kronor, which was spent on projects in 25,000 workplaces chosen largely by the fund's branch organizations in the counties.

After two years operation, however, the private sector, and so predominantly male workplaces, were swallowing the lion's share of these resources. Not a single project, for instance, had been started in homecare, which was notorious for its high rate of absenteeism through occupational injury and stress. The fund thereupon set up a special umbrella project, ALFA-Q, to address women's working environment, and of the five occupational areas it prioritised, three fell within Kommunal's area — cleaners and workers in homecare and medical care. The resources the fund could provide were considerable. Within home care 400 workplace programmes together received 340 million kronor and involved 95,000 women and 5,000 men. Medical care was considerably larger — 704 million kronor was spent on 1,100 workplaces and involved 350,000 women and 73,000 men (Boman, 1995, pp. 8-21, 55 and 74).

The projects employed the techniques already reviewed, above all networks and study circles, to mobilise both the frontline workers and their often 'silent knowledge,' and to maximise the diffusion of new, democratic methods for work development. Like Kommunal's own projects in the same spirit, then, ALFA-Q's consciously employed 'the popular movement model' (Boman, 1995, p. 11; see also Aronsson, Astvik, Freed Solfeldt and Svensson, 1995). But the latter made explicit its break with the gender neutral approach 'which in reality is gender blind' as ALFA-Q's final report avers (Boman, 1995, p.

16). The fund's director, as well as those who guided the projects, insisted instead on a 'gender perspective,' and on the projects' being kept separate from conventional gender equality programmes. The projects were intended to see that women reorganised their workplaces themselves with starting points in their own 'life patterns' that were quite different from men's.

Gunilla Fürst, one of the main figures in ALFA-Q, argued that, with this perspective, one could address the main causes of women's subordination on the labour market and unfavourable working conditions. First, cultural assumptions present women's occupations as mere extensions of their domestic work, and therefore not to be enriched through training. Second, women's working and employment conditions usually do not take into consideration their overall life patterns. Third, women's initial subordination at work initiates a vicious circle as their low status gives them low priority in work development and training (Fürst, 1993). These factors, it is worth repeating, are likely to be further activated if LO's solidarity work policy based on work development is implemented in a gender neutral way so as to leave women in their role of 'guest workers in male society.'

In sum, the valuable experiences won through ALFA-Q's temporary intervention in women's workplaces have boosted and highlighted the line of worklife reform that Kommunal has pioneered. Both break with the Swedish gender model, and thus prefigure a real democratization of work and wider social relationships.

## Conclusion

The developments in Kommunal's organization, strategies and political profile that I have traced above, have occurred in hard times — times of drastic cuts in local government budgets, job losses and a technocratic offensive against humane working conditions and welfare services. While the union has checked the last mentioned danger, the economic pressure is likely to continue for some time, given the country's large budget deficit and economic policy direction. As private-sector unions make substantial gains in the present economic climate, the gap between private- and public-sector wages will tend to widen. But these sorts of conditions have stimulated as well as constrained the union's development in the past, and they have little prospect of arresting it now.

A characteristic of political unionism is to rework a sectional interest into a universal one. In company with the women's movement, I suggest, Kommunal has done so in two ways. First, it has defended and enriched the older social democratic ideal of a labour market and comprehensive welfare state that together underpin a just and egalitarian social order by securing the autonomy and dignity of the individual within the context of a democratic associational life. It is a painful irony that it must now defend this ideal against a social democratic government. Second, its policies and practices challenge the longstanding gender model that has arrested progress towards this ideal in the past.

Kommunal is just one union and represents the least empowered and lowest paid corps of workers on the Swedish labour market. Yet its size and new political profile make it impossible to ignore, and it now has considerable avenues for influence and collaboration. It provides LO with the most advanced and widely diffusable strategy for workplace development; it models the transcendence of blue-collar unionism's baneful, male-dominated organizational culture that LO headquarters itself is now trying to reform; and it provides a leading example of the intensifying co-operation between blue- and white-collar unions. It will, as well, continue to receive inspiration from the women's movement and provide the latter with a valuable arena of practical reform. The recurring organizational formats of Sweden's popular movements — study circles and networks — provide both models of reform and means of cross-fertilization within these relationships. Today Kommunal is unique in having given institutional form to a strategy that makes organized labour the driving force rather than the passive object of worklife reform.

The international significance of Kommunal's pioneering project of self-reform and worklife reform lies in its highly replicable approach to deepening workplace democratization and to getting to the vocational roots of the gender system. The efficacy of its approach points to the need for progressive unions to creatively build their commitment to reform into their very structures, as with Komanco. More importantly, Kommunal can have a powerful demonstration effect in showing how one union can go it alone and defy the profoundly anti-democratic and inegalitarian political currents of the day to restore genuine reform to the national political agenda.

## References

Acker, J. (1992), 'Reformer och kvinnor i den framtida välfärdsstaten', in Acker, J. et al, *Kvinnors och mäns liv och arbete,* SNS, Stockholm.

Acker, J. et al (1992), *Kvinnors och mäns liv och arbete*, SNS, Stockholm.

Aronsson, G., Astvik, W., Freed Solfeldt, M. and Svensson, L. (1995), *Kvalitet genom inflytande: Om förändring och utveckling i hemtjänsten*, Arbetslivsinstitutet, Stockholm.

Baude, A. (ed.) (1992), *Visionen om jämställdhet,* SNS, Stockholm.

Bergkvist, C. (1994), *Mäns makt och kvinnors intressen*, Acta Universitatis Upsaliensis, Uppsala.

Boman, A. (1995), *Arbete i utveckling - på kvinnors vis: Slutrapport från Arbetslivsfondens ALFA-Q program*, Arbetslivsfonden, Stockholm.

Boréus, K. (1994), *Högervågen: Nyliberalismen och kampen om språket i svensk offentlig debatt 1969-1989*, Tiden, Stockholm.

Curtin, J. and Higgins, W. (1995), 'Feminism and unionism in Sweden', paper presented to the Fifth Women and Labour Conference at Macquarie University, Sydney.

Dahlström, E. (ed.) (1962), *Kvinnors liv och arbete*, SNS, Stockholm.

Eduards, M. (1991), 'The Swedish gender model: Productivity, pragmatism and paternalism', *West European Politics*, vol. 14, no. 3.

Eduards, M. (1992), 'Against the rules of the game: On the importance of women's collective actions', in Eduards, M. et al, *Rethinking change: Current Swedish feminist research*, HSFR, Stockholm.

Eriksson, A. (1995), 'Kvinnor och jämställdhet: En intervjustudie av nio kvinnor på förbundsnivå inom facket', stencil, Beteendevetenskapliga linjen, Stockholm University.

Fürst, G. (1993), *Satsa på kvinnors arbetsmiljö*, Arbetslivscentrum and Arbetslivsfonden, Stockholm.

Hedlund, G. (1994), 'Kvinnorna och välfärdsstaten: En strid i kommuner och landsting', in *...å andra sidan: Om kvinnors och mäns villkor*, Rabén/Kommunal, Stockholm.

Hermansson, A.-S. (1993), *Arbetarrörelsen och feminismen*, Brevskolan, Stockholm.

Higgins, W. (1985), 'Political Unionism and the Corporatist Thesis', *Economic and Industrial Democracy*, vol. 6, no. 3.

Hirdman, Y. (1987), 'Makt och kön', in Petersson, O. (ed.), *Maktbegreppet*, Carlssons, Stockholm.

Jenson, J. (1989), 'The talents of women and the skills of men: Flexible specialization and women', in Wood, S. (ed.), *The transformation of work?*, Unwin Hyman, London.

Jónasdóttir, A. (1992), 'Har kön någon betydelse för demokratin?', in Åström, G. and Hirdman, Y. (eds.), *Kontrakt i kris*, Carlssons, Stockholm.

Karlsson, E. (1981), 'De kvinnliga livsmedelsarbetarnas historia', in Baude, A. (ed.), *Rapport om jämställdhet i sju livsmedelsföretag*, Arbetslivscentrum, Stockholm.

Kommunal (1993), *Vårt arbete: Vår framtid*, Kommunal, Stockholm.

Kommunal (1994a), *Kvinnorna i Kommunal och deras villkor i arbetet och på fritiden*, Kommunal, Stockholm.

Kommunal (1994b), *Jämställdhet: Vår framtid*, Kommunal, Stockholm.

Kommunal (1995a), Vår *utbildning: Vår framtid*, Kommunal, Stockholm.

Kommunal (1995b), *Arbetsvärdering: En metod för rättvisa löner och uppvärdering av kvinnors arbete*, Kommunal, Stockholm.

*Kommunalnytt* (1994), no. 17.

Kyle, G. (1979), *Gästarbetarska i manssamhället*, Liber Förlag, Stockholm.

Lindroth, C. (1994), *Projektet 'Kom vidare i vården': En utvärdering*, Institutet för arbetslivsforskning, Stockholm.

LO (1993/4), *Röster om facket och jobbet* (5 vols.), LO, Stockholm.

LO (1994), *Women in the Swedish labour market*, LO, Stockholm.

*LO granskar* (1995), no. 2.

Mahon, R. (1994), 'From solidaristic wages to solidaristic work: A new historical compromise for Sweden?' in Clement, W. and Mahon, R. (eds.), *Swedish social democracy: A model in transition*, Canadian Scholars' Press, Toronto.

NORD (1994:3), *Women and men in the Nordic countries*, The Nordic Council, Stockholm.

Pateman, C. (1988), *The sexual contract*, Stanford University Press, Stanford.

Quick, M. (1994), 'Tjejligan: LO-kvinnornas motståndrörelse', stencil, Political Science Dept., University of Stockholm.

Qvist, G. (1974), *Statistik och politik: Landsorganisationen och kvinnorna på arbetsmarknaden*, Prisma/LO, Stockholm.

Sandgren, K. and Baude, A. (1993), 'Rapport från KOM-projekten i Gävle kommun', stencil, Gävle kommun.

Socialstyrelsen (1994), *Barns villkor i förändringstider: Slutrapport*, Socialstyrelsen, Stockholm.

SOU 1987:19, *Varannan damernas: Slutbetänkande från utredningen om kvinnorepresentation*, Arbetsmarknadsdepartementet, Stockholm.

Svensson, L. (1986), *Grupper och kollektiv: En undersökning av hemtjänstens organisation i två kommuner*, Arbetslivscentrum, Stockholm.

Svensson, L., Aronsson, C. and Höglund, S. (1990), *Kan byråkrati förändras?*, Ordfront, Stockholm.

Svärd, I. (1994a), *Omstrukturering i offentlig sektor: Uppsala kommun - ett lokalt exempel*, Arbetslivscentrum, Stockholm.

Svärd, I. (1994b), *Barnomsorg - ett sorgebarn i Uppsala: Ett exempel på effekter av nedskärningar i kommunal verksamhet*, Institutet för arbetslivsforskning, Stockholm.

Thorgren, G. (1994), 'Facklig kvinnokamp', *Pockettidningen R*, vol. 24, nos. 3-4.

Utbult, M. (1995), 'Tre fackliga företrädare samtalar kring arbetsutveckling', in von Otter, C. et al (eds.), *Det människonära arbetet: Om arbetets organisation inom offentliga sektorn*, Brevskolan, Stockholm.

von Otter, C. and L. Svensson (1995), 'Det utvecklande arbetet som strategi: Om förändringar i den offentliga sektorn', in von Otter C. et al, *Det människonära arbetet: Om arbetets organisation inom offentliga sektorn*, Brevskolan, Stockholm.

Waldemarsson, Y. (1992), 'Kontrakt under förhandling: LO-kvinnorna och makten', in Åström, G. and Hirdman, Y. (eds.), *Kontrakt i kris*, Carlssons, Stockholm.

Wikander, U. (1992), 'Delat arbete, delad makt: Om kvinnors underordning i och genom arbetet', in Åström, G. and Hirdman, Y. (eds.), *Kontrakt i kris*, Carlssons, Stockholm.

Åström, G., and Hirdman, Y. (eds.) (1992), *Kontrakt i kris*, Carlssons, Stockholm.

# 14 Engendering union democracy: Comparing Sweden and Australia

*Jennifer Curtin*

Freeman and Medoff (1984, pp. 3-5) argue that one of the responsibilities of trade unions is to provide workers with a voice at the workplace and in the political arena. However, although representative democracy is considered fundamental to union organization, questions have been raised as to whether trade unions encourage women to participate in union activity, and if the structures of trade unions allow for the representation of women and their interests at decision-making levels (Cook, Lorwin and Daniels, 1992, p. 43).

The aim of this chapter is to discuss the issue of women's voices within trade unions, and the strategies taken by women to have their voices heard. I examine the policies that have been and are currently being adopted to promote women's representation in trade unions in Sweden and Australia. I argue that there has been an increasing emphasis on explicitly 'woman-centred' strategies to increase women's representation. While the historical contexts from which these strategies have arisen differ between the two countries, the perceived lack of responsiveness by trade unions to the varied interests of women workers undermines their legitimacy as democratic institutions.

## Mapping women's representation within trade unions

Lovenduski (1986, p. 166) argues that increases in women's labour force participation should lead to, amongst other things, an influx of women into

---

Thanks go to the Swedish Institute for the provision of a scholarship which enabled me to conduct my research in Sweden. Address correspondence to Jennifer Curtin, Public Policy Program, Australian National University, Canberra, ACT 0200, Australia.

trade unions and an increase in women on the decision-making bodies of unions.

Certainly the first of these two effects is evident. Between 1960 and 1989 there were increases in female union density in six of the nine countries presented in Table 14.1; the Netherlands, Austria and United States being the exceptions. However, also evident from the data in the table is that for period 1980-1989, female union density declined in five countries. Such patterns reflect what has occurred with respect to overall union density during the same period (see Neumann, Pedersen and Westergaard-Nielsen, 1989; Rothstein, 1992).

**Table 14.1**
**Changes in female union density 1960-1989**

| | Female union density change 1980-1989 | Female union density change 1960-1989 |
|---|---|---|
| Australia | -3.5 | 2.7 |
| Austria | -8.5 | -6.9 |
| Canada | 6.2 | 14.5 |
| Germany | 1.8 | 4.6 |
| Ireland | -4.9 | 12.3 |
| Netherlds | -3.3 | -1.5 |
| Sweden | 11.1 | 42.5 |
| UK | -4.5 | 11.1 |
| US | * | -4.4 |

* Not known

*Sources:* Ebbinghaus, B. and Visser, J., DUES data set, University of Mannheim; Australian Bureau of Statistics; United States Labour Bureau; Statistics Canada.

However, this growing membership of women in trade unions has not led to a corresponding increase in the numbers of women in decision-making positions. According to the European Trade Union Confederation (ETUC, 1994) only two confederations had women leaders in 1993: the French CFDT and the Belgian FGTB. By 1995, the Swedish white collar confederation (TCO) and the Australian Council of Trade Unions also had women leaders.

At the executive committee level the comparative position of women in national confederations is slightly better. The data in Table 14.2 indicates there has been an increase or at least a maintenance in the levels of women's representation in most of the countries listed.

**Table 14.2**
**Women on executive committees in national trade union confederations**

| Country | Confede-ration | % women 1981 | % women 1990 | % women 1993 | % of women members 1991-93 | Policy for increasing women on Executive |
|---|---|---|---|---|---|---|
| Austria | OGB | 14 | 9 | 8 | 31 | yes R |
| Australia | ACTU | 0 | 18 | 29 | 33 | yes R |
| Belgium | FGTB | | 8 | 7 | 40 | yes A |
| Denmark | LO | 12 | 17 | 14 | 49 | no |
| France | CGT | 27 | | 25 | 32 | yes R+A |
| (W) Germ | DGB | 7.7 | | 13 | 32 | no |
| Ireland | ICTU | 0 | 11* | 17 | 38 | yes R |
| Italy | CGIL | 16.7 | 24 | 30 | 28 | yes Q |
| | UIL | 0 | 13* | 12 | 41 | no |
| Netherlds | FNV | 0 | 17 | 19 | 22 | no |
| Norway | LO | 6.7 | 20 | 25 | 42 | yes A |
| Sweden | LO | 6.7 | 13 | 13 | 45 | yes A |
| | TCO | 20 | | 20 | 59 | no |
| Swiss | SGB/US | 8.7 | 15 | 16 | 13 | no |
| UK | TUC | 13.7 | 29 | 31 | 36 | yes R |
| US | AFL-CIO | 9 | 9 | | 43 | no |

* figures for 1988
nk = not known, R = reserved seats, Q = quota, A = other measures
*Sources:* ETUC (1983, 1994); ICFTU (1991)

An increase of women on the executive is evident in over half of the confederations listed. Several of the confederations have a system of reserved seats, which appears to ensure at least a minimum level of representation, although in the cases of Australia, Italy and the UK it has served to increase the representation of women quite substantially. Such developments have focused on rule changes concerning the selection of representatives, which is usually done by adding seats rather than displacing the existing seat holders (Trebilcock, 1991, p. 420).

While such strategies appear promising, the picture is still grim: the data in Table 14.2 reflect approximately fifteen years of trade unions advocating policies to promote women, yet in only six confederations does the number of women on executives come close to matching the proportion of female membership. The under-representation of women in the Swedish trade unions included in this study appears less pronounced at lower levels in the hierarchy. In the Municipal Workers Union, the largest blue collar union in Sweden, 80 percent of members are women, and so too are 60 percent of the organisers and shop stewards. Within the Metalworkers Union, 12 percent of the members are women with 14 percent female shop stewards, although the position of women shop stewards reflects the gender segregated nature of the work force. Some white collar unions with around half their membership female also manifest almost proportionate representation at the local levels.

In recent years there have been considerable increases in women delegates to union confederation conferences. Between 1975 and 1985 the percentage of women delegates at the Swedish Confederation of Trade Unions Congress increased from 13 to 25 percent, while women delegates at the Swedish Confederation of Salaried Employees Congress grew from 20 to 39 percent. However, compared to their proportion of membership, women remain under-represented by 50 percent in both cases (Bergqvist, 1991, pp. 114-115).

Within Australia, women remain under-represented at lower levels of the union hierarchy. In 1975 only 3 percent of the delegates to the ACTU national conference were women. This increased from 7 percent in 1979 to 17 percent in 1987. Estimates suggest an increase in women's share of full time union positions from less than 5 percent in 1971 to about 12 percent in 1985, although women still predominate in the appointed rather than elected positions (Pocock, 1995, p. 8). With respect to industrial officers (who participate in direct negotiation with employers), recent figures for South Australia indicate there are 41 percent women in these positions, and 28 percent in Victoria (Pocock, 1995, p. 14). At the workplace level women made up 40 percent of employees, but only 29 percent of the shop stewards (Callus, Morehead, Cully and Buchanan, 1991, p. 106).

## Why is representation by women important?

Although the statistics on women's representation provided above reveal that gender variation exists in the realization of political rights within trade union structures, it has been argued that representative democracy is more about the activities than description of representatives. Representation involves acting in the interests of the represented, 'in a manner responsive to them' (Pitkin, 1967, p. 209). In so far as representatives are to be held accountable to a position, who the representatives are becomes inconsequential.

Yet, if democracy is a matter of representing particular policies and ideas, rather than particular categories such as gender, how can we suggest that representation by women matters? In answering this question I draw predominantly on the work of Phillips (1991, 1994, 1995). While she concentrates primarily on parliamentary democracy it is not uncommon to find the literature on labour movements using the parliamentary and representative practices of liberal democratic states as a model for analysing democracy within the union movement.

The first of Phillips' arguments revolves around a notion of justice. If no systemic or structural discrimination existed, 'all positions of political influence would be randomly distributed between both sexes and across all ethnic groups that make up society' (Phillips, 1994, p. 8). However, the composition of trade union hierarchies indicates that women are being denied access to rights and opportunities currently available to men. Without equal access to political participation (which may in turn impact on access to representation) the democratic nature of trade unionism comes into question (cf. Phillips, 1994).

Theoretically, everyone by virtue of their union membership has the right to attend meetings, air their views, and vote on relevant issues. In terms of equal access to participation, however, for many women, carrying out both paid and unpaid work makes it difficult for them to take on a third set of responsibilities as a union office-holder. The existing literature highlights a number of obstacles that impede women's participation, including the organizational structure and culture of trade unions (Trebilcock, 1991; ICFTU, 1991; ETUC, 1994). Yet if unions are to be considered democratic institutions, it seems only fair that unions seek to remove such barriers, especially since participation in union activity at workplace level is a requirement for advancement in union office (Cook, 1991, p. 243).

The second of Phillips' arguments deals with the notion of a distinct women's interest which, without representation, would otherwise be overlooked. She suggests that specific interests and needs that arise from women's experience would not be adequately addressed in a politics dominated by men. Over the last decade or so, ideas about an objective set of interests shared by all women have come under scrutiny by feminists (Nicholson, 1990; Butler, 1992). Phillips argues that it is precisely this ambiguity concerning women's interests which strengthens the case for increasing women representatives. If women's interests are varied, fluid, even still in the process of formation, it becomes impossible to separate out what is to be represented from who is to do the representation. Thus, representation concerns the formulation of identities and interests as well as how they are dealt with. As a result, Phillips maintains there is a stronger case for more women as representatives to participate in the definition and construction of policies (Phillips, 1994, p. 15).

To date, there is limited evidence to suggest that women are more likely than men to bring women's issues forward when in positions of representation in trade unions (Heery and Kelly, 1988), primarily because a critical mass of women do not yet exist in decision-making positions within most unions. And certainly the election of women will not ensure the representation of all women's interests. However, as Phillips has argued, democratic process should allow for the representation of different interests and perspectives via political presence. If women are not present, interests particularly relevant to women may fall off the agenda (1991, p. 65).

The argument for the existence of 'women's' interests feeds into the notion of responsiveness as a requisite of representative democracy. Arguably the more general theory concerning responsiveness and accountability is weak in that it rests on a prior assumption of shared knowledge or understanding between the representative and the represented of what issues require attention. However, while male union representatives may be able to represent the workers' general interests, for example with respect to wages, it may be questionable that they could represent the specific interests of women without an awareness or comprehension of what those interests are. In this sense, it could be argued that women are needed within leadership to provide such an awareness, and allow for women's interests to surface.

A final argument for increasing women's representation concerns role modelling. While Phillips does not pursue this argument, Hernes and Voje (1980) have referred to this as symbolic representation. They argue that even when women representatives are the exception rather than the rule they represent women symbolically in that they may be viewed as 'a vision of the future possibilities for women', which is of particular importance to both younger women and the public at large (Hernes and Voje, 1980, p. 180). While women's union membership is not declining as rapidly as men's, trade unions in many countries are in a state of decline (Curtin 1993). In response then, it could be considered increasingly important that workers, in this case women workers, feel they and their interests are being adequately represented. In this sense, addressing the under-representation of women in unions is an instrumental as well as a moral concern.

## Method

Primary research material was collected from interviews conducted between September 1994 and June 1995 with 25 women trade union officials working as equality or women's officers in national trade unions in Sweden and Australia. A cross-section of unions was targeted to reflect the different proportions of women members, as well as various occupations and industries. In both countries I also interviewed officials from the trade union confederations: the Australian Council of Trade Unions (ACTU), the Swedish Confederation of Trade Unions (LO), the Swedish Confederation of Salaried Employees (TCO) and the Association of Professional Employees and Civil Servants (SACO) Reference to the material gained from interviews will be made using the abbreviation of the trade union title.

I compare Sweden and Australia for a number of reasons. There are several similarities with respect to the significance of trade unions at a political level. Both have had high levels of unionization, although in Sweden these high levels have continued while more recently Australia is experiencing a decline in union membership (Curtin, 1993). Trade unions have played an active role in public policy-making in both countries, albeit in Australia predominantly over the last thirteen years. While the democratic internal workings of trade unions are important in their own right, they take on an increased salience when trade unions represent workers in the policy-making arena.

Applying a comparative approach makes possible a simultaneous focus on both similarity and difference in an attempt to account for patterns of country variation. While many comparative analyses seek to establish generalizations which may then be used to explain the past and predict the future (Lane and Ersson, 1994, pp. 10-11), comparison is also a mode of locating and exploring a phenomenon as yet insufficiently understood (Castles, 1989, p. 9). Few studies have focused on the gender dimension of union democracy (for exceptions see Cook et al., 1984; 1992). Comparing Sweden and Australia therefore contributes to a better understanding of the historical and cultural discourses which help shape women's collective actions within trade unions in the drive for increased representation.

## Promoting women's representation in Sweden and Australia

### *Sweden*

In an institutional sense, Swedish unions have, since the sixties, avoided acknowledging the existence of a special women's interest and instead have concentrated on equality between the sexes as a 'gender-neutral' interest. This followed the adoption of a new concept of equality, representing the equal standing of both men and women in all areas of social life (Acker, 1994, p. 9). Within the union movement, the move away from ideas of the interests of women toward an inclusion of men in the equation led the major trade union confederations to abolish their women's divisions and establish instead family and equality councils. Equality officers rather than women's officers have become the means by which equal opportunity issues in unions are addressed.

This emphasis on gender-neutrality has meant that strategies involving overt positive action for women have been rarely considered. In 1987, the Clerical and Technical Workers Union set the objective of proportional representation of women on the board, but in general unions have appeared ambivalent toward quotas. Neither of the white collar union confederations provide special programs to increase women's representation as this is seen as the responsibility of the affiliates, although they do undertake a monitoring role in this regard. Until recently, LO had a similar stance.

Underlying this gender-neutral discourse remained an explicit 'universal' class politics. Swedish unionism had grown out of a social-democratic labour movement which, while acknowledging the 'woman question' in the 1880s, saw this as secondary to the belief that women's liberation would automatically be resolved with working class liberation (Dahlström and Liljeström, 1983, p. 11). Separate organising by women's groups was seen as a bourgeoise threat to working class solidarity. In pursuing gender equality through gender neutral, class-based reforms, much has been gained for women in Sweden. There has been a massive increase of the numbers of women in the labour force supplemented by welfare state development which provides care for dependants and enviable parental leave provisions. Anti-discrimination legislation, tax reform and wage solidarity have also benefited women workers (Baude, 1978).

Yet despite these reforms, the political representation of women has (re)surfaced as a contentious issue. In 1986 a high profile Commission on Women's Representation reported on the gender patterns of representation in other commissions and the state administrative boards. These institutions are of great significance for the political decision-making process in Sweden and they are also institutions where organised interests, including trade unions, are represented. The Commission found that women were rarely appointed as trade union representatives (Bergqvist, 1994).

In addition, after the 1991 election, women's parliamentary representation dropped from 38 percent to 33.5 percent which, combined with the Conservative Government's intention to scale down welfare state spending, undertake privatization, reduce municipal spending and cut public employment, 'shocked political women into action' (Acker, 1994, p. 20). Networks began to develop all over Sweden, and a separate women's political party was touted as an alternative and a threat to mainstream political parties.

Within trade unions the renewed emphasis on women's collective actions has expressed itself through an increase in women's networks over the last five years. Special women's projects now exist in every one of LO's seventeen districts and a number of different kinds of women's groups, seminars and networks operate within several of unions (Police, Clerical, Metal, TCO, SACO). In 1994, women conference delegates from the Metalworkers Union met before the conference to network for support. This was the first time that women from this union had officially come together separately.

Perhaps the most impressive new network is Tjejligan (the 'women's gang') established by a few LO women in 1991. Tjejligan now has 14,000 members although it is still very informal, with no constitution. Much of the emphasis is on increasing women's representation within all levels of politics, but particularly within trade unions. A large number of women from Tjejligan were actively involved in the Social Democratic Party's election campaign of 1991. The motive of this was twofold: to increase women's self confidence about participating and to maintain a profile on women's issues during the campaign. This was considered a highly successful strategy as many of these women have gone on to stand for local government and trade union election.

Overt attention has also been given to the under-representation within LO headquarters. Recently the executive board made a decision that, within the LO headquarters, all vacant positions should be filled by women. Suitable justification must be made to the executive if women cannot be found for the positions. There is also a verbal commitment that when research committees are set up for particular investigations, fifty percent of the participants should be women. This is seen as a substantial step for women.

In 1989, the gender representation of the LO executive also changed with the election of a woman as chairperson of the largest blue collar union in Sweden, the Municipal Workers Union. During her time in office (up until 1995), she maintained a high media profile, displayed a determined commitment to the equal status of class and gender, and openly referred to feminism. Having such women in visible positions was cited as crucial in increasing women's participation and representation (Factory, LO). While there is also a female head of TCO, at the time of interviewing it was deemed too early to assess if her appointment had made an impact on the affiliates' women members.

Women unionists openly acknowledge the existence of barriers to their participation and representation within trade unions. Strategies to counter this involve changing meeting times and size, education programmes for both women and men on union culture, and providing child care at meetings. In addition, amendments made to the Equality Act (1992) have also forced unions to more actively address issues of equal access to participation and representation of women. Employers, including trade unions, who employ more than ten people must now design an equality plan every year which outlines measures that the employer intends to take in facilitating the combination of employment and parenthood, overcoming sex-segregation, and eliminating discrimination with respect to promotion, training, and pay. Implementation and the evaluation of outcomes must then be listed in the following year's report.

It appears that many women in Sweden have perceived a failure in the responsiveness of the various political institutions, including trade unions, to the proposed cuts to the welfare state, and the undermining of women's political power through a decrease in their representation. Struggle against such threats has produced a spontaneous identification and solidarity between many Swedish women, with women arguing that the political representation of women has become necessary in protecting their economic, social and political interests.

### *Australia*

Since the early 1970s, women in the Australian unions have been quite explicit in identifying the representation of women in gender specific terms and have adopted strategies which reflect this. Union women have mobilized the ACTU into developing policies relating to the needs of working women through the creation of women's conferences and committees at branch, state and national level. While these structures do not always have a formal position within the union and may not be constitutionally based, they do make policy recommendations which, if accepted, are forwarded to other union decision-making bodies. Women's committees also facilitate the participation of rank and file women in union activities, providing them with an environment which is comfortable and where they can meet other union women. In some unions this is the only form of representation and participation to which women have access (Metal, Construction, Public Service, Services, Clothing).

The separate presence of women has also led to the politicization of issues of explicit interest to women, which have then reached the union movement's policy agenda. This began with the adoption of the Working Women's Charter in 1977; implementation of its objectives has in turn been dependent on the continual pressure of women unionists both within and outside of the ACTU executive. As a result, several women's issues, including sexual harassment, parental leave and equal pay, have begun to gain currency in the mainstream industrial arena. In this sense, women's representation has been seen as critical in undermining the male-dominated agenda-setting process of the union movement.

Participation by women in union activities has been facilitated by education courses, the provision of child care at meetings, informal networks, and more recently by the Anna Stewart Memorial Project. This project allows women to come out of their jobs, fully paid, for two weeks, to work with their union, and gain experience with industrial issues. The individual union finances this, and so participation is ultimately dependent on funding. However, it is viewed by many women unionists as a positive way of encouraging women to become more active (Clothing, Metal, Construction, Nurses, Teachers, Clerical, Public Service).

While still few in number, women are becoming increasingly obvious in the upper echelons of the union movement in Australia. 1983 saw the first woman on the ACTU national executive and in 1987 she became the first woman assistant secretary on the same body. Two other women National Secretaries have lent a female face to the ACTU executive in recent years, as have the three Affirmative Action delegates, first appointed in 1987. The most recent significant achievement in this regard is the election of a woman as ACTU President in September 1995.

In addition to ideas about 'women's interests', arguments for increasing women's representation in Australian unions have been made in the name of justice and democracy, as well as symbolism. In 1977, the Working Women's Charter emphasised the need for more women to be elected if union executives were to become fully representative (Deery et al., 1991, p. 294) and, in 1989, the ACTU Secretary stated that 'the Australian trade union movement cannot pretend to be representative of women if we have within the ranks of Congress and union leadership far fewer women than is warranted' (*The Age*, 25 September, 1989).

In a symbolic sense, having women in high profile and powerful positions within the union movement is seen as a necessary, but not sufficient, condition to further the participation and representation of women (Clothing). Women's visibility may help to change members' perceptions of unions, undermine the dominant images of the ACTU as a 'bastion of male superiority' and controlled by 'out of touch men' (Teachers, Clothing, Public Service), and has implications for recruitment in that it may give women workers a feeling of association with the union movement. Finally, an increase of women in leadership positions may allow for women actually to influence the debate and decisions made within trade unions (Metal, Clerical, Construction).

Although women-centred strategies are common, acknowledgement is made of the differences that exist between women in the Australian union movement. Politically, women are divided between right and left, blue collar-white collar and public-private sectors. There are mixed feelings as to whether notions of sisterhood can override these differences (Clothing, ACTU, Services, Public Service, Nurses). However, maintaining solidarity between women is cited as necessary while the numbers of women in leadership are few. This means seeking to contain and deal with the differences between women inside the women's committee, thus avoiding an ill-afforded splintering at national executive level (Services, Teachers, Metal).

Perhaps the most progressive move yet, however, has been the promotion of affirmative action strategies. In 1991, the ACTU put up a proposal for a target of 50 percent women's representation by the year 2000 and designated three affirmative action places on its executive. Similar appointments have been made in many state level confederations. At branch level, however, it is ultimately up to the unions themselves to implement affirmative action strategies, and not all unions have been completely supportive of the idea (see Manning, 1994). However, by law any union with more than 100 employees must develop an affirmative action program and submit an annual report to the Affirmative Action Agency. With the amalgamations that have taken place over the last five years, more unions are now bound by this ruling.

Within the Australian context it has been suggested that amalgamations 'offer unique opportunities for unions to ... build up structures that are more responsive to women's needs' (Nightingale, 1991, p. 19). The amalgamation process includes the creation of new constitutions, and several amalgamated unions have sought to address the issue of women's representation by writing specific rulings into the constitution guaranteeing women greater representation (Teachers, Services, Clerical). However, more research is required before these examples are accepted as the rule rather than the exception.

Various feminist writers have argued that the labourist tradition in Australia has embodied an ethos of mateship, which has strongly encouraged male bonding and enhanced the exclusion of women (Sawer and Simms, 1993; Pocock, 1995; Lake, 1986). In the call to workers for solidarity, this notion of mateship continues to be an integral part of union rhetoric (Kelty, 1995).

I would argue that the gender-specific, overtly feminist interventions undertaken within trade unions in Australia have been constituted by and through this (ever-changing) masculine class rhetoric (cf. Yeatman, 1995). In other words, to gain entry into trade unions and have the various interests of women workers addressed, women unionists have had to struggle against an exclusive class politics in ways that have highlighted and named this exclusion. While this has meant organising as women and increasing the representation of women, it has not meant representing women's interests as fixed, but rather as formulated out of particular political dialogues. The various and changing strategies employed by women unionists over time is evidence of this.

## Conclusion

In comparing the arguments and strategies employed by women trade unionists in Sweden and Australia, several similarities and differences are evident. When we compare the numbers of women in representative positions within trade unions we see that women remain under-represented at most levels of the trade union hierarchy. In Australia there is a higher percentage of women represented at the union confederation level than in Sweden. This increased level has resulted from the creation of affirmative action delegates within the ACTU. At lower levels however, it appears that women are better represented in Swedish unions.

In both countries, women unionists cited domestic commitments, negative attitudes about women's capabilities with respect to union work and lack of confidence as barriers to women's participation. Similar strategies have been applied in both countries in an effort to overcome these barriers, with a particular emphasis on meeting times and styles, education and informal networks for moral support. Women in both countries also commented on the importance of symbolic representation in making unions appear more 'women-friendly' thereby encouraging women to both join, participate and seek representation.

The most striking similarity is the explicit use of separate collective actions by women in both countries. Within Sweden, a gender-neutral approach was taken from the mid 1960s until the early 1990s which for many years provided Swedish women with comparatively high levels of gender equality. However, as a result of threats to the welfare state and continual barriers to equal political voice, new feminist organising has emerged within trade unions to stand beside the dominant universal class politics discourse. In contrast, union women in Australia have regularly applied overtly feminist discourses to achieve policy outcomes in reaction to the explicitly exclusive masculine character of trade unionism: an approach which has proved successful in mainstreaming many issues of particular concern to women.

That women in both countries have felt it necessary to organise with other women to achieve better representation, albeit in different historical contexts, indicates that in terms of responsiveness and quality of representation, trade unions in the past have often been perceived as remiss in addressing the interests of women unionists. While accountability is an important facet of representative democracy, this does not appear sufficient if particular needs of a group of workers are being ignored.

So what implications do such collective actions have for trade union policy-making, the democratic nature of trade unions, and for union strength in general? The first section of this chapter outlined the increase in women's trade union membership that has occurred over the last thirty years. Despite this increase, in many countries, including Australia, women make up a large proportion of potential union members. While recruitment is a major issue for the union movement as a whole in Australia, women have yet to be recognised as the explicit recruitment challenge. Having trade unions appear more 'women friendly', through better representation of the interests of working women and of women themselves, if necessary with affirmative action strategies, could be seen as a means by which these potential members become actual members and thereby increasing union strength.

Although trade unionism is predicated on a collective identity and seeks to represent a unified working class interest, feminist challenges amongst others continue to undermine the feasibility of this assumption. While organization around gender (and other experiences) fractures the insistence by trade unions on the commonality of work experience, it also has the potential to destabilize the white, male, full time worker 'norm' embedded in unionism in the advanced industrial democracies, and thus enable the provision of more appropriate policies for an increasingly diverse union movement (Ellem, 1992, p. 364).

Finally, in this period of globalization and internationalization, trade unions are having to adjust to substantial changes to the environment in which they operate. In Australia, this has recently involved the undermining of trade union involvement in shaping economic and social policy. Accepting, acknowledging and providing voice for different groups of workers within trade unions therefore becomes increasingly necessary if unions are continued to be viewed by governments and employers as representative of 'the working class' in public policy making arenas.

## References

Acker, J. (1994), *Two discourses of reform: Women in the future Swedish welfare state*, mimeo, Department of Sociology, University of Oregon.

Baude, A. (1978), 'Public policy and changing family patterns in Sweden 1930-1977', in Blumen, J., Lipman and Bernard, J. (eds.), *Sex roles and social policy: A complex science equation*, Sage, London.

Bergqvist, C. (1994), 'The declining corporatist state and the political gender dimension in Sweden', in Karvonen, L. and Selle, P. (eds.), *Closing the gap: Women in Nordic politics*, Dartmouth.

Bergqvist, C. (1991), 'Corporatism and gender equality: A comparative study of two Swedish labour market organizations', *European Journal of Political Research*, vol. 20, pp. 107-125.

Butler, J. (1992), 'Contingent foundations: Feminism and the question of "postmodernism"', in Butler, J. and Scott, J. (eds.), *Feminists theorise the political*, Routledge, New York.

Callus, R., Morehead, A., Cully, M. and Buchanan, J. (1991), *Industrial relations at work: The Australian Workplace Industrial Relations Survey*, Australian Government Printing Service, Canberra.

Castles, F. G. (1989), 'Introduction: Puzzles of political economy', in Castles, F. G. (ed.), *The comparative history of public policy*, Polity Press, Cambridge.

Cook, A., Lorwin, V. and Daniels, A. K. (eds.) (1984), *Women and trade unions in eleven industrialised countries*, Temple University Press, Philadelphia.

Cook, A. (1991), 'Women and minorities', in Strauss, G., Gallagher, D. and Fiorito, J. (eds.), *The state of the unions*, University of Wisconsin, Wisconsin.

Cook, A., Lorwin, V. and Daniels, A. K. (1992), *The most difficult revolution*, Cornell University Press, Ithaca.

Curtin, J. (1993), 'The feminization of trade unions: A comparative perspective', Paper presented to the New Zealand Political Studies Association Conference, Christchurch.

Dahlström, E. and Liljeström, R. (1983), 'The patriarchal heritage and the working class women', *Acta Sociologica*, vol. 26, pp. 3-20

Deery, S. J. and Plowman, D. H. (1991), *Australian industrial relations* (3rd edn.), McGraw-Hill, Sydney.

Ellem, B. (1992), 'Organising strategies for the 1990s: Targeting particular groups: Women, migrants, youth', in Crosby, M. and Easson, M. (eds.), *What should unions do?* Pluto Press, Leichhardt.

European Trade Union Confederation (ETUC) (1983), *Women's representation in trade unions*, ETUC, Brussels.

ETUC (1994), *Women in decision-making in trade unions*, ETUC, Brussels.

Freeman, R. B. and Medoff, J. L. (1984), *What do unions do?*, Basic Books, New York.

Heery, E. and Kelly, J. (1988), 'Do female representatives make a difference', *Work, Employment and Society*, vol. 2,pp. 487-505.

Hernes, H. and Voje, K. (1980), 'Women in the corporate channel in Norway: A process of natural exclusion' *Scandinavian Political Studies,* vol. 3, pp. 163-186.

International Confederation of Free Trade Unions (ICFTU) (1991), *Equality: The continuing challenge - Strategies for success*, ICFTU, Brussels.

Kelty, B., *AM*, ABC Radio,14th November, 1995.

Lake, M. (1986), 'Socialism and manhood: The case of William Lane', *Labour History*, no. 50, pp 54-62.

Lane, E. and Erson, S. (1994), *Comparative politics: An introduction and new approach*, Polity, Oxford.

Lovenduski, J. (1986), *Women in European politics*, Wheatsheaf Books, Brighton.

Manning, H. (1994), 'Women and union politics in Australia', *Policy Organization and Society*, vol. 9, pp. 38-52.

Neumann, G., Pedersen, P. J. and Westergard-Nielsen, N. (1989), 'Long-run international trends in aggregate unionization', Working Paper 90-4, Centre for Labour Economics, University of Aarhus and Aarhus School of Business.

Nicholson, L. J. (1990), *Feminism/postmodernism*, Routledge, New York.

Nightingale, M (1991), *Facing the challenge*, Victorian Trades Hall Council, Melbourne.

Phillips, A. (1995), *A politics of presence*, Oxford University Press, Oxford.

Phillips, A. (1994), 'Democracy and representation', Paper presented at Australian National University, Canberra.

Phillips, A. (1991), *Engendering democracy*, Polity Press, Cambridge.

Pitkin, H. (1967), *The concept of representation*, California University Press, Berkeley.

Pocock, B (1995), 'Women in unions: What progress in South Australia?', *Journal of Industrial Relations*, vol. 37, pp. 3-23.

Rothstein, B. (1992), 'Labor-market institutions and working-class strength', in Steinmo, S., Thelen, K. and Longstreth, F. (eds.), *Structuring politics,* Cambridge University Press, Cambridge.

Sapiro, V. (1981), 'When are interests interesting? The problem of political representation of women', *American Political Science Review*, vol. 75, pp. 701-716.

Sawer, M. and Simms, M. (1993), *A woman's place,* Allen and Unwin, Sydney.

*The Age*, 25 September, 1989, Melbourne.

Trebilcock, A. (1991), 'Strategies for strengthening women's participation in trade union leadership', *International Labour Review*, vol. 130, pp. 407-426.

Yeatman, A. (1995), 'Interlocking oppressions', in Caine, B. and Pringle, R. (eds.), *Transitions: New Australian feminisms*, Allen and Unwin, St Leonards.

# 15 Toward a better understanding of union planning

*Kay Devine and Yonatan Reshef*

Planning is fundamental to all organizations, receiving widespread research attention in numerous disciplines. Oddly enough, industrial relations scholars have virtually ignored union planning. The little available research centers on the popular topic of strategic planning, while other forms of union planning have been submerged. This may be a result of either business policy frameworks guiding much of the research, or the introduction of the strategic choice framework by Kochan, McKersie and Cappelli (1984). We argue that researchers must approach *union planning* from a *union context*. To facilitate a systematic investigation of union planning, we propose a research framework and articulate future research directions.

## Research background

Discussions of union planning typically result in one of two polarized viewpoints: (1) that union leaders are unable, or extremely limited, to act proactively; or (2) that union leaders should, and occasionally do, exhibit proactive behavior vis-à-vis their environment. Advocates of the first view focus almost exclusively on strategic planning and state that the strategic-

---

The authors thank the Faculty of Business, University of Alberta for funding this research. Kathy Haryett's research assistance is greatly appreciated. A version of this chapter has been accepted for publication in *Relations Industrielles*. The authors thank the editor of *Relations Industrielles*, Dr. Jean Sexton, for granting permission to publish this chapter. All correspondence concerning this chapter should be referred to Yonatan Reshef, University of Alberta, Faculty of Business, Edmonton, Alberta, Canada T6G 2R6.

choice orientation is not viable for unions. Union leaders' strategic choices are constrained as they possess few discretionary powers to deal with external circumstances. Labour can only react to environmental changes (Gereluk, 1990; Lewin, 1987).

Proponents of the second orientation believe that the environment creates pressures with which traditional union practices are not suited to deal. Union leaders must adopt a new perspective, one feature of which is strategic planning (Murray and Reshef, 1988). In Canada, for example, several major unions, such as the Canadian Auto Workers, the Communications, Energy and Paperworkers Union, and the Public Service Alliance of Canada, have developed blueprints for union involvement in quality improvement initiatives (Kumar, 1995). At the center of the plans is the integration of workplace unions' interests in maintaining, and improving, their institutional security with management's interests in improved competitiveness and profitability. In principle, then, where constraints do not curtail alternatives, and union leaders possess discretion over issues such as structure and internal functions, leaders can plan the future paths the union should pursue (Stratton and Reshef, 1990).

Both viewpoints include cogent supportive arguments. Little convincing empirical work has resulted to support either view, perhaps because past research has been limited by several problems. Semantic, operational, and measurement problems exist due to a confusion in the nomenclature and conceptualization of planning in general. Moreover, when conceptualizing planning in a trade-union context, researchers have used pre-existing, business models, disregarding the fact that unions are unique organizations, structurally and politically different from corporations.

Unions are political entities with distinct mandates and values. They lack the profit orientation that drives the corporation, and noneconomic considerations may influence internal processes. Union officials' work is defined through a constitution. They are accountable to a range of stakeholders and must represent all members fairly through due process (Dunlop, 1990; Godard, 1994). Being 'democratic people-involved institution[s]' (Quaglieri, 1989, p. 8), unions are required to conduct periodic elections of officers, which do not always result in executives who are chosen for their administrative skills (Dunlop, 1990). Most incumbents are reinstated, but re-election is not guaranteed. Officers must respond to their constituents' concerns or else risk their political future (Dunlop, 1990). In such cases where tenure is unstable, officers may have little regard for long-term development, and may concentrate instead on short-term success.

There is also a need to communicate effectively and quickly with a large number of interest groups, agendas change constantly, membership diversity is increasing, and the coalitions with which leaders work may be unstable (Bryson, 1988a; Bryson, 1988b; Dunlop, 1990; Rankin, 1990). Labour leaders rarely enjoy the administrative work required to deal with these challenges, as they are 'doers', and would prefer to be out among their members rather than in an office (Quaglieri, 1989). These factors influence planning by either dictating the type of planning, or even mitigating against it.

In North America, unions are also conservative organizations, typically reluctant to abandon the status quo (Craft, 1991; Hecksher, 1988; Godard, 1994). A pragmatic 'business unionism' philosophy reflecting a drive to advance and protect members' economic interests has existed in North America since late in the 19th century (Godard, 1994). Officers thus might be averse to committing resources to experiment with new processes or strategies. This leads to an inability of most unions to cope quickly with change, or 'strategic rigidity' (Lawler, 1990, p. 46). This, coupled with a 'sluggishness of spirit', makes unions 'prisoners of inertia' (Raskin, 1986, p. 3).

In sum, research programs must acknowledge the political and conservative nature of unions which, in turn, influences the content, scope, range, and pace of planning.

## Union planning framework

To discover the nature of union planning and develop a research framework, we used a qualitative approach combining interviews and document analysis. Twenty-eight interviews with personnel from 16 different organizations were conducted. A detailed explanation of the data sources and collection is provided in Stratton-Devine and Reshef (forthcoming).

Due to a dearth of empirical work in this area, we have relied on the data when creating the following union planning framework (see Stratton-Devine and Reshef [forthcoming] for an explanation of the data analysis). The data indicate that union planning processes differentiate along three key criteria: planning type (reactive, operational, and strategic), union level (local, regional/intermediate, national/international and federation), and variable dimensions (explicit/implicit, short/long range, top-down/bottom-up, internal/external focus, or global/local issues). These criteria constitute the framework presented by Figure 15.1.

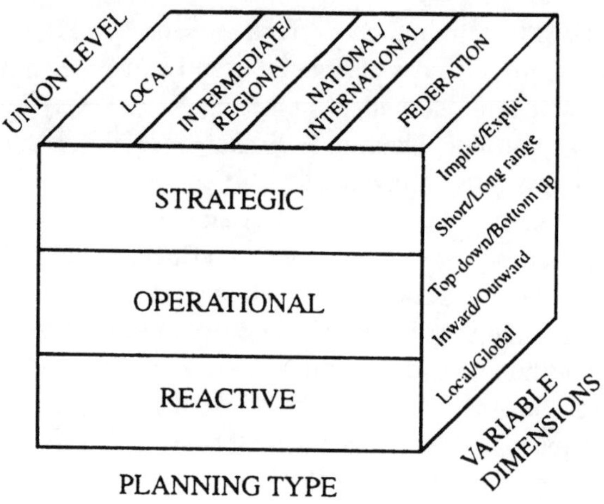


**Figure 15.1 Union planning framework**

*Types of planning*

Descriptions of planning processes revealed that unions engage in three types of planning: (1) reactive; (2) operational; and (3) strategic. Reactive planning consists of quick, ad hoc plans in reaction to unexpected stimuli. Such planning occurs in all unions, and consists of incremental, disjointed decisions.

One interviewee characterized reactive planning as an

> 'action by the seat of the pants' mentality. For example, corporations make plans as to the direction they would like to go [and are in] the driver's seat. We don't have that latitude... Decisions to change the workplace have come to our attention with such short notice that it's not even funny.

Operational planning is the development of plans that guide a union's daily operations. Compared to reactive plans, operational plans are more orderly, following a predetermined schedule. According to interviewees, operational planning addresses issues such as budgeting, collective bargaining, staffing, and general operations of the union. As stated by one local president, 'operational planning would be more appropriate in my job...I am, by and large, doing the day to day work at the union'. All of the participants recognized the existence of, and the need for such planning.

Finally, interviewees describe what they call strategic planning as: (1) futuristic thinking based on a vision for the union; (2) an evaluation of potential opportunities and threats; (3) the formulation of strategies chosen from various alternatives which are designed to cope with future challenges; and (4) involvement of, or consideration of, member needs, wants and ideas from all levels of the organization. The first three aspects mirror corporate planning processes, but the fourth element, the inclusion of rank and file, distinguishes union from traditional business planning. One union mission is to represent the concerns and interests of the rank and file, so many leaders firmly believe that member input is critical to the planning process. Also, because leaders are elected they must acknowledge their members' concerns.

All but one of the officers used the term 'strategic planning'. When describing the process, however, a variety of responses was received. One federation executive distinguished strategic from operational planning by saying, 'you can have long-term goals, but they aren't strategic. Unions must look at their existence and examine their needs'. Another representative stated that strategic planning produces a 'game plan, or a theory that will take unions through a period of time'. Each union has its own definition and process, for there are no universal guidelines driving the phenomenon. This coincides with Burgelman's (1983) observation that when it comes to strategy formulation, different organizational contexts are associated with different strategic processes.

### *Union level*

The data indicate that the higher up in the union hierarchy, the more global, sophisticated and strategic the planning becomes. This finding supports Lawler's (1990, p. 39) statement that 'choice processes may reasonably be expected to differ across hierarchical levels within unions'. The second union planning differentiation factor is based on the vertical dimension of union structure. For the purposes of this framework, the vertical dimension includes four tiers, with the lowest tier consisting of local unions, the second tier being regional bodies or intermediate units of national unions, the third consisting of national or international bodies, and the fourth representing umbrella federations such as the American AFL-CIO, the Canadian Labor Congress (CLC), or provincial federation.

Local level unions primarily engage in reactive and operational planning, while at the national, international, or federation levels, it is more likely that all three types of planning occur. Interviewees attributed this to the availability of resources and the role and responsibilities expected from officials at each level. At the federation, national or international level, resources and expertise are more plentiful. Individuals at these levels are further removed from the day-to-day 'firefighting' activities typically found on the local level. Furthermore, they possess a broader view of the organization and environment, and feel it is their role to blaze a trail or formulate a mission to guide unions into the 21st century.

*Variable dimensions of planning*

As already stated, planning differs considerably from one union to another. As such, each union represents a distinct point along the following continua.

*Implicit/explicit* One continuum of union planning is represented by implicit, unwritten processes on one end, and explicit, written processes on the other.

A deliberate implicit approach is adopted by some leaders. Plans are not always written, and frequently are found only in the president's head. S/he communicates them when the timing seems right (Steiner, 1963). For example, one officer, in speaking about how one of their union programs started, said

> It developed up here [pointing to his head] for a period of about two years...I got my senior staff together...It was a beautiful May afternoon, so we walked to [local café], sat down, ordered a glass of wine, and I said what about this...and everybody agreed to it.

This officer tacitly planned the program, and then shared the idea with his staff to implement, without proposing it in writing, or delineating action plans. An international staffer observed,

> There's so little [explicit] planning because it takes the direction of the organization out of the hands of the president. The president wants to call all the shots. They don't want anything in writing.

In contrast, other interviewees described formalized processes, ranging from scheduled, ongoing sessions to weekend retreats with staff and representatives. It seems that size, in terms of personnel and discretionary resources available (Kimberly, 1976), and degree of centralization affect how implicit or explicit planning processes are. One large, fairly autonomous local within a decentralized (inter)national union structure, engaged in very explicit, detailed planning. The smaller locals in the sample engaged in no explicit planning processes. This finding supports past research which concluded that increased size is related to increased formalization of organizational activities (Hall, 1987), and that decentralization leads to more decisions being made at lower levels (Melcher, 1975).

*Short/long-range* Another dimension is time frame. In some cases, the plan implementation time is fairly short, while other plans demand a longer period. According to one national organizer,

> In organizing, we do plan...and we have long-term projects and, of course, we have numerous short-term projects where we set targets for ourselves...Long-term [projects], we're talking about 5, 6 years.

A local president stated,

> The plan of action must be flexible depending on circumstances of the environment around you. We started with our values, and now have set short term goals. With the short term plans, you want early success, so you can build on it...We're still working on our long term goals, which are concerned with things like major growth and reorganization.

Interviewee responses indicate the time frame of planning varies dependent upon the environment, the issues of concern, and the need for immediate action.

*Top-down/bottom-up direction* Leadership style also differentiates union planning, as management styles 'run the gamut from participatory to autocratic' (Quaglieri, 1989, p. 7). For example, one local president said,

> The leader is the key to it. If there's not someone with vision, it doesn't happen. If someone below in the ranks has vision and the leader doesn't, then you end up with an internal conflict.

Other individuals made it clear that the planning is not strictly an executive function. A national organizer stated,

> The strategic overall planning for our union is done on several different levels. The people who are responsible for actually implementing planning are the directors...They make decisions about where we're going to go and when we're going to do it...But the input to strategic planning comes from a number of sources: our members, through the local unions, because it's not an individual voice — it's a collective voice; staff certainly have a great say. The districts then merge, or form part of the national scene, and the national scene makes a decision about Canada.

Most interviewees emphasized that while the union's vision emanates from the officers, issues and suggestions are generated by the general membership and staff. A few interviewees, however, argued that the process may also be concomitantly top-down and bottom-up.

*Inward/outward focus* The focus of the planning also varies. Most plans concentrate on issues dealing with factors external to the union such as collective bargaining, political action, or environmental issues. However, some participants mentioned that their plans also contain an inward focus, for example, in staffing or budgeting.

*Local/global issues* Planning issues present another variable dimension. On the local level, issues center on topics such as collective bargaining, job security, budgets, and items salient to direct membership gains and services. On the national or federation level, issues are more global in scope, encompassing areas such as environmental concerns, women's issues, freedom and democracy issues, or international affairs. For example, a construction trades local officer, when asked to compare their planning issues with those of a federation said,

> The people at the Fed [Federation], you know, are the save the whales, and owls, and seals, and save the world. Construction unions aren't like that...We insist on buildings that comply with safety standards.

On the intermediate, or regional level, there is a mix of local and national topics. A regional research director stated that, 'one predominant issue is organizing. Second are contract issues. Third are legislative concerns'. On the national level, the scope is much broader, as suggested by one national union president who commented on the work of his union's planning committee:

> In a sense, the Committee decided to try and identify global trends, to then see where Canada fit within those global developments, and to design a set of responses, both structural and policy, to these developments, globally and nationally. We decided to build our own crystal ball and then to gaze into it and build our future.

In sum, there is a range of planning issues, from local bargaining and organizing, to national politics, to international environmental concerns.

## Discussion

The proposed framework captures the main union planning differentiation variables. While any variable combination is possible, the likelihood of some combinations seems more feasible than others. For example, national leaders are more likely to engage in strategic planning than local leaders. Still, the framework provides for the inclusion of any option, such as local strategic planning.

This framework suggests several research directions. First, the three differentiating criteria must be operationalized and empirically validated. Although the framework is appropriate for our sample, there may be additional elements or changes required before it represents all union planning.

Attention should be directed toward (1) further descriptive analyses of processes and content; and (2) evaluative studies of planning outcomes. Both descriptive and evaluative research will assist leaders by exposing them to what other unions are doing, and by relating planning to performance.

*Descriptive analyses*

Researchers should investigate what planning processes occur for each type of planning at each union level, and which variable dimensions are appropriate. For instance, we propose that locals mainly engage in reactive planning which is implicit, short-range, bottom-up, inwardly focused, and concentrated on local issues. In contrast, international bodies or federations are more likely involved in strategic planning which is explicit, long-range, top-down, outwardly focused, and concentrated on global issues.

Another line of research could determine whether or not there is a trickle down, or cascading effect whereby lower union levels are more likely to engage in the various planning types when higher levels engage in such processes. The current data indicate that, in many cases, the local union explicitly plans when its (inter)national is also involved in such processes.

Second, questions abound when describing what union personnel actually do in their planning processes. For example, who is involved in the sessions at each level for each planning type? The role of officers should be explored, for leaders must be able to weigh options, make decisions and secure member support for those decisions.

A third research path should target content questions. Guided by the framework, research should determine what issues are most likely to be addressed at each level for each planning type. Moreover, inwardly focused union functions, such as budgeting or staffing, and outwardly focused activities, such as political action, collective bargaining, or organizing may require different processes involving different personnel. For example, it is unknown if unions engage in piecemeal planning, addressing each activity individually, if they develop one master plan for all activities, or both. Research, therefore, is needed on what topics are addressed and how, or if, they are integrated into a holistic scheme.

Fourth, research should address the determinants of the propensity to plan by examining various contextual contingencies. For example, a union's sector (public vs. private; and in the private sector, manufacturing vs. service) may influence leader propensity to plan strategically. Organizational size or resources may also determine the existence of different types of planning. Finally, leader characteristics such as beliefs, values, or skills may provide a key as to which processes may occur.

*Evaluative analyses*

This chapter and the proposed framework focus on planning processes, thus neglecting planning outcomes. The most crucial question is whether there is a linkage between planning and performance. It has been claimed that planning may be a 'sterile process, one which is oriented merely to the production of documents, the existence of which frequently fails to result in any meaningful change' (Higgins, 1978). It is important to determine if union plans are realized, and what resultant changes occur. For unrealized plans, it may be that individuals or coalitions within the union have low commitment to the decisions, thus creating implementation roadblocks (Guth and MacMillan, 1986). Research could determine potential roadblocks, thus informing union leaders of possible hazards.

The role of organizational context and its relationship to planning effectiveness must also be determined, for each organization exhibits unique contextual characteristics. As already suggested, the degree of centralization and the role of leaders may affect planning type and effectiveness. An interesting question is whether or not the vision and strategic direction for a union should emanate from the top to increase the likelihood of plan implementation, or whether success in plan implementation is more likely if such matters are decided jointly by top leaders and rank and file members.

To sum, today's unstable environment of global competition, technological changes, deregulation, and privatization together with developments such as the transition to high-commitment work systems, seriously challenges the viability of many unions in North America and beyond. To guide their organizations successfully, union leaders must rethink and reformulate basic assumptions about union practices. Part of this process involves planning, a function at which union leaders must be proficient in terms of process, content, implementation, and evaluation.

In this chapter, we have proposed a general union planning framework using the elements of type of planning, union level, and variable dimensions to differentiate the varied components. While past research has portrayed union planning as a dichotomy of whether unions do or do not plan, or can or cannot plan, we propose that it is a complex, multifaceted, multilevel phenomenon which requires a new perspective and further study. This chapter provides a framework that integrates the fragmented literature on the topic and future research paths. For too long, research has ignored union administrative practices. Given today's environment, unions must plan. In so doing, it is critical for research to determine what is being done, and what is effective so that resources are not wasted on unnecessary or ineffective processes.

## References

Bryson, J. M. (1988a), *Strategic planning for public and nonprofit organizations*, Jossey-Bass, San Francisco.

Bryson, J. M. (1988b), 'A strategic planning process for public and non-profit organizations', *Long Range Planning*, vol. 21, no. 1.

Burgelman, R. A. (1983), 'Corporate entrepreneurship and strategic management: Insights from a process study', *Management Science*, vol. 29, no. 12.

Craft, J. A. (1991), 'Unions, bureaucracy, and change: Old dogs learn new tricks very slowly', *Journal of Labor Research,* vol. 12, no. 4, Fall.

Dunlop, J. T. (1990), *The management of labor unions*, Lexington Books, Lexington.

Gereluk, W. (1990), Interview on 5 november, in Edmonton, Alberta.

Glaser, B. G. and Strauss, A. L. (1967), *The discovery of grounded theory: Strategies for qualitative research*, Aldine, Chicago.

Godard, J. (1994), *Industrial relations: The economy and society*, McGraw-Hill Ryerson, Toronto.

Guth, W. D. and Macmillan, I. C. (1986), 'Strategy implementation versus middle management self-interest', *Strategic Management Journal*, vol. 7.

Hall, R. H. (1987), *Organizations: Structures, processes and outcomes*, 4th Edition, Prentice-Hall, Englewood Cliffs.

Hecksher, C. C. (1988), *The new unionism*, Basic Books, New York.

Higgins, J. (1978), 'Strategic decision making: An organizational behavior perspective', *Managerial Planning*, vol. 26, no. 5.

Kimberly, J. R. (1976), 'Organizational size and the structuralist perspective: A review, critique, and proposal', *Administrative Science Quarterly*, vol. 21, no. 4.

Kochan, T. A., McKersie, R.B. and Cappelli, P. (1984), 'Strategic choice and industrial relations theory', *Industrial Relations*, vol. 23, no. 1.

Kumar, P. (1995), 'Canadian labour's response to work reorganization', *Economic and Industrial Democracy*, vol. 16, no. 1.

Lawler, J. J. (1990), *Unionization and deunionization: Strategy, tactics and outcomes*, University of South Carolina Press, Columbia.

Lewin, D. (1987), 'Industrial relations as a strategic variable', in Kleiner, M. M., Block, R. N., Roomkin, M. and Salsburg, S. (eds.), *Human resources and the performance of the firm*, Industrial Relations Research Association, Madison.

Martin, P. Y. and Turner, B.A. (1986), 'Grounded theory and organizational research', *Journal of Applied Behavioral Science*, vol. 22, no. 2.

Melcher, A. L. (1975), *Structure and process of organizations: A systems approach*, Prentice-Hall, Englewood Cliffs.

Miles, M. B. and Huberman, M.A. (1984), *Qualitative data analysis*, Sage, Newbury Park.

Murray, A. I. and Reshef, Y. (1988), 'American manufacturing unions' stasis: A paradigmatic perspective', *Academy of Management Review*, vol. 13, no. 4.

Quaglieri, P. L. (1989), *America's labor leaders*, Lexington Books, Lexington.

Rankin, T. (1990), *New forms of work organization: The challenge for North American unions*, University of Toronto Press, Toronto.

Raskin, A. H. (1986), 'Labor: A movement in search of a mission', in Lipset, S.M.(ed.), *Unions in transition*, ICS, San Francisco.

Steiner, G. A. (1963), *Managerial long-range planning*, McGraw-Hill, New York.

Stratton, K. and Reshef, Y. (1990), 'Private sector unions and strategic planning: A research agenda', *Relations Industrielles*, vol. 45, no. 1.

Stratton- Devine, K. and Reshef, Y. (1996), 'Union planning: A framework and research agenda', *Relations Industrielles*, vol. 13, no. 4.

# Part IV

## MEMBER-UNION RELATIONS

# 16 Union attitudes as a perceptual filter

*E. Kevin Kelloway, Julian Barling and Victor M. Catano*

Unionization has been defined as the process of individual attachment to labour unions (Barling, Fullagar and Kelloway, 1992) and a great deal of data has now accumulated on the factors that lead an individual to join, become active in, and retain membership in a labour union. In reviewing this literature, Barling et al. (1992) pointed to the central role of union attitudes in the unionization process. For example, research on union joining (e.g. Brett, 1980), union commitment (Fullagar, McCoy, and Schull, 1992), union participation (Anderson, 1979; Glick, Mirvis and Harder, 1977; McShane, 1986), and union decertification (Bigoness and Tosi, 1984) have all reported significant relationships between individual attitudes toward labour unions and the criteria under investigation.

Deshpande and Fiorito (1989) drew a distinction between general and specific union attitudes, noting that the former term refers to 'beliefs about the effects of all unions at all workplaces' (p. 885) while the latter refers to 'beliefs about union effects at the respondents' own workplaces' (Deshpande and Fiorito, 1989, p. 885). Thus, beliefs about the general effectiveness of labour unions are typically viewed as measures of general union attitudes (McShane, 1986) while beliefs about the instrumentality of a specific union constitute specific union attitudes. Researchers who have made this distinction have generally concluded that specific union attitudes provide a better prediction of union-relevant criteria than do general attitudes (e.g. Barling et

Preparation of this manuscript was supported by grants from the Social Sciences and Humanities Research Council of Canada. Correspondence regarding this chapter should be addressed to Kevin Kelloway, Department of Psychology, University of Guelph, Guelph, Ontario, Canada, N1G 2W1.

al., 1992; Deshpande and Fiorito, 1989). This observation is consistent with the more general finding that attitudes toward specific behaviours offer stronger prediction than do more diffuse attitudes (e.g. Ajzen and Fishbein, 1980).

In practice, the importance of specific union attitudes suggest that unions focus on highlighting the positive advantages to be gained from union membership at a specific worksite. While we do not dispute this basic conclusion, we do suggest that the current empirical literature has understated the role of general union attitudes in the unionization process. More specifically, based on Brett's (1980) model of the unionization process, we suggest that general union attitudes provide a 'gatekeeping' (Barling et al., 1992) function in the unionization process. After outlining the nature of this gatekeeping function, we review four empirical studies that have tested, and supported the hypothesis. We conclude by considering the practical implications of our suggestion for unions.

## General union attitudes as a 'gatekeeper'

Researchers (e.g. Barling et al., 1992; Brett, 1980, Wheeler and McClendon, 1991), have suggested that the decision to vote for a union is based on three considerations. First, individuals must feel dissatisfied with some aspect of their employment. Certainly, there is a great deal of empirical evidence for job dissatisfaction as the 'trigger' (Youngblood, DeNisi, Molleston and Mobley, 1984) for unionization (for a review see Barling et al., 1992). Anecdotally, union organizers often recognize the importance of job dissatisfaction with the observation that 'the best organizer is the employer' (Brett, 1980). As a result, most models of unionization accord a pivotal role to job dissatisfaction (e.g. Brett, 1980; Premack and Hunter, 1988, for a review see Barling et al., 1992). Second, Brett (1980) suggested that job dissatisfaction would be unlikely to result in unionization unless individuals also held the perception that the union would be instrumental in redressing specific dissatisfactions. Again, the empirical data support this suggestion with a number of studies reporting moderate to high associations between perceptions of union instrumentality and interest in unionization (e.g. Beutell and Biggs, 1984; DeCotiis and LeLouarn, 1981; Deshpande and Fiorito, 1989; Montgomery, 1989; Premack and Hunter, 1988). While job satisfaction has been considered to be a 'trigger' for unionization (Youngblood et al., 1984), instrumentality beliefs have been labelled the 'augmenter' (Youngblood et al., 1984). Specifically, the suggestion is that job dissatisfaction will only lead to unionization if employees also perceive the union to be instrumental (Brett, 1980; Youngblood et al., 1984). Consistent with this suggestion,

Youngblood, Mobley and DeNisi (1981) reported that instrumentality perceptions moderated the prediction of union voting intentions by job satisfaction.

Finally, while most of the available literature focuses on the linear, additive effects of job dissatisfaction and union instrumentality as predictors of unionization, Brett (1980) has suggested that general union attitudes play a 'gatekeeping' role in the unionization process. In the absence of pro-union attitudes (e.g. attitudes toward the labour movement as a whole) a pro-union vote is unlikely even when other conditions (e.g. high job dissatisfaction, perceptions of union instrumentality) favour unionization. Similarly, Youngblood et al. (1984) describe attitudes toward labour unions (i.e. labour union image) as exerting a 'veto' in the unionization decision.

Although the available literature has supported the importance of both job dissatisfaction, general union attitudes, and union instrumentality as predictors of interest in unionization, this hypothesized moderating effect of general union attitudes remains untested to date (Barling et al., 1992). In the one empirical test we located in the literature, Youngblood et al. (1984) tested and failed to support the three way interaction of job dissatisfaction, instrumentality beliefs and union attitudes, however they did not examine the component two way interactions (e.g. dissatisfaction X attitudes, instrumentality X attitudes, dissatisfaction X instrumentality).

## The empirical evidence

In four recent studies, we have investigated the proposed 'gatekeeping' model of general union attitudes. All offer considerable support to the moderating role of general union attitudes.

First, Kelloway, Barling, Fullagar and Laliberte (1996) surveyed two samples of non-unionized faculty members (an American and a Canadian sample) and found that general union attitudes moderated the relationship between perceptions of union instrumentality and interest in unionization in both samples. Following Youngblood et al. (1984), Kelloway et al. (1996) tested for, but did not support the existence of a three-way interaction between job dissatisfaction, instrumentality perceptions, and general union attitudes. However in both samples, perceptions of instrumentality were related to interest in unionization for those individuals holding positive union attitudes (American Sample: b = .54, $p < .01$; Canadian Sample: b = .33, $p < .01$) and unrelated for those holding negative union attitudes (American Sample: b = .14, n.s.; Canadian Sample: b = -.09, n.s.). For the Canadian sample a similar moderating effect was found for the relationship between job dissatisfaction and interest in unionization; dissatisfaction was related to the criterion for those holding positive union attitude (b = .52, $p < .01$) but unrelated for those individuals who held negative union attitudes (b = .05, $p < .01$).

Similar results were obtained from our re-analysis of data taken from Kelloway and Barling's (1993) study of union members' participation in local union activities. In the original study, Kelloway and Barling (1993) reported that union members' feelings of loyalty to the union were predicted by (a) their perceptions of shop steward's transformational leadership styles and (b) their socialization experiences in the first year of union membership. In our reanalysis of the data, both predictions were moderated by respondents' general union attitudes. Specifically, perceptions of shop stewards' transformational leadership predicted union loyalty for those who held positive union attitudes (b = .26, $p < .01$) but not for those who held negative union attitudes (b = .00, n.s.). Similarly, first year socialization experiences predicted union loyalty for those who held positive general union attitudes (b = .27, $p < .01$) but not for those who held negative attitudes (b = .05, n.s.).

Kelloway, Barling, and Catano (1995) also supported the moderating role of general union attitudes in their study of union members. Based on data from 155 union members, general union attitudes again moderated the prediction of union loyalty from both shop stewards' leadership characteristics and recent (i.e. the last six months) union socialization experiences. In both cases, the predictor was associated with union loyalty for individuals holding positive union attitudes (Leadership b = .37, $p < .01$; Socialization: b = .34, $p < .01$) and unrelated to the criterion for those holding more negative perceptions of labour unions (Leadership b = .14, n.s.; Socialization b = .11, n.s.).

Taken together, the findings of the three studies discussed thus far offer considerable support for Brett's (1980) suggestion that general union attitudes play a 'gatekeeping' role in the unionization process. First, as predicted by Brett's (1980) model, job and specific union attitudes were related to interest in unionization only for those individuals holding positive attitudes toward the labour movement. Second, in the latter two studies, the model was extended to the case of union members and, again, the relationship between union experiences (e.g. shop stewards' leadership, socialization) and union loyalty was moderated by general union attitudes. Finally, in each case the nature of the interaction has the exact form predicted by Brett's hypothesis: positive union experiences or specific union attitudes have an impact only for those who also hold positive attitudes toward unions in general.

These findings give rise to the suggestion that general union attitudes may act as a perceptual filter in the unionization process. Specifically, the suggestion is that general union attitudes serve as a 'filter' through which union and job experiences are translated into attachment to (or disengagement from) the union. In this manner, general attitudes toward unions may serve as a predisposition for unionization. The fourth study to be reviewed here, directly assessed this suggestion.

Grace and Kelloway (1995) recently provided a rigorous test of the suggestion that general union attitudes may act as a perceptual filter. In contrast to the studies previously cited, Grace and Kelloway (1995) based their analysis on a sample of undergraduate students. The limited generalizability of this sampling decision was offset by the use of an experimental design in contrast to the reliance on cross-sectional survey data evidenced in earlier studies. Specifically, undergraduate students were randomly assigned to view one of two movies. The first movie *The Battle for Eastern Airlines* was a documentary on the labour-management disputes at Eastern Airlines during the 1980's. The second movie, *Twelve Angry Men*, was a dramatic presentation of conflict among a jury and made no reference to labour unions. Students completed measures of union attitudes immediately prior to seeing the movie, immediately after seeing the movie, and again two weeks after seeing the movie.

The results of the study substantially replicated the results cited earlier. For students who held positive union attitudes prior to the study, viewing a union-relevant movie resulted in increased union attitudes both immediately after seeing the movie (b = .46, $p < .01$) and again two weeks later (b = .32, $p < .05$). For students holding negative attitudes toward labour unions, there was no effect of viewing the union film either immediately afterward (b = -.24, n.s.) or two weeks later (b = -.19, n.s.). While the findings of Grace and Kelloway (1995) are consistent with the previous studies reviewed, it is important to note the need for replication with a non-student population to assess the generalizability of the results.

## Implications for research and practice

The data reviewed thus far, offer strong support for the notion that general union attitudes play a crucial role in the unionization process, acting as a perceptual filter through which union experiences are interpreted. These findings validate an important component of contemporary models of unionization. In contrast to the focus on the linear effects of job dissatisfaction and union instrumentality on unionization (see Barling et al., 1992), we hypothesized that union attitudes served a 'gatekeeper' function in moderating the relationship between job and union experiences and union-relevant outcomes. Although previous researchers have rarely empirically considered these non-linear effects, such effects clearly underlie model development (e.g. Brett, 1980).

One implication of this finding is that models of the unionization process that focus only on linear effects may be truncated in that they fail to take into account the additional variance attributable to the interaction of predictors and general union attitudes. Our results largely support Brett's (1980) suggestions which, until now, have not been empirically examined. The importance of the moderated relationships is underscored by the observation that the effect sizes obtained in the reported studies are large compared to the effect sizes typically attributed to interactions in non-experimental research (Aiken and West, 1991).

More pragmatically, our findings have considerable practical implications for labour unions. Organization of a union often relies on the politicization of the workforce by identifying and drawing attention to dissatisfying aspects of the job. Correspondingly, organizers frequently point to the successful history of the union in resolving dissatisfactions in other workplaces; a direct attempt to increase perceptions of union instrumentality. Our review suggests that this strategy alone is not likely to be productive without a concomitant focus on union attitudes. That is, simply identifying sources of dissatisfaction in the workplace and pointing to the previous instrumental achievements of the union is unlikely to result in individuals turning toward labour unions unless the individuals also hold a favourable attitude toward labour unions.

Shostak (1991) has noted the steady decline in the image of labour unions and emphasizes how critical the public image of unions is for the perceived power of organized labour. It has also been documented that politicians are responsive to public opinions about labour (Goldfield, 1987). Both observations point to the need for labour organizations to focus on developing positive union attitudes among both unionized and non-unionized employees.

To do so, we suggest that a consideration of general union attitudes and their determinants has considerable potential for advancing our understanding of the unionization process. For example, at least three studies (Fullagar et al., 1992; Fullagar, Clark, Gallagher and Gordon, 1994; Fullagar, Gordon, Gallagher and Clark, 1995) suggest the importance of union experiences as a predictor of union attitudes. In particular, this research has highlighted the role of new-member socialization as a predictor of union attitudes and behaviors.

There are also now data suggesting that individuals acquire union attitudes long before they enter the workforce (Barling, Kelloway and Bremermann, 1991) at least partially through a process of family socialization (Barling et al., 1991; Kelloway and Watts, 1994; Kelloway and Newton, 1996).

Moreover, family socialization continues to exert an effect on union attitudes long after individuals have acquired substantial experiences with labour unions. For example, in their survey of shop stewards, Kelloway, Catano and Carroll (in preparation) found that parental union activity predicted both the general union attitudes and militancy of shop stewards.

Although most of the research on the origin of general union attitudes has focused on family socialization influences, there are other factors that certainly play a role in shaping general union attitudes. The portrayal of labour organizations in news and entertainment media is unfailingly negative (Puette, 1992). Most commonly, media portrayals reinforce stereotypes of labour union corruption and the perception that unions are violent and disruptive influences in the workplace (Puette, 1992). Although no empirical data exist, such portrayals undoubtedly influence individual attitudes toward unions.

Our findings to date suggest that labour organizations would benefit from attempts to improve attitudes toward unions. Toward this end, ensuring positive union experiences for current members and working toward more positive portrayals of labour in the entertainment and news media would seem to be avenues worthy of further exploration. Similarly, given that union attitudes develop prior to entry into the workforce (Barling et al., 1992; Kelloway and Newton, 1996; Kelloway and Watts, 1994), labour organizations could benefit from strategies designed to inform young people about unions (e.g. the development of labour-oriented curricula). We suggest that the 'payoff' for such strategies would be seen in both certification campaigns and the development of a committed and active union membership.

## References


Aiken, L. S. and West, S. G. (1991), *Multiple regression: Testing and interpreting interactions*, SAGE, Beverly Hills.

Ajzen, I. and Fishbein, M. (1980), *Understanding attitudes and predicting social behavior*, Prentice-Hall, Englewood Cliffs, NJ.

Anderson, J.C. (1979), 'Local union participation: A reexamination', *Industrial Relations*, vol. 2, pp. 18-31.

Barling, J., Fullagar, C. and Kelloway, E. K. (1992), *The union and its members: A psychological approach*, Oxford University Press, New York.

Barling, J., Kelloway, E. K. and Bremermann, E. H. (1991), 'Preemployment predictors of union attitudes: The role of family socialization and work beliefs', *Journal of Applied Psychology*, vol. 76, pp. 725-731.

Beutell, N. J. and Biggs, D. L. (1984), 'Behavioral intentions to join a union: Instrumentality X valence, locus of control and strike attitudes', *Psychological Reports*, vol. 55, pp. 215-222.

Bigoness, W. J. and Tosi, H. L. (1984), 'Correlates of voting behavior in a union decertification election', *Academy of Management Journal*, vol. 27, pp. 654-659.

Brett, J. M. (1980), 'Why employees want unions', *Organizational Dynamics*, vol. 8, pp. 47-59.

DeCotiis, T. A. and LeLouarn, J. (1981), 'A predictive study of voting behavior in a representation election using union instrumentality and work perceptions', *Organizational Behavior and Human Performance*, vol. 27, pp. 103-118.

Deshpande, S. P. and Fiorito, J. (1989), 'Specific and general beliefs in union voting models', *Academy of Management Journal*, vol. 32, pp. 883-896.

Fullagar, C., Clark, P., Gallagher, D. G. and Gordon, M. E. (1994), 'A model of the antecedents of early union commitment: The role of socialization experiences and steward characteristics', *Journal of Organizational Behavior*, vol. 15, pp. 517-533.

Fullagar, C., Gordon, M.E., Gallagher, D. G. and Clark, P. E. (1995), 'Impact of early socialization on union commitment and participation: A longitudinal study', *Journal of Applied Psychology*, vol. 80, pp. 147-157.

Fullagar, C., McCoy, D. and Shull, C. (1992), 'The socialization of union loyalty', *Journal of Organizational Behavior*, vol. 13, pp. 13-26.

Glick, W., Mirvis, P. and Harder, D. (1977), 'Union satisfaction and participation', *Industrial Relations*, vol. 16, pp. 145-151.

Goldfield, M. (1987), *The decline of organized labour in the United States*, Chicago University Press, Chicago, IL.

Grace, K. A. and Kelloway, E. K. (1996), 'Union attitudes as a perceptual filter: An experimental investigation', Manuscript submitted for publication.

Kelloway, E. K., and Barling, J. (1993), 'Members' participation in local union activities: Measurement, prediction and replication', *Journal of Applied Psychology*, vol. 78, pp. 262-279.

Kelloway, E. K., Barling, J. and Catano, V. M. (1995), 'Union attitudes as a perceptual filter: Implications for training shop stewards', Paper presented at the 2nd International Conference on Emerging Union Structures, Stockholm, Sweden.

Kelloway, E. K., Barling, J., Fullagar, C. and Laliberte, M. (1995), 'Perceived need for unionization: The "gatekeeping" role of union attitudes', Manuscript submitted for publication.

Kelloway, E. K., Catano, V. M. and Carroll, A (in preparation), 'Predictors of shop steward militancy'.

Kelloway, E. K. and Newton, T. (1996), 'Preemployment predictors of union attitudes: The roles of parental union and job experiences', *Canadian Journal of Behavioral Science*, vol. 28, pp. 113-120.

Kelloway, E. K. and Watts, L. (1994), 'Preemployment predictors of union attitudes: Replication and extension', *Journal of Applied Psychology*, vol. 79, pp. 631-634.

McShane, S. L. (1986), 'General union attitude: A construct validation', *Journal of Labour Research*, vol. 8, pp. 402-417.

Montgomery, B. R. (1989), 'The influence of attitudes and normative pressures on voting decisions in a union certification election', *Industrial and Labour Relations Review*, vol. 42, pp. 262-279.

Premack, S. L. and Hunter, J. E. (1988), 'Individual unionization decisions', *Psychological Bulletin*, vol. 103, pp. 223-234.

Puette, W. (1992), *Through jaundiced eyes: How the media view organized labour*, ILR Press, Ithaca, NY.

Shostak, A. B. (1991), *Robust unionism: Innovations in the labour movement*, ILR Press, Ithaca, NY.

Wheeler, H. N. and McClendon, J. A. (1991), 'The individual decision to unionize', in Strauss, G. Gallagher, D. G. and Fiorito, J. (eds.), *The state of the unions*, Industrial Relations Research Association, Madison, WI.

Youngblood, S. A., DeNisi, A. S., Molleston, J. L. and Mobley, W. H. (1984), 'The impact of work environment, instrumentality beliefs, perceived labour union image, and subjective norms on union voting intentions', *Academy of Management Journal*, vol. 27, pp. 576-590.

Youngblood, S. A., Mobley, W. H. and DeNisi, A. S. (1981), 'Attitudes, perceptions, and intentions to vote in a union certification election: An empirical investigation', in *Proceedings of the 34th annual meeting of the Industrial Relations Research Association* (pp. 244-253), Industrial Relations Research Association, Madison, WI.

# 17 The business cycle theory and individual unionization decisions: A comparison of macro- and micro influences on union membership

*Coen van Rij and Annelies Daalder*

Trade-union membership varies in different historical periods (Visser, 1987). In the Netherlands, for example, trade-union density dropped from about 40 percent after the second World War to 25 percent in the 1980s. The question is why? Why are some employees organized, while others are not? And how is the union status of individuals affected by historical and macro-economic circumstances?

Within an international and comparative perspective the predominant focus of earlier studies is on the structural determinants of union density (Visser, 1987). Time series models or business-cycle models of trade union membership showed strong evidence for effects of economic circumstances. The literature is almost unanimous about the importance of the development of unemployment, prices and wages, and the annual level of unionization (see for example, Ashenfelter and Pencavel, 1969; Bain and Elsheikh, 1976; Fiorito and Greer, 1982; Visser, 1987; van Ours, 1991; van den Berg, 1995).

The business-cycle models are based on a macro-economic theory of behaviour. They explain annual fluctuations in aggregate unionism, e.g. the annual percentage of change in trade union membership. A basic assumption is that the economic factors influence workers' decisions about joining and

Coen van Rij is working as a researcher at the Centre for European Studies and Employment Relations (CESAR, University of Amsterdam). Annelies Daalder is project manager at Motivaction Amsterdam B.V., research and strategy development agency. The authors wish to thank J. Visser, D.G. Gallagher and J. Waddington for their comments on an earlier version of this chapter. Address correspondence to Coen van Rij, University of Amsterdam, CESAR, Oude Hougstraat 24, 1012 CE Amsterdam, Netherlands.

leaving a trade union. Generally, 'what the business cycle theory sets itself to explain is how individual decisions about joining or not joining the union are shaped by economic variables' (Visser, 1987: 64). Economic changes influence individual perceptions and expectations of the costs and benefits of being a trade-union member and when benefits outweigh costs a (rational) worker will join a trade union. Consequently, economic developments are expected to affect aggregate unionism.

In predicting individual decisions and aggregate levels of membership the business-cycle models strongly rely upon economic variables. The question is whether employees perceive their situation and choices in this way. The models deny factors related to the individual and workplace level (e.g. occupation, attitudes, values, etc.). Sociological and psychological studies have shown the importance of these personal factors with regard to membership decisions (Booth, 1986; Guest and Dewe, 1988; Hartley, 1992; Klandermans and Visser (eds.), 1995). What remains empirically untested is to what extent workers' joining decisions can be predicted from historical-economic circumstances (unemployment, wages, prices, etc.) and to what extent such decisions should be related to individual characteristics (for example: occupation, attitudes, values). A model and measurement scheme which considers the relative weight of both explanations is therefore needed. In this chapter such a model will be developed. More specifically: the model tests whether there is a direct effect of macro economic circumstances on individual decisions of joining and leaving a trade union. This approach bridges economic and sociological-psychological explanations with regard to joining and leaving a trade union.

It should be noted that the decision whether or not to join or leave a trade union is optional in the Netherlands. 'Closed shops' and 'union shops' are rare though there is an exception in the graphics industry.

## The business-cycle theory reconsidered

According to the business-cycle theory increases in monetary wages (nominal as well as real) affect unionization through the 'credit effect': the tendency of workers to credit wage rises to unions and to support them in the hope of doing as well or even better in the future (Bain and Elsheikh, 1976). Thus the higher the wages the stronger the 'credit effect', and the higher the level of unionization (or the number of members) in that year is likely to be. A positive relation is also assumed for prices. As Bain and Elsheikh argue, if prices rise workers seek protection for their lost income: the so-called 'threat effect'.

Since unions may provide such (inflation) protection this may lead to a higher union density rate.

Unemployment may have an effect on unionization in several ways. In times of high unemployment employers are confronted with a declining level of consumer demand. They therefore have to lower production and/or production costs, for example by lowering wages. If unemployment is high, it is relatively easy for employers to recruit an alternative part of the labour force — a cheaper part of course. They may be better able (and perhaps more willing) to oppose unionism. Consequently, employed workers may be reluctant to unionize for fear of antagonising their employers and thereby losing their jobs, and unemployed workers will have little incentive to unionize because unions can do little for them (Bain and Elsheikh, 1976). Moreover, during periods of high unemployment union members may perceive that it is not easy for unions to obtain concessions from their employers and come to feel that their membership is no longer worthwhile. Thus, it is anticipated that unemployment will have a negative impact upon unionization.

Finally, there is often a negative relation found between the level of unionization in the previous year and aggregate unionism in the current year. It is explained by a 'saturation effect': as the density gets higher it is more difficult to persuade the remaining non-members to become union members, as a result union growth declines. Every extra step becomes more difficult and this is especially the case for the final steps, or as Bain and Elsheikh point out, the (free) trade-union market is 'saturated'.

From several points of view the business-cycle model of trade union membership has been criticized. Criticism is usually directed to: (1) its variants on grounds of predictive ability, (2) the meaning attached to variables, (3) its structural stability and (4) the intercorrelations between variables (Fiorito and Greer, 1982). But, the basic assumption that individual decisions and cost-benefit considerations are directly influenced by macro-economic developments is seldom tested empirically or criticized. Although the relations between economic circumstances and individual decision making as discussed above are straightforward, and in the literature doubts are seldom stated with regard to this 'macro to micro links', it is questionable how and why macro factors have an effect on individual behaviour. Four issues are of particular concern.

Firstly, business-cycle models have been applied in many countries, and sometimes different effects are found. Rising unemployment may lead to both rising and declining unionism; in the US one finds a positive relation while in the UK and other European countries it is negative (van Ours,

1991).The problem is that under the *same* economic developments or threats (i.e. rising unemployment) people react quite differently, some join a trade union while others in apparently the same situation don't (or even resign).

Secondly, it is odd that there is no single business-cycle model that fits all historical periods. For example, Carruth and Disney (1988) concluded that the factors that appeared to explain union growth for Britain in the 1970s were less useful as union membership plummeted in the 1980s. van den Berg (1992) also encountered many difficulties in fitting one model covering a period of almost 80 years for the Netherlands. Moreover, her final models differed markedly from the original business-cycle models (Ashenfelter and Pencavel as well as Bain and Elsheikh).

The third argument comes from an individual perspective. If trade-union members are asked: "Why did you join a trade union?", they never mention general economic situations or changes like wage rise or rising unemployment. The three most important groups of motives are (1) egocentric motives: employees join because they believe that they will benefit personally; (2) sociocentric motives: employees join for reasons based on their social and political beliefs and collective interest; (3) social control motives: employees join because of 'pressure' (or norms) of social groups they belong to (van de Vall, 1963; Klandermans, 1986; van Rij, 1995).

Finally, the business-cycle model claims to explain joining and leaving at the same time but it actually compares members and non-members at several points in time (or for some period of time). Being a member or not in a particular year is the result of two processes, joining and leaving. These processes should be studied separately because different factors influence these different processes (van Rij and Saris, 1993; Klandermans and Visser (eds.), 1995). Furthermore, the effects may differ. On the one hand a wage rise may stimulate members to remain members (the credit effect), but on the other hand a wage rise will not necessarily stimulate non-members to join because they get a 'reward' for having a 'free ride' (see also Olson, 1965).

In this chapter we will therefore consider two models ('join' and 'leave'): the first model for the decision whether or not to join a trade union and the second model for the decision whether or not to resign. The problem with the business-cycle model is that only the (net) outcome of the decision processes is modelled.

## Joining and leaving: Two dynamic models

Decisions to join or leave a trade union are taken by individuals at some time in their life histories. Let us first look at the process of joining. On acquiring the first job after leaving school and entering the labour market, the individual becomes a potential union member. An important question is: How long does it take before someone decides to join a trade union? Do people join shortly after they find their first job? Or does it take several years before they decide to do so? Or do they perhaps never join? In other words: at what *rate* do non-members become members? The rate to join, j($t$), is defined as the 'instantaneous probability' to join a trade union at time t, given that one is still a non-member.[1] The rate of joining depends on personal factors as well as the macro-economic environment. This can be formalized using the Cox-model (see van Rij, 1994).

In the Cox model (1972) the rate of joining is modelled by assuming:

$$j(t) = j_0(t)\, e^{\gamma' \mathbf{x}(t)} \tag{1}$$

where $j_0(t)$ is the baseline hazard rate and g is a vector of coefficients and **X** a vector of covariates (that may change over time): wages, unemployment, level of unionization, etc. This is a ('regression') model which directly relates macro-economic variables to the individual rate of joining a trade union.

From the moment that one is a union member, it is possible to resign. Now the question is how much time does it take before someone decides to resign. Do people decide to resign soon after they have become members? Or does it take several years? These questions lead to the same formalization as for the process of joining. The rate to leave, h($t$), is defined as the 'instantaneous probability' to leave a trade union at time t, given that one is still a member:

$$h(t) = h_0(t)\, e^{\beta' \mathbf{y}(t)} \tag{2}$$

where $h_0(t)$ is the baseline hazard rate and b is a vector of coefficients and **Y** a vector of covariates that may vary over time.

The parameters of the vectors ($\gamma$ and $\beta$) in formulas 1 and 2 are estimated with partial likelihood estimation (Blossfeld, Hamerle and Mayer, 1989). The parameters give us the effect of wages, prices, unemployment etc. on the rate of joining (1) or the rate of leaving (2).

Please note that in these models historical time (i.e. the macro-economic changes over the years) as well as biographical time (i.e. the working career of an individual) are integrated. In formulae 1 'time' ($t$) is related to the working career, that is the years workers are not unionized since the first job, and **X** (with time-varying variables) is related to the historical context, i.e. the time during which the decisions took place. Since this context may change from year to year, its value in the first year of the first job may differ from the value in the second or third year. The data needed to estimate these models come from different levels: micro and macro.

## Data

After starting his or her working career, the worker may or may not join a trade union and, as has been discussed, this decision may take place at any time. A hypothetical union history may be: someone starts the first job at 18 years of age, joins a trade union at the age of 25, and resigns at the age of 40.

To calculate the rate of joining or leaving one has to collect this kind of information for every person. We did this using a computer assisted retrospective interview. All respondents are members of a computer panel (STP): a representative sample of the Dutch population in 1992 (n=1500).[2] Firstly, we asked the respondents questions to reconstruct their 'union history' (Are you a trade union member? If yes, when did you join? If no, have you ever been a trade union member? Etc.). Secondly, some questions about attitudes, networks, contacts with the unions, the working career and job characteristics were asked for. For the network variable, for example, the respondents were asked to guess the level of unionization at the beginning of every job on a six point scale and it was also asked if there was an expectation in the workplace that one should be a trade-union member (on a seven point scale). The choice of the variables is mainly based on older research (Klandermans, 1986; Guest and Dewe, 1988). For these variables it is anticipated that when attitudes towards trade unions and trade union membership are positive, the (social) network is 'pro-union' and there are (personal) contacts between the union and (potential) members, the rate of joining will increase and the rate of leaving will decrease. In the model these factors represent the personal situation and will be used as control variables to investigate the effect of the macro-economic circumstances.

Of course not all personal histories are complete, for example for someone who is 25 years of age and not a member in 1992 (the year of the interview) we do not know whether she or he will join a trade union after 5 years. Some part of the information is therefore missing or censored. In the calculation, censoring is incorporated (Blossfeld et al., 1989).

The historical-economic developments are based on data from the Central Bureau of Statistics (CBS, 1989) in the Netherlands, Visser (1989) and van den Berg (1992). In Table 17.1 an overview of the variables is given. The variables in Table 17.1 are measured after the beginning of the working career until the year of the interview. If a change after the first job occurs, the value of the variable is updated.

**Table 17.1**
**An overview of variables**

| Variable | Operationalization |
|---|---|
| **Economic developments 1947-1990** | |
| Unemployment | unemployment in year t |
| Prices | annual % change in consumer prices |
| Wages | annual % change in nominal hourly wages of male industry workers |
| Price/wage index | annual % change in real wages |
| Level of unionization | union density rate in year t: ratio of membership and dependent labour force (employed only) |
| Strikes | number of strikes in a year |
| **Personal opinions** (5 point scales) | |
| Trade union attitude | very negative(1) - very positive (5) |
| Cost > benefits | strongly disagree(1) - strongly agree(5) |
| **Network** | |
| Level of unionization at workplace | 10% or less(1) - more than 51%(6) |
| Pro-union atmosphere at workplace | very negative(1) - very positive(5) |
| Was/is either parent a union member | no(0), yes(1) |
| **Contacts with trade union** | |
| Personal help | no(0), yes(1) |
| Meeting attendance | no(0), yes(1) |
| Recruitment campaign | no(0), yes(1) |
| Strike within industry | no(0), yes(1) |
| **Personal background** | |
| Gender | man(0), woman(1) |
| Number of previous jobs | number 1-14 |
| Unemployed in year t | no(0), yes(1) |
| Joined for personal benefits | no(0), yes(1) |

## Results

The analyses are restricted to respondents who started to work after 1947 and before 1990. Since van den Berg (1992) has shown that there is a structural break in the business-cycle model in the Netherlands, we restricted the analyses to the post war period. The models in Table 17.2 incorporate macro-economic variables that have been important in the Netherlands (after 1947): level of unemployment, changes in real wages (i.e. price/wage index). In the model of van den Berg the number of strikes is added. It is predicted that workers are more inclined to join a trade union during a period when there are more or longer strikes. This membership accretion is called 'war-profits'. During a strike workers do not get wages; in order to receive strike pay they have to first join the union. Therefore, a positive relation is expected between the number of (successful) strikes and individual decisions about joining trade unions.

For joining as well as leaving we estimated two models: one with only these macro-economic variables and one with macro-economic as well as personal variables. For the latter we investigated whether or not the macro-economic variables could be deleted from the model without decreasing the fit of it. At the bottom of the table the results are given.[3] We also investigated other economic variables or lagged influences (see Table 17.1) but no significant effects were found and these effects are therefore not presented in Tables 17.2 and 17.3. The final choice is based on the model of van den Berg. We have to conclude that with regard to joining as well as leaving a trade union the macro-economic variables may be omitted because the fit of the models do not decrease (significantly).

### *Joining a trade union*

Looking at the complete model the first impression is that gender, contacts, occupational networks and personal opinions are important in explaining the tendency for joining a trade union (see Table 17.2). Men are more likely to join than women; if one contacts or is contacted by a trade union one will also sooner join (personal help and recruitment campaigns are the most important contacts); if the level of unionization at the job is perceived to be high or personal attitudes are positive, again the rate of joining rises significantly. For the number of previous jobs a negative effect is found. Most people decide whether or not to join during the first years of the working career, i.e. before the age of 35. So, if the number of jobs increases (and generally people are older) the rate of joining decreases.

After controlling for individual differences, macro-economic circumstances are of minor importance. None of these effects are significant. But, if all personal variables are deleted and a model with only macro-economic factors is estimated, we find a small significant effect for unemployment. In the complete model this effect however vanishes. The effects of unemployment and real wage change are in the expected direction. A negative effect of unemployment and a positive effect of wages. For strikes a positive effect was expected but the contrary was found.

**Table 17.2**
**Cox models for joining and leaving a trade union**

| | Business-cycle model | | Complete model | |
|---|---|---|---|---|
| | Joining | Leaving | Joining | Leaving |
| **Economic developments** | | | | |
| Unemployment | -0.0008* | 0.0006 | -0.0003 | 0.0004 |
| Price/wage index | -0.0033 | -0.0128 | 0.0282 | -0.0068 |
| Strikes | 0.0021 | 0.0025 | -0.0003 | 0.0004 |
| **Personal opinions** | | | | |
| Trade union attitude | | | 0.8203* | -0.2103* |
| Cost > benefits | | | -0.1454* | 0.1030* |
| **Network** | | | | |
| Level of unionization at workplace | | | 0.1068* | -0.0112 |
| Pro-union atmosphere at workplace | | | 0.1976* | -0.1217* |
| Was/is either parent a union member | | | 0.1225 | -0.2623 |
| **Contacts with regard to joining** | | | | |
| Personal help | | | 0.8970* | - |
| Meeting attendance | | | 0.5654* | - |
| Recruitment campaign | | | 0.9946* | - |
| Strike within industry | | | 0.8568* | - |
| **Personal background** | | | | |
| Gender | | | -0.4808* | 0.5750* |
| Number of previous jobs | | | -0.0797* | 0.0828* |
| Unemployed | | | - | 1.2563* |
| Joined a union for personal benefits | | | - | -0.3647* |
| Number of respondents[a] | 927 | 460 | 927 | 460 |
| % censored | 61.9% | 57.2% | 61.9% | 57.2% |
| Log (L) | -2780.65 | -1083.29 | -2494.64 | -1044.36 |
| Likelihood ratio test (df=3) | | | 7.02 | 2.61 |
| p-value | | | 0.0712 | 0.4560 |

*Notes* * significant at 5% level

[a] Because workers generally only join a trade union when they have a paid job we used for the analyses of joining a trade union 'job spells' instead of the time since the first job. See for a more detailed discussion of this procedure Van Rij (1994).

*Leaving a trade union*

For the model of leaving a trade union 'having a job or not' seems to be the most important factor. Also here the effects of the macro-economic environment are small non-significant. Unemployment gets important if one becomes unemployed or may become unemployed. Besides the effect of having a paid job or not, gender, number of previous jobs, atmosphere and personal attitudes towards trade unions are significant. In the exit model we also included one of the reasons people could mention for joining the trade union. Workers who join for individual benefits (insurance, shopping discounts, legal help, etc.) have a lower rate of leaving than workers who do not join for this reason.

In Table 17.2 the parameters of both models are estimated. The interpretation of the parameters is not always easy. Some of the effects are positive and others are negative. If an effect is positive then an increase of the exogenous variable will result in an increase of the rate (of joining as well as leaving). The question is: How much does the rate change? In other words: What will be the effect of a change in one of the variables on the rate? In Table 17.3 one can see an overview of the estimated change of the rate if one of the variables is increased by one unit.[4] For the process of joining the effect of the number of previously held jobs is negative. Every additional job decreases the rate of joining by almost 8 percent. On the other hand, if an individual contacts a trade union (or the union contacts the individual) during a recruitment campaign the rate of joining rises by 170 percent. And with regard to leaving a trade union one can see in Table 17.3 that if one becomes unemployed the rate of leaving rises by 250 percent.

## Conclusions and discussion

The literature is almost unanimous about the importance of the development of unemployment, prices and wages, and the annual level of unionization on the decisions of workers about joining or leaving a trade union. The arguments seem very plausible. Nevertheless, a basic assumption concerning individual behaviour is untested in these models. Ashenfelter and Pencavel (1969) and Bain and Elsheikh (1976) (see also Fiorito and Greer, 1982) identified relationships between macro-economic factors and trade-union membership, for example the 'credit effect' and the 'threat effect', but their approach is weaker in determining whether the explanations they offer are accurate (Hartley, 1992).[5] Is this how employees perceive their situation and possibilities? When the individual rate of joining or leaving a trade union over time is investigated a direct effect of macro-economic features or the structural context on the decision making processes may be rejected.

**Table 17.3**
**Change in the rate of joining and leaving**

| | Joining | Leaving |
|---|---|---|
| **Economic developments** | | |
| Unemployment | -0.03% | 0.04% |
| Price/wage index | 2.86% | -0.68% |
| Strikes | -0.03% | 0.04% |
| **Personal opinions** | | |
| Trade union attitude | 127.12% | -18.97% |
| Cost > benefits | -13.53% | 10.85% |
| **Network** | | |
| Level of unionization at workplace | 11.27% | -1.11% |
| Pro-union atmosphere at workplace | 21.85% | -11.46% |
| Was/is either parent a union member | 13.03% | -23.07% |
| **Contacts with regard to joining** | | |
| Personal help | 145.22% | - |
| Meeting attendance | 76.02% | - |
| Recruitment campaign | 170.36% | - |
| Strike within industry | 135.56% | - |
| **Personal background** | | |
| Gender | -38.17% | 77.71% |
| Number of previous jobs | -7.66% | 8.63% |
| Unemployed | - | 251.24% |
| Joined a union for personal benefits | - | -30.56% |

If no direct macro-economic effect is found the question rises: Can we do without these structural explanations with regard to the understanding of union membership changes? Probably not. Although a direct effect must be rejected, an *in*direct effect may still exist. Thus, the actual place of the factors within the behavioural framework should change. In the business-cycle model they are given a central position, i.e. close to the decision processes. These factors should however be regarded as shaping the environment, the context within which individuals' decisions take place. Unemployment gets important if one becomes unemployed or may become unemployed. If that is the case, the personal situation changes due to an (external) event. At that moment employees may reconsider a former decision; remain a member, resign membership or perhaps join. The personal situation is crucial and this situation explains why people react differently in apparently the same economic situations.

The present research also implies some recommendations for trade unions that want to increase the rate of joining and decrease the rate of leaving. A pro-union attitude and a pro-union (working) network are important for joining as well as leaving a trade union. The attitude and the network can best be 'shaped' at the plant. It is therefore important to contact members as well as potential members. These contacts should take place at the beginning of the working career. The findings show that young workers have a higher propensity of joining than older workers; the decision to join is typically made before the age of 35. However, the outflow is greatest among young people, women, and members who are temporary unemployed. Generally, these groups have a lower number of contacts with trade unions and, as contacts are so important, trade unions will have to considerably improve their presence and services at the plant level if they want to increase their membership again. Within an environment of increasing flexibilization of working relations, this will become more and more difficult in the future.

Although there is not a direct effect of historical-economic circumstances, the environment may still serve as a 'gateway' for decisions of joining and leaving a trade union. Future research might focus more on this 'gateway' function. Economic explanations should therefore not be treated as opposed to sociological-psychological explanations (as has been done in this chapter), but as being in line with individual factors. This will enhance our understanding of unionization decisions of (individual) workers.

## Notes

1. Although a worker may join or leave a trade union several times during the lifetime we split the model into two single event models.
2. Every household in the sample is supplied with a computer and a modem. The questionnaires are sent to the households through the telephone line and the data are returned to the central computer at the University automatically after the respondents have filled in the the answers. The household members fill in the questionnaires at home without interviewers present.
3. The logarithms of the maximized likelihood's can be used to compute likelihood ratio tests for models that are nested. With large samples this test is chi-square distributed with m (the number of constraints) degrees of freedom. All tests are performed at an $\alpha$ level of .05. When the three economic factors are deleted, the fit of the model of joining and leaving decreases, respectively with a $\chi^2$ of

7.02 and a $\chi^2$ of 2.61. And with a critical value of 7.81 and 3 degrees of freedom this decrease is not significant.

4. If the value of a covariate changes by one unit than the rate changes by $\Delta\ rate = (\exp(\hat{\beta}) - 1) * 100\%$.
5. The business-cycle theory does not pretend nor claim to give a complete answer to the question of union growth or decline and the decision making processes facing choices of joining and leaving trade unions (Visser, 1987).

## References


Ashenfelter, O. and Pencavel, J.H. (1969), 'American trade union growth: 1900-1960', *Quarterly Journal of Economics*, vol. 83, pp. 434-448.

Bain, G.S. and Elsheikh, F. (1976), *Union growth and the business cycle: An econometric analysis*, Blackwell, Oxford.

Berg, A. van den (1992), *Building a time-series model on trade union growth in the Netherlands, 1910-1989*, Research Memorandum 9227, Faculty of Economics, University of Amsterdam.

Berg, A. van den (1995), *Trade union growth and decline in the Netherlands*, Thesis publishers, Amsterdam (dissertation).

Blossfeld, H.P., Hamerle, A. and Mayer, K.U. (1989), *Event-history analysis: Statistical theory and application in the social sciences*, Hillsdale, New Jersey.

Booth, A. (1986), 'Estimating the probability of trade union membership: A study of men and women in Britain', *Economica*, vol. 53, pp. 41-61.

CBS, Centraal Bureau voor de Statistiek (1989), *Negentig jaren statistiek in tijdsreeksen*, Staatsuitgeverij, Den Haag.

Cox, D.R. (1972), 'Regression models in life-tables', *Journal of the Royal Statistical Society*, vol. 34, pp. 187-220.

Carruth, A. and Disney, R. (1988), 'Where have two million trade union members gone?', *Economica*, vol. 55, pp. 1-19.

Fiorito, J. and Greer, C.R. (1982), 'Determinants of US unionism: Past research and future needs', *Industrial Relations*, vol. 21, pp. 1-32.

Guest, D.E. and Dewe, P. (1988), 'Why workers belong to a trade union?: A social psychological study in the U.K. electronics industry', *British Journal of Industrial Relations*, vol. 26, pp. 178-193.

Hartley, J.F. (1992), 'Joining a trade union', in Hartley, J.F. and Stephenson, G.M. (eds.), *Employment relations: The psychology of influence and control at work*, Blackwell, Oxford.

Klandermans, P.G. (1986), 'Participatie in de vakbond: Een overzicht van theorie en onderzoek', *Tijdschrift voor Arbeidsvraagstukken*, vol. 2, pp. 14-29.

Klandermans, P.G. and Visser, J. (eds.) (1995), *De vakbeweging ná de welvaartstaat*, van Gorcum, Assen.

Olson, M. (1965), *The logic of collective action: Public goods and the theory of groups*, Harvard University Press, Cambridge.

Ours, J.C. van (1991), *Union growth in the Netherlands 1961-1989*, Research Memorandum 1991-3, Faculty of Economics, Free University Amsterdam.

Rij, J.C. van and Saris, W.E. (1993), 'Time dependency of trade union membership', *Quality and Quantity*, vol. 27, pp. 73-93.

Rij, J.C. van (1994), *To join or not to join: An event-history analysis of trade union membership in the Netherlands*, NIMMO, Amsterdam (dissertation).

Rij, J.C. van (1995), 'Naar de bond', in: P.G. Klandermans and J. Visser (eds.), *De vakbeweging ná de welvaartstaat*, van Gorcum, Assen.

Vall, M. van de (1963), *De vakbeweging in de welvaartstaat: Een macro- en micro-sociale analyse*, Boom, Meppel.

Visser, J. (1987), *In search of inclusive unionism: A comparative analysis*, University of Amsterdam (dissertation).

Visser, J. (1989), *European trade unions in figures*, Kluwer, Deventer.

# 18 Abstaining from voting in union certification elections

*C. Gail Hepburn, Catherine A. Loughlin and Julian Barling*

Trade unions are facing a crisis with respect to membership in North America (Goldfried, 1987). In the United States, the proportion of unionized workers has decreased from 35 percent in the 1950s to 11.2 percent in 1993 (Gordon, Barling and Tetrick, 1995). Union density in Canada has risen from 30 percent in 1961 to 38 percent in 1986 (Barling, Fullagar and Kelloway, 1992), but the fact remains that most workers are not unionized, and little if any growth is occurring. One probable reason for the decline of unions in the United States is the decreased union success in organizing employees through representation elections[1] (Deshpande and Fiorito, 1989; Goldfried, 1987). To understand this, a considerable body of research has examined individual voting behaviour in union representation elections and the decision to join a union (e.g. Brett, 1980; Premack and Hunter, 1988).

Numerous studies have shown that job satisfaction has a significant impact on individuals' voting intentions and behaviour in representation elections. Specifically, job dissatisfaction (especially, but not only, dissatisfaction with *extrinsic* work related issues) consistently predicts pro-union intentions or pro-union voting (see Barling et al., 1992, pp. 48-53).

---

Portions of this research were supported by a grant from the Social Sciences and Humanities Research Council of Canada to Julian Barling and Kevin Kelloway. The authors express their appreciation to Mike Groom, of the Canadian Union of Educational Workers, and Kevin Kelloway and Kathleen Grace for their assistance in different phases of this project. Correspondence concerning this chapter should be addressed to Julian Barling, School of Business, Queen's University, Kingston, Ontario, Canada K7L 3N6.

Research findings also show that positive general union attitudes predict pro-union voting intentions and behaviour. For example, Getman, Goldberg and Herman (1976) showed that knowing general union attitudes enables one to predict a union vote correctly with 79 percent accuracy.

In addition, the possible effects of peer pressures on union voting have long been acknowledged (Bakke, 1945; Chamberlin, 1935; Whyte, 1944). Several studies have examined the impact of normative or social pressures on pro-union voting intentions and behaviours. These studies showed that peer attitudes influence respondents' own union attitudes and voting (Davy and Shipper, 1993; Montgomery, 1989; Youngblood, DeNisi, Molleston and Mobley, 1984; Zalesny, 1985). Voting in favour of the union in certification elections, therefore, is associated with job dissatisfaction, positive general union attitudes and peer pressures.

However, at this stage we do not know what factors lead individuals to choose to abstain from voting altogether, i.e. *not* to vote in certification elections. This is a major omission in our knowledge of the predictors of union voting behaviour. From a practical perspective, this group of potential voters cannot be ignored. Not only is the margin of victory for a union in a certification election typically very small, but the number of potential voters in a certification election who opt to abstain may well be sufficient to alter the outcome of the election (Roomkin and Block, 1981). As Barling et al. (1992, p. 31) have noted '... votes from each and every employee could well constitute the deciding factor in a labour or management victory'. Moreover, it may be easier to persuade people to vote rather than to change the direction of their vote once they have decided. Thus, in the present study we focused on why individuals choose not to vote in union certification elections. We surveyed a group of university teaching and research assistants, and contract sessional faculty following a union organizing drive.

We suggest that abstainers can be distinguished from individuals who choose to vote in the certification election. In general, the decision to abstain from voting is not unusual: Roughly 30 percent of the eligible voters in the United Kingdom and 50 percent of the eligible voters in the US fail to vote in political elections (Fife-Schaw and Breakwell, 1990). In fact, one rational question is why people choose to vote at all (Dunleavy, 1992), given that the difficulties associated with voting (e.g. registering, travelling to the polling station) may well outweigh the likelihood of one's vote being decisive in determining the outcome of the election if a ballot was cast. Therefore, in the same way that the perceived instrumentality of the union is critical in determining whether individuals will participate in union activities (Barling et al., 1992; Kelloway and Barling, 1993), we propose that perceiving one's vote as instrumental or crucial to the outcome of the certification election is critical in determining whether or not someone will vote. In this sense, voting in a certification election would reflect a rational decision only if one believes that his/her vote matters (Dunleavy, 1992).

Personal interest in the certification election and in voting is also suggested as a predictor of whether individuals will choose to vote in the certification campaign or not. Our reason for this supposition emanates from the literature on voting in political elections (Traugott and Tucker, 1984). Fife-Schaw and Breakwell (1990) investigated the intention not to vote among 17 and 18-year-olds in the United Kingdom, and found that a lack of interest in politics was the factor that most strongly differentiated between those intending to vote and those not intending to vote.

Finally, the question remains of where abstainers stand with respect to the variables that traditionally have separated those voting in favour of union representation from those voting against union representation, namely job satisfaction, general union attitudes and peer pressures. In the present study we specifically chose to examine satisfaction with administration instead of general job satisfaction because it was one of the central issues raised in the certification election, and is also one of the factors identified by Premack and Hunter (1988) as critical in the decision to vote for or against union representation.

Maintaining the view that abstaining from voting is a rational choice, the literature on abstaining from voting in political elections has suggested the notion of 'indifference' to explain abstaining from voting. Brody and Page (1973) showed that individuals who could not differentiate their own opinions concerning political candidates (i.e. did not favour one over another) did not vote. Zipp (1985) included the views of the voter in his conceptualization of indifference in American voters. He found that as the level of indifference of a voter increased, or the further away all the political candidates' interests or views on an issue were from the voter's own views, the less likely an individual was to vote. Voting is more likely to occur when there is a clear choice, such as when the voter's own opinions are closely aligned with one candidate's yet are far from another's. In this instance a real benefit or impact can be achieved by voting.

In the context of the present study, if an individual was dissatisfied with administration a vote in favour of union representation could achieve an outcome desirable to the individual — input into decisions regarding wages. Alternatively, an individual satisfied with administration may have wished to maintain the status quo and a vote against union representation would result in the more favourable outcome. Individuals holding neutral views, i.e. neither satisfied nor dissatisfied with administration, would see no clear advantage in voting one way or the other and may choose not to vote. Similarly, those individuals with strong positive or negative union attitudes would see a clear choice and vote appropriately. Those individuals with more neutral views regarding unions may not favour union representation over management (or the reverse) and may abstain. This logic can be extended to include peer pressure. Those individuals perceiving environments strongly in favour or against unions would vote accordingly, but those perceiving their peers as neutral will see no gain in voting and will abstain. Thus, variables traditionally used to differentiate yes votes and no votes may reflect a continuum ranging between a vote in favour of union representation and a vote against union representation, with the decision to abstain lying somewhere between these extremes. Therefore, we predict that abstainers would lie on the middle of such a continuum with respect to satisfaction with administration, union attitudes and peer pressures.

## Method

### *The certification context*

We studied a group of teaching and research assistants and contract and sessional faculty at one university in Ontario, Canada. The central issue for the teaching and research assistants was the desire to participate in decisions regarding pay. For the contract faculty, the basic issue prompting the unionization drive was wages; secondary issues included seniority, child care and harassment policy. These two groups voted together; however, the university subsequently appealed to the Ontario Labour Relations Board and they were recognised as two separate bargaining units.

There were 778 eligible voters among the teaching and research assistants; 366 voted, there were 2 spoiled ballots, and 410 abstentions. Of the 364 valid votes (47 percent voter turnout), 184 were cast in favour of union representation, 180 against. Among the contract faculty, there were 113 eligible voters, 48 of whom voted. Thirty five voted for union representation and 13 against union representation.

### *Participants and procedure*

Almost four weeks after the election, 891 individuals from the university whose names appeared on a voter list for the union representation election received our questionnaire via the internal campus mail. A total of 270 questionnaires (30 percent response rate) were returned to the researchers (who were from a different university). Of these, 12 were received more than one month following the original mailout of the questionnaire and were excluded from the analyses because of concerns about the retrospective nature of the data; 12 others were excluded because of incomplete data. This resulted in a sample of 246 respondents: 83 who had not voted, 79 who voted in favour of union representation and 84 who voted against union representation. Of those who had not voted, 41 were excluded from the analysis because they indicated that external events had prevented them from voting. Excluding these individuals is important to ensure that not voting was a function of an explicit decision, and that the remaining respondents were true abstainers, thereby reducing error variance in this group. This procedure left us with 42 abstainers. The remaining respondents (100 males, 103 females; 2 unstated) ranged from 19 years to 65 years of age ($M$ = 28.61 years, $SD$ = 6.20).

### *Measures*

*Union vote* Respondents were asked two questions to identify their voting behaviour: First, they were asked 'Did you vote in the recent union representation election?'. For those who had not voted, they were asked 'Did external events (e.g. illness, out of town, field trip) prevent you from participating in the vote?'. If they reported that they had voted, they were then asked 'Did you vote for the union?'.

All other measures were rated on seven-point scales (1 = strongly disagree, 7 = strongly agree). The score used for each measure was the mean of the items.

*Voting instrumentality* Four items adapted from Chacko's (1985) perceived union instrumentality measure were used to measure perceived voting instrumentality in the representation election (alpha = 0.70). The items were 'Voting in a representation election gives me a chance to express my opinion', 'Voting in a representation election gives me a say in the outcome of the election', 'Voting in a representation election allows me to influence other people' and 'Every vote in a representation election is critical'.

*Interest* Three items were designed specifically for this survey to measure respondents' interest in the election and voting (alpha = 0.87). The items read 'I am interested in voting in general union votes', 'I was interested in the recent representation election' and 'The issues in the recent representation election were of interest to me'.

*Satisfaction with administration* Four items derived from Zalesny (1985) were used (alpha = 0.83). Respondents were asked to indicate how satisfied they were with 'The power and decision-making structure', 'Your rate of pay', 'The way your workplace is managed' and 'The way financial decisions are made'.

*Union attitudes* General attitudes toward unions in academic institutions were measured with three items used by Zalesny (1985) (alpha = 0.96). The items were 'Collective bargaining for teaching assistants/research assistants/ sessionals is consistent with my professional values', 'Collective bargaining is an appropriate form of representation for people in my position' and 'Collective bargaining is an appropriate form of representation for academic institutions'.

*Peer pressures* Two items derived from Zalesny (1985) were used (alpha = 0.60). The items were 'My fellow departmental teaching assistants/research assistants/sessionals at this university generally approve of unionization for teaching assistants/research assistants/sessionals' and 'The faculty in my department generally approve of unionization for teaching assistants/research assistants/sessionals'.

## Results

Descriptive statistics, intercorrelations and internal consistency of the measures appear in Table 18.1. A direct discriminant function analysis was performed using five predictors (voting instrumentality, interest, satisfaction with administration, union attitudes and peer pressures) and three groups (eligible voters who abstained from voting, those voting in favour of union representation and those voting against union representation).

**Table 18.1**
**Descriptive statistics, intercorrelations and internal consistency for study variables**

| Predictor | *M* | *SD* | Alpha | 1 | 2 | 3 | 4 |
|---|---|---|---|---|---|---|---|
| 1. Voting instrumentality | 5.07 | 1.19 | 0.70 | | | | |
| 2. Interest | 4.55 | 1.80 | 0.87 | 0.37** | | | |
| 3. Satisfaction with admin. | 4.60 | 1.32 | 0.83 | -0.15* | -0.28** | | |
| 4. Union attitudes | 3.97 | 2.02 | 0.96 | 0.35** | 0.51** | -0.51** | |
| 5. Peer pressures | 3.30 | 1.23 | 0.60 | 0.11 | 0.22** | -0.26** | 0.48** |

*Note:* * $p < .05$, [b] $p < .01$

With these groups two discriminant functions were obtained, and the combined functions were significant, $\chi^2(10, N = 205) = 242.08, p < .001$. Removal of the first discriminant function resulted in a significant Chi Square, $\chi^2(4, N = 205) = 58.27, p < .001$. Thus, two discriminant functions, the second function orthogonal to the first, distinguish between the groups. Further, the second function employs associations among the predictor variables not used in the first function. The first and second function accounted for 81.67 percent and 18.33 percent of the between group variance respectively. Figure 18.1 shows that the first function discriminated participants who voted in favour of union representation from the abstainers and those voting against union representation in a linear fashion. The second function discriminated the abstainers from both groups of voters.

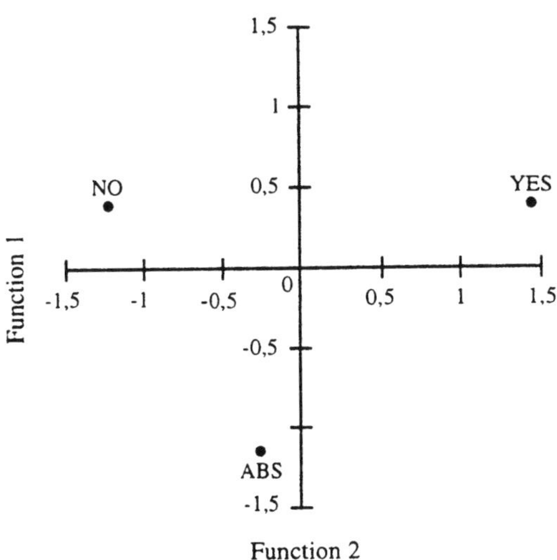


**Figure 18.1 Plots of three group centroids on the two discriminant functions**

Correlations between the predictor variables and the discriminant functions are shown in Table 18.2. These correlations reveal that the predictors that best distinguished between the three groups were union attitudes, satisfaction with administration and peer pressures. The predictors that best distinguished between the abstainers and those who voted were interest and voting instrumentality.

**Table 18.2**
**Correlations of predictor variables with discriminant functions**

| Predictor | Discriminant function 1 | 2 |
|---|---|---|
| Union attitudes | 0.92 | 0.13 |
| Satisfaction with administration | -0.50 | -0.14 |
| Peer pressures | 0.40 | -0.21 |
| Interest | 0.31 | 0.85 |
| Voting instrumentality | 0.19 | 0.48 |

A comparison of the mean scores for the three groups on all study variables was conducted using one-way ANOVA's (see Table 18.3). All *F* ratios were significant. Newman-Keuls post hoc tests were used to isolate specific group differences in the mean scores.

**Table 18.3**

**Scores of the three groups on predictor variables and *F* ratios**

| | Abstainers M *(SD)* | 'Yes' Vote M *(SD)* | 'No' Vote *M* *(SD)* | *F* |
|---|---|---|---|---|
| **Function 1** | | | | |
| Union attitudes | 3.41 (1.51) | 5.83 (1.04) | 2.51 (1.49) | 129.90* |
| Satisfaction with administration | 4.94 (1.23) | 3.72 (1.21) | 5.24 (0.99) | 39.51* |
| Peer pressures | 3.43 (1.12) | 3.91 (1.04) | 2.67 (1.15) | 25.94* |
| **Function 2** | | | | |
| Interest | 2.94 (1.39) | 5.52 (1.19) | 4.43 (1.85) | 38.93* |
| Voting instrumentality | 4.39 (1.37) | 5.49 (0.90) | 5.00 (1.17) | 13.42* |

*Note:* * $p < .001$

Group differences on the variables that best distinguished between the three groups were as follows: Those voting in favour of the union had significantly more favourable union attitudes, expressed significantly less satisfaction with administration and reported peer pressures indicating significantly greater acceptance of unionization from fellows and faculty, than both the abstainers and those voting against the union. Further, the abstainers had significantly more favourable union attitudes and reported peer pressures indicating significantly greater acceptance of unionization from fellows and faculty than those voting against the union. These two groups did not significantly differ on satisfaction with administration.

Group differences on the variables that best distinguished between the abstainers and those who voted were as follows: Abstainers reported significantly less interest and perceived significantly less voting instrumentality than either those voting in favour or those voting against union representation. Those voting in favour of the union reported significantly more interest and perceived significantly more voting instrumentality than those voting against union representation.

Classification compares participants' actual group membership with their predicted membership based on the two discriminant functions. Due to there being three groups of differing sizes, 35.84 percent of the eligible voters would be correctly classified by chance alone. Chance alone would result in the correct classification of 20.49 percent of abstainers, 38.53 percent of those voting in favour of unionization and 40.98 percent of those voting against unionization. Overall, 169 (82.44 percent) of the 205 eligible voters were correctly classified. Using sample proportions as prior probabilities, 59.52 percent of the abstainers were correctly classified. The voters in favour of union representation (93.67 percent) and those voting against union representation (83.33 percent) were more often correctly classified.

## Discussion

The results of this study show that individuals who choose to abstain from voting in certification elections can be significantly differentiated from those who do choose to vote. As predicted, abstainers' scores on union attitudes, satisfaction with administration and peer pressures were on a continuum between the scores of individuals who voted in favour of and those who voted against union representation. This reflects the notion that abstaining from voting is a rational choice. Those individuals whose opinions or views were removed from both the positions held by the union and administration could see no clear choice or benefit from voting either for or against union representation and ultimately chose not to vote. Following from this logic those individuals who did not perceive either strong peer support for or opposition to union representation abstained from voting.

Although these results were statistically significant, it is possible that the ways job dissatisfaction and peer pressures were assessed may have served to underestimate differences between abstainers and voters. First, while dissatisfaction with administration was one of the manifest factors in the certification election, it is still likely that differences between those in favour of and those against union representation may have been even more pronounced had other salient aspects of job dissatisfaction been assessed (e.g. supervision dissatisfaction). Likewise, in assessing peer pressures, we only assessed the perceived influence of workplace pressures (i.e. faculty and associate teaching or research assistants). Research shows that family pressures on union intentions and voting are also significant (Barling, Kelloway and Bremermann, 1991; Kelloway and Watts, 1994; Montgomery, 1989); and had family influences been assessed in this study, it is possible that the effects of social pressures might have been greater, especially because the sample was relatively young, and family influences may be greater in such groups (Dekker, Greenberg and Barling, 1996).

More important, however, was the fact that abstainers could be differentiated from individuals who voted, irrespective of the direction of their vote. Specifically, abstainers perceived their vote in the certification election as significantly less likely to make a difference to the outcome of the representation election than either individuals who voted for or against representation. Abstainers also expressed much less interest in the election than did those who voted in the election. Given the argument that most union certification elections are closely fought, and that the votes of any abstainer could make a difference to the outcome of the election (Roomkin and Block, 1981), these findings provide some practical suggestions for union organizers and management alike. It is incumbent to identify individuals who report that they will not vote, and to convince them of the instrumentality of their vote, i.e., that their vote could well make a difference to the outcome. In addition, it would also be useful in such communications to raise the general level of interest in the election.

Given that abstainers can be differentiated from individuals who choose to vote in certification elections, an initial agenda for research on individual voting decisions in certification elections can be suggested. We chose not to label respondents who indicated that they had not voted because of some external restraint as 'abstainers'. Because of the retrospective nature of the study, it was possible that this explanation reflected a 'self-serving' bias. Thus, we chose to follow the more conservative route, choosing to exclude this group in an effort to minimize within-group variance among individuals who did not vote. This does point to the possibility that individual decisions not to vote are a function of several different factors. While individuals may be abstaining because of indifference, a belief that their votes will not be effective, or a lack of interest, it is also possible that they choose not to vote simply because they are ill or are undecided between a vote in favour of or against certification. Future research may profit from a more in depth focus on the reasons for not voting (e.g. indecision, external constraints preventing the vote).

Ragsdale and Rusk (1993) examined nonvoters in an American senate election and suggested that there are, in fact, different types of abstainers. For example, there are politically ignorant nonvoters, indifferent nonvoters and those who choose not to vote because they dislike all the candidates. The reasons why people may choose not to vote could have direct relevance for the way that union organizers and management approach and communicate with potential voters. In addition, Summers, Betton and DeCotiis' (1986) notion that abstainers may be more susceptible to campaign influence may be assessed. Future research should involve longitudinal data collection, where predictor variables are measured before the actual vote. However, the short term nature of certification campaigns, together with legislation that often makes any access to the bargaining unit problematic, reduces the likelihood that longitudinal research will be feasible. Replication of these findings with diverse bargaining units is also important, because the nature of the sample studied here is somewhat atypical (i.e. relatively young part-time workers). As Cook and Campbell (1976) note, external validity is an empirical issue that awaits replication. Lastly, some would believe a 30 percent response rate to be a cause for concern. However, Schalm and Kelloway's (1996) recent reanalysis of data from five meta-analyses found no correlation between response rates and effect size.

In conclusion, we have identified two sets of factors that discriminate between individuals who vote and choose not to vote in union certification elections. The results of this study have practical implications for both labour organizers and management, and point to the need for further research on 'abstainers', a previously neglected group that may well be able to influence the outcome of certification elections.

## Note

1. The North American unionization process has two steps. Initially, those employees interested in unionizing their work place sign certification cards. If a large enough percentage of employees sign certification cards a representation election is held. If the majority of employees vote in favour of the union all eligible employees become union members.

## References


Bakke, E. W. (1945), 'To join or not to join', *Personnel*, vol. 22, pp. 2-11.

Barling, J., Fullagar, C. and Kelloway, E. K. (1992), *The union and its members*, Oxford University Press, New York.

Barling, J., Kelloway, E. K. and Bremermann, E. H. (1991), 'Pre-employment predictors of union attitudes: The role of family socialization and work beliefs', *Journal of Applied Psychology*, vol. 76, pp. 725-731.

Brett, J. M. (1980), 'Why employees want unions', *Organizational Dynamics*, vol. 8, pp. 47-59.

Brody, R. A. and Page, B. I. (1973), 'Indifference, alienation, and rational decisions', *Public Choice*, vol. 15, pp. 1-17.

Chacko, T. J. (1985), 'Member participation in union activities: Perceptions of union priorities, performance, and satisfaction', *Journal of Labour Research*, vol. 4, pp. 363-373.

Cook, T. D. and Campbell, D. T. (1976), *Quasi-experimentation: Design and analysis issues for field settings*, Houghton Mifflin, Boston.

Chamberlin, E. N. (1935), 'What labour is thinking', *Personnel Journal*, vol. 14, pp. 118-123.

Davy, J. A. and Shipper, F. (1993), 'Voter behaviour in union certification elections: A longitudinal study', *Academy of Management Journal*, vol. 36, pp. 187-199.

Dekker, I., Greenberg, L. and Barling, J. (1996), 'Predictors of part-time students union attitudes', manuscript submitted for publication, School of Business, Queens University.

Deshpande, S. P. and Fiorito, J. (1989), 'Specific and general beliefs in union voting models', *Academy of Management Journal*, vol. 32, pp. 883-897.

Dunleavy, P. (1992), *Democracy, bureaucracy and public choice*, Prentice Hall, Toronto.

Fife-Schaw, C. and Breakwell, G. M. (1990), 'Predicting the intention not to vote in late teenage: A U.K. study of 17- and 18-year-olds', *Political Psychology*, vol. 11, pp. 739-755.

Getman, J. G., Goldberg, S. B. and Herman, J. B. (1976), *Union representation elections: Law and reality*, Russell Sage Foundation, New York.

Goldfried, M. (1987), *The decline of organized labour in the United States*, University of Chicago Press, Chicago.

Gordon, M. E., Barling, J. and Tetrick, L. E. (1995), 'Some remaining challenges', in Tetrick, L. E. and Barling, J. (eds.), *Changing employment relations: Behavioral and social perspectives*, American Psychological Association, Washington, DC.

Kelloway, E. K. and Barling, J. (1993), 'Members' participation in local union activities: Measurement, prediction and replication', *Journal of Applied Psychology*, vol. 78, pp. 262-279.

Kelloway, E. K. and Watts, L. (1994), 'Preemployment predictors of union attitudes: Replication and extension', *Journal of Applied Psychology*, vol. 79, pp. 631-634.

Montgomery, B. R. (1989), 'The influence of attitudes and normative pressures on voting decisions in a union certification election', *Industrial and Labour Relations Review*, vol. 42, pp. 262-279.

Premack, S. L. and Hunter, J. E. (1988), 'Individual unionization decisions', *Psychological Bulletin*, vol. 103, pp. 223-234.

Ragsdale, L. and Rusk, J. G. (1993), 'Who are nonvoters? Profiles from the 1990 senate elections', *American Journal of Political Science*, vol. 37, pp. 721-746.

Roomkin, M. and Block, R. (1981), 'Case processing time and the outcome of representative elections: Some empirical evidence', *University of Illinois Law Review*, vol. 1, pp. 75-97.

Schalm, R. L. and Kelloway, E. K. (1996). 'The relationship between response rate and effect size in organizational survey research: A meta-analysis', manuscript submitted for publication, Department of Psychology, University of Guelph.

Summers, T. P., Betton, J. H. and DeCotiis, T. A. (1986), 'Voting for and against unions: A decision model', *Academy of Management Review*, vol. 11, pp. 643-655.

Traugott, M. W. and Tucker, C. (1984), 'Strategies for predicting whether a citizen will vote and estimation of electoral outcomes', *Public Opinion Quarterly*, vol. 48, pp. 330-343.

Whyte, W. F. (1944), 'Who goes union and why', *Personnel Journal*, vol. 23, pp. 215-230.

Youngblood, S. A., DeNisi, A., Molleston, J. L. and Mobley, W. (1984), 'The impact of work environment, instrumentality beliefs, perceived labour union image and subjective norms on union voting intentions', *Academy of Management Journal*, vol. 27, pp. 576-590.

Zalesny, M. D. (1985), 'Comparison of economic and noneconomic factors in predicting faculty vote preference in a union representation election', *Journal of Applied Psychology*, vol. 70, pp. 243-256.

Zipp, J. F. (1985), 'Perceived representativeness and voting: An assessment of the impact of "choices" vs. "echoes"', *American Political Science Review*, vol. 79, pp. 50-61.

# 19 Union attitudes: Ideologues and instrumentalists

*Clive Fullagar, Renee Slick, Canan Sumer and Paul Marquardt*

Union attitudes have consistently been acknowledged as playing an important predictive role in various aspects of individual attachment to, and detachment from, unions. For example, general attitudes toward labour organizations have been shown to be associated with the decision to join a union, to become committed to the union, to actively participate in union activities, and voting to decertify the union (Barling, Fullagar and Kelloway, 1992). It is surprising, therefore, that despite the acknowledged importance of general attitudes toward unions, little research has investigated the nature of the construct, or treated union attitudes as a dependent rather than an independent variable. Furthermore, most of the research on union attitudes has been undertaken in North America, where unions have been classified as 'business' unions, and support for unions described as 'instrumental' or 'utilitarian' (Wheeler and McClendon, 1991). These calculative/rational models of unionization have been contrasted with ideological models of union attachment found in those countries where a social movement type of unionism is more typical. One purpose of the present chapter is to describe research that attempts to develop a broader, multidimensional conceptualization of the construct of union attitudes by including both instrumental and ideological attitudes.

In addition, recent research (Barling, Kelloway and Bremermann, 1991; Kelloway and Watts, 1994) has shown that personal, work-related beliefs are predictive of union attitudes, but that these do not fully account for individuals' attitudes toward unions. Furthermore, Barling et al. (1991) have shown that union attitudes are relatively stable and already formalized before employment

Comments should be addressed to Clive Fullagar, Department of Psychology, Kansas State University, 492 Bluemont Hall, Manhattan, Kansas 66502, U.S.A.

has even occurred. It would appear that our implicit theories about unions and our attitudes toward them are strongly influenced by family socialization factors, and specifically by our parents' attitudes and involvement in unions. The more favourable our parents' attitudes toward unions are perceived to be, the more likely we are to hold positive attitudes ourselves. This is not surprising given that parental occupational attitudes have been shown to be strong predictors of children's own career choice (Gottfredson, 1981). In a similar vein, culture-specific beliefs have been shown to mentally program many of our individual attitudes. For example, culture-specific beliefs have been found to explain at least 50 percent of the variance in workplace attitudes and behaviours (Hofstede, 1981). It is highly probable that culture impacts strongly on members' general attitudes toward unions. Consequently, another objective of this chapter is to investigate the interaction between culture-specific beliefs and union attitudes and to answer some fundamental questions: Are certain cultural beliefs more predictive of certain types of attitudes toward unions? What cultural beliefs are predictive of ideological union attitudes? Do these differ from the cultural beliefs that are associated with instrumental union attitudes?

## *Toward an understanding of union attitudes*

Drawing upon the literature on union commitment, we would like to distinguish between two types of attitudes to unions; instrumental and ideological attitudes. Instrumental attitudes have been most commonly used in behavioural research and they imply a calculative attitude toward unions where the individual reacts to the union in terms of its perceived instrumentality in maximizing his/her self-interest. Sverke (1995), drawing on Weber's (1968) theory of social action, refers to this as an instrumental rationality-based attitude. For example, instrumental rationality-based commitment depicts a utilitarian relationship between the member and the union, in which the individual rationally considers the costs and benefits of being involved in the union, and makes a decision based on his/her perceptions of the union's instrumentality in achieving certain valued outcomes. Such rational choice models have been most frequently used to describe individual attitudes toward unions (Wheeler and McClendon, 1991).

Recently however, the focus has shifted toward defining ideological attitudes. For example, Newton and Shore (1992) define ideological attachment to the union as being driven by the extent to which individuals identify with and internalize the values and beliefs of organized labour. Unions are perceived as being positive social, organizational and political institutions rather than instruments for maximizing individual self-interest. This kind of ideological attachment infers what Etzioni (1975) referred to as moral involvement with the union as opposed to the calculative involvement implied by instrumental attachment. In a similar vein, Sverke (1995) defines value rationality-based commitment as attachment to the union based on the individual's internalization of the goals and values of the union and organized labour in general. Here social action is not based on individual expectations of personal gain, but rather engaged in for ideological reasons (Sverke, 1995).

### *Union attitudes and cultural beliefs*

It is highly likely that union attitudes vary across cultures, with different industrial relations climates fostering differing levels of adherence to ideological and instrumental attitudes. Bain and Elsheikh (1976), for example, found that instrumental values were predominant in Australia, the United Kingdom, and the United States, whereas ideological attitudes are argued to be more prevalent in European countries (Wheeler and McClendon, 1991).

Another culturally-related factor that possibly impacts on union attitudes is the nature of unions. Business unionism (such as that found in the United States) that focuses on job-related concerns and economic issues is more likely to foster instrumental attitudes. Social movement or political unionism (such as in Europe and South Africa) has broader concerns that emphasize industrial and economic democracy and political reform of the society. Such unionism is more likely to be associated with ideological attitudes (Sverke, 1995; Wheeler and McClendon, 1991).

Despite the fact that union attitudes probably vary with cultural factors, very little research has investigated the association between cultural beliefs and attitudes toward labour unions, especially at the level of the individual. One factor that explains the scarcity of research on culture-specific values and union attitudes is the lack of a theoretical cultural framework. The work of Geert Hofstede has provided a significant advance here (Triandis, 1994). For the purposes of the research described here, we focussed on two of Hofstede's cultural dimensions; Individualism-Collectivism and Power Distance (Hofstede, 1981).

Individualism-Collectivism reflects the extent that people emphasize personal as opposed to group goals. Individualistic cultures expect people to take care of themselves, identity is based in the individual and involvement with organizations is believed to be calculative. At the societal level, individualism is reflected in laws and norms which encourage individuality, individual freedom, and preference for individual work. Some antecedents of individualism include affluence, geographic mobility, and exposure to the mass media (Triandis, 1994). Individualistic themes are more likely to be found in Northwestern Europe and North America.

In collectivist cultures people distinguish between in-groups and out-groups; they expect their in-groups to look after their interests, people are dependent on organizations, involvement with organizations is moral, and emphasis is placed on collectivities. Some of the major antecedents of collectivism are cultural homogeneity, high population density, and occupations that require interdependence. Collectivist themes are more likely to be found in East Asia, Latin America, and Africa. We hypothesized that individualistic beliefs would be associated with more instrumental attitudes toward unions, where unions were evaluated in terms of their ability to maximize individual self-interest (i.e. improve the individual's wages, working conditions, benefits and job security). Collectivist beliefs, on the other hand, would be more associated with moral attachments to unions, where individuals see unions as collective organizations representing and protecting the interests and rights of the in-group (i.e. their memberships or the working class in general).

Hofstede's concept Power Distance indicates the extent to which power is unequally distributed in institutions and organizations, and the degree to which society maintains inequality among its members by stratification of individuals and groups with respect to power, authority, prestige, status, wealth, and material possessions. Power distance is manifested at the societal level in the form of deference to authority, treatment of workers as inferior to managers, the maintenance of class distinctions, and concentration of power among a minority of the population.

In small power distance societies inequality is minimized, all people are seen as having equal rights, and latent harmony exists between the powerful and powerless, and managers are more satisfied with a participative superior. In large power distance societies, inequalities are believed to be a natural part of social hierarchy and latent conflict exists between the powerful and powerless, and managers are more satisfied with a directive or persuasive superior. Hofstede found large power distance countries to be the Philippines, Mexico, and Venezuela, and low power distance countries to be Austria, Israel and Denmark. We hypothesized that those individuals who perceive their society as being relatively large in power distance would tend to adopt more ideological attitudes toward unions as mechanisms for establishing greater equality between the powerful and the powerless. Individuals who perceive their society as being low in power distance were hypothesized as holding more instrumental attitudes toward labour unions.

The present study had two purposes. First, we wanted to establish the dimensionality of union attitudes. Specifically we wanted to determine whether two different types of union attitudes could be discerned, namely ideological attitudes and instrumental attitudes. Second, we wanted to determine the association between these two different types of attitudes and two cultural specific beliefs defined by Hofstede (1981), individualism-collectivism and power distance. Furthermore we wanted to ascertain the unique variance in union attitudes explained by these culture specific beliefs, over and above the variance explained by those work values which have been found to be predictive of union attitudes (Barling et al., 1991; Kelloway and Watts, 1994).

## Method

### *Subjects and Procedure*

It was our belief that there would be a tremendous amount of variation in culture-specific beliefs within any one culture, and that cultural homogeneity in values is a tenuous assumption. Consequently, in this study, we looked at variability in cultural beliefs in a sample of American students. The subjects in the study consisted of 196 students at a Midwest State university in the United States of America. All subjects were taking a General Psychology class and volunteered to participate as part of an experimental credit requirement. All subjects were provided with an informed consent form and completed the surveys anonymously. The mean age of the sample was 21 years ($SD = 4.48$), and it consisted of 89 females (45 percent). The majority of the sample (88 percent) was white Americans. Having completed the survey the subjects were then debriefed about the nature of the study.

### *Questionnaires*

In addition to questions about demographic characteristics, the survey instrument contained three questionnaires, each using the same 5-point response format (1 = 'Strongly Disagree'; 3 = 'Neither Agree Nor Disagree'; 5 = 'Strongly Agree').

Union Attitudes consisted of a 12-item scale adapted from McShane (1986) and Deshpande and Fiorito (1989) scales. The items were chosen to measure both ideological (e.g. 'Unions help workers stand together') and instrumental (e.g. 'Unions improve the wages of workers') attitudes.

Individualism-Collectivism was measured using 22 items from Hui's (1988) scale. The items were chosen to measure individualism-collectivism as it relates to friends (e.g. 'I like to live close to my good friends') and coworkers/classmates (e.g. 'One needs to return a favour if a classmate lends a helping hand') as these were the dimensions believed to be most pertinent to union attitudes (Hofstede, 1981). This scale operationally defines collectivism as a 'set of feelings, beliefs, behavioral intentions, and behaviours related to solidarity and concern for others' (Hui, 1988, p.17). An overall individualism-collectivism score was calculated by averaging the scores on these 22 items. Higher scores indicate greater adherence to individualistic beliefs, whereas lower scores indicate collectivist beliefs. The internal consistency of this scale was found to be satisfactory (Cronbach's $\alpha$ = .79).

No scale has been developed to assess power-distance beliefs and so we constructed an 18-item scale that was based on Hofstede's (1981) definition of the construct, that is that power-distance reflects the perceptions that society and organizations maintain inequality among members by stratifying individuals and groups. Examples of items include 'Those in power in an organization are inaccessible,' and 'Inequality in society should be minimized'. Higher scores indicated high power distance perceptions. Again, the reliability of this scale was acceptable ( $\alpha$ = .83 ).

The survey also included measures of various work-related beliefs as these have been shown to be associated with attitudes toward unions (Barling et al., 1991; Fullagar and Barling, 1989). In determining the association between culture-specific beliefs and union attitudes, we wanted to covary out the effects of these work beliefs. Work-related beliefs were assessed using Buchholz's (1978) Marxist-related (11 items), Humanistic (9 items), Organizational (8 items), Work Ethic (8 items) and Leisure (7 items) beliefs. Briefly defined, Marxist related beliefs reflect the opinion that work is fundamental to human fulfillment but as currently organized represents exploitation of the worker and consequent alienation. The Humanistic belief system has the view that individual growth and development in the job is more important than output. Organizational beliefs indicate that work takes on meaning only as it effects the organization and the in-group, and contributes to one's position at work. The Work Ethic is the belief that work is good in itself, offers social status to the individual, and that success is a result of personal effort. Finally, the Leisure ethic regards work as a means to personal fulfillment through its provision of the means to pursue leisure activities. All the scales indicated acceptable internal consistency (Range $\alpha$ = .73 - .91).

## Results

Principal components analysis of the union attitudes items extracted three reliable factors that accounted for 52 percent of the variance (see Table 19.1). As indicated by the squared multiple correlations (*SMC*s), all three factors were internally consistent and well defined by the variables (smallest *SMC* = .79). Orthogonal rotation was retained because of conceptual simplicity and ease of description. Furthermore, if two factors emerged that resembled instrumental and ideological attitudes, we believed that they would be independent of each other. The three factors that were extracted were interpreted using the loadings of the items that contributed to them.

**Table 19.1**
**Factor loadings, communalities and percents of variance for principal components analysis with varimax rotation**

| | Factor | | | |
|---|---|---|---|---|
| Items | 1 | 2 | 3 | $h^2$ |
| Unions are too involved in political activities | .79 | | | .62 |
| Unions stifle individual initiative | .67 | | | .50 |
| Unions force members to go along with deicisions they don't like | .65 | | | .44 |
| Unions have too much power in this country today | .65 | | | .49 |
| Unions increase the risk that companies will go out of business | .54 | | | .36 |
| Unions improve the the working conditions of workers | | .82 | | .68 |
| Unions improve the wages of workers | | .72 | | .52 |
| Unions give members thir money's worth for the dues they pay | | .66 | | .45 |
| Unions work to get legislation that helps their members | | .51 | | .43 |
| Everyone who works should have to belong to a union | | .79 | .63 | |
| Without unions this country would be less democratic | | .64 | .60 | |
| Unions help workers stand together | | | .56 | .53 |
| Eigenvalues | 3.53 | 1.63 | 1.08 | |
| Percent of variance | 29.5 | 13.6 | 9.0 | |

*Note:* Loadings < .45 have been left blank.

The first factor, which accounted for 29.5 percent of the variance, was labeled Union Intrusiveness Attitudes (5 items): these attitudes indicated that unions are regarded as being politically intrusive, interfering with individual initiative, having too much power, ignoring individual needs, and increasing companies economic risk. The second factor was labeled Instrumental Attitudes (4 items) and explained 13.6 percent of the variance. This factor consisted of attitudes that perceived unions as being effective mechanisms for improving wages and working conditions, giving members their money's worth, and introducing legislation that benefits the worker. Finally, the third factor was termed Ideological Attitudes (3 items; 9 percent of the variance) and consisted of attitudes that indicated that unions are seen as important for the protection of workers' rights, helping workers stand together, and necessary for the facilitation of social democracy.

Simple factor scores were calculated by averaging the scores on those items which loaded on each factor. Descriptive statistics (means, standard deviations, intercorrelations and internal consistencies) for all the study variables are provided in Table 19.2.

The factors derived from the principal components analysis were then used as dependent variables in three hierarchical regression analyses. Work beliefs were entered first into the equations as these have already been found to explain a proportion of the variance in union attitudes. Individualism-Collectivism and Power Distance were then entered in the second step to ascertain if these culture-specific beliefs could explain any additional variance in the three types of union attitudes that was unique from work beliefs. The results of these regression analyses are reported in Table 19.3.

The results of the regression analyses indicated that for each type of union attitude, addition of information regarding culture-specific values significantly improved the prediction of union attitudes. Furthermore, for all three types of union attitude, culture-specific beliefs were stronger predictors than any of the individual work values. This included Marxist-related beliefs which have consistently been found to be associated with union attitudes (Barling et al., 1991; Fullagar and Barling, 1989).

More specifically, union intrusiveness attitudes were significantly correlated with individualistic values ($\beta = .31, p < .01$) and negatively associated with power-distance ($\beta = -.32, p < .01$). Instrumentality attitudes were also significantly associated with individualistic values ($\beta = .49, p < .01$), as well as being positively correlated with Humanistic beliefs ($\beta = .35, p < .01$) and negatively correlated with Organization beliefs ($\beta = -.24, p < .01$) and Marxist-related beliefs ($\beta = -.15, p < .05$). Finally, ideological union attitudes were significantly correlated with high power distance ($\beta = .51, p < .01$), collectivist

**Table 19.2**
**Descriptive statistics for the study variables**

| Variable | *M* | *SD* | α | 1 | 2 | 3 | 4 | 5 | 6 | 7 | 8 | 9 |
|---|---|---|---|---|---|---|---|---|---|---|---|---|
| **Union attitudes** | | | | | | | | | | | | |
| 1. Union Intrusiveness | 3.22 | 0.58 | 0.87 | | | | | | | | | |
| 2. Instrumental Attitudes | 3.49 | 0.57 | 0.83 | -.33 | | | | | | | | |
| 3. Ideological Attitudes | 2.63 | 0.66 | 0.92 | -.39 | .36 | | | | | | | |
| **Culture-specific beliefs** | | | | | | | | | | | | |
| 4. Individualism-Collectivism | 2.98 | 0.43 | 0.79 | .42 | .31 | -.29 | | | | | | |
| 5. Power Distance | 3.05 | 0.54 | 0.83 | -.23 | .02 | .50 | .16 | | | | | |
| **Work beliefs** | | | | | | | | | | | | |
| 6. Humanistic Beliefs | 4.24 | 0.41 | 0.89 | -.21 | .26 | .01 | -.35 | -.17 | | | | |
| 7. Marxist Beliefs | 3.17 | 0.49 | 0.91 | -.26 | -.17 | .49 | -.22 | .40 | .02 | | | |
| 8. Organizational Beliefs | 3.40 | 0.46 | 0.82 | -.20 | -.18 | .31 | -.45 | -.18 | .30 | .24 | | |
| 9. Leisure Beliefs | 3.24 | 0.59 | 0.73 | .05 | .03 | .06 | .06 | .21 | .01 | .37 | -.01 | |
| 10. Work Ethic | 3.36 | 0.52 | 0.78 | .21 | -.02 | -.11 | .28 | .01 | .11 | -.19 | .03 | -.27 |

**Table 19.3**
**Results of hierarchical regression analyses**

| Variables | $\beta$ | $R^2$ | $F_{equ}$ | $\Delta R^2$ | $\Delta F$ |
|---|---|---|---|---|---|
| **DV (Union Intrusiveness Attitudes)** | | | | | |
| *STEP 1:* | | | | | |
| Work Beliefs | | .19 | 9.18* | .19 | 9.18* |
| *STEP 2:* | | | | | |
| Individualism-Collectivism | .31 | .24 | 10.11* | .05 | 12.07* |
| Power Distance | -.32 | .32 | 12.57* | .08 | 21.04* |
| **DV (Instrumentality Attitudes)** | | | | | |
| *STEP 1:* | | | | | |
| Work Beliefs | | .16 | 7.43* | .16 | 7.43* |
| *STEP 2:* | | | | | |
| Individualism-Collectivism | .49 | .31 | 14.25* | .15 | 40.61* |
| Power Distance | .08 | .31 | 12.40* | .00 | 1.20 |
| **DV (Ideological Attitudes)** | | | | | |
| *STEP 1:* | | | | | |
| Work Beliefs | | .30 | 16.58* | .30 | 16.58* |
| *STEP 2:* | | | | | |
| Individualism-Collectivism | -.14 | .31 | 14.57* | .01 | 3.43 |
| Power Distance | .51 | .50 | 27.36* | .19 | 71.50* |

*Notes:* * $P < .01$

beliefs (b = -.14, $p < .01$), Marxist-related values (b = .48, $p < .01$), and Organization beliefs (b = .22, $p < .01$). Such differential correlations suggest that the three union attitude dimensions are indeed distinct constructs.

## Discussion

The first purpose of this study was to establish the dimensionality of union attitudes. Previous research has conceptualized union attitudes as uni-dimensional. We hypothesized at least two types of union attitude; instrumental and ideological attitudes. Our data partially supported this two dimensional model in that two of the factors extracted from principal components analysis were interpreted as instrumental and ideological in nature. However, a third unanticipated factor was derived from the analysis which we labeled Union Intrusiveness attitudes.

Instrumental attitudes consisted of perceptions of unions as being instrumental in advancing individual interests, such as improving working conditions, getting better wages, and politicking for legislation that benefits their memberships. This interpretation was partially validated in that instrumental attitudes were found to be correlated with high individualism beliefs, suggesting that these attitudes are associated with calculative involvement in unions. It was not surprising, given the nature of business unionism in the United States, that, of all the types of union attitudes, instrumental union attitudes should have the highest mean in this study.

Ideological attitudes, on the other hand, consisted of perceptions of unions as solidaristic institutions that are essential mechanisms for the representation of workers and social democracy. In this instance, unions were not seen as instruments for self-satisfaction. Although ideological and instrumental attitudes were positively correlated, their distinctiveness is indicated by the finding that they were predicted by different types of work and culture-specific beliefs. Ideological attitudes toward unions were associated with beliefs that (a) power discrepancies in society were large, (b) work takes on meaning only as it effects one's coworkers, (c) society and work institutions should be collectivist in orientation, and (d) work, as it is currently organized, exploits workers.

The third factor extracted by principal components analysis, which explained the largest proportion of variance, was Union intrusiveness. These attitudes expressed a perception that unions are intrusive, from a political, individual, and business perspective, and they were found to be correlated with work ethic values, individualism and perceptions of low power distance in society. The existence of this factor is probably due to cultural influences. Currently, an image of unionism in the United States has evolved which is negative in nature and to some extent has been associated with the decline in American unionization levels. Such a factor may not be as important in other cultures where the union climate is more positive. Intrusive attitudes may be extremely important when it comes to explaining breakdowns in the unionization process (such as decertification and quitting the union). Although specific union instrumentality perceptions have been shown to be predictive of both collective and individual actions against the union, more research is needed to ascertain the impact of different types of union attitude on the unionization process (Barling et al., 1992).

These findings would suggest that previous uni-dimensional operationalizations of union attitudes may be too narrow. Although not investigated here, we would expect the different types of union attitudes to facilitate different kinds of attachment to unions. Instrumental attitudes are likely to be associated with calculative attachment and more likely to be predominant in industrial-relations climates that are characterized by business unions.

Ideological attitudes, on the other hand, will foster more moral attachments to labour organizations and will be more strongly associated with social movement unionism. Union intrusiveness attitudes will be associated with union detachment or low levels of participation in union activities. Not only will these different types of union attitudes produce different outcomes, but, as shown by the current results, they will also be predicted by different values and beliefs (Sverke, 1995; Wheeler and McClendon, 1991).

The second purpose of the current study was to investigate the impact of culture-specific beliefs on union attitudes. Demographic trends indicate an increasing diversification of the labour force. For various historical and fundamental reasons, organizational psychology is still very parochial in the United States (Triandis, 1994). The neglect of this field has resulted in an underdeveloped theory of the way culture influences union-related behaviours and attitudes. North America and Northwestern Europe have been the centers of both industrial development and the development of organizational theory. These cultures are characterized by high individualism, as a result, many theories of unionization underestimate the importance of groups, cultures, and other human-made entities outside of the individual.

The present results suggest that different types of union attitude, whether instrumental, ideological, or intrusive, are predicted by different culturally specific beliefs and different work values, confirming both the differential validity of the three dimensions of union attitudes and the importance of such cultural beliefs. Culture specific beliefs (individualism-collectivism, and power distance) were found to add significantly to the amount of variance explained in all types of union attitudes, over and above the variance explained by individual work values. The current data were collected on a culturally homogeneous American sample of pre-employed students. Although previous research has suggested that union attitudes are stable and already established before individuals become employed (Barling et al., 1991), the generalizability of the present results is obviously restricted. In the current research only individual variations of culture-specific beliefs were measured. It is predicted that such variation will increase across cultures making the above distinctions even more obvious.

The implications of the research are that in those cultures where there is a high emphasis on individualism and below average power distance, attitudes toward unions will either be antagonistic or instrumental and attachment to unions will be calculative. Consequently union organizing efforts should focus on promoting the individual benefits that the union has accrued for its membership in order to convince potential members of the union of the instrumentality of the union in improving working conditions. In cultures which are collectivist in nature and where there are large discrepancies between the powerful and powerless, attitudes toward unions will be more ideological and attachment to unions of a moral nature. In these instances, union organizing efforts should focus on the democratization and political functions of unions (Sverke, 1995; Wheeler and McClendon, 1991). Future research needs to investigate these phenomena in different cultures to ascertain the way culture affects union behaviour and attitudes. As we evolve toward a global economic and sociopolitical system, it becomes particularly important that psychologists become more involved in such theoretical issues as the impact of culture on attitudes and values, and how these are linked to social behaviour.

## References

Bain, G. S. and Elsheikh, F. (1976), *Union growth and the business cycle: An econometric analysis*, Basil Blackwell, Oxford.

Barling, J., Fullagar, C. and Kelloway, E. K. (1992), *The union and its members: A psychological approach*, Oxford University Press, New York.

Barling, J., Kelloway, E. K. and Bremermann, E. H. (1991), 'Preemployment predictors of union attitudes: The role of family socialization and work beliefs', *Journal of Applied Psychology*, vol. 76, pp. 725-731.

Buchholz, R. (1979), 'An empirical study of contemporary beliefs about work in American society', *Journal of Applied Psychology*, vol. 63, pp. 219-227.

Deshpande, S. P. and Fiorito, J. (1989), 'Specific and general beliefs in union voting models', *Academy of Management Journal*, vol. 32, pp. 883-897.

Etzioni, A. (1975), *A comparative analysis of complex organizations*, Free Press, New York.

Gottfredson, L. S. (1981), 'Circumscription and compromise: A developmental theory of occupational aspirations', *Journal of Counseling Psychology*, vol. 28, pp. 545-579.

Hofstede, G. (1981), *Cultures consequences: International differences in work related values*, Sage Publications, New York.

Hui, H. C. (1988), 'Individualism and collectivism', *Journal of Research in Personality*, vol. 22, pp. 17-36.

Kelloway, E. K. and Watts, L. (1994), 'Preemployment predictors of union attitudes: Replication and extension', *Journal of Applied Psychology*, vol. 79, pp. 631-634.

McShane, S. L. (1986), 'The multidimensionality of union participation', *Journal of Occupational Psychology*, vol. 59, pp. 177-187.

Newton, L. A. and Shore, L. M. (1992), 'A model of union membership: Instrumentality, commitment, and opposition', *Academy of Management Review*, vol. 17, pp. 275-298.

Sverke, M. (1995), 'Instrumental and value rationality-based commitment to the union: Conceptualization, operationalization, and validation', *Reports from the Department of Psychology, Stockholm University, 1995, No. 795*, Stockholm.

Triandis, H. (1994), 'Cross-cultural industrial and organizational psychology', in Triandis, H., Dunnette, M. D. and Hough, L. M. (eds.), *Handbook of industrial and organizational psychology (2nd Edition): Volume 4*, Consulting Psychologists Press, Inc, Palo Alto, CA, pp. 103-172.

Weber, M. (1968), *Economy and society*, University of California Press, Berkeley, CA.

Wheeler, H. N. and McClendon J. A. (1991), 'The individual decision to unionize', in Strauss, G., Gallagher, D. G. and Fiorito, J. (eds.), *The state of the unions*, Industrial Relations Research Association, Madison, WI.

# 20 Ideological and instrumental union commitment

*Magnus Sverke and Anders Sjöberg*

In the literature, union commitment has frequently been defined as an attitude concept (Fullagar and Barling, 1987) reflecting members' identification with the union and with its goals and values (Kuruvilla, Gallagher and Wetzel, 1993). An assumption common to most approaches to union commitment is that this identification will increase the likelihood of participating in union activity (Barling, Fullagar and Kelloway, 1992). Thus, commitment is crucial for effective union functioning. As noted by Gallagher and Clark (1989, p. 52), 'the effectiveness of unions in organizing, bargaining, retaining membership, and political action depends on the level of commitment the organization is able to build among present and potential union members'. Besides being of obvious practical value to the unions, research on union commitment also contributes to knowledge about the psychological processes involved in organizational attachment and social action within organizations (Gordon and Nurick, 1981).

In connection with a growing recognition of the double-sided nature of unions as utilitarian and normative organizations (Schein, 1980), recent developments in research on union attachment (e.g. Fiorito, 1992; Gordon, 1996; Newton and Shore, 1992; Sverke and Kuruvilla, 1995) have emphasized the importance of ideology and instrumentality as the major bases for identification with labour organizations. A focus on both ideology and instrumentality has characterized a substantial amount of trade union research (see, for instance, Adams, 1974; Dunlop, 1958; Goldthorpe, Lockwood,

---

This research was conducted when the first author worked at the Swedish Institute for Work Life Research. All correspondence should be addressed to Magnus Sverke, Department of Psychology, Stockholm University, 106 91 Stockholm, Sweden.

Bechofer and Platt, 1968; Spinrad, 1960) even if, at least when it comes to the study of member-union relationships, the inclusion of also the ideological aspect has been more characteristic of European rather than North American research (Wheeler and McClendon, 1991). The distinction between instrumentality and ideology has been drawn also in the literatures on organizational attachment (Etzioni, 1975; Wiener, 1982) and collective action (Abrahamsson, 1993; Knoke, 1990; Sen, 1982). The basic premise of this distinction is that both instrumentality perceptions and ideological beliefs can motivate individuals to involve in pro-organizational behaviour and, in turn, that the 'organization's existence depends upon the perception by potential participants that some advantages will be gained by cooperation with others — whether these benefits accrue directly to individuals or to the collective whole' (Knoke, 1990, p. 6).

This chapter draws upon the organizational attachment and collective action literature, and focuses on the nature and consequences of ideological and instrumental commitment to the union. We investigate if these two dimensions of commitment are empirically distinct and examine how they are related to members' involvement in the union. As noted by Kelloway and Barling (1993), a typical problem of research on union member attitudes and behaviour is that most studies rely on data from single research settings. Given that the use of data from independent samples minimizes the risk of capitalizing on chance (Bollen, 1989) and provides a means of establishing external validity (Cook and Campbell, 1979), we also evaluate to what extent the empirical results generalize across three different samples of Swedish blue-collar workers. More specifically, the first purpose of the study is to examine the dimensionality (i.e. factor structure and internal consistency) of union commitment using a scale designed to reflect ideological and instrumental commitment (Sverke and Kuruvilla, 1995). The second research objective is to investigate whether the parameters of the measurement model generalize across samples. Finally, our third purpose is to predict members' involvement in the union and to evaluate the extent to which the relationships of commitment dimensions with postulated outcome variables are similar in the three samples.

## Ideological and instrumental commitment

Consistent with the literatures on organizational (Mowday, Porter and Steers, 1982; Wiener, 1982) and union attachment (Gordon, Philbot, Burt, Thompson and Spiller, 1980; Newton and Shore, 1992; Sverke and Kuruvilla, 1995), we define union commitment as an attitude, developed through both positive instrumentality perceptions and an identification with organizational goals, which predisposes individuals to act on behalf of the organization. Ideological attachment refers to member-union value congruence (Newton and Shore, 1992). As noted by Offe and Wiesenthal (1980), unions require solidarity and an ideology, i.e. a collective identity, to express the interests of their members. Sverke (1996) suggested that the degree of ideological commitment is dependent on the extent to which the individual member identifies with this collective identity by internalizing the goals, the values and the mission of the union. This type of commitment thus represents concern for the union and support of union ideology.

Instrumental union commitment, on the other hand, reflects a utilitarian relationship between member and union. Both Newton and Shore (1992) and Sverke and Kuruvilla (1995) defined instrumental attachment as a calculative bond to the union based on cognitive appraisals of the costs and benefits associated with membership. Exchange theory, which is the foundation of this definition, implies that 'the member becomes committed to the union in exchange for the union's provision of improved wages, working conditions, and benefits' (Barling et al., 1992, p. 72). Thus, the more the union is perceived as capable of satisfying utilitarian goals (e.g. job security, better wages), and the more strongly these goals are valued, then the more instrumentally committed to the union the individual is likely to be.

These two dimensions of union commitment are proposed to have important, but differential, consequences for members' involvement in union activity. While 'highly committed members are more likely to support their union in strikes or political activities and to assist in organizing campaigns' (Gallagher and Strauss, 1991, p. 139), a primary feature distinguishing ideological and instrumental commitment is the nature of the underlying motives for supporting the union (Sverke and Kuruvilla, 1995). For instance, even if instrumentally committed members as well as ideologically committed members are likely to remain in the union they will, however, have different reasons for retaining membership; instrumental members stay because they evaluate the benefits associated with prolonged membership as exceeding the costs, while ideological members consider prolonged membership ideologically or morally 'right'. Given that members' participation in union activity can take many forms (Klandermans, 1986; McShane, 1986), it is important both to specify how the two commitment dimensions may relate to various forms of involvement in the union and to evaluate if these postulated relationships hold true in different empirical settings.

Theories on organizational commitment (e.g. Mowday et al., 1982) and collective action (e.g. Knoke, 1990) generally assume that the more intensely an individual appreciates a certain incentive or benefit, the more inclined he/she will be to contribute to the realization of that incentive or benefit. Undoubtedly, as long as members perceive the benefits associated with membership as exceeding the costs, they will have a strong motive for retaining their membership. Instrumentality perceptions have also been found to relate to the propensity to join a union (Beutell and Biggs, 1984) and union meeting attendance. Thus, instrumental commitment appears to guide pro-organizational behaviour to the extent that the behavioural act is associated with low degrees of personal effort and has a duration in time that is limited (Sverke and Sjöberg, 1995).

Instrumentality as a motive for participation in activities requiring active involvement may be more problematic, however, among other things for reasons that are best summarized under the term 'the free rider problem' (Olson, 1971). The advantages entailed by membership are public goods; all members share the benefits of membership while only the active members carry the costs. According to Olson, this means that members have no rational reason to involve actively because they benefit from others' efforts without contributing themselves to the attainment of the public goods. Whereas Olson suggests that free rider problems can be overcome only through the provision of selective incentives (individually targeted rewards) or coercion, other authors (e.g. Abrahamsson, 1993; Robinson, 1990; Sen, 1982) have noted that the alternative is reliance on moral, or ideological, commitment.

A central characteristic of ideologically based commitment is that it 'should reflect personal sacrifice made for the sake of the organization' (Wiener, 1982, p. 421). Research suggests that members who experience individual-organizational value congruence are more likely to involve in activities that primarily benefits the organization rather than the individual (Abrahamsson, 1993; Newton and Shore, 1992; O'Reilly and Chatman, 1986; Sverke and Sjöberg, 1995). Newton and Shore (1992) go so far as to argue that, even among instrumentally attached members, only little participation could be expected in the absence of an ideological attachment to the union. Ideological commitment, therefore, is likely to predict any form of involvement in the union, irrespective of the degree of effort that is associated with it, while instrumental commitment, in referring to self-interest, is expected to influence such participation that involves little time and personal effort.

## Method

### *Research setting and participants*

The data used in this study were drawn from three national blue-collar unions affiliated to the Swedish Trade Union Confederation (LO). Union membership is voluntary in Sweden and the total union density is around 84 percent (Statistics Sweden, 1994). In the LO, workers are organized on a vertical basis characterized by industrial unionism and a strong adherence to the principle of 'one workplace — one union — one collective agreement' (LO, 1991, p. 27). For all three samples, two percent of the members were randomly selected from the membership files of the national unions, and questionnaires were mailed to participants' home addresses. Participation in the study was entirely voluntary.

*Sample 1* The first sample was drawn from the membership roster of a union organizing workers in fields like oil refineries, chemical industries and the rubber industry. Of the 1,434 members selected for the survey, 53 percent ($N$ = 755) provided usable responses. The mean age of the sample was 38 years, the average length of union membership 10 years and the proportion of males 67 percent. A comparison with demographic data from the parent population (extracted from union records) revealed no significant differences between the respondent group and the total union in terms of age and sex distribution.

*Sample 2* This sample was drawn from a survey of 418 members of a union that organizes workers producing, for instance, garment, carpets, shoes and leather products. Questionnaires were returned by 237 members for a response rate of 57 percent. The respondents' mean age was 42 years and they had been members of the union for an average of 12 years. The male proportion of the sample was 37 percent. Data made available by the union allowed for the comparison of the respondent group with the union as a whole in terms of age and sex. In neither case did differences emerge.

*Sample 3* The third sample included members of a union with jurisdictions covering the food industry (e.g. slaughter-houses, dairies, canneries and tobacco plants). Usable responses were obtained from 51 percent ($N$ = 494) of the 979 food workers sampled for the survey. The mean age of the respondents was 38 years and the average length of union membership 10 years. Males constituted 58 percent of the sample. There were no significant differences between the respondent group and the national union in terms of mean age and sex distribution.

### *Measures*

Respondents in the three samples completed identical questionnaires. The order of items on the questionnaire was random. Variable indices were constructed by averaging responses on items comprised by the respective scales.

*Union commitment* Ideological and instrumental commitment to the union were assessed using Sverke and Kuruvilla's (1995) scale of rational union commitment (alluding to Weber, 1968, Sverke and Kuruvilla used the terms value rationality-based commitment and instrumental rationality-based commitment in referring to ideological and instrumental commitment). Nine items, scored on a five-point Likert scale, were used to measure ideological commitment. These items focus on members' psychological attachment to the union based on the perceived degree of similarity between union and personal goals. While ideological commitment was assessed using a *direct* attitude measure, scores on the instrumental dimension were obtained using an *indirect* attitude measure (i.e. instrumental beliefs weighted by outcome evaluations) frequently employed by expectancy-valence researchers interested in instrumental attitudes (e.g. Ajzen and Fishbein, 1980; Beutell and Biggs, 1984). Accordingly, each of the seven instrumental commitment items was measured as the product of a behavioural belief (e.g. 'My union's chances of improving my pay are great'; 5-point disagree-agree scale) and a corresponding outcome evaluation (e.g. 'For me, to get better paid is...'; scale ranging from 1 [very unimportant] to 5 [very important]). Thus, beliefs about benefits and costs associated with membership do not in themselves constitute indicators of commitment; a measure of instrumentally based psychological attachment to the union is obtained first when the beliefs are weighted with subjective evaluations of these outcome beliefs. The square root of the products were used in order to obtain a range from 1 to 5 in the final instrumental commitment measure.

*Outcome variables* Three outcome variables, associated with varying degrees of personal effort, were used in the present study. Union meeting involvement was assessed using six bipolar items (1 = no, 2 = yes) reflecting members' attendance at union meetings and their participation in discussions and voting at meetings ($\alpha$ = .76 for sample 1, $\alpha$ = .69 for sample 2, and $\alpha$ = .77 for sample 3). Two additional outcome variables, scored on five-point Likert scales, were also included in the present study. Membership intention (i.e. the intention to retain union membership) was measured by three items ($\alpha$ = .84, .83 and .84 for the three samples respectively). Union office intention was assessed using a single item reflecting members' propensity to take on a representative position in the union.

## Results

### *Dimensionality of union commitment*

The first purpose of the study, that is, to examine the dimensionality of union commitment, was addressed using confirmatory factor analysis methods of Lisrel 7 (Jöreskog and Sörbom, 1989) and computation of internal consistency reliabilities. In this confirmatory approach, an explicit causal structure is posited to give rise to the observed covariances among questionnaire items and is, then, evaluated to determine whether the proposed model fits the data. More specifically, the nine items designed to reflect ideological commitment, and the seven instrumental commitment items, were constrained to load on their respective proposed latent factors.

Model-data consistency was checked both via an evaluation of the overall model fit and by comparing the magnitudes, signs and significance of parameter estimates to those hypothesized. Due to the chi-square statistic's sensitivity to sample size (Bentler, 1980), several other fit indices were, as recommended by Bollen (1989), relied upon in determining overall model fit: the goodness-of-fit index (GFI; Jöreskog and Sörbom, 1989), the normed fit index (NFI; Bentler and Bonett, 1980), the root mean square error of approximation (RMSEA; Browne and Cudeck, 1993) and the ratio of chi-square to degrees of freedom. GFI and NFI values above .90 indicate good fit (Bentler and Bonett, 1980); RMSEA values of .08 or less indicate reasonable errors of approximation while values of .05 or less indicate close fit of the model to the data (Browne & Cudeck, 1993); ratios of chi-square to degrees of freedom of 5:1 or less indicate good fit (Bollen, 1989).

The hypothesized two-factor model was first evaluated using data from sample 1 and resulted in a significant chi-square test of overall model fit ($\chi^2_{[103]} = 402.51$; $p < .001$), thus suggesting that the model did not fully reproduce the observed covariances. The remaining fit indices, however, indicated that the model provided an acceptable approximation of the observed covariances (RMSEA = .07) and a satisfactory fit to the data (GFI = .93; NFI

= .92; $\chi^2/df$ = 3.91). To investigate the generalizability of the two-dimensional model, data from samples 2 and 3 were used for replication. The fit indicators suggested that the hypothesized model provided an acceptable, but not completely satisfactory, fit to data for sample 2 (GFI = .88; NFI = .87; RMSEA = .08; $\chi^2_{[103]}$ = 233.88; $p < .001$; $\chi^2/df$ = 2.27) and a satisfactory fit for sample 3 (GFI = .90; NFI = .90; RMSEA = .08; $\chi^2_{[103]}$ = 381.02; $p < .001$; $\chi^2/df$ = 3.70). These results are supportive of the proposition that two dimensions of union commitment underlie the data in all three samples.

Standardized maximum likelihood estimates of factor loadings are presented in Table 20.1. For sample 1, all items hypothesized to measure ideological commitment loaded strongly on this factor while the instrumental items evidenced strong loadings on the proposed instrumental commitment factor. The magnitudes of parameter estimates were similar for both replication samples. Thus, all loadings were strong, significant and of the right sign for all three samples. The inter-factor correlations were .70 (sample 1), .69 (sample 2) and .81 (sample 3). As can be seen from the table, computations of Cronbach's alpha indicated adequate internal consistency reliabilities for both ideological ($\alpha \geq .90$ in all samples) and instrumental commitment ($\alpha \geq .85$ in all samples). For descriptive purposes, means and standard deviations in ideological and instrumental commitment are also shown in the table.

### *Factorial consistency across samples*

The second purpose of the study, to investigate whether the measurement model parameters generalize across samples, was addressed using the multi-group confirmatory factor analysis methods of Lisrel 7. This procedure allows for analyzing the same model in several samples simultaneously by constraining some or all parameters to be equal across samples (Jöreskog and Sörbom, 1989). The first analytical step involved testing the hypothesis that the number of common factors (i.e. two) was the same for all three samples without imposing any equality constraints on parameters. The second step comprised, in addition, the test of the hypothesis that the magnitudes of factor loadings were invariant across samples. In the third step equality constraints were imposed on both the factor loadings and the inter-factor correlation. Finally, in the fourth step the hypothesis was tested that the factor loadings, the factor correlation and the measurement errors were all invariant across samples. Also for the multi-sample analyses the chi-square statistic, the GFI, the NFI, the RMSEA and the ratio of chi-square to degrees of freedom were used to evaluate overall model fit while chi-square difference tests were relied upon for comparisons between the nested models.

**Table 20.1**
**Factor loadings on ideological (IDEOL) and instrumental (INSTR) commitment to the union**

| Union commitment item | Sample 1 IDEOL | Sample 1 INSTR | Sample 2 IDEOL | Sample 2 INSTR | Sample 3 IDEOL | Sample 3 INSTR |
|---|---|---|---|---|---|---|
| 1. I believe in the goals of the union movement | .73 | | .75 | | .76 | |
| 2. My union and I have approximately the same basic values | .68 | | .79 | | .70 | |
| 3 The decisions made by my union mostly reflect my opinions | .65 | | .69 | | .64 | |
| 4. My union's problems are my problems | .66 | | .72 | | .70 | |
| 5. I feel that I am an important part of my union | .73 | | .67 | | .76 | |
| 6. My union means a great deal to me personally | .76 | | .76 | | .80 | |
| 7. I have a strong sense of belonging to my union | .81 | | .81 | | .82 | |
| 8. The sense of community one feels in the union is unique | .67 | | .68 | | .70 | |
| 9. I have strong bonds to my union, bonds that would be hard to cut off | .69 | | .71 | | .75 | |
| 10 My union's chances of improving my pay are great | | .56 | | .63 | | .61 |
| 11. My union's chances of improving my physical work environment are great | | .74 | | .72 | | .76 |
| 12. My union's chances of offering me employment security are great | | .54 | | .51 | | .53 |
| 13. My union's chances of making my job more interesting are great | | .60 | | .58 | | .66 |
| 14 My union's chances of working upon the employer to make company operations function in a better way are great | | .70 | | .78 | | .78 |
| 15. My union's chances of bringing about an improvement of my work situation are great | | .82 | | .82 | | .82 |
| 16. My union's chances of giving me more influence over my work are great | | .72 | | .78 | | .80 |
| Inter-factor correlation | | .70 | | .69 | | .81 |
| Coefficient alpha reliability | 0.90 | 0.85 | 0.91 | 0.86 | 0.91 | 0.87 |
| Mean | 2.47 | 3.35 | 2.53 | 3.28 | 2.46 | 3.35 |
| Standard deviation | 0.92 | 0.64 | 0.97 | 0.67 | 0.98 | 0.70 |

*Notes:* Standardized maximum likelihood estimates of factor loadings. All loadings are significant ($p < .001$). For instrumental commitment (items 10 to 16), the behavioral beliefs listed in the table are weighted by corresponding outcome evaluations (e.g. 'For me, to get better paid is...'; scale ranging from 1 [very unimportant] to 5 [very important]).

Table 20.2 shows the results of the sequence of tests, starting with the model that imposed the same factor structure (i.e. two factors) across samples (Model 1). As no equality constraints were specified in Model 1, the chi-square value obtained for this model ( $\chi^2_{[309]} = 1017.41$; $p < .001$) was equal to the sum of the chi-square estimates resulting from the three sample-specific tests of the two-dimensional model. The remaining fit indices (GFI = .90; NFI = .91; RMSEA = .04; $\chi^2/df = 3.29$) indicated that Model 1 provided a satisfactory fit to the data, suggesting that the two-factor model generalizes across samples.

**Table 20.2**
**Tests for equality of factor structures across samples.**

| Model | *df* | $\chi^2$ | $\chi^2/df$ | NFI | PFI | RMSEA | $\Delta\, df$ [a] | $\Delta\, \chi^2$ [a] |
|---|---|---|---|---|---|---|---|---|
| 1. Two factors; Freely estimated | 309 | 1017.41* | 3.29 | .91 | .89 | .04 | – | – |
| 2. Two factors; Equal factor loadings | 341 | 1043.51* | 3.06 | .90 | .90 | .04 | 32 | 26.10*n.s.* |
| 3. Two factors; Equal loadings and factor correlations | 343 | 1051.70* | 3.07 | .90 | .90 | .04 | 34 | 34.29*n.s.* |
| 4. Two factors; Equal loadings, factor correlations, and residuals | 375 | 1083.67* | 2.89 | .90 | .90 | .04 | 66 | 66.26*n.s.* |

*Notes:* * $p < .001$; *n.s.* = not significant; *N*=1295.
[a] Based on a comparison with Model 1.

In Model 2, equality constraints were imposed on the factor loadings. The fit of this model ($\chi^2_{[341]} = 1043.51$; $p < .001$; GFI = .90; NFI = .90; RMSEA = .04; $\chi^2/df = 3.06$) was essentially the same as for Model 1 and the change in chi-square was not significant ($\Delta\, \chi^2_{[32]} = 26.10$; $p > .05$). This indicates that the parameters constrained to be equal (i.e. the factor loadings) did not differ between samples. In Model 3, both the factor loadings and the inter-factor correlation were constrained to be equal across samples. Also this model provided a satisfactory fit ($\chi^2_{[343]} = 1051.70$; $p < .001$; GFI = .90; NFI = .90; RMSEA = .04; $\chi^2/df = 3.07$), and the chi-square difference test suggested no statistically significant impairment of fit as compared to Model 1 ($\Delta\, \chi^2_{[34]} = 34.29$; $p > .05$). Model 4, in which equality constraints were imposed not only on the factor loadings and the inter-factor correlation but also on the measurement errors, still provided a satisfactory fit to the data ($\chi^2_{[375]} = 1083.67$; $p < .001$; GFI = .90; NFI = .90; RMSEA = .04; $\chi^2/df = 2.89$). The chi-square difference between this model and Model 1 was not significant ($\Delta\ \chi^2_{[66]} = 66.26$; $p > .05$), thus indicating that none of the factorial parameters differ between samples.

### *Generalizability of relationships with outcome variables*

The third purpose of the study was addressed using multiple regression analysis. For each outcome variable, we first estimated the effects of ideological and instrumental commitment separately in the three samples. We subsequently constrained the effect of each commitment dimension to be equal across samples and used chi-square tests to examine the generalizability of relationships across samples. A significant chi-square estimate indicates that the fit of the regression model is impaired when equality constraints are imposed, while a non-significant estimate suggests that the commitment dimension subjected to the test has similar effect sizes in all three samples. The results of these analyses are reported in Table 20.3.

Ideological commitment evidenced strong positive relationships with membership intention in all three samples. Instrumental commitment showed positive relationships with the same outcome variable in two of the samples while it did not predict the intention to retain membership in sample 2. These results indicate, as expected, that the more strongly members identify with the goals and values of their union, and the more they perceive that the benefits associated with membership exceed the costs, the more inclined will they also be to remain members of their union. Taken together, ideological and instrumental commitment accounted for approximately 35 percent of the variance in membership intention ($R^2 = .33$ for sample 1, .36 for sample 2 and .35 for sample 3). The tests for equality of regression coefficients showed that the relationship with membership intention did not differ significantly between samples for ideological commitment ($\chi^2_{[2]} = 3.59$, $p > .05$) or instrumental commitment ($\chi^2_{[2]} = 4.61$, $p > .05$). This suggests that the results generalize across samples.

The intention to hold union office was, as expected, predicted by ideological commitment, and the effect sizes did not differ significantly between samples ($\chi^2_{[2]} = 0.41$, $p > .05$). Also consistent with our predictions, instrumental commitment was not related to union office intention, a finding which generalized across the three samples ($\chi^2_{[2]} = 0.28$, $p > .05$). These results indicate that an identification with the goals and values of the union appears to be necessary for members' involvement in such union activities that require substantial personal effort. Union commitment accounted for 15 percent of the variance in union office intention in sample 1 and 18 percent in samples 2 and 3.

**Table 20.3**
**Multiple regression effects of ideological and instrumental commitment on three outcome variables: Generalizability across samples**

| | Sample 1 | Sample 2 | Sample 3 | $\chi^2 (df=2)$[a] |
|---|---|---|---|---|
| **Membership intention** | | | | |
| Ideological commitment | .46*** | .57*** | .41*** | 3.59*n.s.* |
| Instrumental commitment | .17*** | .05 | .23*** | 4.61*n.s.* |
| $R^2$ | .33*** | .36*** | .35*** | |
| **Union office intention** | | | | |
| Ideological commitment | .36*** | .43*** | .39*** | 0.41*n.s.* |
| Instrumental commitment | .05 | .01 | .04 | 0.28*n.s.* |
| $R^2$ | .15*** | .18*** | .18*** | |
| **Union meeting involvement** | | | | |
| Ideological commitment | .40*** | .45*** | .50*** | 1.48*n.s.* |
| Instrumental commitment | .10* | .21** | .14*** | 3.32*n.s.* |
| $R^2$ | .12*** | .13*** | .14*** | |

*Notes:* *** $p < .001$; ** $p < .01$; * $p < .05$; *n.s.* = not significant.
[a] Test for equality of regression coefficients. A nonsignificant chi-square value indicates that the effect of the commitment dimension on the outcome variable is not statistically different between the three samples.

Union meeting involvement, a form of participation that requires more effort than retaining membership, but is less arduous than serving in elected office, was predicted by both dimensions of commitment. As is apparent from the table, ideological commitment was more strongly related to meeting involvement than instrumental commitment. The relatively large effect sizes for ideological commitment were similar across samples ($\chi^2_{[2]} = 1.48$, $p > .05$), so, too, were the more moderate effects obtained for instrumental commitment ($\chi^2_{[2]} = 3.32$, $p > .05$). The amount of variance in meeting involvement accounted for by the commitment dimensions was relatively similar in sample 1 ($R^2 = .12$), sample 2 ($R^2 = .13$) and sample 3 ($R^2 = .14$).

## Discussion

This study focused on two dimensions of union commitment, one of which is based on member-union value congruence (ideological commitment) and the other on member-union exchange relationships (instrumental commitment). Our first research objective involved examining if the theoretical distinction between these two dimensions is also empirically valid. Results of confirmatory factor analysis based on data from a sample of Swedish blue-collar union members rendered strong empirical support for the proposed two-dimensional representation of commitment. The reiteration of these analyses using data from two replication samples drawn from other blue-collar unions showed, once again, that the proposed two-factor model provided an acceptable fit to data, thus lending support for the external validity of the model.

The second purpose of the study was to investigate whether the measurement model parameters generalize across samples. Results of multi-group confirmatory factor analysis once again revealed a striking similarity between unions. Not only was the same measurement model found to hold for the three samples, but the results suggested, in addition, that the magnitudes of parameter estimates (factor loadings, inter-factor correlation, measurement errors) were equal across samples. Indeed, with the addition of each set of equality constraints, the various fit indicators remained essentially the same, indicating that imposing equality constraints across samples did not result in impairments in model fit to the data.

Our third research objective was to predict three important outcome variables (union membership intention, union office intention and union meeting involvement) from ideological and instrumental union commitment, and involved evaluating the extent to which the relationships between commitment dimensions and outcome variables were similar across samples. Consistent with the theoretical assumptions, the multiple regression analyses showed that ideological commitment evidenced stronger relationships than instrumental commitment with the three outcome variables. Instrumental commitment was positively related to the two less effort-consuming forms of involvement in the union (membership retention and meeting involvement), but not to the more arduous form (union office intention). In neither of the analyses were the regression effects of the commitment dimensions on the outcome variables found to differ significantly between samples, which means that the results cannot be attributed to capitalization of chance within a single research setting.

Our results indicate that both ideological and instrumental commitment affect the intention to remain a union member, although at this point it is not known whether a high degree of commitment in only one of the dimensions is a sufficient condition for actual membership retention. Also unanswered by this research is the question of whether there is a minimum level of commitment that is required for membership retention. While both commitment dimensions appear to be important for the membership retention decision, the results also highlight that subsequent active involvement in union affairs depends more on ideological commitment and less on instrumental commitment. Given the generally low rates of actual union participation found in many studies (see e.g. Kuruvilla and Sverke, 1993, for Sweden and the U.S.), these results may suggest that active union members are committed largely on an ideological basis, and that most union members are only instrumentally committed to the union, thus explaining the low levels of participation.

The present results have some important implications for unions. Unions must attempt to develop an ideological bond with their members if they want an active and involved membership body. Pure 'bread and butter' unionism may not generate the ideological commitment that is necessary for members' active participation in union activity. A strong identification with the values of the union appears to be crucial for the decision to engage in union activity (cf. Offe and Wiesenthal, 1980), a finding which contradicts Olson's (1971) thesis that only selective incentives can stimulate members' contributions to the collective system. Thus, our results are, at least to a certain extent, congruent with Newton and Shore's (1992) assertion that in the absence of an ideological attachment to the union, even a high degree of instrumentality is an insufficient motive for union participation. The results do indicate, however, that instrumentality may be a sufficient motive for less effort-consuming forms of involvement such as the propensity to retain membership.

Although similar results were obtained for the three samples included in the present study, thus providing support for the external validity of ideological and instrumental commitment, our samples were all drawn from Swedish blue-collar unions. Naturally, therefore, our results need replication in samples drawn from other kinds of union members (i.e. white-collar workers and professionals) and from other countries before any firm conclusions as to the generalizability of the findings can be drawn.

For instance, while work on an ideological basis is not unknown in the U.S. trade union movement (Freeman and Medoff, 1984), American unions, and to some extent Australian and British unions, can best be described in terms of business unionism (Poole, 1981). In contrast, the union movements in several European countries adhere more strongly to the social unionism model, with its emphasis on ideological matters and broad political reform of the society. It is possible that in other cultural settings the relative importance of ideological and instrumental commitment for membership retention and union participation decisions may differ from what was found here. Bain and Elsheikh (1976), for example, found that instrumental attitudes accounted for up to 70 percent of union density changes in Australia, the U.K. and the U.S., while in Sweden only a small proportion the changes in union density could be explained by instrumental motives. As shown in this chapter, recent developments in research on members' psychological attachment to their unions embraces the possibilities and constraints that structure such relative importances of ideology and instrumentality.

## References

Abrahamsson, B. (1993), *Why organizations? How and why people organize*, Sage, Newbury Park, CA.

Adams, R. J. (1974), 'Solidarity, self-interest and the unionization differential between Europe and North America', *Relations Industrielles*, Vol. 29, pp. 497-512.

Ajzen, I. and Fishbein, M. (1980), *Understanding attitudes and predicting social behavior*, Prentice-Hall, Englewood Cliffs, NJ.

Bain, G. S. and Elsheikh, F. (1976), *Union growth and the business cycle: An econometric analysis*, Basil Blackwell, Oxford.

Barling, J., Fullagar, C. and Kelloway, E. K. (1992), *The union and its members: A psychological approach*, Oxford University Press, New York.

Bentler, P. M. (1980), 'Multivariate analyses with latent variables: Causal modeling', *Annual Review of Psychology*, Vol. 31, pp. 419-456.

Bentler, P. M. and Bonett, D. G. (1980), 'Significance tests and goodness-of-fit in the analysis of covariance structures', *Psychological Bulletin*, Vol. 88, pp. 588-606.

Beutell, N. J. and Biggs, D. L. (1984), 'Behavioral intentions to join a union: Instrumnetality x valence, locus of control, and strike attitudes', *Psychological Reports*, Vol. 55, pp. 215-222.

Bollen, K. A. (1989), *Structural equations with latent variables*, Wiley, New York.

Browne, M. W. and Cudeck, R. (1993), 'Alternative ways of assessing model fit', in Bollen, K. A. and Long, J. S. (eds.), *Testing structural equation models* (pp. 136-162), Sage, Newbury Park, CA.

Cook, T. D. and Campbell, D. T. (1979), *Quasi-experimentation: Design & analysis issues for field settings*, Houghton Mifflin, Boston, MA.

Dunlop, J. (1958), *Industrial relations systems*, Holt, New York.

Etzioni, A. (1975), *A comparative analysis of complex organizations*, Free Press, New York.

Fiorito, J. (1992), 'Unionism and altruism', *Labour Studies Journal*, Vol. 17, pp. 19-34.

Freeman, R. B. and Medoff, J. L. (1984), *What do unions do?*, Basic Books, New York.

Fullagar, C. and Barling, J. (1987), 'Toward a model of union commitment', in Lewin, D. and Lipsky, D. (eds.), *Advances in industrial and labour relations* (pp. 43-77), JAI Press, Greenwich.

Gallagher, D. G. and Clark, P. F. (1989), 'Research on union commitment: Implications for labour', *Labour Studies Journal*, Vol. 14, pp. 52-71.

Gallagher, D. G. and Strauss, G. (1991), 'Union membership attitudes and participation', in Strauss, G., Gallagher, D. G. and Fiorito, J. (eds.), *The state of the unions* (pp. 139-174), Industrial Relations Research Association, Madison, WI.

Goldthorpe, J. H., Lockwood, D., Bechofer, F. and Platt, J. (1968), *The affluent worker: Industrial attitudes and behavior*, Cambridge University Press, Cambridge, MA.

Gordon, M. E. (1996), 'Ideology and union commitment', in Pasture, P. Verberckmoes, J. and De Witte, H. (eds.), *The lost perspective? Trade unions between ideology and social action in the new Europe, Vol. 2, Significance of ideology in European trade unionism* (pp. 241-258). Avebury, Aldershot.

Gordon, M. E. and Nurick, A. J. (1981), 'Psychological approaches to the study of unions and union-management relations', *Psychological Bulletin*, Vol. 90, pp. 292-307.

Gordon, M. E., Philbot, J. W., Burt, R., Thompson, C. A. and Spiller, W. E. (1980), 'Commitment to the union: Development of a measure and an examination of its correlates', *Journal of Applied Psychology*, Vol. 65, pp. 479-499.

Jöreskog, K. G. and Sörbom, D. (1989), *LISREL 7: A guide to the program and applications*, Scientific Software, Chicago.

Kelloway, E. K. and Barling, J. (1993), 'Members' participation in local union activities: Measurement, prediction, and replication', *Journal of Applied Psychology*, Vol. 78, pp. 262-279.

Klandermans, B. (1986), 'Psychology and trade union participation: Joining, acting, quitting', *Journal of Occupational Psychology*, Vol. 59, pp. 198-204.

Knoke, D. (1990), *Organizing for collective action: The political economies of associations*, Aldine de Gruyter, New York.

Kuruvilla, S., Gallagher, D. G. and Wetzel, K. (1993), 'The development of members' attitudes towards their unions: Sweden and Canada', *Industrial and Labour Relations Review*, Vol. 46, pp. 499-515.

Kuruvilla, S. and Sverke, M. (1993), 'Two dimensions of union commitment based on the theory of reasoned action: Cross-cultural comparisons', *Research and Practice in Human Resource Management*, Vol. 1, pp. 1-16.

LO (1991), *Organisationen i framtiden* (The organization in the future), LO, Stockholm.

McShane, S. L. (1986), 'The multidimensionality of union participation', *Journal of Occupational Psychology*, Vol. 59, pp. 177-187.

Mowday, R. T., Porter, L. W. and Steers, R. M. (1982), *Employee-organizational linkages*, Academic Press, New York.

Newton, L. A. and Shore, L. M. (1992), 'A model of union membership: Instrumentality, commitment, and opposition', *Academy of Management Review*, Vol. 17, pp. 275-298.

Offe, C. and Wiesenthal, H. (1980), 'Two logics of collective action: Theoretical notes on social class and organizational form', in Zeitlin, M. (ed.), *Political power and social theory* (pp. 67-115), University of California Press, Los Angeles.

Olson, M. (1971), *The logic of collective action: Public goods and the theory of groups*, Harvard University Press, Cambridge, MA.

O'Reilly, C. and Chatman, J. (1986), 'Organizational commitment and psychological attachment: The effects of compliance, identification, and internalization on prosocial behavior', *Journal of Applied Psychology*, Vol. 71, pp. 492-499.

Poole, M. (1981), *Theories of trade unionism: A sociology of industrial relations*, Routledge and Kegan Paul, London.

Robinson, E. I. (1990), 'Organizing labour: Explaining Canada-US union density divergence in the post-war period', Unpublished doctoral dissertation, Yale University.

Schein, E. H. (1980), *Organizational psychology* (3rd ed.), Prentice-Hall, Englewood Cliffs, NJ.

Sen, A. (1982), 'Rational fools? A critique of the behavioural foundations of economic theory', in Sen, A. (ed.), *Choice, welfare and measurement*, Blackwell, Oxford, U.K.

Spinrad, W. (1960), 'Correlates of trade union participation: A summary of the literature', *American Sociological Review*, Vol. 25, pp. 237-244.

Statistics Sweden (1994), *Arbetskraftsundersökningarna* (The labour force surveys), Statistics Sweden, Stockholm.

Sverke, M. (1996), 'The importance of ideology in trade union participation in Sweden: A social-psychological model', in Pasture, P. Verberckmoes, J. and De Witte, H. (eds.), *The lost perspective? Trade unions between ideology and social action in the new Europe, Vol. 2, Significance of ideology in European trade unionism* (pp. 353-376). Avebury, Aldershot.

Sverke, M. and Kuruvilla, S. (1995), 'A new conceptualization of union commitment: Development and test of an integrated theory', *Journal of Organizational Behavior*, Vol. 16, pp. 505-532.

Sverke, M. and Sjöberg, A. (1995), 'Union membership behavior: The influence of instrumental and value-based commitment', in Tetrick, L. E. and Barling, J. (eds.), *Changing employment relations: Behavioral and social perspectives*, American Psychological Association, Washington, DC.

Weber, M. (1968), *Economy and society*, University of California Press, Berkeley, CA.

Wheeler, H. N. and McClendon, J. A. (1991), 'The individual decision to unionize', in Strauss, G., Gallagher, D. G. and Fiorito, J. (eds.), *The state of the unions*, Industrial Relations Research Association, Madison, WI.

Wiener, Y. (1982), 'Commitment in organizations: A normative view', *Academy of Management Review*, Vol. 7, pp. 418-428.

# 21 Modelling the influence of steward satisfaction and participation on perceived union performance

*Robert R. Sinclair, James E. Martin, Lois E. Tetrick and Michael McMillan*

Recent structural changes in political, social, and economic systems, coupled with changes in employer-employee relations and human resource policies and practices (e.g. strategic compensation systems, participative management programs, contingent workers, team work structures), are associated with a decline in the proportion of working individuals who belong to labour unions in several Western industrialized nations (Hartley, 1995). In this context, researchers interested in labour unions have begun to develop methods to build union commitment and increase union participation. While stewards are recognized as an important influence on members' attitudes and behaviours, relatively little research has examined the antecedents or consequences of steward behaviour. Therefore, the purpose of this chapter was to develop and test a model of the relationship between stewards' satisfaction, participation, and perceptions of union performance.

Social exchange theory suggests that individuals interpret the actions of key agents of organizations as actions of the global organization (Levison, 1965). Further, individuals personify the actions of the organization and, thus, develop exchange relationships with organizations (Eisenberger, Huntington, Hutchison and Sowa, 1986; Levison, 1965). Accordingly, individuals' attitudes toward and behaviours concerning the global organization are influenced by the actions of these agents. In labour unions, stewards are the organizational agents who have the most day to day contact with rank and file members and, thus, are an important influence on the rank and file. This is supported by

---

Please address all correspondence concerning this manuscript to Robert R. Sinclair, University of Tulsa, Department of Psychology, 600 South College Ave.,Tulsa, Oklahoma 74104, USA.

research indicating that stewards' leadership behaviour is related to members' satisfaction with the union (Kelloway and Barling, 1993), judgements of the performance of the union (Johnson and Johnson, 1992), attitudes toward grievance procedures (Clark and Gallagher, 1988), and union participation rates (see Barling, Fullagar and Kelloway, 1992, for a review). However, differences are typically obtained in the correlates of stewards' attitudes and behaviour as compared with the correlates of rank and file members' attitudes and behaviour (e.g. Dalton and Todor, 1987; Magenau, Martin and Peterson, 1988). Therefore, new theoretical models and corresponding empirical studies are required to identify the correlates of stewards behavior.

While little research has directly applied social exchange theory to research on union stewards, the theory suggests that individuals who have satisfactory experiences as stewards feel a sense of obligation toward the union and a greater willingness to fulfill their day to day responsibilities (e.g. Shore, Tetrick, Sinclair and Newton, 1994; Sinclair and Tetrick, 1995). Further, the organizational citizenship literature (Organ, 1988) suggests that stewards who are satisfied with the union are more likely to engage in behaviour that exceeds normal expectations and that these behaviours result in better union performance. Thus, the literature suggests that causality flows from union satisfaction to participation and from participation to performance.

Understanding the effects of steward satisfaction and participation on union performance requires that two types of potential temporal effects be examined. The first is the degree of consistency of attitudes or behaviours across time. Consistency is typically attributed to the influence of relatively stable dispositions (e.g. Staw and Ross, 1985) or by the observation that given conceptually similar situations, individuals will engage in conceptually similar behaviours as in ecology models of biodata (Mumford, Stokes and Owens, 1990). Assessing consistency is particularly important for researchers and practitioners interested in changing union attitudes or behaviours because highly stable constructs are more difficult to change. For instance, if attitudes are primarily influenced by relatively stable dispositions, developmental efforts to change members' attitudes toward their union may not be worth the required investment of resources.

Second, social psychological theories such as consistency theory (Festinger, 1957), self perception theory (Bem, 1970) and self presentation theory (see Leary and Kowalski, 1990, for a review) suggest the dynamic and reciprocal nature of the relationship between attitudes and behaviours. Most models of union participation treat attitudes as a causal influence on members behaviour (e.g. Kelloway and Barling, 1989). However, individuals also adjust their attitudes to be consistent with their past behaviour. Over time, this suggests reciprocity in the relationship between attitudes and behaviours. Stewards who are more satisfied with their union will be more involved in the union and thus positively impact the performance of the union and stewards who see the union as more effective will describe themselves as more satisfied with the union.

Based on the discussion above, Figure 21.1 presents a hypothesized model of the relationship between stewards' satisfaction, participation and ratings of union performance (all relationships are positive). Three types of effects are presented. The first concerns the effects of one construct upon another. As described above, causality was hypothesized to flow from satisfaction to participation and from participation to performance. The second type of effect concerns cross lagged relationships. A path is hypothesized between union performance at time 1 and union satisfaction at time 2. Finally, the model includes three paths for the autoregressive effects, that is, the paths linking the two measures of the same construct at different time periods (the values of these paths are used to assess consistency across time).

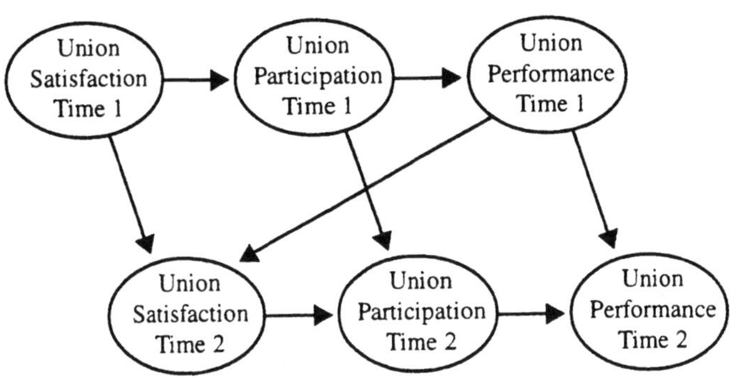


**Figure 21.1 Hypothesized longitudinal model of relations among satisfaction, participation and performance**

## Method

### *Subjects*

The subjects were 408 stewards from a union local representing more than 30,000 members from over 60 retail stores, several located in the midwestern United States. The stewards participated in telephone surveys administered in January and September of 1994 by business agents (full-time union staff members) who serviced the stores where the stewards were employed. During the first phase, 355 stewards (87 percent) were contacted, during the second phase 349 stewards (86 percent) were contacted. Completed questionnaires for both phases were obtained from 241 stewards (representing 59 percent of the total sample).

### *Measures*

The questionnaire contained items from three content areas, all of which were scored with four point response scales. Five items tapped Union Satisfaction (e.g. 'Overall, I am usually satisfied with the treatment I receive when I call the Local Union'), with response options ranging from strongly agree to strongly disagree. Four items tapped Union Participation (e.g. 'Which of the following statements best describes the number of grievances you have filed in the last year'), with response options indicating the frequency of each behaviour and appropriate to individual items such as the number of grievances filed in the last year and the frequency with which the stewards attended union meetings and functions. Two items tapped Union Performance (e.g. 'Overall, how would you rate the contract negotiated for your workplace by [the local]') with response options ranging from very poor to very good. The internal consistency estimates (coefficient alphas) for the scales were $a_{time\ 1} = .77$ and $a_{time\ 2} = .74$ for satisfaction, $a_{time\ 1} = .59$ and $a_{time\ 2} = .62$ for participation, and $a_{time\ 1} = .59$ and $a_{time\ 2} = .49$ for union performance. While the internal consistency estimates for participation and performance are low, this is, in part, a function of the low number of items in each scale (see Cortina, 1993). Further, the average inter-item correlations for each scale ranged from .27 to .43 suggesting an adequate degree of internal consistency.

## Results

### *Univariate and bivariate analyses*

Table 21.1 presents the means, standard deviations and intercorrelations from both waves of data collection. The temporal stability of the measures was examined by computing correlations between the two measures of each construct (i.e. the test-retest reliability coefficients). These correlations suggested that the measures have moderate degrees of temporal stability (satisfaction: $r_{time\ 1.time\ 2} = .45$; participation: $r_{time\ 1.time\ 2} = .61$; performance $r_{time\ 1.time\ 2} = .49$). Since the test-retest coefficients provide information on the stability of the rank order of individuals on the measures but do not provide information on changes in absolute standing, matched pairs t-tests were conducted comparing the mean of each measure at time 1 with the corresponding mean at time 2. These tests indicated that the mean levels of participation and performance did not change (participation: $t[241] = .90$; performance: $t[241] = -1.04$). The mean for union satisfaction was slightly lower at time 2 ($t[241] = -2.06$; $p < .05$). However, examination of the means (3.49 and 3.43 for time 1 and 2, respectively) suggests that the practical significance of this difference is not large, particularly given the statistical power of the test. Taken as a whole, these results suggest a moderate degree of temporal stability of the measures, both in terms of individuals' relative standings and overall means for the measures.

**Table 21.1**
**Descriptive statistics for all variables at both time periods**

| | Time 1 | | Time 2 | | | | |
|---|---|---|---|---|---|---|---|
| Variable | Mean | SD | Mean | SD | 1 | 2 | 3 |
| 1. Satisfaction | 3.49 | 0.43 | 3.44 | 0.49 | 0.<u>45</u>*** | 0.06 | 0.22** |
| 2. Participation | 2.80 | 0.56 | 2.77 | 0.56 | 0.20*** | 0.<u>61</u>*** | 0.36*** |
| 3. Performance | 3.08 | 0.54 | 3.12 | 0.49 | 0.35*** | 0.33*** | 0.<u>48</u>*** |

*Notes:* The lower half of the matrix contains the intercorrelations at time 1, the upper half contains the intercorrelations at time 2, and the test-retest correlations are underlined on the diagonal.
*** $p < .001$; ** $p < .01$

Some differences were obtained in the two sets of synchronous correlations (correlations within a time period). The correlation between satisfaction and participation was significant at time 1 ($r = .20, p < .001$) but not at time 2 ($r = .06$). The correlation between satisfaction and performance was similar at time 1 and time 2 ($r$'s = .35 and .36, respectively; both $p$'s < .001). Finally, the relationship between participation and performance was statistically significant at both time periods but was somewhat stronger at time 1 ($r = .33, p < .001$) than time 2 ($r = .22, p < .01$). These results suggest support for the hypothesized relationship between steward participation and union performance; stewards who report higher levels of participation also tend to describe the union as more effective. However, only partial support was obtained for the hypothesized relationship between satisfaction and participation as there was a positive relationship at time 1 but not at time 2. The correlational analyses suggested a relationship between satisfaction and performance rather than between satisfaction and participation.

The final set of correlations of interest are the cross lagged correlations (because of space considerations, these are not shown in the table). Satisfaction at time 1 was related to performance at time 2 ($r = .39$, $p < .001$) but not to participation. Participation at time 1 was related to both satisfaction at time 2 ($r = .14$, $p < .01$) and performance at time 2 ($r = .27$, $p < .001$). Finally performance at time 1 was related to both satisfaction at time 2 ($r = .23$, $p < .001$) and participation at time 2 ($r = .19$, $p < .001$). Taken as a whole, these results suggest support for the hypothesized model. At the bivariate level, four of the five hypothesized relationships among the variables were supported. The only rèlationship not supported by the these analyses was the time 2 relationship between satisfaction and participation which was not statistically significant.

### *Multivariate analyses*

A structural equations analysis was performed to test the full system of hypothesized relationships. This approach requires two caveats with respect to the present research. First, this study used two waves of correlational data. While structural equations analyses can be used to test theoretical models with a temporal dimension, they do not, in and of themselves, allow researchers to conclude that a causal relationship exists. The strength of the causal inference is dependent on the strength of the theory guiding the data analysis and requires experimental replication before strong causal inferences can be drawn. Second, the hypothesized model considers three variables from a rich system of interrelationships among numerous organizational, environmental, individual and interpersonal factors. Since this model is not self contained (i.e. does not include every relevant variable) the analyses should be viewed as a multivariate multiple regression rather than a complete test of a theoretical model (James, Mulaik and Brett, 1982).

We chose four criteria to evaluate the fit of each model tested: (1) that the ratio of chi square to degrees of freedom be 5:1 or less (Bollen, 1989), (2) that the root mean square error of approximation (RMSEA) be .08 or less (Browne and Cudeck, 1993), (3) that the incremental fit index (IFI) be .90 or greater to indicate good fit, and (4) that hypothesized parameters be statistically significant. In instances where we compared multiple models we used a chi square difference test to compare them (see Bollen, 1989, for a description of this technique).

Following procedures recommended by Anderson and Gerbing (1989), a two stage approach was used to conduct the analysis. In this approach, confirmatory factor analysis is used to assess the adequacy of the hypothesized 'measurement model' (the correspondence between items and latent variables) prior to evaluating the relationships between the latent variables. Two models were evaluated for each phase of data collection: a three factor model, where each item was hypothesized to tap the latent variable it was designed to tap, and a one factor model where all items were hypothesized to load on a single latent variable. In each case the three factor model fit the data well (phase 1: chi square ratio = 2.13, RMSEA = .06, IFI = .94; phase 2: chi square ratio = 2.85, RMSEA = .07, IFI = .87) and significantly better than the one factor model (phase 1: $\Delta \chi^2 = 128.99$, df = 3, $p < .001$; phase 2: $\Delta \chi^2 = 146.24$, df = 3, $p < .001$). Further, all parameters linking items to latent variables were statistically significant. These results indicate the adequacy of the hypothesized measurement model.

We then tested the hypothesized structural model using a manifest variables approach. Table 21.2 presents the chi square, degrees of freedom, RMSEA and IFI for each model tested. None of the fit indices met our criteria for the hypothesized model (Model 1). Therefore, modification indices were examined as an exploratory method of assessing where the model might be improved. These indices indicate, for each fixed parameter, the minimum expected improvement in the value of the chi square for a model estimated with that parameter allowed to vary. Since models with any additional freed parameters will obtain higher fit indices and the modification indices capitalize on chance variation, it is commonly recommended that only substantively interpretable parameters be tested (e.g. Jöreskog, 1993).

**Table 21.2**
**Results of the structural equations analysis**

| Model | $\chi^2$ | df | $\chi^2$/df | $\Delta \chi^2$ | RMSEA | IFI |
|---|---|---|---|---|---|---|
| Model 1 | 56.03** | 7 | 8.00 | — | 0.17 | 0.85 |
| Model 2[a] | 32.10** | 6 | 5.35 | 23.93** | 0.14 | 0.92 |
| Model 3[b] | 10.63 | 5 | 2.13 | 21.47** | 0.07 | 0.98 |
| Model 4[c] | 3.21 | 4 | 0.80 | 7.42** | 0.00 | 1.00 |

*Notes:* ** $p < .01$
[a] similar to model 1 but includes path from satisfaction at time 1 to performance at time 1
[b] similar to model 2 but includes path from satisfaction at time 2 to performance at time 2
[c] similar to model 3 but includes path from satisfaction at time 1 to performance at time 2

Three subsequent nested models were examined. In each case, the chi square difference test indicated a significant improvement in model fit. In the first alternative model (listed as Model 2 in Table 2), the path from union satisfaction to union performance at time 1 was freed. This resulted in substantial improvement in all fit indices although the chi square ratio (5.35) and RMSEA (.135) were still not within acceptable limits. The next model estimated (Model 3) differed from Model 2 in that the path from union satisfaction to union performance at time 2 was freed. This model also resulted in substantial improvement in the fit indices, all of which met our established criteria for good fit. Finally, Model 4 differed from model 3 in that it included a path from union satisfaction at time 1 to union performance at time 2. This model also obtained substantial improvement in the fit indices with the chi square ratio dropping to 0.80, the RMSEA dropping to 0.0 and the IFI increasing to 1.0.

Figure 21.2 presents the statistically significant parameter estimates ($\beta$ and $\gamma$) and the variance accounted for ($R^2$) in each endogenous variable from the standardized solution for Model 4. Two hypothesized paths were not significant, the path from union performance at time 1 to union satisfaction at time 2 and from union satisfaction at time 2 to union participation at time 2. All other hypothesized paths were significant with coefficients ranging from .13 to .42 for path coefficients and autoregressive effects ranging from .35 to .61. Contrary to the hypotheses, union satisfaction influenced union participation at time 1 but not at time 2. Both the path coefficients and the squared multiple R's are generally of small to moderate magnitude (e.g. values of $R^2$ ranging from .04 to .37) indicating the lack of self containment in the model. However, the results demonstrate the importance of both steward attitudes and steward participation for predicting union performance.

## Discussion

This chapter reports the results of a longitudinal study of the relationship between steward satisfaction, participation and perceptions of union performance. A structural equations analysis was conducted using two waves of questionnaire data from 241 union stewards who were members of a union local in the midwestern United States. The results suggested that self reports of satisfaction, participation and performance are somewhat stable over time and demonstrated the influence of stewards' satisfaction and participation on perceptions of union performance. Finally, steward satisfaction was found to predict union performance nine months later.

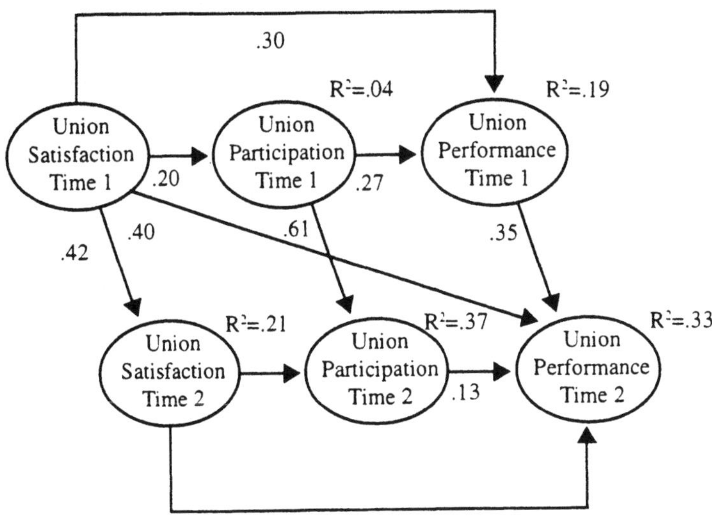


**Figure 21.2 Structural equations analysis results for Model 4**

This study has three limitations which influence the strength of inferences drawn from the data. First, the reliance on self report data raises the possibility that the findings are attributable to common method variance effects (Podsakoff and Organ, 1986) or bias in stewards' judgements of union performance. Second, the results may not generalize to unions representing individuals in occupations that are not in the retail/service sector of the economy or in cultural milieus other than the midwestern United States. For instance, North American unions emphasize instrumental issues to a greater extent than unions in other countries which may emphasize ideological issues (Wheeler and McClendon, 1991). Finally, longitudinal designs employing two waves of cross sectional data are not the ideal method for drawing causal inferences. Future research could address these concerns by using independently obtained and, where possible, objective measures, particularly for participation and performance. Further, alternate research designs, such as field studies, can be employed to draw stronger causal inferences.

The results of this study suggest that union performance is, in part, a function of the attitudes and behaviours of union stewards. This has both practical and theoretical implications. For practitioners, the moderate correlations between measures of the same variables at two different time periods suggest that while steward attitudes and behaviours are somewhat stable, there is clearly room for change. When coupled with the data concerning the linkage of steward attitudes and behaviours to ratings of union performance these findings suggest the efficacy of organizational development interventions that focus on improving steward attitudes and involvement.

An emerging body of research suggests that employees' perceptions of the extent to which their organizations are committed to them and value them as individuals are important predictors of attitudes and behaviour. Eisenberger et al. (1986) term these perceptions as perceived organizational support. Recent research indicates that union members form perceptions of union support (Shore, et al., 1994; Sinclair and Tetrick, 1995); however, little is known about the antecedents of perceived union support, either for rank and file members or stewards. Efforts to improve union performance by improving the quality of the exchange relationship between stewards and their union could focus on steward recruitment, selection, training and/or socialization. For instance, research could examine the effects of early socialization experiences into the role of union steward on the attitudes and behaviours of stewards and rank and file members and link these socialization processes to both objective and subjective measures of union effectiveness.

Further research on the construct of union performance would be of value to practitioners. While previous research suggests the influence of stewards' behaviour on members' satisfaction and perceptions of union performance (e.g. Kelloway and Barling, 1993; Johnson and Johnson, 1992; Martin and Magenau, 1993) less research has focused on steward satisfaction and steward perceptions of union performance. Linking these perceptions with objective measures of performance such as ratification or strike votes, increases or decreases in union membership (in organizations where union membership is optional), or even the fiscal status of the union would be interesting to academics and valuable to practitioners.

This study suggests that the relationship between steward satisfaction and participation is similar to relationships obtained in research on rank and file union members. However, this study focused exclusively on administrative measures of participation (e.g. attending union meetings). Fullagar and Barling (1989) distinguish between formal and informal union participation where informal participation refers to 'frequently occurring but unscheduled extrarole behaviours that reflect support for the union but are not crucial to its survival' (Fullagar et al., 1995, p. 149). The organizational citizenship literature suggests that satisfaction is a better predictor of extrarole behaviours than of inrole behaviours (Organ, 1988). This suggests that stewards' satisfaction with the union may be more strongly related to informal participation. While the dimensionality of union participation continues to be debated in the same fashion as the dimensionality of union commitment, further research examining the relationship between satisfaction and both formal and informal participation measures would clearly be valuable.

We began this chapter by suggesting that behavioural research can aid unions in the process of building member commitment and participation. Our findings indicate that one strategy unions may adopt to enhance their future viability is to improve stewards' satisfaction with the union, thereby increasing the involvement and participation of both stewards and rank and file members. Many organizations are beginning to recognize the importance of developing and maintaining high quality relationships with their members. Clearly unions can benefit from pursing similar strategies.

## References

Anderson, J. C. and Gerbing, D. W. (1989), 'Structural equation modeling in practice: A review and recommended two-step approach', *Psychological Bulletin*, vol. 103, no. 3.

Barling, J., Fullagar, C. and Kelloway, E. K. (1992), *The union and its members: A psychological approach*, Oxford University Press, New York.

Bem, D. J. (1970), *Beliefs, attitudes, and human affairs*, Brooks Cole, Monterey, CA.

Bollen, K. A. (1989), *Structural equations with latent variables*, Wiley, New York.

Browne, M. W. and Cudeck, R. (1993), 'Alternate ways of assessing model fit', in Bollen, K. A. and Long, J. S. (eds.), *Testing structural equation models*, Sage, London.

Clark, P. F. and Gallagher, D. G. (1988), 'The role of the steward in shaping union member attitudes toward the grievance procedure', *Labour Studies Journal*, vol. 13, no 3.

Cortina, J. M. (1993), 'What is coefficient alpha? An examination of theory and applications', *Journal of Applied Psychology*, vol. 78, no. 1.

Dalton, D. R. and Todor, W. D. (1981), 'Grievances filed and the role of the union steward vs. the rank and file member: An empirical test', *International Review of Applied Psychology*, vol. 30, no. 2.

Eisenberger, R., Huntington, R., Hutchison, S. and Sowa, D. (1986), 'Perceived organizational support', *Journal of Applied Psychology*, vol. 71, no 3.

Festinger, L. (1957), *A theory of cognitive dissonance*, Stanford University Press, Stanford, CA.

Fullagar, C. and Barling, J. (1989), 'A longitudinal test of the antecedents and consequences of union loyalty', *Journal of Applied Psychology*, vol. 74, no 2.

Fullagar, C., Gallagher, D. G., Gordon, M. E. and Clark. P. F. (1995), 'Impact of early socialization on union commitment and participation: A longitudinal study', *Journal of Applied Psychology*, vol. 80, no 1.

Hartley, J. (1995), 'Challenge and change in employment relations: Issues for psychology, trade unions and managers', in Tetrick, L. E. and Barling, J. (eds.), *Changing employment relations: Behavioral and social perspectives*, American Psychological Association, Washington, D.C.

James, L. R., Mulaik, S. A. and Brett, J. M. (1982), *Causal analysis: Assumptions, models, and data*, Sage, Beverly Hills.

Johnson, W. R. and Johnson, G. J. (1992), 'Union performance and union loyalty: The role of perceived steward support', *Journal of Applied Social Psychology*, vol. 22, no. 9.

Jöreskog, K. G. (1993), 'Testing structural equation models', in Bollen, K. A. and Long, J. S. (eds.), *Testing structural equation models*, Sage, London.

Kelloway, E. K. and Barling, J. (1993), 'Member participation in local union activities: Measurement, prediction, and replication', *Journal of Applied Psychology*, vol. 78, no 2.

Leary, M. R. and Kowalski, R. M. (1990), 'Impression management: A literature review and two component model', *Psychological Bulletin*, vol. 107, no.1.

Levison, H. (1965), 'Reciprocation: The relationship between man and organization', *Administrative Science Quarterly*, vol. 9, no 1.

Martin, J. E. and Magenau, J. M. (1993), 'A longitudinal examination of the antecedents and consequences of union commitment among union stewards', paper presented at the invited International Workshop on Union Commitment, Amsterdam.

Magenau, J. M., Martin, J. E. and Peterson, M. M. (1988), 'Dual and unilateral commitment among stewards and rank and file members', *Academy of Management Journal*, vol. 31, no. 2.

Mumford, M. D., Stokes, G. S. and Owens, W. A. (1990), *Patterns of life adaptation: The ecology model of human individuality*, Lawrence Earlbaum, Hillsdale, NJ.

Organ, D. W. (1988), *Organizational citizenship behavior: The 'good soldier syndrome'*, Lexington Books, Lexington, MA.

Podsakoff, P. M. and Organ, D. W. (1986), 'Self-reports in organizational research: Problems and prospects', *Journal of Management*, vol. 12, no 4.

Shore, L. M., Tetrick, L. E., Sinclair, R. R. and Newton, L. A. (1994), 'Validation of a measure of perceived union support', *Journal of Applied Psychology*, vol. 79, no 6.

Sinclair, R. R. and Tetrick, L. E. (1995), 'Social exchange and union commitment: A comparison of union instrumentality and union support perceptions', *Journal of Organizational Behavior*, vol. 16, no. 6.

Staw, B. M, and Ross, J. (1985), 'Stability in the midst of change: A dispositional approach to job attitudes', *Journal of Applied Psychology*, vol. 70, no. 3.

Wheeler, H. N. and McClendon, J. A. (1991), 'The individual decision to unionize', in Strauss, G., Gallagher, D. G. and Fiorito, J. (eds.), *The state of the unions*, Industrial Relations Research Association, Madison, WI.

# 22 A test of the exit-voice hypothesis in an Australian work setting

*Donna M. Buttigieg and Roderick D. Iverson*

Since the late 1970s, economic studies have explored the possibility of a positive union impact on output and employment. In particular, debate has flourished around Freeman and Medoff's (1984) hypothesis of collective voice, which argues that unions provide a grievance mechanism for employees to voice job dissatisfaction. This alternative to the individual response of exiting or quitting, is said to provide beneficial externalities to the firm, which counter, at least in part, the negative effects traditionally associated with unionism.

Freeman and Medoff's (1984) hypotheses have been widely tested, particularly with respect to turnover (Freeman, 1980; Freeman and Medoff, 1984; Miller and Mulvey, 1991). In the process of testing the exit-voice dichotomy, however, a curious empirical paradox has been exposed. While union members display a lower propensity to exit, they are more inclined to express dissatisfaction with their jobs.

The paradox has been argued to be consistent with exit-voice theory because of the politicization role that unions play within the workforce. Borjas (1979) argued that unions highlight existing problems at the workplace, thereby simultaneously raising employee expectations and levels of job dissatisfaction. However, this dissatisfaction is not genuine and will not necessarily lead to quits. The extent to which it will lead to quits is expected to vary with tenure.

---

The authors would like to thank Stephen Deery, Peter Gahan, Christina Cregan, Peter Turnbull and Dan Gallagher for their suggestions on earlier drafts of this chapter. The research reported in this chapter was supported by a research grant awarded to the second author and Stephen Deery by the Faculty of Economics and Commerce. Direct all correspondence to Donna M. Buttigieg, Department of Management and Industrial Relations, University of Melbourne, Parkville, Victoria, Australia 3052.

That is, new recruits are hypothesized to be more likely to express dissatisfaction by quitting, while longer tenure employees (with greater firm specific investment) are expected to have a higher dissatisfaction-quit threshold.

Early studies by Bartel (1981), and Kochan and Helfman (1981) provided some support for the politicization argument by illustrating that levels of satisfaction may not be congruent with objective working conditions. Other studies utilized a multi-dimensional measure of job satisfaction (Berger, Olson and Boudreau, 1983; Kochan and Helfman, 1981; Schwochau, 1987) and found that union members tended to be more satisfied than non-union members over pecuniary benefits of employment (i.e. pay) but were more dissatisfied with their job overall and with non-pecuniary aspects of the job (i.e. autonomy, role clarity and job security).

However, two recent American studies that examined quits and job satisfaction concurrently, did not find support for the paradox. In a study of three separate organizations, Gordon and DeNisi (1995) found insignificant differences between union membership and both job satisfaction and quit behaviour. In an earlier study, Hersch and Stone (1990) detected a negative relationship between union membership and job satisfaction, but following insignificant tests for interactions between union membership and job satisfaction on quits, concluded that this dissatisfaction was real. A study by Miller and Mulvey (1993), which replicated Hersch and Stone's methodology, confirmed these findings.

Gordon and DeNisi (1995) have noted the methodological problems associated with the concentration of probability samples in previous research. Namely, that job satisfaction may have inadvertently been a proxy for working conditions in these studies because they effectively compare unionized and non unionized work environments with very different work contexts. Indeed, the issue of endogeneity of membership had been raised earlier by Borjas (1979) who argued that job dissatisfaction could be a determinant as well as an outcome of membership, given that workers with unpleasant working conditions will also be those more inclined to unionize. Studying the attitudes of unionized and non-unionized employees in a single organization resolves the statistical problem of endogeneity as the objective working conditions for all employees are homogeneous (Gordon and DeNisi, 1995).

In this chapter, we examine the impact of union membership on three dependent variables (job satisfaction, intention to quit and voluntary absenteeism) within a single public service organization. The first stage of the model involves a test of the job satisfaction-union membership nexus. Several methodological deficiencies have been identified in the existing research. This study modifies the basic job satisfaction model developed by Borjas (1979) to include several important, but neglected variables, such as labour market conditions, union-management relations and job-contextual factors. The analysis is then extended to examine the effect of union membership on two modes of exit behaviour: voluntary turnover (measured by intention to quit) and absenteeism. Turnover is the most obvious form of labour withdrawal; however, less attention in the empirical literature has focused on the impact of unions on other possible modes of exit. This chapter suggests that voluntary absenteeism may be categorized as a temporary form of exit behaviour (Price and Mueller, 1986).

## Model specification

### *Job satisfaction*

Borjas' (1979) study has formed the basis of most subsequent economic research on the effects of union membership on job satisfaction. Borjas' model regards job satisfaction as a function of the full wage (F), which is determined as the sum of the money wage (W) and non-pecuniary job attributes measured in monetary terms (N):

$$F = W + N \tag{1}$$

In order to appropriately quantify N, a basic assumption underlying previous economic literature is that individuals performing the same job (with similar characteristics) have identical tastes. This assumption ensures that a unique full wage exists for each particular occupation (Borjas, 1979; Hersch and Stone, 1990). In a perfectly competitive labour market, equalization should similarly occur with levels of job satisfaction, with empirical differences attributed to imperfections in the labour market, such as unionism (U).

The unobservability of N has led to the reliance in most studies on traditional controls such as demography, industry and occupation to capture differences between individuals on job satisfaction (Bartel, 1981; Borjas, 1979; Hersch and Stone, 1990; Miller, 1990). This is based on the crucial assumption that F is stable for each occupation. It is generally acknowledged, however, that there are intra-industry and intra-occupational differences that confound the problem of estimating union membership effects. Specifically, Hersch and Stone (1990) suggest that if proxies for N are omitted it may lead to a spurious negative correlation between N and the union factor if the partial correlation between U and N is negative (as may be the case if poor jobs are dominated by union members).

One way of reducing variance between individual perceptions of job satisfaction is to test for exit-voice *within* organizations, rather than *between* organizations (probability samples). The obvious advantage of probability samples is the generalizability of results, which cannot be said for organization specific data. However, specification errors are reduced in the latter because union membership is no longer confounded with working conditions that affect job satisfaction and unionization (Gordon and DeNisi, 1995). Similarly, an examination of a single workplace validates a relaxation of the assumption of homogeneous tastes. The empirically testable model can therefore be correctly specified to include individual responses to non-pecuniary job characteristics as proxies for N identified in the psychological and sociological literature (Brooke and Price, 1989; Iverson and Roy, 1994; Locke, 1976; Steers and Rhodes, 1978; Vroom, 1964), as well as controls for demography (Z) and context (C).

The model of job satisfaction used in this study is defined as:

$$S = a_0 + a_1W + a_2N + a_3Z + a_4C + a_5U \tag{2}$$

where W = pay ; N = f (promotional opportunity; job security; distributive justice; autonomy; routinized work, role clarity ); Z = f (white collar; full time employment; sex; education; tenure and health [mental and physical]); C = f (union-management relations; external job opportunities ) and U = union membership.

The model includes three measures of extrinsic rewards that are hypothesized to have a positive impact on job satisfaction: Promotional opportunity (the availability of movement between different status levels in an organization; Martin, 1979), job security (the extent to which an organization provides stable employment for employees; Herzberg, 1968) and distributive justice (the degree to which an organization treats employees fairly; Price and Mueller, 1981). Conceptually, their relationship with job satisfaction (defined as the overall degree to which an individual likes his/her job) may be equated, in some respects with that of pay (positive association). Intrinsic job characteristics are measured by autonomy and routinization. Autonomy refers to the degree of influence that an individual may have over his/her work (Tetrick and LaRocco, 1987), while routinized work represents the degree of repetitiveness in a job (Price and Mueller, 1981). The level of job satisfaction that an individual experiences is expected to have a positive and inverse relationship with autonomy and routinized work, respectively. Role ambiguity has been defined in the literature as the degree to which an individual's expected job role is unclear and has been consistently associated with measures of job stress (Kahn, Wolfe, Quinn, Snoek and Rosenthal, 1964). The existence of role clarity should therefore reduce stress and raise levels of job satisfaction.

Two additional controls added to Borjas' model can be broadly defined as contextual variables: union-management relations (defined as the degree of harmony between management and the unions) and external job opportunities (defined as the availability of alternative jobs outside the organization; Price and Mueller, 1981). Kochan and Helfman (1981), and Gordon and DeNisi (1995) suggest that the way in which employers adjust to unions (i.e. substitute capital for labour) will have direct implications for job satisfaction. A positive relationship between unions and management can be expected to be closely associated with higher levels of job satisfaction, as consultative arrangements should result in a better fit of preferences for unions on the employment-wage tradeoff. Additionally, the existence of external job opportunities (which are normally proxied by education) will affect the manner in which an individual perceives his/her job. External job opportunities are a measure of the opportunity costs of remaining within an organization. Therefore, its relationship with job satisfaction is hypothesized to be negative.

Other control variables which are included in the model are consistent with previous economic research. White collar occupations are expected to have a positive relationship with job satisfaction as they are associated with high job content (Miller, 1990). Similarly, full time employment is also expected to have a positive impact (Bartel, 1981; Miller, 1990) because of greater extrinsic rewards such as promotional opportunity and job security. Demographic control variables include sex, education and organizational tenure. Education has consistently been found to have a significant negative impact on job satisfaction (Bartel, 1981; Hersch and Stone, 1990; Miller, 1990). However, the inclusion of a job alternatives factor is expected to subsume any direct impact that education may have on job satisfaction. Tenure is similarly expected to have a significant (negative) relationship with job satisfaction (Borjas, 1979). Finally, controls for mental health (degree of an individual's state of mental well-being) and physical health (degree of an individual's physical well-being) have also been included and are consistent with Borjas (1979) and Bartel (1981). Both authors have found a significant positive association between good health and job satisfaction.

*Exit behavior*

Intention to quit (Q) and absenteeism (A) have been specified by equations (3) and (4):

$$Q = a_0 + a_1S + a_2W + a_3Z + a_4C + a_5U \quad (3)$$

$$A = a_0 + a_1S + a_2W + a_3Z + a_4C + a_5U \quad (4)$$

*Intention to quit* Voluntary turnover is proxied by the employee's intention to leave the organization within the near future. While actual quits are a more desirable and objective assessment of exits, other studies have used similar proxies (Drago and Wooden, 1991; Hersch and Stone, 1990). Moreover, the association between quit intentions and actual behaviour has been found in psychological studies to be reliable (Kirschenbaum and Weisberg, 1990).

Although relatively few studies have explicitly incorporated a measure of job satisfaction within econometric models of quit behaviour its inclusion is entirely congruent with job search models (Akerlof, Rose and Yellen, 1988; Hersch and Stone, 1990; Miller and Mulvey, 1991, 1993). Clearly, the utility derived from an individual's current job is partially dependent upon the full wage. That is, non pecuniary benefits, such as distributive justice and job security (mediated by job satisfaction), as well as monetary wages will contribute to an individual's decision to leave an organization. While attention in the economic literature focuses on the latter as a key determinant of quits, Akerlof et al. (1988) stress that most job quits do not involve large wage increases, but are associated with significant non pecuniary gains. This suggests that job satisfaction (which is often neglected in economic models) has an important role in explaining turnover behaviour.

Additionally, Miller and Mulvey (1993) have stated that perceptions of the external labour market regarding the full wage in alternative employment will crucially determine quit intentions, particularly where the nexus between job dissatisfaction and quits is positive. However, the difficulties of measuring alternative wages have meant that most studies exclude this variable. This study controls for job alternatives by including individual assessments of the labour market (external job opportunity). While criticisms may be directed to the subjectivity of the measure it is argued that individuals formulating the decision to quit will necessarily rely on perceptions (rather than perfect assessments) of search costs because of the existence of imperfect information (Iverson and Roy, 1994).

Union-management relations has been included as a control variable, although its net impact on exits is difficult to predict *a priori*. Freeman and Medoff (1984) suggest that if the beneficial effects of collective voice (via reduced turnover) to an organization are to outweigh the monopoly effects, then a relatively co-operative (rather than conflictual) industrial relations climate should exist. However, Freeman and Medoff have done little to explain the process by which this might occur. Turnbull (1988) is highly critical of this 'black box' approach regarding climate and productivity because it ignores the inherently conflictual aspects of the relationship between unions and management. While a co-operative climate might suggest that union voice will be enhanced, a counter argument can easily be made. If unions and management are seen to be co-operative, members may interpret this as a *reduced* capacity for union voice, especially where there may be an imbalance of power, or a perception that managerial interests have 'captured' the union's agenda. This contention will be more closely explored with interaction tests between union-management relations and union membership.

The costs and benefits of quitting are predicted to differ according to personal characteristics such as sex, education and tenure. Human capital theory suggests that employees with accrued firm specific skills (proxied by tenure) will internalize greater costs by leaving an organization. With respect to unionism, however, it could also be said that the preferences of the median voter (who is assumed to hold greater tenure) will determine the preferences of the union. Subsequently, the prospect of voice rather than exit may appear to be the more attractive option for older, tenured employees. Previous literature also suggests that blue collar and part time workers will have a higher propensity to quit than white collar or full time employees respectively (Miller and Mulvey, 1993; Wooden and Baker, 1994).

*Absenteeism* Defining absenteeism as a mode of exit is legitimate, although problematic. Allen (1984) argues that the difficulties are twofold: first, absences may be involuntary and unrelated to job dissatisfaction (i.e. illness); and second, absenteeism resulting from job dissatisfaction may be interpreted as a form of voice by signalling employee discontent. We argue that *voluntary* absenteeism is more appropriately viewed as exiting because it represents an *escape* from unsatisfactory working conditions (Erwin and Iverson, 1994). Additionally, the high noise factor of the signal (i.e. the difficulties of distinguishing voluntary from involuntary absence) creates obstacles in interpreting it as a voice mechanism (Allen, 1984).

Indeed, in the context of tight labour market conditions, absenteeism may be deemed the more logical manifestation of exit behaviour than turnover.

However, this is not to suggest that there are no costs to absenteeism as a form of exit. A tight labour market may also raise fears for job security, which could in fact constrain absenteeism as well as quit behaviour.

In order to establish voluntary absenteeism (as opposed to absence due to illness) absenteeism is defined in terms of the frequency of uncertified leave (of one or two days duration where a medical certificate was not supplied) provided by matched organization records of that year (Erwin and Iverson, 1994). This objective measure is a significant improvement on other studies using self-report measures, which tend to be unreliable and underestimate absenteeism (Drago and Wooden, 1992).

While evidence largely suggests that the impact of trade unionism on absenteeism is positive (Allen, 1984; Balchin and Wooden, 1992; Leigh, 1981, 1986) it is difficult to predict this relationship *a priori.* Allen (1981a) argues that the additional job security unions provide (by increasing the costs of disciplining employees) may encourage the formation of an absence culture. Alternatively, assuming that individuals dislike shirkers and that unions are responsive to majority preferences, unions may discourage avoidable absenteeism.

Similarly, the uncertainty of the relationship between absenteeism and turnover makes it difficult to hypothesize the impact of external job opportunities on absenteeism. Job opportunities may have a positive relationship with absenteeism in the continuous exit model as individuals take days off to job search or 'use up' their sick leave before quitting. However, where absenteeism is an alternative to quits (such as a situation where external jobs are not available) the impact should be negative.

The relationship between the wage (pay) and absenteeism is also ambiguous. The labour-leisure choice model predicts that if absence is a normal good then an increase in the wage should cause greater consumption of that good (income effect). However, if we ignore the possible provision of sick leave, an increase in wage also raises the opportunity cost of absence and will discourage absence from work (substitution effect). Where sick leave is provided, the effect of an increase in wage on absence is unambiguously positive (Preston, 1990). The reality, however, is that there are penalties (reduced promotional opportunities, decreased job security) associated with using all paid sick leave and these will increase with the wage.

If absenteeism is a response to poor job satisfaction, then absenteeism will be negatively related to the union-management relations variable. Kenyon and Dawkins (1989) who observed that strike activity is preceded by periods of high absenteeism, provide some support for this hypothesis.

Controls for occupation and status are included in this model. Blue collar workers are more likely to be absent because they are associated with more hazardous employment (Leigh, 1982). Full time employees are also more likely to be absent as standard hours of work are associated with greater constraints in meeting non-work obligations (Allen, 1981a). Additionally, demographic (sex, tenure and education) and health controls have been included in this model. Several studies have found significantly higher levels of absence amongst female employees because of greater family responsibilities (Allen, 1984; Leigh, 1981). With regards to the health variables, physical and mental health are expected to be insignificant if the measure of absenteeism accurately predicts motivation rather than ability to attend.

## Data and methodology

### *Data collection*

The data used in this analysis was collected in a public hospital located in the inner centre of Melbourne, Australia, employing 1,750 blue and white collar employees. A voluntary survey was administered to a random sample of 740 employees. The questionnaire provided information on 165 items regarding attitudes to work, unions, the employer as well as data on absenteeism and quit intentions using well established scales of measurement. Absenteeism figures (over a 12 month period) were obtained from computerized organizational records and matched to employees who voluntarily provided identifying information.

### *Sample*

Of the 740 employees surveyed, 473 questionnaires were returned, representing a response rate of 64 percent. Following the matching of respondents to their absence records and the listwise deletion of missing data procedure, a total of 328 questionnaires were used in the analysis. To maintain a consistent sample, matched cases were used in all three regressions. Chi-square analysis was undertaken to evaluate the representativeness of the final sample (N=328) compared to the initial sample (N=473) (before listwise deletion of cases). The results indicate that there were no differences in the characteristics of sex ($\chi^2[1]=1.67$, $p>.05$), status (i.e. full or part time) ($\chi^2[1]=1.33$, $p>.05$), and union membership ($\chi^2[1]=0.06$, $p>.05$).

The final sample consisted of 250 union members (77 percent female, 23 percent male) and 78 non-union (74 percent female and 26 percent male) members. Although there was a relatively low number of non-union members in the sample, it was proportional (24 percent) to the hospital population generally. Furthermore, other studies that have employed single organizational designs have similar problems of sample size (Gordon and DeNisi, 1995). The average age, education and organizational tenure of the sample were 38.85, 12.91 and 6.08 years, respectively.

### *Measurement and statistical techniques*

A 5-point Likert scale was employed to measure employees' perception to each item, ranging from strongly disagree (1) to strongly agree (5). The variables were constructed from established scales where possible. Cronbach's (1951) alpha was calculated for all variables with greater than one item (reported in Table 1) to ascertain internal consistency between items in a single scale. Exploratory factor analyses employing both orthogonal and oblique rotations confirmed that the factors displayed discriminant and convergent validity (Kim and Mueller, 1978).

Single indicators were used for the following exogeneous variables: Pay (measured by the natural log of fortnightly net salary); union membership (1=union member, 0=non member); white collar (1=white collar, 0=blue collar); full time (1=full time; 0=part time); sex (1=female; 0=male); tenure (measured in years) and education (measured in years).

Two statistical techniques are used in the model: ordinary least squares (OLS) and tobit. The absenteeism equation has been estimated using Tobit because of the skewed nature of absenteeism data (a disproportionate number of individuals have never been absent). Tobit analysis is a superior technique designed to address truncation and is preferable to the commonly used procedures of OLS (Allen, 1981a, 1981b, 1984; Leigh, 1981).

## Results

### *Descriptive statistics*

Mean difference tests on the explanatory and dependent variables have been performed between the unionized and non-unionized groups (Table 22.1). In examining the issue of job satisfaction, all means of the job characteristics which have been predicted to have a positive impact upon job satisfaction are lower for union members, although only three are significant (promotional

**Table 22.1**
**Descriptive statistics, items and reliabilities**

| Variable | Scale Source | Mean | |
|---|---|---|---|
| | | Union (n=250) | Non-union (n=78) |
| **Dependent Variables** | | | |
| Intention to quit* | Porter et al (1974), 1 item | 2.76 | 2.49 |
| Absenteeism* | Frequency of uncertified leave (of one or two days duration where medical certificate not supplied) taken from personnel records during the year Chadwick-Jones et al (1982), 1 item | 1.10 | 0.78 |
| Job satisfaction | Price and Mueller (1981), 6 items (α =.83) | 3.63 | 3.73 |
| **Non Pecuniary Job Attributes** | | | |
| Promotional opportunity* | Price and Mueller (1981, 1986), 3 items (α = .56) | 2.47 | 2.74 |
| Job security | Oldham et al (1986), 3 items (α =.76) | 2.83 | 2.97 |
| Distributive justice* | Price and Mueller (1981), 3 items (α =.82) | 3.04 | 3.34 |
| Autonomy* | Tetrick and LaRocco (1987), 3 items, (α =.47) | 3.32 | 3.58 |
| Routinized work | Price and Mueller (1981, 1986), 3 items, (α =.76) | 2.67 | 2.50 |
| Role clarity | Rizzo et al (1970), 3 items (α =.64) | 3.95 | 3.95 |
| **Money Wage** | | | |
| Pay(log) | Fortnightly salary (after tax) (natural log) | 6.60 | 6.65 |
| **Union Variable** | | | |
| Union membership | | – | – |
| **Contextual Variables** | | | |
| Union-management relations | Dastmalchian et al (1989), 10 items (α =.91) | 2.93 | 3.01 |
| External job opportunity | Price and Mueller (1981, 1986), 3 items (α =.89) | 2.51 | 2.65 |
| **Control Variables** | | | |
| White collar | | 0.71 | 0.79 |
| Full-time | | 0.72 | 0.71 |
| Sex | | 0.77 | 0.74 |
| Tenure* | | 6.44 | 4.96 |
| Education* | | 12.79 | |
| 13.32 | | | |
| Physical health | Cyphert (1990), 3 items (α =.70) | 3.99 | 4.10 |
| Mental health* | Goldberg (1972), 3 items (α=.67) | 3.83 | 3.99 |

* Significantly different between the union and non-union samples at the 0.05 (2-tailed) level.

opportunities, distributive justice and autonomy). This result is consistent with Miller (1990) who finds that unionists are more likely to complain about specific issues.

What is interesting, however, is that job satisfaction, although lower for unionized employees, is insignificantly different from non-unionized workers. Similarly, results regarding exit behaviour (quits and absences) appear to contradict the hypotheses of the exit-voice model. Union members have a greater propensity to express an intention to leave the organization and are also more inclined to be absent (although the overall mean of 2.69 indicates that the tendency is for employees not to leave).

Other significant differences are expected. Union members possess higher tenure and have significantly lower education. They also suffer from lower mental health, which may reflect greater job stress experienced in unionized occupations (e.g. blue collar environmental settings).

### *Multivariate analysis*

The results (one tailed unless otherwise stated) for job satisfaction, intention to quit and absenteeism are presented in Table 22.2, and will be discussed in turn.

*Job satisfaction* The adjusted $R^2$ for the OLS regression indicates that the model explains 51 percent of variance. Although not directly comparable to previous economic models of job satisfaction, this represents a substantial improvement in predictive power. Miller (1990), for example, was able to explain only 3 percent of variance.

The non-pecuniary aspects of the job provide considerable explanatory power to the job satisfaction model. In particular, job satisfaction is associated with lower routinized work ($\beta$ =-.39; p<.001), and greater distributive justice ($\beta$ = .12; p<.01), role clarity ($\beta$ = .08; p<.05) and job security ($\beta$ =.09; p<.05). This contrasts with the insignificance of the pecuniary aspect of the full wage, pay, but is consistent with Akerlof et al.'s (1988) hypothesis that intrinsic rewards are more important determinants of job satisfaction than monetary payment.

Of the environmental factors, external job opportunity has a significant negative (b =-.14; p<.002) impact on job satisfaction. The result is consistent with *a priori* expectations that job satisfaction is sensitive to the opportunity cost of alternative employment. Union-management relations, however, does not appear to be a predictor of job satisfaction.

**Table 22.2**
**Job satisfaction, quit intentions and absenteeism**

| Variables | Job satisfaction (OLS) | Intent to quit (OLS) | Absenteeism (TOBIT) |
|---|---|---|---|
| **Non Pecuniary Job Attributes** | | | |
| Promotional opportunity | 0.06 | — | — |
| Job security | 0.09* | — | — |
| Distributive justice | 0.12** | — | — |
| Autonomy | 0.05 | — | — |
| Routinized work | -0.39*** | — | — |
| Role clarity | 0.08* | — | — |
| **Money Wage** | | | |
| Pay(log) | -0.05 | 0.04 | -0.01 |
| **Union Variable** | | | |
| Union membership | 0.02 | 0.09* | 0.70*** |
| **Contextual Variables** | | | |
| Union-management relations† | 0.05 | -0.06 | 0.07 |
| External job opportunity | -0.14*** | 0.09* | -0.04 |
| **Control Variables** | | | |
| White collar | 0.05 | -0.15** | -0.16 |
| Full-time | 0.13** | 0.05 | 0.16 |
| Sex | 0.01 | -0.00 | -0.09 |
| Tenure | -0.00 | -0.10* | 0.01 |
| Education | -0.03 | 0.03 | -0.04 |
| Physical health | 0.10** | 0.03 | 0.02 |
| Mental health | 0.19*** | -0.14** | 0.21 |
| **Job Satisfaction** | | | |
| Job satisfaction | — | -0.28*** | -0.77*** |
| Adj. $R^2$ | 0.51 | 0.16 | |
| Sample size | 328 | 328 | 328 |
| -2Loglikelihood | | | 1087.48 |

* p<.05 (1 tailed) or p<.10 (2 tailed)
** p<.01(1 tailed) or p<.02 (2 tailed)
*** p<.001 (1 tailed) or p<.002 (2 tailed)
† Significant interaction between union member and union management relations for intention to quit.

Of the occupational and status controls, full-time (b =.13; p<.01) workers, as expected, are significantly more satisfied than part-time employees. White collar employment, however, does not impact on job satisfaction. The two controls for health indicate that job stress may be mediated by good physical (b = .10; $p<.01$) and mental health (b = .19; $p<.001$). Interestingly, however, the demographic controls have no impact on job satisfaction. The insignificant impact of tenure on job satisfaction, rejects Borjas' (1979) hypothesis regarding interactions between union membership, and job satisfaction. Schwochau (1987) and Miller (1990) similarly rejected this hypothesis.

*Intention to quit* The adjusted $R^2$ for the OLS regression indicates that this model explains 16 percent of variance. Job satisfaction ($\beta$ =-.28; $p<.001$), white collar employment ($\beta$ =-.15; $p<.01$) and mentaβ l health ($\beta$ =-.14; $p<.01$) appear to be the most important determinants of quit intentions. This is consistent with previous literature, indicating that the probability of quit intentions increases amongst individuals in blue collar employment, sufferers of stress, and individuals with high levels of dissatisfaction. The contextual variable, external job opportunity ($\beta$ =.09; $p<.05$), is also significant in the hypothesized direction.

Individuals with higher tenure have a lower propensity to express an intention to leave ($\beta$ =-.10; $p<.10$). Union membership, however, (weakly) relates to quit intentions in a positive direction (two tailed test) ($\beta$ =.09; $p<.10$). This is in contrast to the previous literature that has found a strong negative relationship.

The quits model was re-estimated to include an interaction term ($\beta$ =.17; $p<.001$) between union membership and union-management relations. As is customary, the sample was divided into two groups according to the median value of the *union-management* measure (high or cooperative union management relations and low or conflictual union management relations). Four variables predict intention to quit amongst individuals that perceived a cooperative union-management relationship: job satisfaction ($\beta$ =-.27; $p<.001$), tenure ($\beta$ =-.15; $p<.05$), white collar ($\beta$ =-.22; $p<.01$) and union membership ($\beta$ =.14; $p<.05$).

The determinants of quit intentions for individuals who perceive a poorer industrial climate differ substantially, with the only common significant predictor being job satisfaction ($\beta$ =-.24; $p<.01$). Of the individuals who intend to leave the organization, external job opportunities ($\beta$ =.17; $p<.05$) are significantly higher, while their mental health ($\beta$ =-.30; $p<.01$) is lower. Union membership, occupation and tenure are no longer significant.

*Absenteeism* Table 22.2, column 3, presents the results for the tobit model of absenteeism. Consistent with the quit intentions model and previous absenteeism literature, the relationship between union membership and absenteeism is positive and significant. The beta coefficient (0.70) and the very high level of significance ($p<.01$) indicate that this is a very strong relationship. Similarly, job satisfaction is also highly significant ($\beta$ =-.77; $p<.01$) and has the expected positive sign. Interaction checks between the two variables, however, are insignificant. That is, while union members overall are more likely to take uncertified leave (i.e. voluntary absence), dissatisfied union members are no more likely to be absent than satisfied union members. While the remaining variables in the model confirm hypothesized signs, they are insignificant. The modest predictive power of the estimated model is a common problem associated with absenteeism research because of the difficulties in differentiating between involuntary and voluntary reasons for work non-attendance (Brooke and Price, 1989).

## Discussion

This study indicates that job satisfaction is primarily determined by objective working conditions and values: that is, individual levels of job satisfaction are influenced by comparisons of job rewards within the current job (especially non-pecuniary) and that of the next best alternative (external job opportunities). Unionism has no direct impact on job satisfaction, *per se*, although it may have some impact on job outcomes, such as job security and promotional opportunity. Organizational specific data has its limitations regarding generalizability but it does provide an excellent control for differences in work environment. Theoretically, if unions politicize their members, then differences in job dissatisfaction should still occur between union members and non-members in the same environment. The insignificance of the trade union variable confirms that it is objective working conditions that determine levels of job satisfaction, for union members and non-union members alike.

Our results suggest that research that has neglected to incorporate non-pecuniary measures (such as routinization, job security and distributive justice) and control for the opportunity cost of remaining in the current job (such as external job opportunity) may have misconstrued the impact of union membership on job satisfaction. This is further compounded by the possibility of endogeneity of membership in probability samples. Macro studies effectively compare unionized and non-unionized work places with heterogeneous work environments (Gordon and DeNisi, 1995). This means that the correlation between membership and job satisfaction may be spurious or that unionization may in fact be the result rather than the cause of job dissatisfaction. In terms of exit-voice theory, this result suggests that union voice cannot be determined or measured by perceptions of job dissatisfaction.

Indeed, Gordon and DeNisi (1995) assert that there is little logic to the argument that unions arouse discontent at the workplace, except when specific grievances are in progress. Several studies have indicated that job satisfaction is a significant determinant of satisfaction with union performance (Fiorito, Gallagher and Fukami, 1988; Freeman and Medoff, 1984). This relationship suggests that there is little incentive for unions to incite dissatisfaction when it becomes a reflection of its own services to members. Disgruntled union members may leave their union (in the absence of a closed shop) or alternatively voice their concerns to the union via internal democratic processes such as elections.

The present study also hypothesized that the definition of exit as permanent separations is too narrow. Specifically, it was argued, that union membership may also have an impact on temporary labour withdrawal (absenteeism). Our research suggests that there is some support for viewing absenteeism as part of a continuous withdrawal process. Common predictors (union membership and job satisfaction) imply that the relationship is not insignificant. Of interest, however, was the direction of the relationship between union membership and the two measures of exit behaviour. Union membership has a positive and significant effect on both absenteeism and (weakly) intention to quit. Moreover, in both instances, it is apparent that the impact is direct and unrelated to job dissatisfaction.

On the issue of absenteeism, a recent study by Balchin and Wooden (1992) may provide some insight to these results. They find that work group norms reduce absenteeism in cases of high job satisfaction, but increase absenteeism where satisfaction is low. The present study does not directly examine work group norms, although it can be argued that unionism reflects the presence of work group cohesion. The additional job security that a union provides for its members should reduce the threat of disciplinary procedures and perhaps encourage the formation of an absence culture (Allen, 1981a). Given the positive association between absenteeism and quit intentions, it may be the case that those individuals who are intending to resign are taking days off to either search for alternative employment, or are exhausting their provision of sick leave.

A more perplexing result is that regarding permanent exits. Interaction tests revealed that union members who perceived union-management relations to be relatively good, were also those with higher quit intentions. It is apparent from our particular study that the function of union voice becomes more complicated where the union's relationship with the organization is not clearly delineated.

Perline and Sexton (1994) have argued that the term cooperation can be interpreted differently by management and unions. They state that many unionists believe that when management refers to cooperation, it is attempting to 'gain knowledge possessed by workers in order to increase productivity, reduce work rules, and in general gain concessions from the union — but not a willingness to permit union input into the decision making process' (Perline and Sexton, 1994, p. 379). There has been some evidence that the benefits of cooperative industrial relations are unevenly distributed between employees and organizations, particularly in periods of economic downturn. In the U.K., Metcalf (1989) argued that an increase in labour productivity during the 1980s was largely due to compliance, rather than cooperation. Concession bargaining in the United States during the same period was viewed with similar concerns (Linsenmayer, 1986).

The problem for unions is that in a climate of high unemployment and uncertain legal status, compliance may be viewed as strategically necessary for its survival as a bargaining agent. However, in terms of the wider problem of declining union density, the union must simultaneously appear attractive to potential union members. Individuals make the decision to join a union (or to remain a member) through cost-benefit calculations. However, benefits may be significantly reduced for members where individuals perceive co-operation to be a weakening of union power or autonomy (from an instrumentality viewpoint) or, because ideologically, this market unionism style approach is associated with the neglect of broader social functions of unions (Martinez Lucio and Weston, 1992).

In terms of exit-voice theory and the union-productivity question, an interesting dilemma is presented. On the one hand, co-operative industrial relations raises productivity by presumably reducing strikes and conflict on a collective level. However, Turnbull (1988) has argued that voice is dependent, in many respects, on monopoly power. That is, union instrumentality is conditional upon the threat of disruption to the production process. Should individual union members perceive that a co-operative arrangement between unions and management reduce the union's effectiveness as an agent of voice, then it is logical to expect that individual forms of protest (exit), may increase, particularly in the case of low tenured employees. Therefore, while co-operative arrangements should improve productivity by reducing collective disruptions to the workplace, the results of this chapter indicate that the erosion of the voice mechanism may reduce these benefits overall.

Although our chapter does not attempt to generalize its findings beyond this public sector organization, it does raise pertinent questions. In particular, this study reminds researchers that the contextual variables of union management relations, the legislative framework and historical relationships between management, employees and their unions are important, and cannot necessarily be determined easily through probability samples. Further research using firm specific data is necessary to try and capture these often neglected effects.

## References


Akerlof, G. A., Rose, A. K. and Yellen, J. L. (1988), 'Job switching and job satisfaction in the U.S. labour market', *Brookings Papers on Economic Activity, 2.*

Allen, S. G. (1981a), 'An empirical model of work attendance', *Review of Economics and Statistics*, vol. 63, no. 1.

Allen, S. G. (1981b), 'Compensation, safety and absenteeism: Evidence from the paper industry', *Industrial and Labour Relations Review*, vol. 34, no. 2.

Allen, S. G. (1984), 'Trade unions, absenteeism and exit-voice', *Industrial and Labour Relations Review*, vol. 37, no. 3.

Balchin, J. and Wooden, M. (1992), 'Absence penalties and the work attendance decision', National Institute of Labour Studies, Working Paper No. 120.

Bartel, A. P. (1981), Race differences in job satisfaction: A reappraisal, *Journal of Human Resources*, vol. 16, no. 2.

Berger, C. J., Olson, C. and Boudreau, J. W. (1983), 'Effects of unions on job satisfaction: The role of work-related values and perceived rewards', *Organizational Behavior and Human Performance*, vol. 32, no. 3.

Borjas, G. J. (1979), 'Job satisfaction, wages and unions', *Journal of Human Resources*, vol. 14, no. 1.

Brooke, P. J. and Price, J. L. (1989), 'The determinants of employee absenteeism: An empirical test of a causal model', *Journal of Occupational Psychology*, vol. 62.

Cronbach, L. J. (1951), 'Coefficient alpha and the internal structure of tests', *Psychometrika*, vol. 16, no. 3.

Chadwick-Jones, J. K., Nicholson, N. and Brown, C. A. (1982), *Social psychology of absenteeism*, Praeger, New York.

Cyphert, S. T. (1990), *Employee absenteeism: An empirical test of a revision of the Brooke model*, Unpublished doctoral dissertation, University of Iowa.

Dastmalchian, A., Blyton, P. and Adamsom, R. (1989), 'Industrial relations climate: Testing a construct', *Journal of Occupational Psychology*, vol. 62, no. 1.

Drago, R. and Wooden, M. (1991), 'Turnover down under: Trade unions and exit behaviour in Australia', *Journal of Industrial Relations*, vol. 33, no. 2.

Drago, R. and Wooden, M. (1992), 'The determinants of labour absence: Economic factors and workgroup norms across countries', *Industrial and Labour Relations Review*, vol. 45, no. 4.

Erwin, P. J. and Iverson, R. D. (1994), 'Strategies in absence management', *Asia Pacific Journal of Human Resources*, vol. 32, no. 3.

Fiorito, J., Gallagher, D. G. and Fukami, C. V. (1988), 'Satisfaction with union representation', *Industrial and Labour Relations Review*, vol. 41, no. 2.

Freeman, R. B. (1980), 'The exit-voice tradeoff in the labour market: Unionism, job tenure, quits and separations', *Quarterly Journal of Economics*, vol. 94, no. 4.

Freeman, R. B. and Medoff, J. L. (1984), *What do unions do?* Basic Books, New York.

Goldberg, D. (1972), *The detection of psychiatric illness by questionnaire*, Oxford University Press, London.

Gordon, M. E. and DeNisi, A.S. (1995), 'A re-examination of the relationship between union membership and job satisfaction', *Industrial and Labour Relations Review*, vol. 48, no. 2.

Hersch, J. and Stone, J. A. (1990), 'Is union job dissatisfaction real?' *Journal of Human Resources*, vol. 25, no. 4.

Herzberg, F. (1968), *Work and the nature of man*, Granada, London.

Iverson, R. D. and Roy, P. (1994), 'A causal model of behavioural commitment: Evidence from a study of Australian blue-collar employees', *Journal of Management*, vol. 20, no. 1.

Kahn, R. L., Wolfe, D. M., Quinn, R. P., Snoek, J. D. and Rosenthal, R. A. (1964), *Organizational stress: Studies in role conflict and ambiguity*, Wiley, New York.

Kenyon, P. and Dawkins, P. (1989), 'A time series analysis of labour absence in Australia', *Review of Economics and Statistics*, vol. 71, no. 2.

Kim, J. and Mueller, C. W. (1978), *Introduction to factor analysis*, Sage, Beverly Hills, CA.

Kirschenbaum, A. and Weisberg, J. (1990), 'Predicting worker turnover: An assessment of intent on actual separations', *Human Relations*, vol. 43, no. 9.

Kochan, T. A. and Helfman, D. E. (1981), 'The effects of collective bargaining on economic and behavioral job outcomes', in Ehrenberg, R. G. (ed.), *Research in labour economics, vol. 4.*, JAI Press, Greenwich, CT.

Leigh, P. J. (1981), 'The effects of union membership on absence from work due to illness', *Journal of Labour Research*, vol. 2, no. 2.

Leigh, P. J. (1982), 'Are unionized blue collar jobs more hazardous than non-unionized blue collar jobs?', *Journal of Labour Research*, vol. 3, no. 3.

Leigh, P. J. (1986), 'Correlates of absence from work due to illness', *Human Relations*, vol. 39, no. 1.

Linsenmeyer, T. (1986), 'Concession bargaining in the United States', *Labour and Society*, vol. 11.

Locke, E. A. (1976), 'The nature and causes of job satisfaction', in Dunnett, M. (ed.), *Handbook of industrial and organizational psychology*, Rand McNally, Chicago.

Martin, T. N. (1979), 'A contextual model of employee turnover intentions', *Academy of Management Journal*, vol. 22.

Martinez Lucio, M. and Weston, S. (1992), 'Human resource management and trade union responses: Bringing the politics of the workplace into the debate', in Blyton, P. and Turnbull, P. (eds.), *Reassessing human resource management*, Sage, London.

Metcalf, D. (1989), 'Water notes dry up: The impact of the Donovan reform proposals and Thatcherism at work on labour productivity in British manufacturing industry', *British Journal of Industrial Relations*, vol. 27, no. 1.

Miller, P. (1990), 'Trade unions and job satisfaction', *Australian Economic Papers*, vol. 29, no. 55.

Miller, P. and Mulvey, C. (1991), 'Australian evidence on the exit/voice model of the labour market', *Industrial and Labour Relations Review*, vol. 45, no. 1.

Miller, P. and Mulvey, C. (1993), 'The effects of union job dissatisfaction and quits', The Western Australian Labour Market Research Centre, Discussion Paper No. 7.

Oldham, G. R., Kulik, C. T., Stepina, L. P. and Ambrose, M. L. (1986), 'Relations between situational factors and the comparative referents used by employees', *Academy of Management Journal*, vol. 29, no. 3.

Perline, M. M. and Sexton, E. A. (1994), 'Managerial perceptions of labour-management cooperation', *Industrial Relations*, vol. 33, no. 3.

Preston, A. (1990), Multivariate analysis of nurses' behaviour', Confederation of Western Australia Industry, Discussion Papers in Economics and Industrial Relations No. 3.

Price, J. L. and Mueller, C. W. (1981), 'A causal model of turnover for nurses', *Academy of Management Journal*, vol. 24, no. 3.

Price, J. L. and Mueller, C. W. (1986), *Absenteeism and turnover of hospital employees*, JAI Press, Greenwich, CT.

Rizzo, J. R., House, R. J. and Litzman, S. I. (1970), 'Role conflict and ambiguity in complex organizations', *Administrative Science Quarterly*, vol. 15.

Schwochau, S. (1987), 'Union effects on job attitudes', *Industrial and Labour Relations Review*, vol. 40, no. 2.

Steers, R. M. and Rhodes, S. R. (1978), 'Major influences on employee attendance: A process model', *Journal of Applied Psychology*, vol. 63, no. 4.

Tetrick, L. E. and LaRocco, J. M. (1987), 'Understanding, prediction, and control as moderators of the relationships between perceived stress, satisfaction, and psychological well-being', *Journal of Applied Psychology*, vol. 72, no. 4.

Turnbull, P. (1988), 'The economic theory of trade union behaviour: A critique', *British Journal of Industrial Relations*, vol. 26, no. 1.

Vroom, V. H. (1964), *Work and motivation*, Robert Kriegler Publishing Company, Florida.

Wooden, M. and Baker, M. (1994), 'Trade unions and quits: Australian evidence', *Journal of Labour Research*, vol. 15, no. 4.

# 23 Peripheral employment contracts: The relationship between part-time employment and union attachment

*Daniel G. Gallagher, Judith W. Tansky and Kurt W. Wetzel*

To varying degrees of determination and effectiveness, labour unions throughout the world have recognized the importance of adapting organizational strategies and structures to meet the changing nature of the external environment in which workers are employed. The accelerated rate of technological change in the workplace, industry sector decline or relocation, and foreign market competition and integration are among the numerous environmental forces which have greatly impacted labour unions in the past decade and will continue to do so into the twenty first century. However, in recent years there has been a significant trend in the industrialized market economies of the world toward a substantial restructuring of employment contracts in the workplace. In particular, a growing number of organizations in Europe, North America and the developed economies within Asia have increased their reliance upon 'contingent' or 'temporary' workers claiming the need for greater 'flexibility' in the scheduling and utilization of human resources. Even more pronounced has been the accelerated growth of employment opportunities for workers on 'part-time' or 'key-time' work schedules which often involve less than 25 hours of paid employment per week (Belous, 1989; de Neubourg, 1985; ILO, 1989; Leighton, 1991). Within such countries as Australia, Canada, Japan, New Zealand, the Netherlands, Norway, Sweden, United Kingdom and the United States, where part-time employment data is available, the percentage of workers employed on part-time work schedules is approximately 18 to 25 percent of the total workforce

Correspondence concerning this chapter may be sent to Dr. Daniel G. Gallagher, Department of Management, James Madison University, Harrisonburg, VA 22807, USA.

(Belous, 1989; de Neubourg, 1985; ILO, 1989). In fact, there is substantial labour market data to argue that the rate of growth of part-time employment opportunities clearly exceeds the development rate of permanent full-time jobs (e.g. Delsen, 1993; de Neubourg, 1985; ILO, 1989; Leighton, 1991).

Accompanying this growth in part-time employment has been a modest debate concerning the extent to which part-time opportunities for workers are driven by supply and/or demand factors. An early explanation of the growth of part-time employment relied considerably on demographic and social changes in the labour force to suggest that the influx in the supply of younger workers and working mothers had generated the increased creation of part-time jobs by employers (Peterson, 1993). This supply side perspective suggests that part-time jobs illustrate a method by which employers satisfy their need for labour and, also, accommodate the needs of an increasing number of workers who desire or need to work part-time schedules in order to balance work with family and/or school. In addition, part-time jobs may represent a means for older workers to retain some continued labour force attachment after retirement. Employers may also respond to supply side shortages in critical occupational groups by using part-time jobs to attract qualified people or as an inducement to retain workers by offering them less hours (Zeytinoglu, 1992).

However, more recent explanations of part-time employment trends have suggested that part-time work is predominately driven by employer demand interests (Appelbaum, 1992; Tilly, 1992; Zeytinoglu, 1992). Some of the benefits for the employer that have been associated with part-time employment include: flexibility of scheduling, reduced costs of compensation, decreases in or the absence of fringe benefits and lower legally required worker welfare payments (e.g. Appelbaum, 1992; Zeytinoglu, 1992). Another argument supporting the demand side theory is the growing shift within many mature industrialized economies from manufacturing to service sector jobs which have traditionally utilized part-time employment (Barling and Gallagher, 1996).

In addition to the debate over the causes of the growth of part-time work, there exists another set of relevant questions which pertain to what, if any, differences exist between workers employed on full-time and part-time schedules. From the perspective of organizational based research, there has been a slow but gradual investigation of these potential differences with regard to such job related attitudes as organizational commitment, job involvement and job satisfaction (e.g. Jackofsky and Peters, 1987; McGinnis and Morrow, 1990). Although this research has become more extensive and has been extended to include behavioural outcome differences between part-timers and full-timers (e.g. absenteeism, turnover), the results are mixed and often contradictory (Feldman, 1990; Lee and Johnson, 1991; McGinnis and Morrow, 1990; Wotruba, 1990). Furthermore, basically all of this research has focused on consequences for the employer organization.

Unfortunately, very little research attention has addressed the potential consequences of the growth of part-time employment upon unions. The rate of unionization of part-time workers in most industrialized nations falls well below that of unionization among full-time workers. In Canada, 35.1 percent of the full-time workforce is unionized, compared to about 23 percent of the part-time workers (Kumar, 1993). In the US with its overall lower rate of unionization, the comparable unionization rates are 18 percent for full-time workers and 7 percent for part-timers (Kumar, 1993). Hartley's (1995) research found that within the British banking industry, full-timers were three times more likely to join a union than were their part-time counterparts. The differential in the unionization rates between full-time and part-time workers is less extensive in the industrialized nations with extremely high rates of unionization (Sundstrom, 1982).

Existing literature suggests that the historic relationship between the labour movement and part-time workers has been either tenuous or one of neglect (e.g. Brooks, 1985; Delsen, 1993; duRivage, 1992; Leighton, 1991). In fact, many unions have historically opposed the introduction of part-time work opportunities as a threat to full-time jobs or as a means to undermine the basis of worker power in the workplace. Although some unions in the service industries have long recognized the importance of organizing part-time workers (e.g. duRivage, 1992; Kahne, 1985), many union leaders have viewed part-timers as being difficult to organize and hard to involve in union activities. In fact, unions have been sceptical that part-time workers are tangitially attached to the workforce and are either not interested in union representation or, if represented, that part-timers will make poor union members due to lower interest in workplace concerns than their full time counterparts (e.g. Duffy and Pupo, 1992; Jecchinis and Koutroukis, 1991; Kahne, 1985). Although evidence does exist to support lower unionization rates among part-time employees relative to full-time workers, less is known about how part-time workers perceive unions not only in the case of the decision to unionize, but also the extent to which unionized part-timers identify with the unions that represent them.

The purpose of this study is to focus on the later question of determining if part-time workers are as committed to the union which represents them as are full-time workers. In addressing this issue, this study also seeks to ascertain the extent to which worker commitment to the union — as expressed in terms of loyalty, willingness to work for the union and responsibility to the union — is a function of employment status *per se* (full-time v. part-time) or perhaps more a function of demographics, tenure in the organization, social influences and union related experiences which may distinguish between full- and part-time workers. This study, also, examines part-time workers to determine if differences in union commitment exist among part-time workers based upon the number of hours worked.

## Literature review and theoretical perspective

### *Correlates of commitment*

In order to further understand the potential relationship between the growth of part-time employment and the commitment of part-time workers to the union which represents them, it is first useful to examine the underlying issue of 'commitment' to a trade union or labour organization. A major issue on the area of commitment research has been the question of whether or not workers could be loyal or committed to the goals and objectives of *both* the employer and the union organization. Much of this so-called 'dual loyalty' research was based upon survey work conducted in blue collar production facilities and tended to support the conclusion that workers are capable of and often evidence loyalty to both the employer and the union organization.

During the 1980s not only was there a reexamination of the dual loyalty hypothesis (e.g. Fukami and Larson, 1984; Gordon and Ladd, 1990; Sverke and Sjöberg, 1994), but also considerable advances in the development of more reliable and alternative multidimensional measures of union commitment (e.g. Gordon, Philbot, Burt, Thompson and Spiller, 1980; Klandermans, 1989; Kuruvilla and Sverke, 1993; Shore, Tetrick, Sinclair and Newton; 1994).

The research evolved into investigations attempting to more systematically identify the antecedents or correlates of worker commitment to the union which represents them and, as a variant of the dual loyalty thesis, the extent to which union and employer commitment shared similar antecedents (e.g. parallel models research; see Barling, Wade and Fullagar, 1990; Deery, Iverson and Erwin, 1993). Although these studies differed considerably on their research designs and focus, the results generally tended to support the conclusion that union commitment is less dependent upon the individual or demographic characteristics of union members, and more a function of worker attitudes toward the job, satisfaction with union representation and the early socialization experiences during tenure in the union and employer organizations (Barling, Fullagar and Kelloway, 1992; Fullagar, Clark, Gallagher and Gordon, 1994).

For example, there are mixed results on the relationships of the independent variables of age, education and tenure with union commitment. In a study of voluntary union members, Peterson and Martin (1986) found that less educated and older workers tended to be more committed to the union. Conversely, Fukami and Larson (1984) found that although older workers and less educated workers are more committed to the organization, they are not significantly committed to the union. Although Peterson and Martin (1986) found tenure to be positively related to union commitment, other studies have found no relationship (Barling et al., 1990; Deery et al., 1993; Fukami and Larson, 1984; Gordon et al., 1980; Sverke and Sjöberg, 1994).

Several studies have examined the relationship between gender and commitment to unions. The findings have been mixed. Using a global measure of union commitment, Sherer and Morishima (1989) and Martin, Magenau and Peterson (1986) found women were higher in union commitment. Gordon et al. (1980) found women to be more loyal to their unions than men. Studies by Barling et al. (1990), Deery et al. (1993) and Wetzel, Gallagher and Soloshy (1991) found that gender is not a significant correlate of commitment to the local union. Based on a three-dimensional analysis of union commitment, Wetzel et al. (1991) found gender was only significantly correlated with willingness to work for the union.

The work of Gordon et al. (1980) identified socialization experiences, early union experiences and union satisfaction as basic determinants of union commitment. Union attitudes of family members and friends may contribute toward a person's overall union commitment as well as the number of early positive experiences that a person has within the union (Fullagar et al., 1994; Gordon et al., 1980). Also, satisfaction with an organization is strongly related to commitment (Gordon et al., 1980). Gordon et al. (1980) and Sverke and Sjöberg (1994) found that workers who are satisfied with the performance of their union tend to be more loyal to it.

### *Employment status*

Despite this increasing emphasis on understanding the antecedents of union commitment, very limited attention has been directed to the relationship between employment status (full-time/part-time) and commitment to the union organization. One issue to be considered is whether, just as the organizational literature on organizational commitment has been used as a model for union commitment, the organizational literature on employment status and job attitudes can be used as a basis for developing literature on employment status and attitudes toward the union.

To date, only a few studies exist which have examined the correlates of union commitment and have also given consideration to the potential impact of employment status. Ironically, these studies have resulted in somewhat contradictory findings. Morishima (1988) found that, among unionized airline employees, part-time status was significantly related to higher levels of union commitment. However, subsequent research by Sherer and Morishima (1989) revealed that when wage tier and job tenure were also considered the employment status effect was nonsignificant. These results are contrary to those of Martin and Peterson (1987) who found that full-time workers are significantly more committed to the employer and union organizations than are their part-time counterparts. While the results are contradictory, they do suggest a consistency in that the employment status/commitment relationship may be moderated by other organizational and job variables such as wage level or wage tier.

### *Theoretical issues*

To date, the preponderance of research examining the commitment of part-time workers to either the employer organization or labour union which represents them has been atheoretical in nature. In situations where broader organizational theories have been applied to the study of commitment among part-time workers, theory has often been used in a post hoc manner to interpret statistical findings. One theory which has been frequently utilized in the comparative analysis of part-time and full-time workers is the concept of 'partial inclusion'. Partial inclusion posits that people (workers) are involved in social systems (e.g. employment) on a segmented or partial basis (Katz and Kahn, 1978). Within the content of organizational research, partial inclusion theory has often been used to suggest that commitment and satisfaction are less important to part-time workers for the reason that work is less central to their lives than full-time employees. Although not directly referenced, partial inclusion theory appears to fit well as the basis for practical concerns by trade unionists that part-timers are less attached to their work and unions, and for such reasons may exist as less active and reliable members of the trade union movement. Alternatively stated, part-time workers are only partially involved in the organizational and union social structure and have other competing demands which may detract from their participation and support for union related activities (Barling and Gallagher, 1996).

Extension of partial inclusion theory to the study of commitment in labour unions would tend to suggest that the level of commitment which a part-time worker has to a labour union may be a function of extensiveness of their part-time hours of employment. More specifically, partial inclusion theory would support the assertion that part-time workers on more extended schedules would tend to be more committed to the union which represents them than part-time workers on more limited part-time schedules. Alternatively stated, partial inclusion theory would be supportive of union commitment differences between full- and part-time workers and levels of commitment among part-time workers.

### *Research questions*

Based upon the literature on organizational commitment, the research that has been done on union commitment and the emerging literature on the differences between full-time and part-time employment status (e.g. Barling and Gallagher, 1996), this research proposes to investigate the following research questions from a sample of workers in two different industries and three different occupational groups:

1 Are part-time workers less committed to the union which represents them than their full-time counterparts and, if so, to what extent are differences a function of part-time status or other factors associated with union commitment?

2 Among part-time workers, to what extent are the hours worked per week positively associated with commitment to the union, after controlling for demographics, tenure, socialization and union performance?

## Methodology

### *Samples*

In order to ascertain the extent to which employment status (full-time/part-time) is related to workers' commitment to the union which represents them in the employment relationship, it was necessary to collect survey data in employment environments which were both unionized and employed a large percentage of workers on part-time work schedules. The three research samples utilized in this study consisted of union members employed in the retail trade and healthcare industries in a western province of Canada.

*Sample 1* The workers in retail trade were employed as clerks, food preparers and warehouse personnel for large food chains and producer owned cooperatives. Data were collected by mail questionnaire surveys which included two follow-up mailings. Survey questionnaires were mailed to 1,054 full-time and part-time workers who were randomly selected from the union membership roster. Complete and usable responses were received from 472 union members for a 45 percent response rate. The response rate among full-time workers was higher than the response rate among part-time workers (47 percent v. 42 percent).

*Sample 2* A second survey was conducted involving full-time and part-time workers in the healthcare industry. Participants included hospital support staff (e.g. housekeeping, maintenance, security, clerical) for large urban hospitals. Similar to the first survey, questionnaires were distributed by mail to a random sample of union members based on the full-time and part-time composition of the union. For the healthcare staff, 728 questionnaires were mailed and 449 usable questionnaires were returned for a response rate of 62 percent. A total of 204 full-timers and 245 part-timers returned the questionnaires for response rates of 61.6 percent and 61.8 percent respectively.

*Sample 3* A third survey involved nurses in the healthcare industry. Based on full-time and part-time composition of the union, 930 questionnaires were mailed to nurses. The response rate was 67 percent (623 usable questionnaires). Full-time workers had a response rate of 75 percent while part-time workers had a response rate of 61.4 percent.

### *Measures*

*Dependent variables* The dependent variable of interest, union commitment, was measured using a shortened, seventeen-item version of the Gordon et al. (1980) union commitment instrument. A confirmatory factor analysis was performed which replicated Kelloway, Catano and Southwell's (1992) three dimensions of union commitment: union loyalty, responsibility to the union and willingness to work for the union.

*Union loyalty* was measured by a seven-item scale representing the degree to which a member demonstrates a sense of pride in the union, awareness of its instrumentality in obtaining benefits and a desire to remain a member of the union (alpha = .88). *Responsibility to the union* consisted of five items assessing the degree to which the member accepts union membership expectations and is willing to fulfil day-to-day membership obligations and duties to protect union interests (alpha = .82). Five items measuring member readiness to do special union work or expend extra effort in service to the union were used to measure *willingness to work for the union* (alpha = .87). All three dimensions of union commitment were scored on a five point Likert scale, with a higher value indicating greater commitment.

*Independent variables* *Full-time* was coded '0' for part-time employees and '1' for full-time employees. Employees' employment status was determined by the membership records of their union and confirmed by employment schedule data provided by the participants. *Workweek* was determined by asking all part-time employees how many hours a week they worked.

Reflecting the research which has examined the correlates of union commitment, a number of other variables were included in the study for the purpose of controlling for the influence of variables other than full-time which may contribute to union commitment. These variables were classified into four groups: demographics, tenure, socialization and union performance.

Among the demographics, *age* was measured in twelve incremental categories of five year intervals beginning with '16-20 years' and ending with 'over 70.' *Gender* was coded '0' for males and '1' for females. *Educational status* was measured by asking retail and healthcare participants if they were students or not. Nonstudents were coded '0' and students were coded '1.' For the sample of nurses, educational status was coded '0' if they did not have a college degree and '1' if they did have a college degree. *Mother* was coded '1' if the respondent was a woman with a child or children.

*Tenure in months* was a continuous variable represented by the number of months the worker had worked for the current employer.

Socialization was based heavily on the work of Gordon et al. (1980) which identified socialization experiences as fundamental determinants of union commitment. *Family* assessed the respondent's opinion of parental attitudes toward unionization. *Friends* measured the members' perception of the degree of union support found among their friends. Both of these social influence variables were measured on a five-point Likert scale (1 = strongly dislike to 5 = strongly support). *Early experiences* was comprised of six items measuring the extent to which the respondent had experienced one or more favourable social interactions with other union members during the first year of membership.

Union performance included two measures of union satisfaction. *Extrinsic* consisted of a three-item scale measuring worker satisfaction with the performance of the union on extrinsic or 'bread and butter' bargaining issues such as wages and benefits (alpha = .86). *Member relations* was a six item scale measuring worker satisfaction with the internal relationship between the local union leadership and the rank and file union members (alpha = .93).

### *Data analysis*

The first part of the analysis consisted of a comparison of means and t-tests on the basis of work status and union commitment to determine if there were significant differences for the retail, healthcare and nurses' samples. Second, t-values or chi-squares were calculated to determine if overall differences existed between full-time workers and part-time workers across demographic variables.

Third, hierarchical multiple regression was used to determine the effect of full-time/part-time work status on each of the dependent variables controlling for the other independent variables. Employment status was entered first, followed by demographics, tenure in months, socialization variables and union performance variables. Finally, hierarchical multiple regression was used with the part-time samples to further test partial inclusion theory and determine the effect of the workweek on each of the dependent variables controlling for the other independent variables.

## Results

A comparison of full-time and part-time respondents' union commitment on each of the three dimensions measured is presented in Table 23.1. The results revealed that in the case of both the retail and healthcare unions, there existed a significantly higher level of commitment among full-time workers in terms of responsibility to the union and willingness to work compared to their part-time counterparts. Since both of these dimensions of union commitment involved an element of 'active' support of the union, the finding that full-time workers are more committed than part-time workers might well reflect a greater emphasis among full-time workers in protecting contractual rights (responsibility to the union) and the behavioral intention of contributing to the functioning of the union organization (willingness to work).

In contrast to the uniform differences between full- and part-time workers across all unions noted above, the comparison between full- and part-time workers indicated a mixed result with regard to the loyalty dimension of union commitment. In particular, within the retail union there existed no significant difference in expressed loyalty to the union between full-timers and part-timers. However, within the healthcare union's support staff and nurses, there existed a significant difference in loyalty on the basis of work status ($p < .05$).

Overall, these results suggest that at least in the case of loyalty, differences between full-time and part-time workers may vary by union or industry.

**Table 23.1**
**Mean comparison between part-time workers and full-time workers: Union commitment**

| | $UC_L$ Mean (Sd) | $UC_{WW}$ Mean (Sd) | $UC_{RTU}$ Mean (Sd) |
|---|---|---|---|
| **Retail** | | | |
| Full-time | 3.05 (0.46) | 3.04 (0.88) | 3.67 (0.63) |
| Part-time | 3.03 (0.43) | 2.71 (0.78) | 3.47 (0.62) |
| *t*-value | -0.49 | -4.26*** | -3.47** |
| **Health care** | | | |
| Full-time | 3.17 (0.37) | 2.92 (0.69) | 3.64 (0.54) |
| Part-time | 3.09 (0.31) | 2.67 (0.68) | 3.46 (0.52) |
| *t*-value | -2.40* | -3.72*** | -3.53*** |
| **Nurses** | | | |
| Full-time | 3.21 (0.35) | 3.04 (0.69) | 3.63 (0.50) |
| Part-time | 3.15 (0.31) | 2.74 (0.62) | 3.49 (0.49) |
| *t*-value | -2.18* | -5.73*** | -3.43** |

*Notes:* $UC_L$ = Union commitment, Loyalty; $UC_{WW}$ = Union commitment, Willingness to work; $UC_{RTU}$ = Union commiment, Responsibility to the union * $p < .05$; ** $p < .01$; *** $p < .001$.

Although the findings are generally supportive of significant differences in union commitment based upon the employment status dichotomy, it remains entirely possible that observed differences in commitment between full-timers and part-timers may be reflective of demographic differences between full- and part-time workers (Feldman, 1990). The data supported the observation

**Table 23.2**
**Hierarchical regression results: Union commitment**

| | Retail | | | Health care | | | Nurses | | |
|---|---|---|---|---|---|---|---|---|---|
| | $UC_L$ | $UC_{WW}$ | $UC_{RTU}$ | $UC_L$ | $UC_{WW}$ | $UC_{RTU}$ | $UC_L$ | $UC_{WW}$ | $UC_{RTU}$ |
| *1. Full-Time* | -.04 | .15* | .14** | -.03 | -.00 | -.01 | .00 | .16*** | .10* |
| *2. Demographics* | | | | | | | | | |
| Age | .06 | .05 | .08 | .11* | .08 | .03 | -.05 | .06 | -.00 |
| Gender | .09 | .03 | .05 | -.01 | -.08 | .04 | .04 | .02 | .01 |
| Educational status | .01 | .02 | -.01 | -.10* | -.12* | -.08 | -.03 | .02 | -.05 |
| Mother | .04 | -.00 | .06 | -.07 | -.11* | -.11* | -.09* | -.06 | -.00 |
| *3. Tenure in months* | .01 | -.01 | -.06 | -.05 | -.03 | .02 | .09* | -.00 | -.02 |
| *4. Socialization* | | | | | | | | | |
| Family | .01 | .11* | .08 | .09* | .19*** | .18*** | .02 | .06 | .06 |
| Friends | .15*** | .14** | .16*** | .20*** | .14** | .11* | .10** | .16*** | .08 |
| Early experiences | .11** | .16*** | .22*** | .10* | .22*** | .22*** | .12** | .11** | .06 |
| *5. Union performance* | | | | | | | | | |
| Extrinsic | .23*** | -.00 | -.03 | .19*** | .02 | -.04 | .15*** | -.06 | -.04 |
| Member relations | .37*** | .39*** | .38*** | .34*** | .08 | .21*** | .37*** | .26*** | .28*** |
| 1. $\Delta R^2$ | .00 | .04*** | .03*** | .01* | .02* | .02** | .01* | .05*** | .02*** |
| 2. $\Delta R^2$ | .07*** | .02 | .04*** | .04** | .04** | .02 | .01* | .01 | .00 |
| 3. $\Delta R^2$ | .01* | .00 | .00 | .00 | .00 | .01 | .02** | .00 | .00 |
| 4. $\Delta R^2$ | .17*** | .18*** | .22*** | .13*** | .13*** | .13*** | .10*** | .08*** | .04*** |
| 5. $\Delta R^2$ | .22*** | .11*** | .09*** | .20*** | .01 | .03*** | .19*** | .05*** | .06*** |
| Total $\Delta R^2$ | .47*** | .35*** | .38*** | .38*** | .20** | .21*** | .33*** | .19*** | .12*** |

*Notes:* $UC_l$ = Union commitment, Loyalty; $UC_{WW}$ = Union commitment, Willingness to work; $UC_{RTU}$ = Union commiment, Responsibility to the union. * p < .05; ** p < .01; *** p < .001

that part-time healthcare support staff were significantly younger while retail workers and nurses were older than their full-time counterparts ($p < .01$). Part-time retail workers and healthcare staff had significantly less tenure compared to full-time workers while nurses had more tenure ($p < .01$). These profiles support the fact that not only are part-time and full-time workers different in term of their demographic profiles, but that the magnitude or direction of these profiles may differ by occupation.

The multiple hierarchical regressions that determined the effect of work status on union commitment after controlling for demographics, tenure, socialization and union performance showed mixed results. As noted in Table 23.2, the employment status (full-time) had an insignificant effect on union loyalty in all three samples after controlling for the relative effects of demographics, tenure, socialization and union performance. Most notable was the fact that the effect of employment status on union loyalty became insignificant immediately after the entry of the demographic characteristics of full- and part-time workers at the second step of the hierarchical regressions. This finding is especially suggestive of the conclusion that union loyalty is more sensitive to the characteristics of the workers than employment status *per se*.

In contrast to the results pertaining to the relationship between employment status and loyalty, the results presented in Table 23.2 appear to support a more direct relationship between employment status and the other two dimensions of union commitment examined in this study. In particular, in the retail and nurses samples, employment status remained a significant predictor of both the willingness to work and responsibility to the union dimensions of union commitment after controlling for demographic, tenure, socialization and union performance variables. These findings, in two of the three samples, again confirm that employment status (full-time v. part-time) is strongly associated with more 'active' forms of union commitment by the membership. The results also confirm prior research findings which emphasize the role of socialization and union performance as factors which influence the level of commitment which members have toward the unions to which they belong (Barling et al., 1992; Fullagar et al., 1994; Gallagher and Clark, 1989).

As indicated, a subsequent analysis of union commitment was conducted of subsamples comprised entirely of part-time workers for the purpose of determining the extent to which greater inclusion in the workplace (hours of work) was associated with higher levels of union commitment. The results of these analyses are presented in Table 23.3.

Contrary to expectations based upon the 'partial inclusion' theory (Katz and Kahn, 1978), the results lend only modest support for a systematic

**Table 23.3**
**Hierarchical regression results: Union commitment among part-timers**

| | Retail | | | HealthCare | | | Nurses | | |
|---|---|---|---|---|---|---|---|---|---|
| | $UC_L$ | $UC_{WW}$ | $UC_{RTU}$ | $UC_L$ | $UC_{WW}$ | $UC_{RTU}$ | $UC_L$ | $UC_{WW}$ | $UC_{RTU}$ |
| *1. Workweek* | -.04 | .14** | .11* | .05 | .02 | .02 | -.00 | .11** | .06 |
| *2. Demographics* | | | | | | | | | |
| Age | .04 | .00 | .07 | -.05 | -.12* | -.11* | -.05 | .07 | .02 |
| Gender | .09* | .03 | .03 | -.00 | -.09 | .03 | .04 | .02 | .01 |
| Educational status | .01 | .02 | -.01 | -.09 | -.13* | -.07 | -.03 | .03 | -.04 |
| Mother | .06 | .05 | .08 | .13* | .06 | .03 | -.09* | -.07 | -.01 |
| *3. Tenure in months* | .00 | .00 | -.05 | -.08 | -.03 | .01 | .08 | -.02 | -.04 |
| *4. Socialization* | | | | | | | | | |
| Family | .00 | .11** | .08* | .10* | .20*** | .18*** | .01 | .06 | .05 |
| Friends | .11** | .16*** | .17*** | .09* | .20*** | .20*** | .11** | .11** | .09* |
| Early experiences | .14*** | .14** | .23*** | .19*** | .17*** | .12* | .112* | .18*** | .07 |
| *5. Union performance* | | | | | | | | | |
| Extrinsic | .22*** | .02 | -.01 | .19*** | .01 | -.05 | .15*** | -.04 | -.03 |
| Member Relations | .37*** | .37*** | .36*** | .32*** | .07 | .22*** | .37*** | .26*** | .29*** |
| 1. $\Delta R^2$ | .00 | .02** | .02* | .03*** | .03** | .02** | .01* | .04*** | .01* |
| 2. $\Delta R^2$ | .07*** | .02* | .04*** | .04** | .05** | .02 | .01 | .01 | .00 |
| 3. $\Delta R^2$ | .02** | .01* | .00 | .00 | .00 | .00 | .01** | .00 | .00 |
| 4. $\Delta R^2$ | .17*** | .19*** | .23*** | .13*** | .04*** | .12*** | .10*** | .09*** | .05*** |
| 5. $\Delta R^2$ | .22*** | .11*** | .09*** | .19*** | .01 | .03*** | .19*** | .05*** | .07*** |
| Total $\Delta R^2$ | .48*** | .35*** | .38*** | .40*** | .22*** | .20*** | .33*** | .19*** | .13*** |

*Notes:* $UC_L$ = Union commitment, Loyalty; $UC_{WW}$ = Union commitment, Willingness to work; $UC_{RTU}$ = Union commiment, Responsibility to the union. * $p < .05$; ** $p < .01$; *** $p < .001$

relationship between the number of hours worked by part-timers and their reported levels of union commitment. In only three of the nine regressions was the number of hours worked by part-time employees (workweek) significantly associated with union commitment after controlling for the relative effects of demographics, tenure, socialization and union performance. Although these results suggest limited applicability of either the partial inclusion theory or the use of 'hours' as a measure of inclusion, the results do strongly confirm the importance of socialization and union performance as a determinant of union commitment among part-time workers.

## Discussion

Based upon an investigation of three different industry/occupational samples, the results of this research suggest that differences in union commitment between full-time workers and part-time workers may vary depending upon the dimensions of union commitment under examination. There is also evidence which provides considerable support for the conclusion that employment status (full-time/part-time), even when significant, has a rather limited relative effect on union commitment.

In the case of union loyalty, the results indicate that employment status, in all three samples, has no significant relationship with union loyalty after controlling for the influence of demographic profile variables. In contrast, for the more active forms of union commitment (e.g. willingness to work for the union, responsibility to the union), there does appear to be a significant employment status effect (full-time/part-time). In particular, even after controlling for demographics, job tenure, socialization and union performance variables, employment status was significantly related to willingness to work for the union and responsibility to the union in two of the three samples (retail workers and nurses). These findings may offer some modest support for the 'partial inclusion' theory by suggesting that although part-time workers may be attitudinally committed to the union that represents them, they may find it more difficult to expend the necessary time and effort associated with demonstrations of more active union commitment.

There was very consistent evidence, across all three samples, that factors associated with socialization influences and union performance were correlates of all three dimensions of union commitment. Particularly important is the observation that socialization variables and union performance variables were found to be significant correlates of commitment for union members employed on both full-time and part-time work schedules.

As suggested by Gallagher and Clark (1989), some determinants of union commitment (e.g. family, friends) may be beyond the immediate control of most unions. However, these findings also support previous research which has indicated that early attempts by unions to recognize and involve new members is important as a long term commitment building strategy (Fullagar et al., 1994). This study further suggests that such socialization strategies should be recognized by unions as especially important in developing union commitment among part-time workers.

The findings also indicate that union performance, as associated with members perceptions, of how the union is handling the relationship between the individual union member and the union organization, is a particularly salient factor contributing to membership commitment. The importance of the perceived quality of the union-member relationship is an important consideration for part-time workers, and a factor that is in large part under the direct control of the union organization.

A surprising aspect of these findings was the absence of a relationship between the level of organizational inclusion (as measured by hours of weekly employment) and union commitment. Such findings cast some doubt upon the applicability of the 'partial inclusion' model to the union commitment research. However, consistent with the alternative theoretical interpretations offered by Katz and Kahn (1978), inclusion may be less a function of hours and more a function of the psychological involvement or intensity of the relationship.

Although the statistical findings in this study are generally consistent across samples and intuitively reasonable, there are a number of limitations of the study which should be addressed in any future research.

First, it is possible that differences in union commitment may vary among part-time workers as a function of their reasons for being employed on part-time schedules. Consistent with the suggestions made by Feldman (1990), part-time workers' commitment to the representing union may depend on whether their work is undertaken as a temporary or permanent arrangement, whether such employment is by economic choice or necessity, and whether it exists as a voluntary option or an involuntary option due to the absence of the availability of full-time employment.

Second, as noted above, greater consideration should be given to determining the extent to which the relationship between hours of employment and union commitment may be nonlinear. It is possible that increased inclusion for part-time workers (i.e. working a greater number of hours) may be associated with decreasing levels of marginal commitment to the union. For example, employees who work long hours but are officially treated as part-time workers may be less committed to the union (and employer) than limited scheduled part-timers. It would also be interesting to determine the extent to which the regular assignment of overtime hours affects the willingness of full-time workers to be more actively committed to the union that represents them.

Third, future research on the relationship between part-time employment and union commitment needs to devote greater systematic attention to the identification of the referent groups or 'significant others' which part-time workers use for comparison in evaluating their jobs and/or the union which represents them. Alternatively stated, do unionized part-time workers compare themselves to other organized part-time workers or to other possible referent groups such as unorganized part-timers, organized full-time workers, or even their own prior work experiences or their own prior union related experiences?

Finally, although this study has directed attention to the issue of union commitment among workers on part-time work schedules, a more serious challenge to labour unions may rest with the growth of other forms of atypical employment. Most notably, within Europe and North America there has been an acceleration in the reliance of employers upon workers on 'temporary' or 'contingent contracts.' Unlike part-time work, which is often permanent in nature, contingent employment is giving rise to a workforce which is often without an identifiable long term employer. Alternatively, workers ranging from unskilled to professionals are becoming self-employed contract labourers moving from employer to employer. In many respects, greater effort may be required of both union practitioners and researchers to understand the nature of contingent workers and the ability of union organizations to address the needs of this growing segment of the labour force.

## References


Appelbaum, E. (1992), 'Structural change and the growth of part-time and temporary employment', in duRivage, V. (ed.), *New policies for the part time and contingent workforce*, M. E. Sharpe, Armonk, N.Y.

Barling, J., Fullagar, C. and Kelloway, E. K. (1992), *The union and its members: A psychological approach*, Oxford University Press, Oxford.

Barling, J. and Gallagher, D. G. (1996), 'Part-time employment', in Cooper, C. L. and Robertson, I. T. (eds.), *International review of industrial and organizational psychology*, vol. 11, pp. 243-277.

Barling, J., Wade, B. and Fullagar, C. (1990), 'Predicting employee commitment to company and union: Divergent models', *Journal of Occupational Psychology*, vol. 63, pp. 49-61.

Belous, R. S. (1989), *The contingent economy: The growth of the temporary, part-time and subcontracted workforce*, National Planning Association, Washington, DC.

Brooks, B. (1985), 'Aspects of casual and part-time employment', *The Journal of Industrial Relations*, vol. 25, pp. 159-171.

de Neubourg, C. (1985), 'Part-time work: An international quantitative comparison', *International Labour Review*, vol. 124, pp. 559-576.

Deery, S. J., Iverson, R. D. and Erwin, P. (1993), 'Predicting organizational and union commitment: A parallel models approach', Working Paper No. 76, Department of Management and Industrial Relations, University of Melbourne, Parkville, Victoria.

Delsen, L. (1993), 'Atypical employment and industrial relations in the Netherlands', *Economic and Industrial Democracy*, vol. 14, pp. 589-602.

Duffy, A. and Pupo, N. (1992), Part-*time paradox: Connecting gender, work, and family*, McClelland and Stewart, Toronto.

duRivage, V. (1992), 'New policies for the part-time and contingent workforce', in duRivage, V. (ed.), *New policies for the part-time and contingent workforce*, M. E. Sharpe, Armonk, NY.

Feldman, D. C. (1990), 'Reconceptualizing the nature and consequences of part-time work', *Academy of Management Review*, vol. 15, pp. 103-112.

Fukami, C. V. and Larson, E. (1984), 'Commitment to company and union: Parallel models', *Journal of Applied Psychology*, vol. 69, pp. 367-371.

Fullagar, C., Clark, P., Gallagher, D. G. and Gordon, M. E. (1994), 'A model of the antecedents of early union commitment: The role of socialization experiences and steward characteristics', *Journal of Organizational Behavior*, vol. 15, pp. 517-533.

Gallagher, D. G. and Clark, P. F. (1989), 'Research on union commitment: Implications for labour', *Labour Studies Journal*, vol. 14, pp. 52-71.

Gordon, M. E. and Ladd, R. T. (1990), 'Dual allegiance: Renewal, reconsideration, and recantation', *Personnel Psychology*, vol. 43, pp. 37-69.

Gordon, M. E., Philbot, J. W., Burt, R. E., Thompson, C. A. and Spiller, W. E. (1980), 'Commitment to the union: Development of a measure and an examination of its correlates,' *Journal of Applied Psychology Monograph*, vol. 65, pp. 479-499.

Hartley, J. (1995), 'Challenge and change in employment relations: Issues for psychology, trade unions and managers', in Tetrick, L. E. and Barling, J.(eds), *Changing employment relationships: Behavioral and social perspectives*, American Psychological Association, Washington, DC.

ILO, International Labour Office (1989), *Conditions of work digest: Part-time work*, vol. 8(1), International Labour Organization, Geneva.

Jackofsky, E. F. and Peters, L. H. (1987), 'Part-time versus full-time employment status differences: A replication and extension', *Journal of Occupational Behavior*, vol. 8, pp. 1-9.

Jecchinis, C. and Koutroukis, T. (1991), 'Part-time work in Greece: Problems and prospects', *The Work Flexibility Review*, vol. 2, pp. 65-67.

Kahne, H. (1985), *Reconceiving part-time work*, Rowman and Allanheld Publishers, Totowa, NJ.

Katz, D. and Kahn, R. L. (1978), *The social psychology of organizations*, Wiley, New York.

Kelloway, E. K., Catano, V. and Southwell, R. (1992), 'The construct validity of union commitment: Development and dimensionality of a shorter scale', *Journal of Occupational and Organizational Psychology*, vol. 65, pp. 197-212.

Klandermans, B. (1989), 'Union commitment: Replications and tests in the Dutch context', *Journal of Applied Psychology*, vol. 74, pp. 869-875.

Kumar, P. (1993), *From uniformity to divergence: Industrial relations in Canada and the United States*, IRC Press, Queens' University, Kingston, Ontario.

Kuruvilla, S. and Sverke, M. (1993), 'Two dimensions of union commitment based on the theory of reseasoned action: Cross-cultural comparisons', *Research and Practice in Human Resource Management*, vol. 1, pp. 1-6.

Lee, T. W. and Johnson, D. R. (1991), 'The effects of work schedule and employment status on the organizational commitment and job satisfaction of full versus part-time employees', *Journal of Vocational Behavior*, vol. 38, pp. 204-224.

Leighton, P. (1991), 'The legal vulnerability of part-timers: Is job sharing the solution?', in Davidson, M. J. and Earnshaw, J. (eds.), *Vulnerable workers: Psychological and legal issues*, Wiley, Chichester, Great Britain.

McGinnis, S. K. and Morrow, P. C. (1990), 'Job attitudes among full-and part-time employees', *Journal of Vocational Behavior*, vol. 36, pp. 82-96.

Martin, J. E., Magenau, J. M. and Peterson, M. F. (1986), 'Variables related to patterns of union stewards' commitment', *Journal of Labour Research*, vol. 17, pp. 323-336.

Martin, J. E. and Peterson, M. M. (1987), 'Two-tier wage structures: Implications for equity theory', *Academy of Management Journal*, vol. 30, pp. 297-315.

Morishima, M. (1988), 'Wage inequity, job security, and union commitment', in *Proceedings of the 40th Annual Meeting of the Industrial Relations Research Association*, IRRA, Madison, WI.

Peterson, J. (1993), 'Part-time employment and women: A comment on Sundstrom', *Journal of Economic Issues*, vol. 27, pp. 909-914.

Peterson, M. P. and Martin, J. E. (1986), 'Personal attachment to the union in small bargaining units', *Canadian Journal of Administrative Sciences*, vol. 3, pp. 204-220.

Sherer, P. D. and Morishima, M. (1989), 'Roads and roadblocks to dual commitment: Similar and dissimilar antecedents of union and company commitment', *Journal of Labour Research*, vol. 10, pp. 311-330.

Shore, L., Tetrick, L. E., Sinclair, R. R. and Newton, L. A. (1994), 'Validation of a measure of perceived union support', *Journal of Applied Psychology*, vol. 79, pp. 971-977.

Sundström, M. (1982), 'Part-time work and trade-union activities among women', *Economic and Industrial Democracy*, vol. 3, pp. 561-567.

Sverke, M. and Sjöberg, A. (1994), 'Dual commitment to company and union in Sweden: An examination of predictors and taxonomic split methods', *Economic and Industrial Democracy*, vol. 15, pp. 531-564.

Tilly, C. (1992), 'Dualism in part-time employment', *Industrial Relations*, vol. 31, pp. 330-347.

Wetzel, K., Gallagher, D. G. and Soloshy, D. E. (1991), 'Union commitment: Is there a gender gap?', *Relations Industrielles*, vol. 46, pp. 564-583.

Wotruba, T. R. (1990), 'Full-time vs. part-time salespeople: A comparison on job satisfaction, performance, and turnover in direct selling,' *International Journal of Research in Marketing*, vol. 7, pp. 97-108.

Zeytinoglu, I. U. (1992), 'A sectoral study of part-time workers covered by collective agreements: Why do employers hire them', *Relations Industrielles*, vol. 46, pp. 401-418.

# 24 Short-term union merger effects on member attitudes and behaviour

*Magnus Sverke and Anders Sjöberg*

Union mergers have occurred since the beginning of unionism and are expected to have a number of beneficial consequences. Many analysts seem to agree that mergers have the potential of enhancing bargaining and organizing power, increasing strike funds, reducing jurisdictional disputes, and entailing economies of scale (e.g. Buchanan, 1992; Chaison, 1986; Williamson, 1995). However, as noted by Chaison (1992, pp. 9-10), the 'costs and benefits of mergers, whether in terms of membership participation or representational and administrative effectiveness, are seldom investigated in a systematic manner'. This implies that the extent to which expected merger outcomes are realized has not been subjected to detailed empirical scrutiny. It also suggests that the knowledge of unintended consequences accompanying intended merger effects is limited. Thus, although mergers may have positive as well as negative effects on members' attitudes and behaviour (Chaison, 1986), very little is known about such psychological aspects of union structural change.

A rapidly changing industrial relations climate, characterized by factors such as internationalization of capital and economic restructuring, has confronted contemporary unionism with numerous challenges to traditional ways of organization and interest representation (Hyman, 1994). For many trade unions, the changing environmental conditions have induced membership decline and financial difficulty. Since the provision of services such as lobbying, strike funds, publications, and bargaining support involves

---

The data collection was financed by the National Institute for Working Life. Address correspondence on this chapter to Magnus Sverke, Department of Psychology, Stockholm University, 106 91 Stockholm, Sweden.

administrative expenditures, a lack of economies of scale may force unions with insufficient numbers of members to reduce their services to the membership unless the financial basis is improved by, for instance, charging unnecessarily high dues (Conant and Kaserman, 1989). Indeed, there appears to be some minimum size below which unions 'have difficulty carrying out their representative, organizing, and administrative capacities' (Chaison, 1986, p. 50).

In order to overcome the problems associated with membership decline and financial difficulty, an increasing number of unions have chosen the merger option. Merger refers to the uniting of two or more trade unions, where at least one relinquishes its independence, into a single organizational entity (Waddington, 1988). For unions in declining sectors, merging with a union with a different jurisdiction may be the only possible way to increase membership. In other economic environments, merger may be considered a more cost-effective way for achieving growth than recruitment. For these reasons merger is a very common method of organization building (Freeman and Brittain, 1977).

Research on trade union mergers has almost exclusively used merger or union as the study object while only a few studies have been concerned with the members of the merging unions. A large proportion of research has predicted the aggregate pattern of merger activity from environmental indicators (e.g. Buchanan, 1981, Freeman and Brittain, 1977; Waddington, 1988). Other studies have examined one or more mergers in detail in order to identify the merger reasons, describe the resulting organization and explain the significance of the merger for issues such as collective bargaining (e.g. Undy, Ellis, McCarthy and Halmos, 1981). Those studies that have explicitly focused on the role of individuals in the merger process have either predicted member support for the merger (Cornfield, 1991; McClendon, Kriesky and Eaton, 1995) or examined unsuccessful merger attempts on the basis of members' expectations of potential negative outcomes of the merger (Chaison, 1986). However, to our knowledge, no attempts have been made at uncovering the effects of mergers on union members. Thus, there is a clear need for research into the consequences of merger activity (Chaison, 1986; Conant and Kaserman, 1989).

The overall aim of the research reported in this chapter was to investigate how union members are affected by a merger. We studied an amalgamation between two Swedish unions affiliated to the Swedish Trade Union Confederation (LO), which is the confederation for blue-collar unions. Included in the study was also a third LO union, which was involved in the initial merger negotiations but was not part of the eventual merger. By surveying representative samples from these unions both before and shortly after the merger, our ambition was to shed light on the short-term merger effects on members' attitudes and behavior.

## The merger

LO was originally composed primarily of artisan unions, but industrial unionism has been its officially stated goal since 1912. The ambition has been to reduce the number of affiliated unions by encouraging voluntary mergers between unions organizing workers in similar industrial or occupational areas. As an example, in the last wave of mergers (1960-1973), the number of unions was reduced from 44 to 25 (Abrahamsson, 1993; Lewin, 1980). Similar trends have been observed also internationally, for instance in North America where the AFL-CIO has encouraged mergers to enhance labour movement effectiveness (Chaison, 1986; Janus, 1978; Stratton-Devine, 1992) and in the U.K. where a small number of unions have come to organize a large proportion of the total membership (Buchanan, 1981; Waddington, 1988).

As noted by Chaison (1986), mergers are usually preceded by several years of merger negotiations, an observation which is true also for the organizational integration we studied. The merger was initiated by the Swedish Clothing Workers Union in 1986 when its convention decided to explore the possibility of merging with other unions. Since its formation in 1972 — actually as the result of a merger between three unions organizing clothing, textile and shoe workers — the union had been confronted with declining employment levels and intense technological change in the domestic clothing industries. As a consequence, the number of members dropped from 60,000 in the early 1970s to around 30,000 in the late 1980s, and the union was involved in several jurisdictional disputes (Abrahamsson, Ahlén, Eriksson and Sverke, 1991).

In 1987 an official investigation to evaluate various merger alternatives was commenced. The resulting report (Färm, 1990) suggested a merger with the Swedish Factory Workers Union and the Swedish Food Workers Union. Formal merger negotiations were initiated and a committee was set up to inspect the dues structure, the regional level structure and the decision making rules and structures of a conjoined union. At the same time, discussions were organized at all levels of all three unions in order to anchor the merger idea among the memberships (Abrahamsson et al., 1991). The formal merger proposition, delivered in February 1991, was rejected by the convention of the food workers' union, while it was approved by the conventions of the unions of clothing workers and factory workers.

A new two-way merger between the latter unions was investigated and extra conventions in late 1992 advocated merger. The constituent assembly was held in April 1993 and the new union formally came into existence on 1 May 1993. The nature of the merger can be described by drawing upon the work of Chaison (1986), who made conceptual distinctions between different forms of merger (amalgamation and absorption) and between various integrating governing structures in merged unions. In Chaison's terms, the merger between the unions of clothing and factory workers was an amalgamation of two unions to form a new organization, which was also manifested in a new name of the merged union (the Industrial Union). It was also characterized by a relatively high degree of integration; the central administrations were combined, the regional organizations were fusioned and members of the pre-merger unions entered the new union on equal conditions.

## Potential consequences

It is widely agreed that the attitudes and behaviour of the rank and file are crucial for effective unionism (Gallagher and Strauss, 1991). Unions require members' support for union goals as manifested in their active participation in the fulfilment of these goals. As McClendon et al. (1995) phrased it: 'Unions survive on the commitment of their members and, to be effective, national unions must have the support of local union rank and file' (p. 10). However, although a vast amount of research has focused on important issues such as members' participation in union activity (e.g. Kelloway and Barling, 1993; McShane, 1986), commitment to the union (e.g. Barling, Fullagar and Kelloway, 1992; Gordon, Philbot, Burt, Thompson and Spiller, 1980) and satisfaction with union representation (e.g. Fiorito, Gallagher and Fukami, 1988; Kuruvilla, Gallagher and Wetzel, 1993), it is not clear how member-union relationships are influenced by mergers.

Union participation can take many forms, such as serving in representative positions and attending membership meetings (Klandermans, 1986; McShane, 1986). Chaison (1983, 1986) observed that mergers may have positive as well as negative consequences for members' active involvement. On the one hand, even if mergers are expected to bring about growth-related advantages, they may also result in more centralized union structures and the replacement of member volunteers with staff specialists which, in turn, may reduce membership participation (Chaison, 1986). On the other hand, the work associated with integrating the merging parties may involve members at different levels; it is therefore 'conceivable that in post-merger periods there may be substantial membership participation and political activity as the members of the pre-merger locals form into political factions' (Chaison, 1983, p. 336).

Union commitment refers to members' psychological attachment to the union based on an identification with the goals and values of the organization and an appreciation of the services it provides (Gordon et al., 1980; Sverke and Kuruvilla, 1995). It has been argued that mergers can lead to decreased levels of member attachment to the union when the interests and craft specialities of multiple unions are fusioned (Chaison, 1986; Cornfield, 1991). On the other hand, it is possible that members' levels of identification with the organization remains unaffected if the merger parties operate within similar jurisdictions and express similar interests and values (cf. Freeman and Brittain, 1977). In the present case, the two merging unions operated mainly in different jurisdictions but, as manifested in a number of jurisdictional disputes between the unions, there was also a certain degree of overlap (Färm, 1990).

Union satisfaction is an evaluative construct reflecting members' contentment with union representation and performance (Fiorito et al., 1988; Kuruvilla et al., 1993). In distinguishing between the attitudinal constructs of commitment and satisfaction, Mowday, Porter and Steers (1982) noted that satisfaction is more short-term and affected by day to day events while such transitory events should not influence the individual's attachment to the organization. Analysts seem to agree that by merging, unions (especially smaller ones) may derive economies of scale which, in turn, might increase organizational effectiveness and services to the membership (Chaison, 1986; Stratton-Devine, 1992). To the extent that such improvements have an impact in the lower levels of the union hierarchy and are also perceived by the members, increasing levels of satisfaction could be expected.

In combination with a lack of empirical evidence, the theoretical ambiguity regarding merger effects makes it difficult to formulate specific hypotheses on how union members' attitudes and behaviour are affected by a merger. Thus, the present study was of an exploratory nature. Our purpose was to evaluate the short-term merger effects on members' participation, commitment and satisfaction.

## Research methodology

### *Design and participants*

The merger between the Swedish Factory Workers Union and the Swedish Clothing Workers Union provided a quasi-experimental situation (the nonequivalent control group design; Cook and Campbell, 1979), the merger serving as the treatment and the Swedish Food Workers Union as a comparison group. We used questionnaires to assess the central variables both before and after the merger. Pre-merger baseline data were collected in winter 1991-92 (time 1) while post-merger data from the same individuals were collected in summer 1993 (time 2), that is, a few months after the official date (1 May 1993) of the merger.

Two percent of the members of the three unions were randomly sampled for the study. Of the 1,434 members of the Swedish Factory Workers Union selected for the survey, 541 (38 percent) provided usable responses at both time 1 and time 2. The mean age of participants was 44 years (*SD* = 12) and they had been members of the national union for an average of 12 years (*SD* = 9); males comprised 66 percent of the sample.

A total of 418 members of the Swedish Clothing Workers Union were selected for the survey. Approximately 42 percent (*N* = 178) provided usable responses at both points of time. The mean age was 48 years (*SD* = 12), the average length of union membership 16 years (*SD* = 12) and the male proportion of the sample 37 percent.

Completed questionnaires at both time 1 and time 2 were returned by 356 of the 979 members of the Swedish Food Workers Union sampled for the study, for a response rate of 36 percent. The mean age of the sample was 44 years (*SD* = 13), the average length of union membership 12 years (*SD* = 10) and the proportion of males 58 percent.

Although the response rates were not altogether satisfactory, relatively low response rates are commonly obtained in surveys of trade union memberships (Cornfield, 1991). Our three samples did not differ from their respective populations in terms of mean age and sex distribution, thus suggesting that they were representative of the unions from which they were drawn.

## Measures

Instrumental and ideological commitment to the union was assessed using Sverke and Kuruvilla's (1995) scale of rational union commitment. Items were scored on five-point Likert-type scales. Instrumental rationality-based commitment was measured by seven items. For all three samples, the internal consistency reliability was satisfactory at both time 1 (Cronbach's $\alpha$ ranged from .84 to .87) and time 2 (range of $\alpha$ = .87 to .90). Value rationality-based commitment, that is, members' ideological attachment to the union, was measured by nine items that also demonstrated a satisfactory reliability ($\alpha$ exceeded .90 in all samples at both points of time).

Union satisfaction was measured using two scales developed by the authors. Responses were given on five-point disagree-agree scales. Satisfaction with the national union was assessed with four items focusing on members' overall contentness with union representation and the information provided by the national union ($\alpha$ ranged from .73 to .81 at time 1 and from .69 to .87 at time 2). Similarly, satisfaction with the local union was assessed with four items focusing on how the local union was perceived to represent and inform the membership (time 1 $\alpha$ = .68 to .74; time 2 $\alpha$ = .62 to .71).

Two forms of union participation were assessed at both times. Union office holding was measured by asking members if they currently had any representative position in the union. To measure union meeting attendance, respondents were asked if they in the recent past had attended a union meeting. Single items, scored on two-point scales (1 = no, 2 = yes), were used to assess the two forms of participation.

## Results

We used analysis of variance with covariate (ANCOVA) to evaluate the short-term merger effects on members' commitment, satisfaction and participation. This method of analysis contrasts each individual's score on the variate (time 2) with that on the covariate (time 1) before the individuals are compared at time 2 on the basis of their union affiliation. The inclusion of the pre-test measure in form of a linear regression serves to increase the precision of the group effect (Cook and Campbell, 1979), in this case the effect of the merger. A significant ($p < .05$) group effect was used as the criterion for determining if the merger contributed to between-union differences in the study variables at time 2. For descriptive purposes, the ANCOVAs were supplemented with exploratory tests for pre-merger differences between unions using analysis of variance (ANOVA) procedures and paired $t$ tests for mean level changes within unions over time.

Table 24.1 displays mean values in union commitment, union satisfaction, and union participation at time 1 and time 2 for the three unions. It also presents results of the baseline comparisons, the tests for mean level changes within unions over time, and the comparisons between merged and non-merged unions at time 2.

**Table 24.1**
**Baseline levels, changes within unions over time, and tests for post-merger differences between unions in commitment, satisfaction and participation**

| Variable (range) | Union[a] | Mean value Time 1 | Time 2 | $t^c$ |
|---|---|---|---|---|
| **Commitment** | | | | |
| Value rationality- | Factory | 2.46 | 2.70 | 7.69*** |
| based commitment | Clothing | 2.55 | 2.71 | 2.82** |
| to the union | Food | 2.48 | 2.67 | 5.30*** |
| (1-5) | ANOVA $F^b$ | 0.50 | | |
| | ANCOVA $F^d$ | | 0.64 | |
| Instrumental rationality- | Factory | 3.31 | 3.39 | 2.90** |
| based commitment | Clothing | 3.29 | 3.37 | 1.69 |
| to the union | Food | 3.37 | 3.35 | 0.48 |
| (1-5) | ANOVA $F^b$ | 1.13 | | |
| | ANCOVA $F^d$ | | 1.74 | |
| **Satisfaction** | | | | |
| Satisfaction with | Factory | 2.92 | 2.91 | 0.33 |
| national union | Clothing | 3.08 | 3.16 | 0.82 |
| (1-5) | Food | 2.96 | 3.03 | 1.03 |
| | ANOVA $F^b$ | 0.75 | | |
| | ANCOVA $F^d$ | | 2.60 | |
| Satisfaction with | Factory | 3.16 | 3.19 | 0.83 |
| local union | Clothing | 3.30 | 3.22 | 1.18 |
| (1-5) | Food | 3.18 | 3.18 | 0.02 |
| | ANOVA $F^b$ | 1.32 | | |
| | ANCOVA $F^d$ | | 0.24 | |
| **Participation** | | | | |
| Union office | Factory | 1.22 | 1.20 | 1.25 |
| holding | Clothing | 1.18 | 1.17 | 0.46 |
| (1-2) | Food | 1.19 | 1.13 | 3.78*** |
| | ANOVA $F^b$ | 1.30 | | |
| | ANCOVA $F^d$ | | 3.32* | |
| Union meeting | Factory | 1.55 | 1.50 | 2.55* |
| attendance | Clothing | 1.56 | 1.42 | 3.55*** |
| (1-2) | Food | 1.56 | 1.52 | 1.25 |
| | ANOVA $F^b$ | 0.05 | | |
| | ANCOVA $F^d$ | | 3.70* | |

*Notes:* *$p<.05$ **$p<.01$ ***$p<.001$.
[a] Merged unions: clothing and factory; comparison union: food.
[b] Oneway ANOVA $F$ test for baseline difference between unions.
[c] Two-tailed paired $t$ test for mean level change within union over time.
[d] ANCOVA $F$ test for post-merger (time 2) mean difference between unions after controlling for time 1 levels in the corresponding variable.

We first turn to the examination of short-term merger effects on union commitment. As can be seen from the table, the baseline levels of value rationality-based commitment did not differ between unions. Thus, members of the three unions were about equally committed to their union on an ideological basis before the merger took place. Value-based commitment increased significantly from time 1 to time 2 for all three unions. The similar baseline levels and the relatively equivalent mean increases over time concerted to produce almost identical aggregated mean levels for the unions at time 2. The non-significant post-merger difference between unions at time 2 thus suggests that the merger did not impact members' value rationality-based commitment to the union. Also in instrumental rationality-based union commitment, the baseline levels were similar across unions. While the mean values were stable over time for the clothing workers and the food workers, members of one of the merger parties (the factory workers union) reported higher levels of instrumental commitment at time 2 than at time 1. After controlling for initial levels of instrumental commitment, however, there was no significant post-merger difference between merged and non-merged unions.

The results for union satisfaction were somewhat similar to those for commitment. The baseline levels of members' satisfaction with their national union did not differ significantly, and the mean values remained stable over time for all three unions. When the unions were compared at time 2, after the initial levels of national union satisfaction had been taken into account, no significant difference emerged. Also in local union satisfaction, the baseline values were similar across unions and the mean values remained essentially the same over time as reflected in the non-significant $t$ values. The similarity between unions was also reflected in almost identical post-merger mean values in local union satisfaction.

While the above results suggest that the merger did not have an effect on any of the commitment or satisfaction variables, an interesting pattern of results emerged for union participation. The baseline levels of office holding and meeting attendance were similar across unions, and post-merger differences between unions emerged. First, there was a significant time 2 difference between the unions in office holding after the initial levels had been taken into account. The $t$ tests revealed that union office holding decreased significantly among the food workers while it remained stable for the two merging unions. These results suggest that the merger did not affect members' frequency of serving in elected office, while union office holding decreased in the comparison union.

Second, after controlling for members' pre-merger scores, the post-test comparison revealed that the degree of meeting attendance differed significantly between unions after the merger. As is apparent from the *t* tests, union meeting attendance decreased for the unions of factory workers and clothing workers, while no significant change over time emerged for the food workers' union. These results indicate that the merger reduced members' participation in union meetings, whereas meeting attendance was stationary in the comparison union. It should be noted, however, that in those cases where participation declined over time, these changes, albeit significant, were small in absolute values.

## Discussion

The previous literature on union mergers has focused on merger motives, and it has predicted the occurrence of mergers and discussed their potential outcomes. Our knowledge is however limited about how members are affected by this type of structural change. Therefore, the purpose of this study was to evaluate the effects of union mergers on members' attitudes and behaviour. By surveying representative samples of two merging Swedish blue-collar unions and a comparison union both before and shortly after the merger, our quasi-experimental design allowed for investigating if members' commitment to the union, satisfaction with union representation and participation in union activity increased or decreased in the post-merger period.

Although mergers may enable unions to increase administrative and financial resources, achieve economies of scale, enhance bargaining power and improve organizational effectiveness, they have also been argued to have some negative consequences for the attitudes and behaviour of the members (Chaison, 1986; Williamson, 1995). For instance, Williamson (1995) noted that mergers, since they require an adaptation to the policies and practices of a new organizational entity, involve 'an abandonment of history and tradition, and a loss of the institution's identity' (p. 24). Further, Chaison (1986) emphasized that after mergers, especially those characterized by high degrees of integration between the merger parties, 'more powerful and centralized governing structures tend to emerge ...[which, in turn,]... can reduce membership participation because of the larger committees and meetings, the creation of additional layers of government between top officers and the membership, and the increased time and effort needed to run for higher level office' (p. 120). This reasoning parallels Child, Loveridge and Warner's (1973) observation that a heterogeneous membership body might provide opportunities for union officers to centralize decision-making and, thereby, reduce membership participation.

The results of the present study provides a more optimistic picture of how union members are affected by a merger. A major finding was that there were no differences in commitment or satisfaction between unions after the merger. Another important finding was that there were small, but significant, post-merger differences between unions in terms of union participation. More specifically, when we contrasted the unions after the merger the results showed that union meeting attendance decreased among members of the merged unions while it remained stable in the comparison union. In contrast to this, the degree of union office holding did not change over time in the merged unions while it decreased in the comparison union. Our results thus imply that the merger had negative short-term effects on members' union meeting attendance, but that it did not affect members' attitudes towards the union or the frequency of union office holding.

One possible explanation for these results is that the merger was carefully planned and therefore several potential negative effects were reduced. In both the amalgamating unions the merger was discussed over a long period of time. Further, the decision-making rules and practices of the new organization were highly integrated, and considerable effort was given to the design of the regional and local union structures. It is conceivable that through all these efforts the structure, goals and policies of the new merged union received support among the memberships, thus facilitating members' involvement in the union. Structural characteristics may have important consequences for members' attitudes and behaviour and, as noted by Barling et al. (1992), it is 'probable that the structure of the labour organization facilitates participation and commitment to the extent that it possesses the structures that encourage democracy' (p. 85).

We do emphasize, though, that our study focused only on short-term merger effects. Janus (1978) observed that, typically, the functions and organizational units of the merging parties are not melded immediately after the merger. Rather, the implementation of mergers is likely to take some time since members and officers have to adjust to the policies and modes of operation of the new union, and local level unions must 'accommodate new members, employers, and collective bargaining relationships' (p. 14). Thus, our results could be taken as preliminary evidence indicating that union mergers do not impact members' attitudes towards their union and have only a limited effect on their participation. While intended as well as unintended changes in the new, merged union might not have become manifest shortly after the official merger date, a more long-term follow-up is required before a firm conclusion is drawn about how members' attitudes and behaviour are affected by a merger.

While the merger studied here was an amalgamation, it is quite possible that other kinds of mergers (i.e. absorptions) may have different consequences for the involved memberships. Members of a small absorbed union may fear that it will be 'swallowed up' by the large absorbing organization (Conant and Kaserman, 1989, p. 247). Indeed, especially highly attached members may apprehend that the sense of community they derive from the union would be jeopardized through merger, thereby possibly leading to impaired commitment and reduced participation. In order to advance the theoretical understanding of union mergers, we therefore urge researchers to investigate how absorption mergers affect members' attitudes and behaviour, preferably by applying quasi-experimental designs as in the present study.

Although the present study focused on a single merger and evaluated only its short-term effects, we feel that our results have some important implications for unions contemplating merger. There is a commonly held vision among both union leaders and labour scholars of a rationalized union structure and revitalized labour movement through mergers (Chaison, 1992). Union mergers are seen as tools for improving cost effectiveness, bargaining power and membership growth, and they occur frequently in industrialized countries. The results presented in this chapter suggest that such beneficial outcomes, to the extent that they are realized, do not have to befall at the expense of impaired member attitudes towards, and active involvement in, their unions.

## References

Abrahamsson, B. (1993), 'Union structural change', *Economic and Industrial Democracy*, vol. 14, pp. 399-421.

Abrahamsson, B., Ahlén, K., Eriksson, A. H. and Sverke, M. (1991), Framtidens fackförbund: Programplan BEFALI, Swedish Center for Working Life, Stockholm.

Barling, J., Fullagar, C. and Kelloway, E. K. (1992), *The union and its members: A psychological approach*, Oxford University Press, New York and Oxford.

Buchanan, R. (1981), 'Mergers in British trade unions 1949-79', *Industrial Relations Journal*, vol. 12, pp. 40-49.

Buchanan, R. (1992), 'Measuring mergers and concentration in UK unions 1910-88', *Industrial Relations Journal*, vol. 23, pp. 304-314.

Chaison, G. N. (1983), 'Local union mergers: Frequency, forms, and national union policy'. *Journal of Labour Research*, vol. 4, pp. 325-338.

Chaison, G. N. (1986), *When unions merge*, Lexington Books, Lexington, MA.

Chaison, G. N. (1992), Union mergers in the United States: Recent trends and questions for research, Paper presented at The Symposium on Emerging Union Structures: An International Comparison, Clark University, March 9-10, 1992, Clark University, Worcester, MA.

Child, J., Loveridge, R. and Warner, M. (1973), 'Towards an organizational study of trade unions', *Sociology*, vol. 7, pp. 71-91.

Conant, J. L. and Kaserman, D. L. (1989), 'Union merger incentives and pecuniary externalities', *Journal of Labour Research*, vol. 10, pp. 243-253.

Cook, T. D. and Campbell, D. T. (1979), *Quasi-experimentation: Design & analysis issues for field settings*, Houghton Mifflin, Boston, MA.

Cornfield, D. B. (1991), 'The attitude of employee assosciation members toward union mergers: The effect of socioeconomic status', *Industrial and Labour Relations Review*, vol. 44, pp. 334-348.

Fiorito, J., Gallagher, D. G. and Fukami, C. W. (1988), 'Satisfaction with union representation', *Industrial and Labour Relations Review*, vol. 41, pp. 294-307.

Freeman, J. and Brittain, J. (1977), 'Union merger process and industrial environment', *Industrial Relations*, vol. 16, pp. 173-185.

Färm, G. (1990), Utredning om framtiden för Beklädnadsarbetarnas Förbund inom LO, Norrköping.

Gallagher, D. G. and Strauss, G. (1991), 'Union membership attitudes and participation, in Strauss, G., Gallagher, D. G. and Fiorito, J. (eds.), *The state of the unions*, pp. 139-174, Industrial Relations Research Association, Madison, WI.

Gordon, M. E., Philbot, J. W., Burt, R., Thompson, C. A. and Spiller, W. E. (1980), 'Commitment to the union: Development of a measure and an examination of its correlates', *Journal of Applied Psychology*, vol. 65, pp. 479-499.

Hyman, R. (1994), 'Changing trade union identities and strategies', in Hyman, R. and Ferner, A. (eds.), *New frontiers in European industrial relations*, pp. 80-107, Blackwell, Oxford.

Janus, C. J. (1978), 'Union mergers in the 1970's: A look at the reasons and results', *Monthly Labour Review*, October, pp. 13-23.

Kelloway, E. K. and Barling, J. (1993), 'Members' participation in local union activities: Measurement, prediction, and replication', *Journal of Applied Psychology*, vol. 78, pp. 262-279.

Klandermans, B. (1986), 'Psychology and trade union participation: Joining, acting, quitting', *Journal of Occupational Psychology*, vol. 59, pp. 198-204.

Kuruvilla, S., Gallagher, D. G. and Wetzel, K. (1993), 'The development of members' attitudes towards their unions: Sweden and Canada', *Industrial and Labour Relations Review*, vol. 46, pp. 499-515.

Lewin, L. (1980), *Governing trade unions in Sweden*, Harvard University Press, Cambridge, MA.

McClendon, J. A., Kriesky, J. and Eaton, A. (1995), 'Member support for union mergers: An analysis of an affiliation referendum', *Journal of Labour Research*, vol. 16, pp. 9-23.

McShane, S. L. (1986), 'The multidimensionality of union participation', *Journal of Occupational Psychology*, vol. 59, pp. 177-187.

Mowday, R. T., Porter, L. W. and Steers, R. M. (1982), *Employee-organizational linkages*, Academic Press, New York.

Stratton-Devine, K. (1992), 'Union merger benefits: An empirical analysis', *Journal of Labour Research*, vol. 13, pp. 133-143.

Sverke, M. and Kuruvilla, S. (1995), 'A new conceptualization of union commitment: Development and test of an integrated theory', *Journal of Organizational Behavior*, vol. 16, pp. 505-532.

Undy, R., Ellis, V., McCarthy, W. and Halmos, A. (1981), *Change in trade unions: The development of U.K. unions since the 1960s*, Hutchinson, London.

Waddington, J. (1988), 'Trade union mergers: A study of trade union structural dynamics', *British Journal of Industrial Relations*, vol. 26, pp. 409-430.

Williamson, L. (1995), 'Union mergers: An update', *Monthly Labour Review*, February, pp. 18-25.

# 25 Evaluating the effectiveness of a political action campaign on union members

*Victor M. Catano and E. Kevin Kelloway*

Today, trade unions are under increasing assault from both politicians and employers. Private sector trade unions in North America and the United Kingdom have had to deal with downsizing, layoffs and the casualization of employment. Public sector unions have had to confront legislation or court decisions which limit their power and growth, the privatization of public corporations; and government action abrogating freely negotiated collective agreements (Catano, Cole and Hebert, 1995). Hartley (1995) recently assessed the impact of changes in the economic, political and social context on these employment relationships. Referring primarily to the situation in the United Kingdom, she noted the dominance of a right wing ideology in the national government which valued the private market above all other organizational relationships. As trade unions are seen as impediments to the operation of the free market, the U.K. government enacted legislation to reduce the power and growth of trade unions and professions. The dominance of these right wing ideologies is reflected in the privatization of the public sector, that is, the selling off of public corporations to the private sector. Hartley identified privatization as causing '... considerable employment uncertainty in parts of the public sector, such as local government, health and the civil service, where the future of jobs is unknown, or where market forces push down wages, make jobs redundant and casualize others' (Hartley, 1995, p. 8). She could just as easily have been describing the political situation in Canada today, at both the federal and, particularly, the provincial levels.

---

We would like to thank the union and its members for their cooperation throughout this project. Correspondence should be addressed to Dr. Victor M. Catano, Department of Psychology, Saint Mary's University, Halifax, N.S., Canada, B3H 3C3.

Political and social trends often are late in coming to Canada; the last recession and the 1990s saw this New Right ideology bloom in the form of new political parties which have forced both centrist and even left wing parties to shift to the right. In Ontario, some would argue that the only difference between the policies of the left-of-center New Democratic Party (NDP) government and those of the right wing Conservative government that replaced it was that the NDP showed more sympathy when it laid off civil servants and cut their wages. Trade unions can sit idly by and surrender to these forces or attempt to direct the collective energy of its membership into opposition. Both organizational psychologists and industrial relations specialists will have to develop more applied research agendas which have immediate, practical implications, if they wish to be of assistance to organized labour during this period when unions are under assault from both politicians and employers (Gordon and Ladd, 1993).

Increasing union members' sense of commitment is one way of bolstering unions against these threats. Greater involvement in union activities, willingness to take strike action and support for a union's political agenda are fundamental to the immediate survival and future strength of unions. Many of these outcomes are directly related to a member's union commitment (Barling, Fullagar and Kelloway, 1992). Recently, Catano et al. (1995) demonstrated that union activities such as training workshops led to increases in union commitment. The purpose of the present study was to assess whether a systematic political action campaign undertaken by a union had an impact on the union members.

## Unions and political action

Although we have developed a considerable data base on union commitment, we have barely begun to scratch the surface in understanding its linkage to political action. In fact, little research has taken place with respect to unions and political involvement (Bennett, 1984; Masters and Delaney, 1987). Bennett and Delaney (1993), while noting a modest increase in research on this topic, identify union political activities as one of seven industrial relations topics on which additional research was most needed. They believe that research on unions' political efforts at all levels of government is particularly timely. In part, this lack of interest may stem from the fact that most trade unions in North America have not had extensive involvement in action, even though they may need to become more overtly political to achieve success (Kochan and Wever, 1991).

In the U.S., both governments and courts have tried to restrict the role of unions to economic matters and to hamper their role as political institutions. For example, the U.S. Supreme Court ruled in *Communications Workers of America v. Beck* (1988) that unions could not use any dues obtained from nonmembers they represent through 'agency' shops for political purposes without the agreement of those nonmembers. Through executive order, President Bush extended this ruling to federal contractors by requiring them to post notices informing members covered by union contracts that they could request dues refunds proportionate to the percentage of money that their bargaining agent spent on political activity. These rulings make it difficult for U.S. unions to participate fully in the political process (Bennett and Delaney, 1993).

Similar attempts have been made to limit union political activity in Canada. However, unlike its U.S. counterpart, the Supreme Court of Canada in *Lavigne v. Ontario Public Service Employees Union* (1991) held that it was legitimate for unions to use dues obtained from nonmembers to obtain political objectives. Canadian unions have shown a willingness to become involved in political action. Many have had direct or indirect associations with the New Democratic Party, including holding formal organizational memberships in the NDP. Masters and Delaney (1985) argue that unions in industries or occupations that are most dependent on government actions are most likely to engage in political activity to influence government policies. It stands to reason, then, that unions which represent public sector or government workers should be most likely to engage in political activity. This has been the case in Canada where public sector unions have been in the forefront of opposing the New Right agenda.

Political action can take many forms. It may involve direct contributions from unions to political parties which support union objectives; the use of union staff, office and research facilities to support political campaigns; mobilizing membership to take specific actions such as letter writing campaigns, participating in demonstrations, or voting in elections; and attempting to persuade members to vote for political candidates that are sympathetic to the objectives of trade unions. Generally, those political activities which are based on union executive decisions, e.g. donating money to political groups, have been more successful than those which require direct action of the membership, e.g. having members vote for a particular candidate. In this latter example, union members may share the economic goals of the union but are not committed to the political philosophy on which those economic goals are based. This argument is similar to the point Barling et al.

(1992) make that after joining a union, the level of members' commitment to, and participation in, the union varies considerably reflecting the union members' attitudes and behaviors.

### *The political action campaign*

Starting in 1991, the Conservative government of an Atlantic Canadian province, acting under the influence of its newly elected leader, adopted a right wing agenda similar to the one reported by Hartley (1995). This program involved government downsizing of services, the privatization of public companies, and a 'rationalization' of health, education and social services. The government emphasized budget restraint over job creation and legislated a two-year freeze on wages and salaries paid to public sector workers. The government's policies had created a great deal of concern among public service workers, particularly those employed directly by the government itself. In response, the union which represented these government employees initiated a political action campaign in opposition to the policies of the government. The campaign was designed to oppose what was perceived to be the unfair and inequitable treatment of public employees and to promote their interests. The campaign involved three phases: (a) distributing information opposing the privatization policies of the government; (b) publicizing the negative impact of the government's policies and actions on the economy and on union members; and (c) working to defeat the government during an election.

The union used a variety of media as part of its political action campaign. These included articles in the union newsletter, pamphlets directed at specific issues, notices on union bulletin boards in the work place, direct mailings to union members' residences and newspaper advertisements. The union also initiated activities, e.g. public talks by union leaders and other public events, designed to publicize the union's positions both to its members and to the general public. In the last stage of the campaign, the focus shifted from opposing the government's policies to opposing the government, itself, which was then seeking re-election. In addition to the previous media, union sponsored political advertisements opposing the government on radio and television. It also provided each union member with a summary of each candidate's views on issues of concern to the union.

The union represents over 13,000 members, 9,000 of whom are civil servants, i.e. direct employees of the government. The civil service members are required to belong to the union as a condition of employment. The union was quite aware that attitudes and opinions about the union, let alone government, varied considerably across these members. The union was also aware that the political action campaign might produce a backlash against the union among its more conservative members. On the other hand, following Fiorito's (1987) argument that union instrumentality is multi-faceted, the union's political activity could improve its members' perceptions of both the union's service and power. Therefore, the union decided to monitor the effects of the political action campaign. This was done through two telephone surveys of its membership; the surveys were taken approximately one year apart. The first survey established baseline measures and provided information for the political action campaign; the second was taken after the conclusion of the election and was used to evaluate the effectiveness of the campaign.

## Method

### *Sample*

The first telephone survey of the union members (*N*= 367) took place over a ten day period in April, 1992 (Time 1). The second telephone survey (*N*=416) took place over ten days in June, 1993 (Time 2). The sample drawn at Time 1 was independent from the sample drawn at Time 2. Both samples were randomly drawn from union membership lists, proportionate to the number of union members residing in each electoral district in the province. Each sample represented approximately 3 percent of the total union membership. Respondents were informed that the survey was being done on behalf of their union. Approximately 31 percent of those called in the first survey declined to participate as did 34 percent of those in the second; these refusal rates are similar to ones found in other telephone surveys done with this union. It was possible that the two independent samples differed in composition with respect to the respondents' sex, income, age, living status and education. Kolmogorov-Smirnov two-sample tests compared the distribution of responses in the Time 1 and Time 2 samples on each of these five demographic variables. These statistical tests did not reveal any significant differences, suggesting that both the Time 1 and Time 2 samples represented the same population.

Given the sample size used in the surveys, the information contained in each is accurate within ±5 percent, 19 times out of 20. This means that if 70 percent of sample respondents answered 'Yes' to a question, the actual percentage of 'Yes' responses in the population from which the sample was drawn is likely to range from a low of 65 percent to a high of 75 percent. Furthermore, if the survey had been repeated with 20 different, independent samples drawn from the same population, the percentage of 'Yes' responses in 19 of the samples would likely fall into the 65 percent to 75 percent interval.

### Survey materials

Each survey contained about 25 substantive questions and was designed to be answered within 15 minutes. The responses for all questions used either a yes-no format or five-point, verbally anchored rating scales. The response options were presented as part of each question. The survey questions were constructed with the assistance of union officers and were designed to obtain information either for use in the political action campaign or as part of its evaluation. In addition to soliciting unique information, both surveys also contained a set of common questions.

The second survey included Chacko's (1985) Perception of Union Power and Union Service items. Because of time constraints, these items were not included in the first survey. However, we had obtained baseline data for these measures previously (Kelloway, Catano and Southwell, 1992) and had established that, without intervention, they remained relatively stable over time (Catano et al., 1995).

### Procedure

The telephone surveys were conducted by five, experienced interviewers. Each interviewer was randomly assigned a list of names with telephone numbers that had been selected for the study from the union's master membership list. Interviewers were given twice as many names as needed in anticipation of refusals, respondents not being at home, or out-of-date phone numbers. They were instructed to continue down their lists until reaching a designated quota of names that had been established for each electoral district. Calls were made between 6:00 pm and 10:00 pm on weekday nights and between 1:00 pm and 6:00 pm on weekends.

### Data analysis

To facilitate statistical analyses of questions which had five response options, the two most extreme options in each direction were combined into one. For example, 'Strongly Agree' and 'Agree' were collapsed into one category, 'Agree', while 'Strongly Disagree' and 'Disagree' were combined into 'Disagree'. For each question, the frequency of responses in each option was converted to a percentage. Chi-square statistical tests ($\chi^2$) then compared the similarity in these response distributions at Time 1 and Time 2 for each substantive item on the survey. Relatively large $\chi^2$ values suggest that there is a significant difference between the Time 1 and Time 2 response distributions;

that is, there is only a very small probability ($p$) that the difference may have occurred by chance. Probabilities of less than 5 percent (noted as $p < .05$) are considered to be significant. The size of the $\chi^2$-value depends as well on the 'degrees of freedom' associated with the value; degrees of freedom (df) are related to the number of response options. Significant differences are indicated below by presenting the probability that the result may be due to chance, e.g. $p < .05$; non-significant differences are represented by the abbreviation 'n.s.'

## Results

### *The anti-privatization campaign*

The majority of the Time 2 survey noticed the anti-privatization campaign materials (80 percent) and believed that they were useful to some degree (74 percent). A third of these respondents (34 percent) reported that they became more opposed to privatization as a result of their union's campaign with only a few (3 percent) reporting less opposition. Similarly, 41 percent felt that their support for the government in the recent election decreased as a result of the anti-privatization campaign, with only 8 percent reporting that the campaign caused them to become more supportive.

Compared to the Time 1 survey, support for privatization decreased significantly by nearly 50 percent, falling from 24 percent to 12 percent ($\chi^2 = 11.25$, df = 3, $p < .02$). Over this same period, the union members' concerns over someone in their household suffering the effects of job loss or reduced employment did not change significantly and remained relatively stable. Table 25.1 shows that members' attitudes toward the consequences of privatization became significantly more negative: the percentage of union members who felt privatization would lead to creation of new jobs dropped significantly from 27 percent at Time 1 to 7 percent at Time 2 ($\chi^2 = 26.20$, df = 3, $p < .01$); those who believed privatization would reduce the number of government employees increased significantly from 79 percent to 88 percent ($\chi^2 = 14.82$, df = 3, $p < .01$). Belief that it would produce cost savings decreased significantly from 34 percent to 19 percent ($\chi^2 = 22.25$, df = 3, $p < .01$) as did the belief that it would increase both the quality (31 percent vs. 16 percent; $\chi^2 = 23.43$, df = 3, $p < .01$) and quantity (10 percent vs. 1 percent; $\chi^2 = 26.52$, df = 3, $p < .01$) of government services. Attitudes concerning the effect of privatization on government services in small communities and on labour problems did not change significantly between the two surveys.

**Table 25.1**
**Percentage of respondents at Time 1 and Time 2 who believed that jobs or services would change as indicated if private companies and businesses performed the work currently done by government employees**

| | Increase[a] | Decrease | Same | Don't know |
|---|---|---|---|---|
| Number of government employees[b] | | | | |
| Time 1 | 5.8 | 78.6 | 15.2 | 0.4 |
| Time 2 | 0.7 | 88.0 | 6.0 | 5.0 |
| Cost of government services[b] | | | | |
| Time 1 | 43.4 | 34.1 | 22.1 | 0.4 |
| Time 2 | 44.1 | 19.3 | 11.6 | 24.8 |
| Quality of government services[b] | | | | |
| Time 1 | 30.7 | 44.4 | 24.9 | 0.0 |
| Time 2 | 15.9 | 52.2 | 15.6 | 16.1 |
| Number of government services[b] | | | | |
| Time 1 | 9.9 | 65.3 | 24.8 | 0.0 |
| Time 2 | 1.2 | 74.5 | 11.1 | 13.0 |
| Number of new jobs[b] | | | | |
| Time 1 | 27.2 | 37.7 | 30.4 | 4.7 |
| Time 2 | 6.7 | 63.9 | 16.1 | 13.0 |
| Government services in small communities | | | | |
| Time 1 | 4.8 | 69.9 | 10.1 | 14.9 |
| Time 2 | 11.3 | 67.5 | 15.6 | 5.8 |
| Strikes and other labour problems | | | | |
| Time 1 | 48.0 | 18.5 | 21.1 | 11.6 |
| Time 2 | 48.2 | 10.6 | 13.7 | 27.2 |

[a] The data represent the percentage of union members choosing each response option.
[b] $p < .01$ (based on $\chi^2$ comparison of response distribution for the two surveys).

*The anti-government campaign*

The majority of respondents at Time 2 noticed the anti-government campaign materials (82 percent); however, they were evenly divided on whether this material was useful (Useful: 49 percent; Not Useful: 51 percent). Printed materials and advertisements were seen as more useful (52 percent) than radio or television commercials (41 percent). Nonetheless, 35 percent of the respondents believed they became more opposed to the government as a result of the anti-government campaign while 42 percent stated that the campaign had made them less likely to support the government in the recent election. In both cases only small minorities (5 percent and 4 percent, respectively) attributed more support for the government and its re-election as a result of the union's campaign.

An overwhelming majority, 95 percent, of Time 2 respondents reported that they had voted in the election; this compared with an election turn-out of 75 percent of all eligible voters. There were significant changes in the member's felt closeness to the major political parties over the period covered by the two surveys ($\chi^2 = 14.55$, df = 4, $p < .01$). There was a significant decrease in felt closeness to both the ruling Progressive Conservatives and the NDP, the socialist party. Only 8 percent of the respondents, compared to 22.5 percent in the Time 1 survey, reported feeling close to the Conservatives; 10 percent expressed closeness to the NDP compared to 20 percent, previously. Felt closeness to the Liberal Party, which won the election increased significantly from 21 percent to 26 percent. Disenchantment with all political parties increased significantly from 20 percent to 27 percent with 29 percent (vs. 15 percent, previously) being either unable or unwilling to identify with any of the parties.

### *The use of union dues*

The Time 2 survey asked members for their views on using union dues to finance certain types of political activities. Survey responses suggested that the union members supported funding for political action that was not overtly partisan in nature and linked to issues that affected their job security. A majority agreed or strongly agreed with the use of union funds to finance the Candidate Survey (52 percent) and the anti-privatization campaign (50 percent) but opposed the use of union money to fund political advertising (62 percent) and the anti-government campaign (44 percent).

### *Perception of union power and union service*

In comparison to data collected prior to the start of the political action campaign, the union members became more definitive in their perception of their union's power. The 'undecided' members decreased significantly, in most cases by over 50 percent; however, those attributing less power to the union increased as did those attributing more power to it. Table 25.2 shows that this trend was consistent across each of the four Power items. This shift was significant for responses to questions on the union's influence over election to public office ($\chi^2 = 18.36$, df = 2, $p < .01$), influence over passage of laws ($\chi^2 = 8.62$, df = 2. $p < .02$) and its influence over how the workplace is run ($\chi^2 = 18.70$, df = 2, $p < .01$). In this last case, the percentage of members who agreed doubled from 26 percent to 55 percent. The change in belief that the union was respected by the employer was only marginally significant ($\chi^2 = 5.84$, df = 2, $p < .06$) with those disagreeing with this proposition increasing from 26 percent to 38 percent.

There was little change in how the members' perceived the service provided by their union; their perception of union service remained relatively constant. They did not significantly change their views with respect to the union protecting them against unfair actions by their employer ($\chi^2 = 1.05$, df = 2, n.s.), to the union improving their job security ($\chi^2 = 3.83$, df = 2, n.s.), or to the union improving their wages and working conditions ($\chi^2 = 3.92$, df = 2, n.s.). They did, however, significantly change their position on whether the union gave them their money's worth for the dues they paid ($\chi^2 = 8.04$, df = 2, $p < .02$). Again, those who were undecided shifted to either positive or negative views. The percentage agreeing with that statement increased from 37 percent to 47 percent; those disagreeing with it increased from 31 percent to 38 percent.

## Discussion

Bennett and Delaney (1993) encouraged researchers to adopt new perspectives and to attempt non-traditional analyses of topics like union political action that have received relatively little attention. They recognized why many academics might be reluctant to delve into such research: the available methodologies and analytic procedures might not find favour with referees who assess the research for publication. In fact, Masters and Delaney (1987) pointed out that almost every attempt at empirical research on union political activities was fraught with methodological problems. The research reported here illustrates these points; there are two methodological issues that should be kept in mind when evaluating the results from this study.

### *Methodological concerns*

There is no means by which the changes in the union members' attitudes that are reported in this study can be directly attributed to the political action campaign. There was no way in which a meaningful control situation could be established; the resulting design is a one group pretest-posttest design. Although this design is frequently used in applied research, it is subject to threats to validity primarily from history, maturation and regression (Cook,

**Table 25.2**

**Perceptions of union power and union service: The percentage of union members who agreed or disagreed with each statement**

| Statement | Percent[a] | | |
|---|---|---|---|
| | Agree[b] | Neither | Disagree[c] |
| **Union power** | | | |
| The union has a lot of influence over who gets elected to public office[d] | | | |
| Time 2, 1993 | 24.1 | 20.7 | 54.3 |
| Kelloway, et al., 1992 | 14.9 | 49.8 | 34.2 |
| The union has a lot of influence over what laws get passed[d] | | | |
| Time 2, 1993 | 21.5 | 27.1 | 51.3 |
| Kelloway et al., 1992 | 15.3 | 47.1 | 36.7 |
| The union is respected by the employer | | | |
| Time 2, 1993 | 36.6 | 24.6 | 38.1 |
| Kelloway et al., 1992 | 34.0 | 39.6 | 26.1 |
| The union has a lot to say about how the work place is run[d] | | | |
| Time 2, 1993 | 55.5 | 16.6 | 27.7 |
| Kelloway et al., 1992 | 26.4 | 36.1 | 37.3 |
| **Union service** | | | |
| The union protects workers against unfair actions of the employer | | | |
| Time 2, 1993 | 73.4 | 14.0 | 12.1 |
| Kelloway et al., 1992 | 67.9 | 18.6 | 12.8 |
| The union improves job security of its members | | | |
| Time 2, 1993 | 67.7 | 17.1 | 15.0 |
| Kelloway et al., 1992 | 69.6 | 22.7 | 7.1 |
| The union improves the wages and working conditions of the members | | | |
| Time 2, 1993 | 66.4 | 13.2 | 20.4 |
| Kelloway et al., 1992 | 71.6 | 17.1 | 10.6 |
| The union gives members their money's worth for the dues they pay[d] | | | |
| Time 2, 1993 | 47.0 | 14.5 | 37.9 |
| Kelloway et al., 1992 | 37.4 | 31.5 | 31.0 |

[a] The data represent the percentage of union members choosing each response option.
[b] Combined response category of 'Strongly Agree' and 'Agree'.
[c] Combined response category of 'Strongly Disagree' and 'Disagree'.
[d] $p < .05$ (based on $\chi^2$ comparison of response distribution for the two surveys).

Campbell and Peracchio, 1990). In this study, maturation effects are not an issue; regression can also be ruled out as the attitudes became more extreme over time, whereas the opposite effect would be more consistent with regression toward the mean. From a methodological perspective, history remains an issue; however, it is not a practical concern to the union whether its campaign changed its members attitudes by itself, or that it helped to reinforce other events that occurred over the period which were the real cause of the attitude change. What is important is that change took place in the appropriate direction. There is some evidence that does suggest the change in attitude occurred because of the campaign. One would expect the harsh economic climate and people reacting to bad times to influence changes in attitude; however, our data show that the respondents did not express more concerns in this area. This suggests that the attitude changes which occurred were specifically directed at the government; that is, the type of change that would be expected from an effective campaign.

The second methodological point concerns the use of two different samples at Time 1 and Time 2. Inferences about changes in the opinions of union members were based on differences between these two independent samples. This is the same methodology used to track changes in public opinion on a wide variety of topics, including preferences for political parties and candidates; it generally produces highly accurate estimates of the population's views. This methodology does, however, leave open the possibility that any change in responding over the two samples is due to sampling error; i.e. the changes may reflect differences in the composition of the two samples rather than true changes in the population's opinion. While there is always a chance of sampling error in any survey, the size of the samples used here suggest the results will accurately reflect those in the population 95 percent of the time.

### *Evaluation of the political action campaign*

The political action campaign opposing privatization and the government was successful. Members' attitudes about privatization became more negative in comparison to their beliefs prior to the start of the campaign. Examination of the results suggest that while some attitudes changed in an outright negative direction, others reflected an increase in 'Don't know' responses; that is, there was less certainty about the positive effects of privatization. This should be considered a positive outcome of the campaign in that the dominant ideology over this period (as reflected in government speeches, news reports, etc.) presented a clear case for downsizing of government. Perhaps sowing uncertainty was the best that could be hoped for in the such an environment.

While changes in attitudes cannot be directly attributed to the anti-privatization campaign, that campaign most likely played an important role in the change that took place.

Members' attitudes about the government also became more negative. Although there were no previous comparative data, as in the case of privatization, this self-reported shift in attitude is consistent with the changes that respondents attributed to the anti-privatization campaign. Given the continuity of the anti-privatization and publicity campaigns, it is likely that most members did not differentiate between the two and perceived both as one continuous campaign opposing the government and its policies. Together, both campaigns had the desired effect of increasing opposition to both the government and its policies among a substantial number of union members. These changes are reflected in the substantial number of respondents who reported that they were more likely to oppose the government as a result of both campaigns.

Union members voted in the recent election at much higher level than the general public. While there is no way to assess the extent to which this increase in participation was influenced by the political action campaign, the responses to other questions in the survey suggest that it most likely influenced a substantial portion of the increase.

Political action campaigns require the expenditure of union funds in pursuit of a common cause to which not all members may subscribe. The results of this survey suggest that union members will support political action if it is not overtly partisan in nature. That is, a campaign directed at a specific policy or action is more likely to be supported than a campaign directed at the government itself. Similarly, providing information on the candidates' views on issues of importance to the Union is acceptable but publicly advertising in support of, or against, candidates is not. This approach is consistent with the members not feeling closely attached to any political party. Over time, however, members may become more tolerant of a broader range of political activities.

Overall the political action campaign appears to have had a positive impact on the members' perceptions of their union. Union members became more definitive in their perception of the Union's power. Increases occurred in the number of members attributing more power to the union as well as those attributing less power to it. The percentage of members who agreed that the union has a lot to say about how the work place is run more than doubled. These results may reflect the fact that while the union's campaign did not deter the government from passing its legislation, it may have initiated a better appreciation of the union's power in the work place and, to a lesser extent, in the public arena. The perception of service provided by the union remained relatively constant; however, more members now agreed that the union gave them their money's worth for the dues they paid. The political action campaign may have increased the perception that union dues are well-spent.

In conclusion, the political action campaign must be judged a success in meeting its objectives. Attitudes towards the government and its policies became more negative and, on the whole, attitudes towards the union became more positive. The results from this survey, as expressed above, offer some suggestions for building on that success. Similar to Catano et al. (1995), these results also show that unions can take actions to change member attitudes.

## References


Barling, J., Fullagar, C. and Kelloway, E. K. (1992), *The union and its members: A psychological approach*, Oxford University Press, Oxford.

Bennett, J. T. (1984), 'Unions and politics: Introductory remarks', *Journal of Labour Research*, vol. 5.

Bennett, J. T. and Delaney, J. T. (1993), 'Research on unions: Some subjects in need of scholars', *Journal of Labour Research*, vol. 14.

Catano, V. M., Cole, G. and Hebert, N. (1995), 'Can union commitment be developed? A quasi-experimental analysis', in Tetrick, L. E. and Barling, J. (eds.), *Changing employment relations: Behavioral and social perspectives* , American Psychological Association, Washington, DC.

Chacko, T. I., (1985), 'Member participation in union activities: Perceptions of union priorities, performance, and satisfaction', *Journal of Labour Research*, vol. 6.

*Communication Workers of America v. Beck*, (1988), 487 U.S. 735.

Cook, T. D., Campbell, D. T and Peracchio, L. (1990), ' Quasi-experimentation', in Dunnette, M. D. and Hough, L. M. (eds.), *Handbook of industrial and organizational psychology* , 2nd ed., vol. 1, Consulting Psychologists Press, Palo Alto, California.

Fiorito, J. (1987), 'Political instrumentality perceptions and desires for union representation', *Journal of Labour Research*, vol. 8.

Gordon, M. E. and Ladd, R. T. (1993), 'Union commitment: An update', paper presented at the International Workshop on Union Commitment, Amsterdam, The Netherlands.

Hartley, J. (1995), 'Challenge and change in employment relations: Issues for psychology, trade unions, and managers', in Tetrick, L. E. and Barling, J. (eds.), *Changing employment relations: Behavioral and social perspectives*, American Psychological Association, Washington, DC.

Kelloway, E. K., Catano, V. M. and Southwell, R. R. (1992), 'The construct validity of union commitment: Development and dimensionality of a shorter scale', *Journal of Occupational and Organizational Psychology*, vol. 65.

Kochan, T. A. and Wever, K. R. (1991), 'American unions and the future of worker representation',. in Strauss, G., Gallagher, D. G. and Fiorito, J. (eds.), *The state of the unions*, Industrial Relations Research Association, Madison, WI.
*Lavigne v. Ontario Public Service Employees Union* (1991), 81 D.L.R. (4th) 545.
Masters, M. F. and Delaney, J. T. (1985), 'The causes of union political involvement: longitudinal analysis', *Journal of Labour Research*, vol. 6.
Masters, M. F. and Delaney, J. T. (1987), 'Union political activities: A review of the empirical literature', *Industrial and Labour Relations Review*, vol. 40.